From Home Guards
to Heroes

T0287903

Shades of Blue and Gray Series

Louis S. Gerteis and Clayton E. Jewett, Series Editors
Herman Hattaway and Jon Wakelyn, Consulting Editors

The Shades of Blue and Gray Series offers Civil War studies
for the modern reader—Civil War buff and scholar alike.
Military history today addresses the relationship between
society and warfare. Thus biographies and thematic studies
that deal with civilians, soldiers, and political leaders are increasingly important to a larger public. This series includes
books that will appeal to Civil War Roundtable groups, individuals, libraries, and academics with a special interest in
this era of American history.

University of Missouri Press
Columbia

From Home Guards *to Heroes*

The 87th Pennsylvania and Its Civil War Community

Dennis W. Brandt

Copyright © 2006 by
The Curators of the University of Missouri
University of Missouri Press, Columbia, Missouri 65211
Printed and bound in the United States of America
First paperback printing, 2018

ISBN 978-0-8262-2173-5 (paperback : alk. paper)

Library of Congress Cataloging-in-Publication Data

Brandt, Dennis W., 1946–
From home guards to heroes : the 87th Pennsylvania
and its Civil War community / Dennis W. Brandt.
      p.   cm. — (Shades of blue and gray series)
Includes bibliographical references and index.
ISBN-13: 978-0-8262-1680-9 (hard cover : alk. paper)
ISBN-10: 0-8262-1680-3 (hard cover : alk. paper)
1. United States. Army. Pennsylvania Infantry Regiment, 87th (1861–1865)
2. Pennsylvania—History—Civil War, 1861–1865—Regimental
histories.   3. United States—History—Civil War, 1861–1865—Regimental
histories.   4. Soldiers—Pennsylvania—York County—History—19th century.
5. Soldiers—Pennsylvania—Adams County—History—19th century.   6. United States.
Army—Military life—History—19th century.   7. Pennsylvania—History—Civil War,
1861–1865—Social aspects.   8. United States—History—Civil War, 1861–1865—Social
aspects.   9. Pennsylvania—History—Civil War, 1861–1865—Campaigns.
10. United States—History—Civil War, 1861–1865—Campaigns.   I. Title.
E527.587th .B73 2006
973.7'448—dc22   ☉™   2006026039

This paper meets the requirements of the
American National Standard for Permanence of Paper
for Printed Library Materials, Z39.48, 1984.

Designer: Stephanie Foley
Title page illustration and jacket design: Jennifer Cropp
Typefaces: Adobe Garamond and Alison

Cover photos (l to r): James Adair (Gil Barret Collection),
unnamed soldier (Gil Barret Collection),
William Henry Lanius (William Henry Lanius III),
Ramsey Hannagan (Gil Barret Collection),
William Bierbower (Gil Barret Collection), and
Daniel Peter Reigle (Gettysburg National Military Park).
Background courtesy Dreamstime.com

For Mark Snell and Denise Messinger,
George Tyler Moore Center for the Study of the Civil War.
It finally happened, thanks to both of you.

Contents

Foreword		ix
Preface		xi
Acknowledgments		xvii
List of Abbreviations		xix
Prologue		1
Chapter 1	Seeds	5
Chapter 2	Initial Test: April–July 1861	15
Chapter 3	Genesis	26
Chapter 4	The Rank and File	39
Chapter 5	Commanders and Their Companies	53
Chapter 6	Discipline Problems	89
Chapter 7	Desertion	115
Chapter 8	Mine Run, Military Law, and Andrew B. Smith	140
Chapter 9	South-Central Pennsylvania and Race	156
Chapter 10	Winter Camp, the Overland Campaign, and Petersburg	179
Chapter 11	Monocacy	195
Chapter 12	Final Days of War	212
Chapter 13	Postwar Politics and Reunions	235

Epilogue: Two Tales of Closure   241

Appendix   243

Selected Bibliography   253

Index   265

Foreword

The city of York, Pennsylvania, and York County—for which the former is the county seat—conjures up the names of manufacturing icons such as York Barbell and York Air Conditioners, but Harley Davidson motorcycles are built there also, and other giants in their field, such as Hanover Foods, are located there. One does not associate York or York County with the Civil War; it is known for manufactured goods and its colonial and Revolutionary War history. To the west, neighboring Adams County and its seat, Gettysburg, are, on the other hand, inextricably associated with the Civil War. These two counties have much in common (Adams once was part of York County), including a shared Civil War regiment, the 87th Pennsylvania Volunteer Infantry, of which two of my great-great-grandfathers were members.

On the surface, the 87th looks like so many other Union regiments raised in the Northeast. Recruited in the spring of 1861 after President Lincoln called for "three-year volunteers," the majority of the company's regiments were raised in the various townships and boroughs of York County (along with some volunteers from three counties to the north and northeast), but two companies were raised in Adams County, including Company F from Gettysburg. The regiment's initial service consisted of guarding railroads in Maryland and what is now West Virginia (it was still the western part of the Commonwealth of Virginia until June 1863), but soon after the Battle of Gettysburg, the 87th joined the Army of the Potomac's Third Corps, which had been so devastated in that great battle. The following spring, George Meade's reorganization shifted the 87th to the Sixth Corps. From then on, the regiment participated in the bloody battles of the Virginia theater, including the Overland campaign, Petersburg, Sayler's Creek, and finally the surrender at Appomattox. Because the regiment was part of the Sixth Corps, it also fought in battles that the rest of the Army of the Potomac missed, such as the Battle of Monocacy and the 1864 Shenandoah Valley campaign.

Service in the Sixth Corps is not what makes this regiment unique, nor is it the fact that one of its companies was recruited from the town that bears the name of the Civil War's most famous battle. York and Adams counties were border counties: they sat astride the Mason-Dixon Line. Many of the counties' residents, especially those in York, were ambivalent about the war; some were even sympathetic to the South because of economic and social ties. On the other hand, citizens of both counties harbored fugitive slaves as the latter made their way to freedom on the Underground Railroad. This regiment also differed from the great majority of Union regiments in that their families suffered the harsh fate of war as Confederate forces invaded both counties in the summer of 1863. Gettysburg and its environs became a battlefield and vast hospital; York was captured and paid a ransom, ostensibly to avoid destruction, while Hanover, a York County town that straddled the border of Adams and York counties, was the scene of a cavalry battle that raged through the streets on June 30, 1863.

This regimental history is not typical of the genre. In fact, it is more social history than military history. It examines a slice of south-central Pennsylvania society during a crucial era of U.S. history. Nor is it merely narrative history, such as the great regimentals on the First Minnesota Infantry by Richard Moe and the Twentieth Maine Infantry by John J. Pullen. Dennis Brandt continues this tradition but goes much further by drawing on the advances of modern social and military historians of the past two decades, such as Joseph Glatthaar, Maris Vinovskis, and Reid Mitchell. Research in the soldiers' compiled military service records and pension files provides Brandt with the raw data for detailed statistical analysis, upon which he draws to support his arguments and conclusions. Yet, Brandt's engaging writing style and thematic approach to the book makes this regimental history interesting, informative, and scholarly at the same time. Here is a regimental history that will set the standard for others to follow. It is the unique story of a Union regiment that truly grew *From Home Guards to Heroes*.

Mark A. Snell
The George Tyler Moore Center for the Study of the Civil War
Shepherd University
January 13, 2006

Preface

The 87th Pennsylvania Volunteer Infantry held a special place in the hearts of nineteenth-century York and Adams counties' residents. It was a region that thrived principally on the individual work ethic of German and Scotch-Irish farmers, craftsmen, and small businessmen, a peaceful area dotted with hundreds of one-room schools and small churches, some of which were the religious abodes of the Society of Friends. Nonetheless, when the nation proclaimed war upon itself, the area sent thousands of its sons and fathers to war, and more men took up weapons to serve militia duty during crisis situations engendered by campaigns that culminated with the great battles of Antietam, Gettysburg, and Monocacy.

Men joined many different units, but the 87th Pennsylvania was the area's only homegrown three-year regiment. York County supplied most of eight companies, supplemented by a small number of men from Cumberland, Dauphin, and Perry counties. Adams County offered two companies, one of them from Gettysburg, which precluded their presence at that legendary battle in their hometown. Other counties will forgive me when I take advantage of superior numbers and refer to the 87th Pennsylvania as "the boys from York." After all, the regiment did muster there.

Washington rushed the regiment into existence with a specific job in mind that initially lured men into ranks but ultimately created unhappy soldiers. The men of the 87th Pennsylvania never wore sprigs of pine or tails of bucks in their hats, although one company used its headgear as an excuse to pester their captain until he almost lost his commission. Neither did they serve in a brigade with a name more colorful than "Cheat Mountain Division." Nineteen months passed between muster and their first battle with a lot of boredom and ruinous marching in between. When they finally "met the elephant," the result was so devastating that the regiment nearly disintegrated. Still, they held their heads high because they had fought bravely in a difficult situation, and most lived to fight again. Fight they did in Ulysses S. Grant's bloody Overland campaign and then under Phil Sheridan in the Shenandoah Valley. In between, fate put them and a few thousand comrades near three vital Maryland bridges to buy time while General Grant reinforced a suddenly threatened Washington. A remnant of the original regiment, by then supplemented with many new faces, concluded the regiment's fighting at Petersburg, Virginia, and were camped a few miles from Appomattox Court House the day Ulysses S. Grant accepted Robert E. Lee's surrender.

The boys from York gathered often after the war, first locally in small groups, but eventually in grand reunions that returned veterans from all parts of the country. As the millennium approached, they were spending an increasing amount of time serving as honor guards at comrades' funerals. Veteran Benjamin Franklin Frick convinced his mates that they needed to write the regiment's story before no one was left to tell it. A history committee sprang into existence that assigned veterans from every company except H—not an inexplicable oversight, as we shall see—to chronicle events from their perspective. The committee approached York historian and educator George Reeser Prowell with a proposition: They would supply the documentation; he would do the writing. The result was *History of the 87th Pennsylvania Volunteers.*

Why, then, a new regimental history of the 87th Pennsylvania? First, this is not a "regimental" in the traditional sense because it explores issues usually omitted in similar publications. I must confess that I tackled this project in part because Prowell's book has never satisfied me. His writing is lifeless and his research shallow, amazing given that he had hundreds of living prime sources to consult. When describing the battle of Carter's Woods, for example, he consumed several pages quoting from official records instead of reporting what the veterans remembered or wrote about the battle. Although Prowell was long associated with the York County Historical Society, none of his research for the regimental history has ever surfaced. A Prowell family researcher who has spent decades studying her family is unaware of its existence. While he may have destroyed some and returned other documents to owners, I have long harbored a suspicion that he never made any notes worth keeping.

Prowell also did not connect the regiment's existence to contemporaneous social and political issues, although that is hardly unusual for a regimental history written during his time. He barely mentioned discipline problems except to shrug off bad behavior with a "boys-will-be-boys" attitude. His roster, for example, omits almost all of the regiment's deserters, and he often refused to identify troublemakers in his narrative. His description of a deserter drummed out of service never mentions that his name was Henry Armprister. Prowell briefly discussed the accidental shooting of John Quincy

Colehouse in the mountains of West Virginia but did not list Alfred Frederick Dustman as the man responsible. Prowell described a lad nicknamed "Squaw" whose keen ability to forage often exceeded orders but never identified him as George Washington Fleming from Oxford Township, Adams County. I readily grant Prowell forgiveness because he was a gentleman who lived in a time when Victorian morality often led men to shy from stepping on the toes of the living—with notable exceptions such as Mark Twain. The passage of time has freed me from such restraints.

From Home Guards to Heroes delves into other subjects that George Prowell touched on briefly, if at all, as well as those of minimal interest in his day: Why men enlisted, why some deserted while others reenlisted, and how they behaved before, during, and after the war. The book touches on the social history of south-central Pennsylvania—what folks here often call "the Susquehanna Valley"—but as overhead illumination rather than a principal light source. Still, a view of York's and Adams's societies is vital to understanding the communities from which the regiment sprang. An army is a grand collection of individual men, good and bad, emerging from a society that has molded their views, who have banded together to form an army greater than the sum of its individual members.

For the ultimate reason why I wrote *From Home Guards to Heroes,* I asked the eminent historian Emory M. Thomas to grant me the honor of quoting, with one critical substitution, the opening words of his biography of Robert E. Lee, and he graciously consented. "I grew up in [York, Pennsylvania]. That explains a lot about this book." While a labor of love provides great satisfaction to an author, it cannot justify publication. The trick is to attract readership from Portland, Maine, to Portland, Oregon, with a stop in Bug Tussle, Oklahoma, not just within the confines of York and Adams counties.

For *From Home Guards to Heroes* to have that kind of draw in spite of its regional-specific nature, I had to provide something unique for the University of Missouri to grant me the honor of publishing. I did so by delving into soldiers' personal lives in a way I hoped would be unprecedented and perhaps open wide a door heretofore only ajar. While it is difficult to get inside the heads of men long dead, to not try is to ignore the connective fiber that tied soldiers to their feelings, regiment, communities, and families. Few travel this earth without leaving some trail of information crumbs that history birds can snatch up and analyze.

The path for accomplishing this daunting project starts at each soldier's compiled military service and pension records, both housed at the National Archives in Washington. I studied the nearly 2,000 of the former and all 1,038 of the latter for the original organization of the 87th Pennsylvania and supplemented that with identical research into thousands of area men. I then extracted data in the same manner for more than 800 others who enlisted in 1861, a "virtual" regiment that I call simply "Non-87th Men." A non-87th recruit had to have enlisted in 1861 for three years in any regiment except the 87th Pennsylvania. He also had to have lived in a primary 87th Pennsylvania recruiting area or been in one of the following organizations principally recruited in the York/Adams counties region:

Company K, 1st Pennsylvania Reserves (30th Pa. Inf.)—principally recruited in Adams County

Company H, 7th Pennsylvania Reserves (36th Pa. Inf.)—principally recruited in Cumberland and York Counties

Company G, 12th Pennsylvania Reserves (41st Pa. Inf.)—principally recruited in York and Dauphin Counties

Companies D and I, 76th Pa. Inf.—principally recruited in Wrightsville and Hanover, York County, respectively.

Battery E, 1st Pennsylvania Light Artillery (43rd Pa.), recruited from a variety of locations including York, also supplied a random sampling of non-87th men. In all, the non-87th group represents approximately fifty different regiments.

The "bookmarks" of postservice correspondence cross-referenced in compiled military service records are a resource that researchers seem to have ignored. Perhaps it is because they reveal nuggets only occasionally and are so buried in the National Archives within a multiplicity of indexing systems that it is somewhat of a struggle to obtain them. Still, I read every one I could find and culled interesting information not available elsewhere. This fact hunt, supplemented with censuses, personal accounts, diaries, and family research resulted in a massive amount of detailed statistical and genealogical data on more than 2,000 area Union soldiers used to create this book. Presentation of statistics within a narrative, however, can cause brain strain if taken to extremes, so I have taken care to present them minimally in a variety of readable formats and use them only to illustrate pertinent issues. The appendix provides charts that reveal the physical character of the regiment.

I chose to slip by tactical and strategic issues with the exception of the battle of Monocacy. That battle most affected the regiment's veterans and is the only battlefield that contains a monument to the 87th Pennsylvania. Otherwise, the book concentrates on human interest, soldiers' lives and foibles, humor and sadness, relationships, politics, prejudices, and memories, some of which the men no doubt would have preferred had remained secret. George Prowell ignored race relations because the attitudes of his day gave him no reason to tackle the subject. I tried to cut through the sensitive topic with a knife sharp enough to cleave the fog of revisionism so I could cast aside the political correctness that often pours history into a mold shaped like certain twenty-first–century viewpoints.

Of course, no history could be complete without the words of the participants themselves. Several authors of letters and recollections have become old friends: Alfred Jameson, Jack Skelly and his brother Charles Edwin, George C. Blotcher, Michael Heiman, and Thomas Oliver Crowl, to name a few. The latter young man was a shoemaker from rural Siddonsburg in the northwest section of York County, but he had a way with words, atrociously spelled as they often were. Some of his statements will stun the racially sensitive, but he stated things as he saw them within his frame of reference. While writing a letter to a friend from camp in Winchester, Virginia, for example, he stopped writing long enough to eat dinner and afterward provided history with a classic bit of sarcasm on the quality of army rations. He dated the letter "March 7th 1863 Dollars" probably because the army had not paid him in seven months.

> Here I stoped and eat my supper and I eat so damed much that I have to open the two uper butons of my pants a fore I comenced riting. I will tell you what our supper consisted of. We had some old mess pork a bout seventeen years old and you ma[y] sware full of little white things that crawls on there bellys. You may name them your self. And also some coffee and a little sugar and also a chunk of bread so infernal dry and hard that it would take a dog with scissered teeth to chaw it.

I use quotes such as Tom's whenever they best serve the narrative but always edit them for relevance and maintenance of narrative flow. I have also risked the wrath of purists by inserting punctuation and paragraphs where necessary to make them more readable. Spelling remains unchanged, but I have clarified a few words rendered incomprehensible by egregious spelling by including the correct spelling in brackets.

Above all, I framed this work on the firm belief that a history of this nature, no matter how intellectually prepared and methodically presented, is storytelling that should not require readers to have preexisting interests or backgrounds to appreciate. To paraphrase classical music comedienne Anna Russell, I have no desire to be a great expert who writes books solely for the edification of other great experts. My fervent wish is that readers will recommend *From Home Guards to Heroes* to friends of all backgrounds and interests because they think it is a good read as well as one that has taught them much.

In the uncovering of events, I cannot help but feel sadness that so many of the accounts here relate negative experiences, as if I were a history highway rubbernecker staring backward at the crashes of past lives. True to human nature and sad to say, good behavior is seldom documented and usually not very interesting when it is. As you read, keep in mind that the 87th Pennsylvania as a whole acted no more egregiously than most regiments.

Enjoy meeting the boys from York (et al). I have grown to love them, warts and all.

Acknowledgments

The first thank-you cannot be made strongly enough. Mark A. Snell, fellow Yorker, retired army major, former history instructor at West Point, and as of this writing, director of the George Tyler Moore Center for the Study of the Civil War (GTMC), Shepherdstown, West Virginia, offered invaluable aid. Without his assistance and guidance, sometimes forcibly and correctly administered, I would never have gotten this book published. Just as much thanks goes to his assistant, Denise E. Messinger, who is, according to Mark, just as much a genius behind the success of the GTMC. She offered her valuable time as a proofreader and cheerleader. Both richly deserve this book's dedication.

Coming in a close second are the wonderful folks at the York County Heritage Trust Library, namely head librarian emerita June Lloyd and her erstwhile assistant and now head librarian, Lila Fourhman-Shaull, admirably assisted by the always sartorially splendiferous Josh Stahlman. They lead as well-organized a historical society library as I have had the pleasure to visit, and it is a place where history is sweetened with a sense of humor. Just as important, they run a place where history is never dull. They have given me the run of the library and its copious sources for the 87th Pennsylvania and deserve my eternal gratitude for their support. Best of all, they laugh at my jokes.

I must applaud the folks at the National Archives in Washington, D.C., who have seen a lot of me over the years. Government offices do not always have the reputation of assisting on a personal level, but many at the Archives have become friends and frequently go the extra mile in assisting with my research. They also laugh at my jokes—usually.

To all those who provided personal data about their descendants: George Hay Kain III, descendant of Col. George Hay, who allowed me to use his private library of the colonel's documents; Tim Smith, Gettysburg historian and battlefield tour guide, who shared his vast knowledge of Adams County history; Cheryl Lutz, descendent of George Felty, and Geoff Spangler, relative of John Edwin McIlvain, who both put me onto delightful stories of their families; Dr. Walter L. Powell, who gave permission to use the James Hersh letters and offered other encouragement; Dr. Richard Sommers of the U.S. Army Military History Institute, Carlisle, Pennsylvania, who provided guidance, who never fails to inquire on the book's status and my welfare, and who, in late 2005, looked quite distinguished sporting a new Robert E. Lee–style beard; Jim Rhea, who sent me a typed copy of Beniah K. Anstine's diary, and Larry Peahl, who provided similar information on Ross L. Harman; Sam Snyder, who shared his knowledge of ancestor Benjamin Snyder, possibly the most intriguing tale in the book; Larry Ellis of Newberry College and Jacob Hay Brown, both of whom were eager to see the Reverend John Allen Brown's story in print; Kerwin Lanz, who gave me a newspaper account written by his descendant John Keses; and Capt. Charles Creekman, 106th New York researcher, who pointed out several interesting anecdotes and whose material now resides beautifully organized at the U.S. Army Military History Institute. To all those generous people go my heartfelt gratitude.

List of Abbreviations

Army Records	Preliminary Inventory of the Records of United States Army Continental Commands, 1821–1920
Bates	Samuel P. Bates, *History of Pennsylvania Volunteers*
CMSR	Compiled Military Service Records of [soldier] [company] [regiment]
Court-Martial	Records of the Office of the Judge Advocate General (Army), Court-Martial Case Files
CWMC	Civil War Miscellaneous Collection U.S. Army Military History Institute, Carlisle, Pennsylvania
Federal Muster Rolls	Muster Rolls of the 87th Pennsylvania Infantry, National Archives and Records Administration
HCWRT	Harrisburg Civil War Roundtable Collection, U.S. Army Military History Institute, Carlisle, Pennsylvania
NARA	National Archives and Records Administration
O.R.	*War of the Rebellion: A Compilation of the Official Records of the Union and Confederate Armies*
O.R. Atlas	*Atlas to Accompany the Official Records of the Union and Confederate Armies*
PA AGO	Pennsylvania Adjutant General's Office
Pattee	Historical Collections and Labor Archives, Pattee Library, Pennsylvania State University
Pension Records	Department of the Interior, Pension Application of [soldier] [company] [regiment]

Secretary of War	Letters of the Office of the Secretary of War: Records Sent by the Secretary of War Relating to Military Affairs
SHSP	Southern Historical Society Papers
Veterans' Affairs	Records of the Department of Military and Veterans' Affairs, Office of the Adjutant General, Harrisburg, Pennsylvania
Worth Infantry	Record Book and Memorabilia of the Worth Infantry
YCHT	Library of the York County Heritage Trust, York, Pennsylvania

From Home Guards
to Heroes

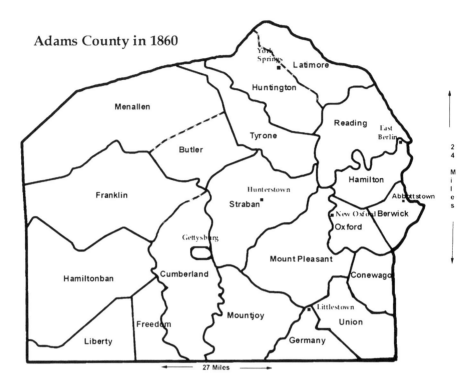

Adams County in 1860

York Springs, Latimore, Huntington, Menallen, Reading, East Berlin, Tyrone, Butler, Hamilton, Franklin, Hunterstown, Straban, Abbottstown, New Oxford, Berwick, Oxford, Gettysburg, Mount Pleasant, Conewago, Hamiltonban, Cumberland, Mountjoy, Littlestown, Union, Freedom, Liberty, Germany

24 Miles

27 Miles

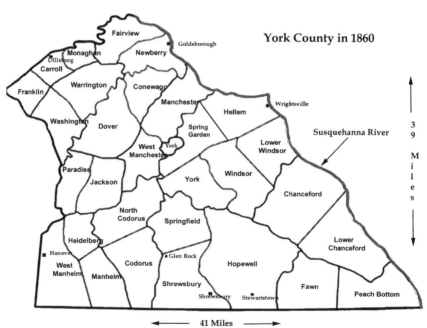

York County in 1860

Fairview, Goldsborough, Dillsburg, Monaghan, Newberry, Carroll, Franklin, Warrington, Conewago, Manchester, Wrightsville, Hellam, Washington, Dover, Spring Garden, West Manchester, York, Lower Windsor, Susquehanna River, Paradise, Jackson, York, Windsor, Chanceford, North Codorus, Springfield, Heidelberg, Lower Chanceford, Hanover, Glen Rock, West Manheim, Codorus, Hopewell, Manheim, Fawn, Peach Bottom, Shrewsbury, Shrewsbury, Stewartstown

39 Miles

41 Miles

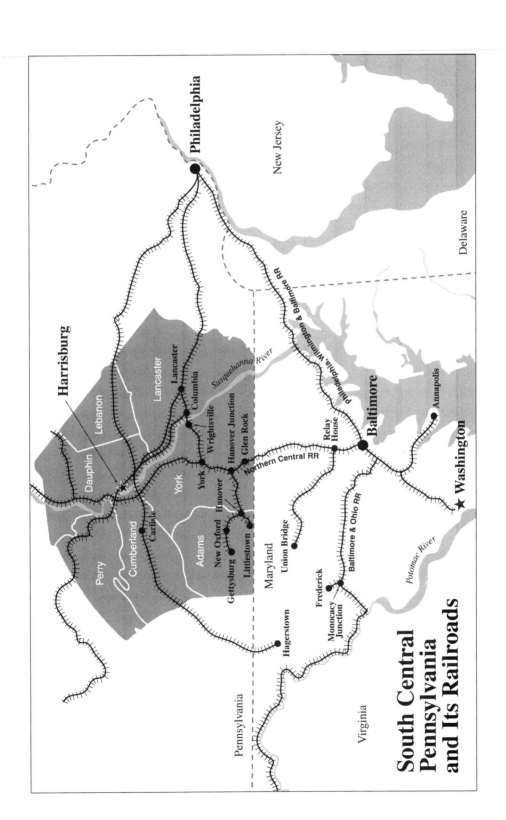

South Central Pennsylvania and Its Railroads

Artist Lewis Miller's view of half the 87th Pennsylvania leaving York (*Sketches and Chronicles, The Reflections of a Nineteenth Century Pennsylvania German Folk Artist*, courtesy York County Heritage Trust)

Prologue

The frantic excitement created by the hourly increasing
probability of a civil war continues unabated in the federal
capital. . . . They think, talk, and dream of nothing but war.

Daily Baltimore Republican, April 9, 1861

Solomon Myers stepped through the schoolhouse doorway into a chill-
ing drizzle and perhaps contemplated days ahead when coming in from
the rain would be a luxury. April 19, 1861, should have been just another
spring day in south-central Pennsylvania. The young season had softened the
ice on the Susquehanna River and brought an end to winter frivolity. Farmers
anticipated the coming of drier weather to begin another spring planting that
would return abundance to fields for as far as anyone could travel in a week
or more.

But this was a spring different from those anyone could recall, a spring
with a terrible distinction, a spring in which long-dreaded events had shoved
the weather from its usual position atop the conversational hierarchy. Troubling events were unfolding that forced Solomon Myers to grant his pupils
an early summer recess and don the second lieutenant's uniform that seventy-
five friends and neighbors of York had elected him to wear. This time, it was
no drill. Myers and his fellow militiamen were about to stake one of several
claims to the title of "Union's First Defenders." They would fight to receive
that recognition until their last breaths.[1]

1. Diary of Solomon Myers, ms. file 12740, York County Heritage Trust Library, York, Pennsylvania; diaries of John Stoner Beidler, courtesy of Beidler descendant Charles Douglas Wilcox
(electronic copies available at http://www.rootsweb.com/usgenweb/pa/york/area.htm); Worth Infantry, Rare Book Collection, YCHT; *York Gazette,* Mar. 31, 1893. Congressman Daniel Franklin
Lafean, son of a militia veteran, introduced House Bill H.R. 27222 to make the claim of "First
Defenders" official. York still celebrates "First Defenders Day."

A week beyond the cannon fire at Fort Sumter, the still-embryonic specter of the American Civil War had shifted northward. Fifty miles and a three-hour train ride south of York, Pennsylvania, citizens of Baltimore, Maryland, had attacked soldiers from Massachusetts as they marched between train stations on their way to defend Washington. Fort Sumter was an exchange of gunfire between soldiers, but this time American soldiers turned guns on American civilians, and the civilians fired back. No one could say who pulled the first trigger, nor did anyone seem to notice that the Massachusetts men were themselves only days and the donning of a uniform removed from civilian status.

In the North, the melee was immediately dubbed the "Pratt Street Riots" for the street on which it occurred. Details of the bloody affair remained sketchy. On York's town square, Jim Small's News Depot, whose running newspaper ads bragged about its wide selection of out-of-town newspapers, now had nothing to fill the space reserved for Baltimore papers. Trains stopped running after Baltimore's mayor ordered rail bridges damaged to keep more trainloads of Federal soldiers out of his city. No one knew when the "cars" might be running again or if the mayor's ruffians might slip across the state line to create more havoc.[2]

York also looked twenty-five miles up the Northern Central to Harrisburg. Recruits were pouring into the state capital so fast that a Harrisburg newspaper gave up printing a daily head count because too many to tally were arriving. These civilian-soldiers' short-term goal was to get to Washington as fast as possible to protect the national capital. During more pacific times, that meant taking the Northern Central Railway to Baltimore and there changing to the Baltimore and Ohio line. Now, the Pratt Street Riots had rendered that route impassable for the foreseeable future. Even if the Union took control of the Northern Central, war could transform its rails into a double-iron fuse linked to the powder keg that Baltimore had become. That fuse would have to burn through York, Pennsylvania.[3]

These events were troubling enough to the nation but especially distressing to a south-central Pennsylvania region that had long enjoyed social and commercial cohabitation with the port and rail city of Baltimore. Nearly four

2. *O.R.* (hereafter, all references to series 1 unless otherwise noted), George P. Kane to Charles Howard, ser. 2, 1:628–30, Report of Edward F. Jones, 2:7–9, Report of Baltimore Police Commissioners, 2:9–10; Report of George W. Brown, 2:12–13, George W. Brown to Thomas H. Hicks, 2:581; Warren Lee Goss, "Going to the Front," in *Battles and Leaders of the Civil War,* 1:150–51; Samuel Penniman Bates, *History of Pennsylvania Volunteers,* 382; *Hanover (Pa.) Spectator and Commercial Advertiser* (hereafter cited as *Hanover Spectator*), May 3, 1861.
3. *O.R.,* message of the mayor of Baltimore, 2:15–16; *York Gazette,* Apr. 23, 1861; *Harrisburg (Pa.) Patriot and Union,* Apr. 22, 1861.

decades before the war, Maryland surveyor George Winchester had predicted, "The salvation of the city of Baltimore must, in great measure, depend upon the Susquehanna Valley." Time proved his prophecy dead-on, especially after a transportation innovation called "the railroad" united the two regions in the wholly lucrative bonds of fiscal matrimony. A spur line from York to Wrightsville opened in 1840 to transport Baltimore-bound goods and passengers to the headwaters of the Susquehanna and Tidewater Canal, a connection that boosted canal shipping levels beyond anything previously imagined. When the town of Hanover got its rail line in 1852, it tied an economic knot that routinely put twenty or more Baltimore business ads into town newspapers.[4]

Adams County, less than half the population of York, had some economic catching up to do, but an absence of mass transportation retarded economic growth. Six years after Hanover got its line, tracks finally stretched through New Oxford. Shortly thereafter, rails entered Gettysburg, and yet another branch line soon sent trains chugging into Littlestown. So invigorating was the railroad to Adams County's economy that a former New Oxford resident returning home after a long absence was amazed how the town had been "roused from a long sleep of half a century."[5]

Blood as much as commerce linked the two regions. York and Adams counties' censuses for 1860 reveal that more citizens were born in Maryland than any other non-Pennsylvania location. Roads that had connected the two states almost since the first white settlements could still reunite families in a matter of hours. York's two militia companies stood on friendly terms with their Baltimore counterparts and united like twenty-first-century reenactors to celebrate the War of 1812's battle of North Point. Gettysburg's militia adopted the name "Independent Blues," the same title held by "one of the most respectable companies in the city of Baltimore."[6]

But as civil war became imminent, that lucrative proximity became a double-edged sword. Maryland was a slaveholding state, and York and Adams

---

4. Robert L. Gunnarsson, *The Story of the Northern Central Railway,* 19, 24–26, 39. The Baltimore and Susquehanna Railroad began service under the name Northern Central in January 1855. *York Democratic Press,* Dec. 31, 1858; Ezra J. Warner, *Generals in Blue: Lives of the Union Commanders,* 218–19; James Weston Livingood, *The Philadelphia-Baltimore Trade Rivalry, 1780–1860,* 56, 60–61, 80. The independently owned York-Wrightsville line needed an expert to resolve problems and hired West Point–trained engineer Herman Haupt, destined to become chief of construction and transportation for United States military railroads during the Civil War.

5. *Hanover (Pa.) Citizen,* Feb. 13, 1862; University of Virginia Library Geospatial and Statistical Data Center, fisher.lib.virginia.edu/collections/stats/histcensus/. In 1860, York had 66,834 white and 1,366 black residents; Adams had 27,532 whites and 474 blacks. More than 20 percent of area soldiers are missing from the 1860 census, so these numbers are low.

6. U.S. Census, 1860, Pennsylvania, York County; *Worth Infantry.*

counties had another railroad—the Underground—that placed them in the dichotomous position of undermining the South's slave-based economic system while transacting business with slave owners. A York newspaper predicted, "If there is a conflict between the North and the South, we will be the first and greatest sufferers." While time proved that fear an overstatement, the prediction was reasonable in 1860 and did contain a grain of truth. The serpent of civil war was waiting to coil around Gettysburg and make its most deadly strike. Before that, York would have to swallow a dose of Southern inhospitality that it would spend more than a century trying to forget.[7]

7. Black History File 630.1–630.4, YCHT; *York Gazette,* Apr. 23, 1861. York's popular historical focus clings to being first capital of the United States, a dubious claim based on the Articles of Confederation being ratified there in 1781.

Chapter 1

Seeds

The United States had struggled with sectional political disputes since its inception. While facing the British foe at Boston in 1775, Gen. George Washington feared his army might disintegrate from the intense intersectional rivalry that existed between various states' militias. Two decades later, Vice President Thomas Jefferson warned that secession was inevitable if the federal government assumed too much power. During the first decade of the nineteenth century, New England grew so unsettled by the South's political domination that it actively pursued secession, a movement that ceased only after the War of 1812 ended. In 1833, President Andrew Jackson quashed South Carolina's first attempt to secede and became convinced that the South's ultimate goal was to form a separate nation with the Potomac River as its northern border.[1]

Fear of Southern secession grew to critical heights during the decade of the 1850s, fueled by a spate of racially charged court decisions, compromise legislation on the expansion of slavery and dealing with runaways, and violent acts by extremists epitomized by John Brown. The word *disunion* or one of its synonyms appeared with alarming frequency in the nation's principal mass-communication media, the newspaper. Few sources better highlight this tumultous period than the duels of wit and rhetoric between rival newspapers that routinely launched salvos of words fully intended to strike fatal political blows against opponents.

York and Adams counties' editors came as rhetorically well armed as their metropolitan counterparts except that small budgets limited publication to one weekly issue on a single duplexed sheet folded into four pages. They filled

1. David McCullough, *John Adams* (New York: Simon & Schuster, 2001), 521.

front pages not with current events but with philosophy, human-interest stories, historical accounts, or romantic tales, all of which could be prepared early and thus shorten weekly preparation time. In what front-page space remained, ads hawked the undeniable health benefits of products such as Ayer's Sarsaparilla, Spalding's Cephalic (headache) Remedy, and various brands of "female pills" that lacked anything resembling estrogen. Even in the first issue after the Confederate invasion of 1863, readers had to turn to page two to read about it.

Unbiased journalism was a rare commodity throughout the newspaper industry, and south-central Pennsylvania was no exception. Only two area newspapers backed no candidates during the 1860 elections and published the names of every nominee. All others listed just their favored candidates and mentioned the opposition primarily in insulting and often outrageous terms. Newspapers as yet contained no op-ed pages, so most editors freely mixed opinion with what we today call "hard news" and turned their pages into a political voice rather than a disseminator of public information.[2]

Arguments over "state rights," a divisive topic since the country's inception, grew hotter. There were other contentious issues: taxes, squabbles over protective tariffs favorable to the North, or whether the federal government should fund internal improvements of infrastructure. While those debates generated heat, the state right involving slavery was the only quarrel fiery enough to set the country alight. When South Carolina's Preston Brooks cracked abolitionist senator Charles Sumner's skull on the Senate floor in 1856, he was reacting to Sumner's personal attack against a relative's proslavery stance, not his position on the transcontinental railroad. John Brown's aborted attack on Harpers Ferry gave the South nightmares of slave revolts, not of increased taxes. So pervasive was the slavery topic that Democrats freely referenced their opponents by tacking the adjective *black* onto the noun *Republican* whatever the subject at hand.

Northern and Southern Democrats made odd bedfellows on the subject of slavery. Southerners generally agreed with a South Carolina senator who insisted that an elite class of slave owners had to maintain a subclass of slaves to perform "menial work." Northern Democrats, on the other hand, had neither love nor need for slavery, and only the elderly could even remember seeing a slave working in their hometown. The two sections of Democrats cohabited politically because they concurred with Thomas Jefferson's concept

---

2. The *York County Star and Wrightsville (Pa.) Advertiser* (hereafter *Wrightsville Star*) and *Hanover (Pa.) Spectator and General Advertiser* were the nonpartisan newspapers. The *Wrightsville Star* ceased publication January 2, 1862, because five staff members had joined the army, but it resumed operation after the war.

than a central government worked best that governed least. States should get what they wanted, Democrats said, including the right to own other human beings until the Constitution said otherwise. Proslavery forces did all they could to keep the Constitution from changing. From May 25, 1836, through December 3, 1844, they used their majority in the House of Representatives to gag all debate on the slavery question. One Republican, frustrated by this perceived single-mindedness, wrote, "So long as the Democratic Party is in power, there will be a ceaseless howl on the Negro question."[3]

The howling was no louder over slavery itself than over its expansion into the territories, especially after a victory in the Mexican War annexed huge amounts of western land and opened new economic possibilities. Whether Kansas was free or slave was of no immediate geographical concern to south-central Pennsylvania, but if enough new free states emerged, the balance of power in Congress could shift Republican, dealing a fatal blow to slavery and making all Republican policies triumphant. To prevent their political adversaries from capturing power, Democrats attacked using words that make the worst modern-day political squabbles seem tame by comparison.

The *York Democratic Press* was the area's foremost journalistic provocateur. Reporting on the first-ever Republican national convention, it did not hesitate to describe delegates as "a congregation of rabid, slimey, frothy creatures . . . [that] go for the niggers first, last and all the time." All area Democratic newspapers agreed that Republicans supported abolition solely to bring freed slaves north to shove whites out of low-paying jobs and further enrich Republican coffers. The *Press,* though, was particularly vicious in its attacks. Referencing the many black family picnics then taking place in Philadelphia parks, a reporter wrote:

> The aroma of their surroundings is so strong that the Lincoln legions are experiencing a little nausea and cry loudly for a nigger non-intercourse act . . . This is only a small taste of what you will get when the "irrepressible conflict" has ended and the four million niggers of the South are set loose upon you. Brace up your nerves, the disease is but in a mild form yet; by and by you will experience its virulence.[4]

3. "Mudsill" speech of South Carolina Senator James Henry Hammond to the United States Senate, Mar. 4, 1858. Text available at Africans in America, www.pbs.org/wgbh/aia/part4/4h3439t .html (accessed Aug. 8, 2004); Jean H. Baker, *Affairs of Party: The Political Culture of Northern Democrats in the Mid-Nineteenth Century,* 141, 145–46, 165–76. "Ceaseless howl" comment from *New York Times,* Sept. 28, 1860.

4. *York Democratic Press,* Feb. 26, 1856, Nov. 6, 1860, and May 22, 1860. "Irrepresible conflict" was a jab at Senator William Henry Seward, who attacked Democrats with the phrase in an 1858 speech. Typical of many Democratic newspapers, the *Press* misjudged Lincoln's potential, printing of his candidacy on Sept. 18, 1860: "We do not fear this ticket. It can have no strength."

Adams County's *Gettysburg Compiler* maintained a calmer approach but shared the *Press*'s philosophy. The *Compiler* pointed to the Underground Railroad as exhibit A in its case against Republicanism. It insisted those "black Republicans" would not hesitate to use weapons of "secrecy, cunning, and trickery" to connive votes and lure slaves north as cheap labor. Foretelling the sound bite familiar in subsequent centuries, the *Compiler* announced during the 1860 presidential campaign, "A vote for Lincoln is a vote for black labor over white labor."[5]

Blacks were not the only ethnic group area Democratic newspapers targeted. Germans of a Republican persuasion also received verbal thumping, surprisingly so since they were the region's majority cultural group. The editor of *York Gazette,* himself descended from German immigrants, slurred not only some of his readership but perhaps his own family when he attacked a German immigrant who was a Lincoln elector.

> In the heart of the foreigner beats no one single noble impulse—no one single throb of patriotism. He is so brutish and degraded that he has no sympathy for anything but cabbage and lager beer, potatoes and butter-milk, or some other abominable outlandish dish only fit for hogs . . . You see a lop eared, wide mouthed mullet-headed Dutchman coming up just from some hut in the land of Krout with the foam of beer still sticking to his horsetail whiskers and his breath smelling of garlick and onions enough to kill a white man [at] three hundred yards.[6]

Even in less insulting moments, area Democratic newspapers sounded downright Southern expressing the party's state-rights platform. In 1860, the *York Gazette* lauded proslavery presidential candidate John Cabell Breckin-ridge when he called Republicans "traitors to the Constitution." Even when the *York Democratic Press* used calmer rhetoric, its words would have been at home in any Southern newspaper.[7]

> The aim and object of the Black Republican party is eternal war upon the institution of slavery . . . The South has been within the Consti-tution . . . [and] demanded naught beyond their just rights under the Constitution . . . The Black Republican party attacks . . . the very Con-stitution itself.[8]

5. *Gettysburg (Pa.) Compiler,* Nov. 6, 1860, and Mar. 25, 1861.
6. *York Gazette,* Oct. 9, 1860.
7. *York Gazette,* Sept. 11, 1860.
8. *Democratic Press,* May 31, 1859.

Gettysburg Compiler editor Henry John Stahle pressed his support for Southern rights so vehemently that military authorities found an excuse to arrest him after the battle of Gettysburg on suspicion of "communicating valuable information to the Rebel military authorities." The rival *Gettysburg Star and Banner* concluded that the charges rendered Stahle "unfit to live here or anywhere else." The *Banner* almost got its wish when Stahle began viewing the world from a cell inside Baltimore's Fort McHenry. The army released him without trial, however, and he returned to publishing his newspaper without restructuring his opinions. Ironically, Henry John was the brother of James Alanza Stahle, who was, at the time of Henry's arrest, serving as lieutenant colonel of the 87th Pennsylvania Infantry. Brother Jim would later serve in Congress—as a member of the Republican Party.[9]

Democratic editors sometimes allowed political petulance to trump reality. The *York Gazette* headlined coverage of a local rally for the 1860 Republican gubernatorial candidate Andrew Gregg Curtin "MAGNIFICENT FAILURE!" When Curtin won the election in October but lost York County, the *Gazette* printed only the York County results. Eventually forced to admit the obvious, the editors pulled out some of their largest headline type to declare that Curtin had won only through "STUPENDOUS FRAUDS!" As a public service, they explained the mechanics of voting in the November presidential election but invited only Democrats to participate. After Abraham Lincoln's victory, the *Gazette* likewise stressed his loss in York Borough but ignored his state and national victories.[10]

On the other side of the political spectrum stood a Republican Party born largely out of opposition to slavery but with convictions on the topic that ran the gamut. A fair, albeit oversimplified, description of Republicans' range of feelings about slavery appeared in a New York newspaper. "There are Republicans who are Abolitionists; there are others who anxiously desire and labor for the good of the slave; but there are many more whose main impulse is a desire to secure the new territories for Free White Labor, with little or no regard for the interests of Negroes, free or slave."[11]

Most radical abolitionists supported the Republican Party, but only a minority of Republicans called themselves radical abolitionists. Ohio's Republi-

9. *Gettysburg Compiler,* Nov. 6, 1860, and Apr. 22, 1861; *Gettysburg Star and Banner,* July 16, 1863; *Star and Sentinel* (Gettysburg, Pa.), Oct. 4, 1898; Biographical Directory of the United States Congress. James A. Stahle served one term in the 54th Congress but refused to stand for reelection. "Stahle" is pronounced "Staley."

10. *York Gazette,* Sept. 11, Oct. 2 and 16, and Nov. 6 and 13, 1860. Elections then were independently scheduled and held throughout the year.

11. Eric Foner, *Free Soil, Free Labor, Free Men: The Ideology of the Republican Party before the Civil War,* 61 (citing the *New York Tribune,* Oct. 15, 1856).

can governor William Dennison wrote, "Our party to this, as in every other state, has its conservative and radical elements." "Conservative" was the byword in the party's platforms in 1856 and 1860. Neither plank advocated outlawing slavery, but both condemned its spread into the territories for reasons that were just as political as moral. York and Adams counties' Republican newspapers toed the conservative line, although the *York Republican* clearly hated the Fugitive Slave Law. Partly because they did not assume a radical slant, area Republican newspapers never reached the name-calling mastery of the *York Democratic Press*. While they often replaced "Democrat" with the derisive expression "locofoco," they largely played down the emotional slavery issue after their presidential whooping in 1856. The banner of radical abolitionism was not going to wave over a winning national ticket in 1860.[12]

The Republican *Gettysburg Star and Banner* and its kindred *Adams Sentinel and General Advertiser* used up much space picking apart almost everything the *Gettysburg Compiler* printed. In one issue, the *Sentinel* printed eight different stories mocking *Compiler* articles, including accusations of *Compiler* anti-Catholicism in heavily Catholic Adams County. Republican papers generally were light on positive reasons to vote Republican and spent much time reacting defensively. When Democrats called Lincoln a man of "violent Abolition prejudices," the *Star and Banner* argued that the Radicals' disfavor with Lincoln proved he was not going to turn America colorblind. The *Sentinel* insisted that a Lincoln presidency would not cause the dreaded influx of black labor and cited Lincoln saying, "I am not . . . in favor of bringing about . . . the social and political equality of the white and black races." A hangman's noose lifted John Brown into martyrdom for many Radical Republicans, but the *York Republican* thought "the whole country breathed freer when John Brown was hung."[13]

If Democratic newspapers leaned on the abrasive edge of journalism, their Republican counterparts tilted to the uninspiring. The *York Republican,* for example, filled the bulk of one issue with the complete text of the Ohio gov-

12. Ibid., 103; 1856 Republican Platform, Lause's Links Web site, www.geocities.com/College Park/Quad/6460/doct/856gop.html (accessed Jan. 4, 2005); Republican National Platform, 1860, in *Documents of American History,* edited by Henry Steele Commager and Milton Cantor, 363–65; *York Republican,* Dec. 24, 1860; *Star and Banner* and *Adams Sentinel and General Advertiser,* any issue Aug.–Oct. 1860.

13. *Star and Banner* and *Adams Sentinel,* any issue Aug.–Oct. 1860, and Nov. 2, 1860. The example of the *Sentinel*'s mockery is from September 19. *York Republican,* Dec. 19 and 24, 1860; Lincoln-Douglas Debates, Department of the Interior, National Park Service, Lincoln Home, www.nps.gov/liho/debates.htm (accessed Sept. 11, 2004); *Democratic Press,* May 22, 1860; *Gettysburg Compiler,* Oct. 1, 1860.

ernor's annual message to his legislature on the dreary subjects of banking and taxes. Another issue grabbed readers' attention with the screaming headline "SOUTHERN WRONGS!" The story was only a number-heavy treatise on how foolish the South would be to secede and lose what the *Republican* judged to be a disproportional benefit from the U.S. postal system. In yet another issue, a long letter from a county resident argued that opening a territory to slavery would lead to lower property values and had all the numbers to "prove" it.[14]

No matter how hard conservative Republicans tried to steer away from the slavery issue, it always popped to the surface. The topic of "Popular Sovereignty" did much to keep the subject in the public sphere during the 1850s. The issue figured heavily in the 1860 presidential race but found little favor in south-central Pennsylvania with either party. The principle's champion, Illinois Democratic senator Stephen Arnold Douglas, wanted territories to decide the slavery question for themselves. Forging a coalition of Southern Whigs and Northern Democrats, he maneuvered the principle into law as part of the 1854 Kansas-Nebraska Act and made matters worse. "Nebraska" infuriated slaveholders and abolitionists alike because each side feared it would lose power. As a result, the Whig Party's already weakened sectional fault line cracked wide open, and the party tumbled into the abyss of history. In its place arose the Republican Party tinted almost exclusively with Northern hues.[15]

By 1860, that issue, coupled with the South's increased dread of slave revolts in the wake of John Brown's violent deeds in Kansas and Harpers Ferry, also had strained the bonds of Democratic sectional brotherhood. *Gettysburg Compiler* editor Henry John Stahle covered the 1860 Democratic Convention in Charleston, South Carolina, and reported disarray from the opening gavel. Delegates arrived arguing seating plans and with opposing platforms, one touted by Stephen A. Douglas and the other by future Confederate general and sitting vice president John Cabell Breckinridge. When the convention leaned toward Douglas's plank, most Deep South delegates walked out. After twelve ballots and no aspirant close to nomination, the convention closed

14. *York Republican,* Jan. 5, 1859, and Dec. 5 and 19, 1860; *Star and Banner,* Sept. 21, 1860. Newspapers then commonly published complete speeches. For examples from elsewhere, see Foner, *Free Soil,* 43–44. For an opinion on how disinterested the public had become regarding taxes and banking long before the Civil War, see Robert V. Remini, *Henry Clay: Statesman for the Union* (New York: W. W. Norton, 1991), 633–35.

15. Daniel Meyer, *Stephen A. Douglas and the American Union;* Kansas-Nebraska Act, in *Documents of American History,* 331–32; David Herbert Donald, *Lincoln,* 201. The death in 1852 of longtime Whig leader Henry Clay also contributed to the party's demise.

without a candidate. Six weeks later, the party reconvened and picked Douglas as their standard-bearer only to see Massachusetts's delegates walk out with the few remaining Southerners.[16]

The fracture was irrevocable. Separate conventions nominated former Tennessee senator John Bell under the Constitutional Union banner and Vice President John C. Breckinridge as the Southern Democratic candidate. Unhappy Pennsylvania Democrats deepened the divide when they convened in Reading to create a "Fusion" ticket, a slate of electors promised to the party but no candidate. If victorious, they could then bargain for political favor with the winner. Once south-central Pennsylvania's vote was counted, Stephen A. Douglas had pulled only 4.7 percent in York County and less than 1 percent in Adams, and John Bell had barely topped 4 percent combined. The rest of the two counties' Democratic votes went "Fusion," but that became irrelevant when Abraham Lincoln won Pennsylvania.[17]

While the Republican Party also had no clear candidate going into their convention, it eventually nominated and rallied behind Abraham Lincoln. South-central Pennsylvania Republicans smarted from the 1856 election when first-ever Republican presidential candidate John Charles Frémont captured barely 10 percent of area votes. Some wondered why, especially those who viewed the party's political base—citing one Illinois Republican—as men "who work with their hands, who live and act independently, who hold the stakes of home and family, of farm and workshop, of education and freedom." That was an apt description of south-central Pennsylvanians, yet not until 1940 did Adams County shift Republican, and York County waited until 1952. Lincoln offered temporary hope to Republicans when he took 46.9 percent in the two counties in 1860. Detailed returns reveal more. Lincoln won a majority in sixteen of York County's thirty reporting districts and a plurality in four others, losing the county largely due to four townships that gave him only 100 votes out of 987 cast. He snatched a small majority in Adams County by winning ten of nineteen districts, including an overwhelming victory in the York Springs area known for its Underground Railroad activity.[18]

16. *Gettysburg Compiler,* Apr. 30 and May 7, 1860; Jeffery A. Jenkins and Irwin Morris, "Spatial Voting Theory and Counterfactual Inference: John C. Breckinridge and the Presidential Election of 1860," http://polmeth.wustl.edu/retrieve.php?id=67 (accessed Nov. 2, 2004); University of Chicago Special Collections Research Center, www.lib.uchicago.edu/e/spcl/excat/douglasint.html (accessed Nov. 2, 2004).

17. *Gettysburg Compiler,* July 16 and Nov. 12, 1860; *York Gazette,* Nov. 13, 1860. Pennsylvania's "Fusion Ticket" was frequently called the "Reading Ticket." No state went "Fusion" in 1860.

18. Foner, *Free Soil,* 34–35 (citing the Springfield, Illinois, *Republican,* Nov. 1, 1856); *Adams Sentinel,* Nov. 10, 1856, and Oct. 10, 1860; *York Gazette,* Nov. 11, 1856, and Nov. 13, 1860; *Gettysburg Compiler,* Nov. 12, 1860. No votes were reported for John C. Breckinridge in 1860. From 1948

The Democratic split gave Lincoln the presidency, provoking the South to rip itself from the Union and making war inevitable. Once the firing started, men from south-central Pennsylvania had to pull together a lifetime of political consciousness to decide which uniform to wear. If state rights had been the overriding factor, the Confederacy might have drawn about half the counties' manpower. Editorial philosophy in the region was balanced in numbers, but Democrats had the momentum in votes and energy. Maryland loomed on the southern border, the only state outside the Deep South that voted for proslavery candidate John C. Breckinridge. Many Marylanders crossed the Mason-Dixon Line for work and no doubt left an influence, while Pennsylvania men went south for employment and mingled with proslavers on their turf. York's own West Point graduate Johnson Kelly Duncan had moved to Louisiana before the war, and during the conflict he would rise to the rank of brigadier general in the Confederate army.[19]

Four 87th Pennsylvania men would risk fighting against brothers. William Crosby Waldman would visit Rebel brother George in Fort Delaware Prison and convince him to sign a loyalty oath to the Union. John Clutter and David N. Hoffman's brother Charles would die at Gettysburg fighting for the Confederate cause alongside their maternal uncle Valentine Clutter. Before the war, John Wesley Culp had gone to Virginia with friends and family members to work in the carriage trade. As war neared, the others returned home, but Wes Culp stayed behind and joined the 2nd Virginia Infantry. He would face brother William and friend Jack Skelly in battle at Winchester, Virginia. Wes's subsequent involvement in the Jack Skelly–Jennie Wade relationship just before his death at Gettysburg arguably made the Culps the war's most famous brother-versus-brother combination. The potential was there for more split family loyalties that could create a situation like that in Kansas and Missouri.[20]

Circumstances were not that simple. Pennsylvania and Maryland had two centuries of history; Kansas and Missouri were yet struggling for identity. Though plantation owners may have been eagerly throwing on gray uniforms and abolitionists donning blue, south-central Pennsylvanians viewed events through a different lens. It is not surprising that area Republicans supported a war to save the Union, but Democrats proved they were not "disunion-

through 2004, only the 1964 Johnson-Goldwater election gave Democrats a majority in York and Adams counties' national races. William J. Switala, *Underground Railroad in Pennsylvania*, 27, 100–110.

19. Ezra J. Warner, *Generals in Gray: Lives of the Confederate Commanders*, 77–78. See also Michael J. Strong, *Keystone Confederate: The Life and Times of General Johnson Kelly Duncan, CSA* (York: Historical Society of York County, 1994).

20. George R. Prowell, *History of York County*, 1:557.

ists" whatever their Southern sympathies. The *York Gazette* still called South Carolina's decision to leave the Union "madness."[21]

One proud York County Democrat defined his reasons for enlisting and expressed the feelings of many in his party:

> I call myself a democrat; and I believe that the Democratic Party is right in the main questions on our national affairs. . . . I did and still believe that by proper action the troubles and calamities now before us might have been averted. . . . I do not sanction the agitation of the slavery question. . . . I said that if the North would commence this warfare, that I would stand by the South; but if they (the South) would fire upon Fort Sumter and seek the destruction of our Republic by making war upon it, I would be against the South and say blow them to h——.[22]

The man was true to his word. The South fired on Fort Sumter, and he enlisted with the 87th Pennsylvania.

However they may have viewed their politics, whatever they may have felt about the institution of slavery, the boys from York were about to prove they were almost entirely Union men. Many of them were going to shed blood proving it.[23]

---

21. *York Gazette,* Nov. 13, 1860.
22. "F" to the *York Republican,* Apr. 1, 1863, letter dated Mar. 12, 1863. The unidentified "F" claimed to be from heavily Democratic Seven Valleys, North Codorus Township, but no 87th man from that township had a last name beginning with "F."
23. As of summer 2005, Gettysburg historian and author Tim Smith had identified only six Adams County men who fought for the South.

Chapter 2

Initial Test

APRIL–JULY, 1861

The sacrifices the Civil War would ultimately demand from the American population were inconceivable as Fort Sumter fell in April 1861. Instead, an almost childlike excitement reigned, reflected in newspapers that dug out their largest type to create stirring headlines. "PENNSYLVANIA A UNIT! PARTY LINES OBLITERATED!" the *Gettysburg Star and Banner* shouted with naive optimism. The politically neutral *Hanover Spectator and General Advertiser* went into gear with the muscular headline "TRAITORS BEWARE!" warning Confederate sympathizers that "every sword will leap from its scabbard." The *York County Star and Wrightsville Advertiser,* the area's other impartial voice, urged readers to "take your place in line." The surprise came from Democratic papers. The *York Gazette,* which had sided so strongly with Southern rights, screamed, "WAR EXCITEMENT" headlining a positive story of how York was rallying to the cause. The *York Democratic Press* joined the war parade with, "Survival is the first law of nature and of nations," and added, "The Union feeling is intensely strong."[1]

The *Gettysburg Compiler* swallowed hardest, but swallow it did.

> What is the duty of the hour? . . . No other honorable course for patriotic and national men but to sustain the Constitutional Authorities in the exercise of their legitimate functions. Much as we opposed the election of Mr. Lincoln, solid as we have deemed Southern grievances,

1. *Star and Banner,* May 6, 1861; *Hanover Spectator,* Apr. 26, 1861; *Democratic Press,* Apr. 23, 1861; *Wrightsville Star,* Apr. 18, 1861; *York Gazette,* Apr. 23, 1861.

we urge with all our power acquiescence in the Constitutional and legal decision of the people.[2]

Red-white-and-blue bunting quickly appeared on many of York's buildings. American flags suddenly fluttered everywhere, one from atop a hundred-foot-tall staff that everyone agreed was the most magnificent sight they had ever seen in "Little York." Crowds pressed the telegraph office for the latest news and snatched newspapers from Jim Small's hands as fast as he could take their money. Citizens jammed meeting halls to pledge emotional and financial support for soldiers and their families. Orators who would never have to dodge a bullet delighted audiences with tales of glory on battlefields yet unknown. The Worth Infantry Band ended each day lip-weary and footsore from performing in countless flag-raising ceremonies and parades.[3]

Suddenly, it seemed as if half the men in the North were descending on south-central Pennsylvania as fast as wheels, hooves, and shank's ubiquitous mare could move them. Men from western states normally would have ridden the Baltimore and Ohio Railroad to Washington, but Virginia forces had cut the line at Harpers Ferry, (West) Virginia. The burden fell to the Pennsylvania Railroad's Pittsburgh-to-Harrisburg route. Passengers then took the Northern Central through York on to Baltimore and changed to the Baltimore and Ohio for the journey's final leg. Getting the Northern Central Railway running was vital to the Union's existence. In the opinion of the United States Army's commanding general, it was the most vital rail line of them all.[4]

That meant York's two militia companies, the Worth Infantry and the York Rifles, were going to war on short notice. They were the militia defined by the Bill of Rights' Second Amendment, but calling them "well ordered" was a stretch. Meetings more resembled those of a modern-day Rotary Club than smart military training and often did little to advance martial skills. Discipline amounted to dismissal from the company if dues went unpaid. Drilling

2. *Gettysburg Compiler,* Apr. 22, 1861. Democratic newspapers throughout the nation behaved much the same way. For examples, see Baker, *Affairs of Party,* 152–53.

3. *York Gazette,* Apr. 16 and 23, 1861; *Adams Sentinel,* Apr. 17, 1861; Adams County Commissioners, minutes, 1841–1860. For New England's reaction, see Thomas R. Kemp, "Community and War: The War Experience of Two New Hampshire Towns," in *Toward a Social History of the American Civil War: Exploratory Essays,* edited by Maris A. Vinovskis. A June 11, 1834, article in the *Pennsylvania Republican* decried using "Little York," but twenty-seven years later, it was still in wide use.

4. *O.R.,* Maj. Gen. Winfield Scott to Maj. Gen. Robert Patterson, Apr. 22, 1861, 2:587. On his trip from Illinois, President-elect Abraham Lincoln was scheduled to ride the Northern Central and pause in York until security learned of an assassination plot and detoured him to Philadelphia. Note: The author will use (West) Virginia in references to events in that area that took place prior to June 20, 1863, the date of West Virginia's admittance to the Union.

occurred irregularly, and the men fired their muskets seldom because ammunition cost money. They marched in parades, went on weekend encampments, and looked good in their uniforms but were little better prepared for war than modern-day reenactors, albeit with live ammunition and thinner waistlines. On the other hand, they were no worse than thousands of other units then forming, and they were available on one day's notice, just as New Englanders had made themselves available at Concord and Lexington ninety years before.[5]

Maj. Gen. George Hay of the state militia galloped through town shouting for men to report at once, and the whole community reacted. Hantz Brothers Hardware supplied gunpowder and P. A. and S. Small's Hardware donated lead to forge bullets. Blacksmith Jacob Dieter and tinsmith George Wantz put aside personal work and set ovens ablaze casting forty rounds of bullets per man. Every endeavor received assistance from "citizens, ladys, & children of the borough." At 11:00 P.M. on April 19, 1861, with the Worth Infantry Band pumping out "The Girl I Left Behind Me" and a crowd cheering them on, the two companies boarded a special train bound for Maryland and, for all they knew, glory.[6]

The boys from York leaped from the train into military life near Cockeysville, Maryland, site of the northernmost bridge damaged by order of Baltimore's mayor. The night was cold, but the rain had stopped, and the temperature rose to a more comfortable level at daylight. Over the next two days, a dozen more trains arrived. Some were crammed with troops or military supplies while others carried materials for callus-handed workers used to repair bridges and damaged track.[7]

The near presence of a Yankee army enflamed an already volatile situation in Baltimore. City newspapers kept close tabs on those Yankee "despots" up at Cockeysville and screamed headlines such as "WARLIKE RUMORS— ANNOUNCEMENT OF PENNSYLVANIA TROOPS APPROACHING

5. Worth Infantry; Reid Mitchell, "The Northern Soldier and His Community," in *Toward a Social History of the American Civil War: Exploratory Essays,* edited by Maris A. Vinovskis, 81. Mitchell compared early unit discipline to that of "a lodge of Elks." For another example of an unprepared militia, see Richard Moe, *The Last Full Measure: The Life and Death of the First Minnesota Volunteers,* 9.

6. Worth Infantry. For additional information on these two militia companies, see www.geocities.com/Heartland/Hills/3916/cwpa/cwpa16a.html and www.personal.psu.edu/users/n/r/nrl108/york/unitdesig.htm (both sites accessed June 1, 2006). "P.A. & S. Small," founded by Philip Albright and Samuel Small, existed as a company name into the late twentieth century.

7. *O.R.,* Report of Edward F. Jones, Apr. 22, 1861, 2:7, Extracts of the report of the Baltimore Police Commissioners, May 3, 1861, 2:10, George William Brown to Thomas H. Hicks, Apr. 20, 1861, 2:581, Report of George William Brown, May 9, 1861, 2:12–13; diary of Solomon Myers; Worth Infantry; *Democratic Press,* Apr. 23, 1861.

—A WILD EXCITEMENT." Who could blame them for being nervous? Since the Pratt Street Riots, Fort McHenry had been aiming its big guns squarely at the city. Northbound roads filled with refugees.[8]

Long-term friendships dissolved overnight. A Maryland friend and militia associate of George Hay was crushed by Pennsylvania's actions and told him so in a letter.

> Little did I think to see the day when the Worth Infantry, the Fenci-
> bles, and others of our comrades would volunteer to march and cut our
> throats. Are they not mad? For what is there between us? On Sunday
> when told they were within a short march of us I refused to believe so
> horrible a story. But they have made their selection and I can only [say]
> good for the nigger. . . . I suppose we shall next hear of them from some
> other source. I say shame, shame.[9]

Washington knew the raw troops at Cockeysville were not quite as dangerous as Baltimore thought and sent Maj. Fitz-John Porter to assist Governor Andrew Curtin. New Hampshire-born Porter, West Point class of '45 and recipient of two Mexican War promotions for gallantry, was the lone army man from a family of distinguished naval officers. He set right to work only to be stunned by Pennsylvania's lack of military supplies. He scrounged three different arsenals for ordnance, pleaded with restaurants and hotels to contribute food until he could form a commissary department, and begged assistance from two railroads to transport everything to where it was needed. After inspecting troops at Cockeysville, he told division commander Col. George Campbell Wynkoop that he needed more than the 3,400 men already in his command. Porter ordered Wynkoop to sit tight while he fetched reinforcements from Harrisburg. By daylight, they would be marching on Baltimore to straighten out those traitors. In truth, Porter was less bothered by inadequate numbers than inexperienced officers, a concern that would prove well founded.[10]

---

8. *Baltimore American and Commercial Advertiser,* Apr. 22, 1861; *Daily Baltimore Republican,* Apr. 24, 1861. The *Republican* was solidly Democratic in spite of its name.

9. Charles Calvert Egerton to George Hay, Apr. 26, 1861, George Hay Kain III Collection; U.S. Census, 1860, Maryland, Baltimore, 11th Ward. Egerton was a Maryland militia leader who commanded Harpers Ferry forces during John Brown's raid in 1859. Hay knew him through interaction of the states' militias.

10. Warner, *Generals in Blue,* 378–80; *O.R.,* Winfield Scott to Robert Patterson, Apr. 21, 1861, 2:585, Simon Cameron to the "Officer in Charge," Apr. 21, 1861, 2:584, Report of Fitz-John Porter, May 1, 1861, LI/1:345–52; Stephen W. Sears, *George B. McClellan: The Young Napoleon,* 70. Pennsylvania was not the only state lacking armaments. About this same time, George B. McClellan unlocked an Ohio arsenal and found more rust than functional equipment.

Porter reached York at midnight and found himself stuck there until a southbound train passed on the line's single track. The train's arrival held him in York longer than expected because it carried new orders, ones that Porter considered so far-fetched he raced to a telegraph key to question Washington about their veracity. Finally convinced they were real and not about to change, he passed them down the line to George Wynkoop and continued to Harrisburg. Solomon Myers and friends were just as bewildered as Porter had been when they heard the orders. After all their rushing to guard the Northern Central Railroad, the secretary of war was sending them back to York. As the last of the militiamen boarded a northbound train, they could hear saboteurs plying their trade on the railroad behind them.[11]

Fitz-John Porter tried to salvage something from the disturbing turn of events. Sacrificing Maryland's bridges was bad enough, but nothing said York County had to abandon theirs. Again, he planted himself beside a telegraph key, this time trying to goad George Wynkoop into a semblance of action. The resulting exchange demonstrated the difference between regular army and militia officers and how unprepared the region's leaders were to fight a war.[12]

"Where are you going with your command?" Porter asked.

Wynkoop replied, "Ordered from Maryland by order of General [Winfield] Scott and Secretary of War," parroting the very orders Porter had given him.

"Can you camp your men at the Junction?" Porter asked, referring to Hanover Junction in southern York County where the Hanover line split from the Northern Central.

"Have nothing but unground coffee, rice, and beef," Wynkoop said, not explaining why his men could not grind coffee and survive a few days on rice and beef. Contradicting himself, he added, "No supper last night, and nothing for the men this morning."

"I will send meals," Porter said, "if you will secure the bridges and road and fix your camp, and maintain your post at all hazards."

"No ground is suitable for the command to encamp here. At York there is good ground . . ."

"The Government orders that this road be secured at all hazards," Porter said "Can you, and will you, do it? . . . Go to Shrewsbury if you can execute your orders."

11. *O.R.,* Report of Fitz-John Porter, May 1, 1861, LI/1:348; James Belger to Fitz-John Porter, Apr. 22, 1861, LI/1:360; diary of Solomon Myers.

12. *O.R.,* Fitz-John Porter to Simon Cameron, Apr. 22, 1861, LI/1:363.

Wynkoop said, "If I take my command out here I cannot hold them without food. The men are in a very bad condition, and must have something to eat. Will come on to York and get their provisions and make any arrangements that will be acceptable to the Government."

"I will supply food immediately if you will say where you determine to locate."

"Give my men their breakfast at York and I can then take them wherever you wish . . . if sanctioned by Secretary of War or General Scott."

"The Secretary of War directs the road to be held at all risk, and if you bring all your men here you will lose your bridges."

"Will stop in the cars until I can find a place to encamp. My men must have tents and provisions."

"I will send provisions immediately," Porter repeated, his words scarcely concealing his frustration. "Tents are to come from the city by order of Governor Curtin." He again asked Wynkoop where he would camp.

"I cannot yet say."[13]

Porter gave up and informed Washington that the city would fall within ten days unless someone found a way to transport soldiers from New York via a water route. He then headed to the nation's capital to give his gloomy report in person.[14]

Wynkoop's force entered York about 10:00 A.M. on April 23 and established camp on the fairgrounds. The men were soon gorging on fresh beef and other rations the community had waiting, supplies that York residents had been loading onto railcars for shipment when they heard the men were returning.

Wynkoop's fear of commanding a starving army was baseless. While complaining of his men's hunger in his telegraph conversation with Fitz-John Porter, he admitted that he had rice and beef on hand. He also failed to report that stores had arrived on April 22, an event Solomon Myers documented in his diary. Even if food stocks had been zero, Porter had repeatedly offered to send supplies as soon as Wynkoop made a decision where to post his forces. A competent commander would have been in touch with York and known that citizens there were gathering rations. The indecisive colonel of militia never offered a thought as to what his men would have eaten had they remained in Maryland as originally planned.[15]

---

13. Ibid., messages between Fitz-John Porter and George Wynkoop, pp. 364–67.

14. Ibid., Report of Maj. Fitz-John Porter, May 1, 1861, pp. 346, 349. Porter traveled by train to Hagerstown, Maryland, and then continued overland to Washington.

15. *York Gazette,* Apr. 23 and 30, 1861; diary of Solomon Myers; *O.R.,* W. H. Sidell to Colonel Fry, Aug. 16, 1862, 16/2:349–50, Report of George C. Wynkoop, 16/1:877–78. While colonel of

Porter's doomsday prediction proved unfounded. Rebel forces did not enter York and Adams counties in 1861 and would not arrive in any great number for another two years. Neither did Washington fall, and none of York County's bridges ever suffered sabotage. Baltimore's mayor had ordered the destruction of Maryland's bridges to save his city from further violence, not as a prologue to attacking Pennsylvania. Porter, however, could not have known that then. His advice to Wynkoop made sense and was within instructions issued by the secretary of war.[16]

Abraham Lincoln's abandonment of the Northern Central cost the rail line seventeen bridges, but they were the necessary cost of keeping Maryland in the Union. Tension gripped Maryland throughout the war but squeezed hardest during those opening weeks. If Maryland had fallen into the Southern camp, it would have leaned the heavy weight of the Confederacy against Pennsylvania and made Washington the meat in a Southern sandwich. Lincoln had decided the day after the Pratt Street Riots to halt troop flow through Baltimore. There were better uses for soldiers than guarding a temporarily functionless railroad. It would not take long before the president would nudge Maryland's governor and legislature into line by pushing pro-Southern Marylanders "behind closed doors," as one Unionist Maryland newspaper put it. Then, the army would clamp Baltimore tightly and give its bridge-busting mayor firsthand appreciation of his prison system.[17]

Shortly after George Wynkoop's men returned to York, companies from Hanover and Gettysburg arrived to share straw in the fairground sheds. Units from other parts of the state followed until five thousand soldiers were milling around town. York's citizenry made the men feel so welcome they called their abode "Camp Delight." Authorities decided to honor the supreme commander with "Camp Scott," a name that would play a dual role three months later. From the base of York and Adams counties' men came the 2nd and 16th Pennsylvania Regiments, signed on for the ninety days considered sufficient

---

the 7th Pennsylvania Cavalry, Wynkoop saw his force routed at Gallatin, Tennessee, and fled the field. *Atlas of York Co. Pennsylvania Illustrated, from Surveys of Beach Nichols,* 68–69. The fairground was located between King Street and Plank Road (Prospect Street), a block east of Queen Street. Wynkoop's non-York regiments returned to Camp Curtin in Harrisburg.

16. *O.R.,* Report of Fitz-John Porter, LI/1:345–52; Simon Cameron to the "Officer in Charge," Apr. 21, 1861, 2:584, George William Brown to Thomas H. Hicks, Apr. 20, 1861, 2:12–13, Report of George William Brown, May 9, 1861, 2:581; diary of Solomon Myers; *Democratic Press,* Apr. 30, 1861.

17. *Democratic Press,* Apr. 23 and 30, 1861, and Sept. 12, 1862. Thomas A. Scott claimed repairs to the Northern Central bridges cost $14,000. *York Gazette,* Apr. 23, 1861; *News* (Frederick, Md.), Sept. 1861; *O.R.,* George William Brown to Thomas Hicks, Apr. 20, 1861, 2:581.

to quash the rebellion. After the first battle of Bull Run (Manassas) proved that the war would run longer than most had expected, many men from the regiments reenlisted and formed the core of the 87th Pennsylvania.[18]

Responsibility for building Pennsylvania's portion of the three-month Union army fell onto Harrisburg's untested shoulders. The inexperience showed. John Taughinbaugh McIlhenny, editor of the *Gettysburg Star and Banner,* was slumming as a corporal with the 2nd Pennsylvania Infantry and filed a series of insider reports. In one, he complained that the shoddy uniforms the state issued made them "look more like a gang of convicts from the penitentiary than a company of soldiers." He deemed their treatment "a disgrace to the State of Pennsylvania" and dropped the blame on their division commander, whom he regarded as "not the man for the place." Corporal McIlhenny suffered no punishment for drubbing a superior in print, a clear demonstration of the militia's weak discipline.[19]

Washington created a new Department of Pennsylvania and handed command of it to sixty-nine-year-old Irish-born Robert Patterson, veteran of both the War of 1812 and Mexican War. General Patterson was about to prove he had stayed beyond his prime by setting a standard of lassitude the Union's most cautious generals later had difficulty emulating. Among the thousands of words he wrote to Washington, none better describes the roots of his inaction of the next three months than, "I am resolved to conquer and risk nothing." Patterson indeed risked nothing and, as events will demonstrate, may have single-handedly guaranteed a long, bloody war.[20]

By July, April's excitement had withered, and the reality of boredom and sickness set in. So, too, did a sense of pointlessness. Robert Patterson kept ordering his army here and there while bragging to Washington of the grand things he was about to do. So suddenly and so often did he change his army's position that one soldier complained they never knew ten minutes in advance of when they were going to march off again. Corporal-editor McIlhenny reported that they had "traveled nearly 150 miles and have only got about 35 miles from Gettysburg." Until mid-July, the closest they came to a fight was a

18. *York Gazette,* Apr. 23, 1861; diaries of John Stoner Beidler; *Star and Banner,* May 10, 1861; *Democratic Press,* Apr. 30, 1861.

19. *Pennsylvania Archives,* 4th ser., vol. 8, *Papers of the Governors 1858–1871,* 420–21; *O.R.,* A. G. Curtin to the War Department, Apr. 29, 1861, ser. 3, 1:132–33; August V. Kautz, *Customs of Service for Officers of the Army: A Handbook of the Duties of Each Grade Lieutenant to Lieut.-General,* 280; *Star and Banner,* May 10, 1861. Gen. William High Keim was McIlhenny's target.

20. *O.R.,* General Orders No. 12, Apr. 27, 1861, 2:607, General Order No. 23, Apr. 29, 1861, 2:611, Robert Patterson to E. D. Townsend, June 12 and 19, 1861, 2:676, 707. The Department of Pennsylvania included Delaware and part of Maryland. Ezra J. Warner omitted Robert Patterson from *Generals in Blue.*

dark night they almost gunned down their own pickets. Even a skirmish with the enemy on July 15 accomplished little, harmed few, and did not directly involve any significant number of York or Adams County men. The only soldier in the 2nd or 16th Pennsylvania who took a bullet was a sergeant who accidentally shot himself in the foot. Inaction did not stop one daydreaming 16th Pennsylvania wag calling himself "Amigo" from dubbing his outfit "the bloody 16th."[21]

Through it all, supplies remained inadequate and of morale-killing quality, as John McIlhenny reported.

> Another screw got loose in the Commissary's department. Our rations ever since we arrived here have been very poor, but yesterday it was unbearable. In addition to the hard sea biscuits, they tried to force on us dirty, stinking oily sides of pork not fit for a dog to eat, while the sugar and coffee not only fell far short of the usual amount, but were also of the very worst quality . . . Those who would thus impose upon the soldier should at once be hurled from position and punished.[22]

Whatever the quality of rations, Washington ordered Patterson to occupy Rebel forces around Winchester, Virginia, a town at the Shenandoah Valley's lower (northern) end destined to become all too familiar to the boys from York. Union forces were about to move on the Rebels at Manassas Junction, and Patterson needed to lock up Confederate forces in the valley while that happened. It was a critical order, and Patterson botched it. Had he deployed for attack right away, he might have held the enemy's attention without engaging in combat. Instead, he stopped at Bunker Hill ten miles north of the goal and wired Washington that he could not move another step. The men would soon be going home, he said, and had voted not to remain one hour longer than required. Instead, Patterson stood his men in line of march for several hours without telling them where they were going. The men assumed it was Winchester, but Patterson turned them around and marched to Charles Town, (West) Virginia.[23]

---

21. Johnston Hastings Skelly Jr. to his mother, July 5 and 16, 1861, Department of the Interior, Pension Records of Johnston H. Skelly, Co. F, 87th Pa., NARA; *Star and Banner,* June 21, 1861, event dated June 17; *Democratic Press,* Apr. 18 and 25, June 18 and 25, and July 16, 1861; diary of Solomon Myers; *O.R.,* Report of Robert Patterson, July 16, 1861, 2:166–67; Pension Records of Jacob L. Stough, Co. A, 16th Pa., and Co. D, 12th U.S. Stough was the man who shot himself in the foot.

22. *Star and Banner,* June 14, 1861, event dated June 11.

23. "Lower" and "upper" Shenandoah Valley are terms relative to the flow of the Shenandoah River. *O.R.,* Winfield Scott to Robert Patterson, July 13, 1861, 2:166, Robert Patterson to E. D.

One of his angry soldiers vented to his hometown newspaper.

> Fierce was our indignation and bitter the curses of the men when we
> learned that we were enroute for Charles Town—an almost retrograde
> movement from the enemy. Our column soon deteriorated into a stag-
> gering horde, the retreat, as we called it having a most demoralizing effect
> on the troop. The opinion was plainly expressed that our commander
> was playing directly into the hands of the rebels; either treacherously or
> through imbecility.[24]

A baffled reporter traveling with the army remarked that Patterson's strategy "would puzzle the spirits of Caesar, Saxe, Napoleon, Wellington, and
all the departed heroes." While Patterson insisted he could accomplish grand
things from Charles Town, the move put his army no closer to the enemy and
in no position to block the railroad to Manassas Junction. The Confederate
force at Winchester plunged through the hole Patterson had left and headed
east on an intact and unguarded railroad. Washington warned him what was
happening, but he refused to believe it. When his own scouts finally convinced him of the truth, he maintained that he still could not move because
many of his men were barefoot and only had a week left in service.[25]

"A week is enough to win victories," Gen. Winfield Scott scolded and reminded Patterson that the enemy had stolen a march on him.

"The enemy has stolen no march upon me," Patterson responded indig-
nantly. It was his last delusion.[26]

The Confederate force Patterson allowed to escape turned the first battle
of Manassas from a potential Federal victory into a Southern rout. Possibility of a short war faded. In recognition of his three-month effort, the War
Department informed General Patterson that his thirty-nine-year military
career was over. In a farewell statement, he complimented his men because
"they had steadily advanced in the face of the enemy."[27]

The boys from York went home without experiencing battle. Joyous as it
was to return home and in spite of their bitter taste of the military, many of

---

Townsend, July 14, 16, and 18, 1861, 2:166–69, 701–2; Johnston H. Skelly to his mother, July 16,
1861, Pension Records of Johnston H. Skelly; *Columbia Spy,* July 20, 1861.

24. "Thirsty Squad" to the *Columbia Spy,* July 27, 1861, letter dated July 14, 1861.

25. *O.R.,* Robert Patterson to E. D. Townsend, July 4, July 9, July 16, and July 18, 1861, 2:157–
58, 162–63, 166–67, 169–70, Joseph E. Johnston to Samuel Cooper, July 18, 1861, 2:982; *Rebellion
Record,* vol. 2, doc. 117, pp. 395–96.

26. *Rebellion Record,* Winfield Scott to Robert Patterson, and Robert Patterson to E. D. Townsend, both July 18, 1861, vol. 2, doc. 117, p. 168.

27. Ibid., War Department General Orders No. 46, July 19, 1861, p. 171; Department of Pennsylvania General Orders No. 33, July 25, 1861, p. 174. Patterson was discharged July 27, 1861.

them had to feel embarrassed about their decision to cut and run. Expired enlistments technically freed them from shame, and their vote to leave the army had occurred before anyone knew there would be a battle of Bull Run. Still, they had left the army during a crisis. No extant communication reveals how they felt about their exit from military service, but their actions during the next few weeks screamed their feelings.[28]

A company of Zouaves greeted them at the train station. Armed and brilliantly attired in red-and-blue French-style uniforms, they had been drawing the eyes of the ladies since their inception on May 10. Capt. James Alanza Stahle had not gone to war but stayed behind to whip together a new seventy-man militia. Stahle announced that his "Ellsworth Zouaves" would lead the way toward a new regiment by opening camp at their own expense. The York Rifles would not be outdone and went on their own overnight excursion to stage drills at Wrightsville and Columbia. Men talked freely of reenlisting. This time, that meant cutting out three years of their lives.[29]

Washington was about to come up with work it considered perfectly suited to the boys from York. Before that, some qualified leaders needed to step forward and volunteer.

---

28. *York Gazette,* July 30, 1861.

29. Diary of Solomon Myers; Prowell, *87th Pennsylvania,* 3; *York Gazette,* June 11 and 23, 1861, and Aug. 6, 1861; "Chaplain" [John Francis Baird] to the *York Gazette,* Sept. 23, 1862, letter dated Sept. 2, 1862. The *Gazette* reported the Zouaves' campsite was located at Neiman's Grove near Weiglestown, but the *Democratic Press* claimed George Meisenhelter's woods where "the Little Conewago Creek crosses the Bull Road." Stahle named his company after the martyred Elmer Ellsworth.

Chapter 3

Genesis

Veterans of the 2nd and 16th Pennsylvania regiments were among many who witnessed how the railroad was going to make this a new type of war. The Bull Run debacle demonstrated that trains could move men and matériel rapidly over long distances and alter the outcome of battle. The penalties for not guarding railroads had been made all too clear. For all their power, though, trains had a weakness. One man could remove a few rail spikes and flip a passing train onto its side, helpless as a belly-up turtle. Even on intact rails, incompetent management could make train travel more dangerous than it already was.[1]

The Union had immediate need for a railroad expert with an extensive résumé, political connections, and people skills that could herd ego-driven personalities toward a common goal. Tough as those requirements seemed, the search was a short one. The governor of Pennsylvania already employed just such a superman of the railroad industry: Thomas Alexander Scott was the man of steel rails, and he was about to find work for the lads from south-central Pennsylvania.

History sometimes smiles on selected individuals. It flashed a toothy grin at Thomas A. Scott, born of humble origins but raised to rare heights of power and wealth. He even had a York County connection. At the young age of seventeen, he began his transportation career just across the Susquehanna River in Columbia but soon left that fledgling business to open a sawmill. After a flood deposited his mill into the Chesapeake Bay, he crossed the bridge into Wrightsville and tried his hand at running an icehouse. It was fortunate

---

1. Scanning through any York or Adams County newspaper c. 1860 reveals an almost weekly incidence of railroad accidents.

for the nation that the new venture also failed because it forced him back
to the transportation industry. He rocketed up the Pennsylvania Railroad
hierarchy to general superintendent, and he used his authority to grease the
skids of rail expansion to Pittsburgh and beyond. By the onset of the Civil
War, visitors entered his office through a door emblazoned with the words
vice president.[2]

Scott's success gained him powerful allies, among them Senator Simon
Cameron, a master of patronage and self-interest notorious among Democrats and even some Republicans. When the Cameron-controlled Pennsylvania delegation needed transportation to the 1860 Republican presidential
convention in Chicago, Thomas A. Scott provided them all with free rail tick-
ets. After Cameron's presidential aspirations went bust, he threw his support
behind Abraham Lincoln but attached a price tag that included the keys to
the office of secretary of war. Once seated, Cameron handed Scott responsibility for keeping the railroads and telegraph lines working. By mid-May,
trains were safely crossing the Northern Central's bridges, and Jim Small once
again sold Baltimore newspapers on the square in York.[3]

Scott now had to keep the railroads running. If the Baltimore lines were
cut again, the city might be lost and the war with it. Problem was, manpower
expended guarding a railroad subtracted from that available for active service.
Given Maryland's unstable situation, Scott argued that Pennsylvania should
muster a special militia to guard the Northern Central. The state adjutant
general politely agreed in principle but was sorry that he could "find no provision authorizing the organization of companies or regiments to constitute
such a reserve force as your suggestions contemplate." The adjutant general
was not being just a stuffy bureaucrat. No state militia could stand duty in
another state except by call of the president. If Pennsylvania was to secure the
Northern Central, Scott had to find another way to do it.[4]

The colonel's rank Simon Cameron had granted Scott failed to impress
generals and gave Scott little direct authority over the military. After the dis-

2. Samuel Richey Kamm, "The Civil War Career of Thomas A. Scott: A Dissertation in History"; *Philadelphia Evening Bulletin,* June 13 and Dec. 27, 1924, and Feb. 29, 1946; *Columbia Spy,*
May 21, 1870. Scott was born December 23, 1823, in Loudon, Franklin County, the son of innkeep-
ers Thomas A. and Rebecca Douglas Scott. At his death on May 21, 1881, he left an estate valued
in excess of $8,000,000, which courts were still distributing after World War II.

3. Gunnarsson, *Northern Central,* 47–52, 58; *O.R.,* 27/3:592, William Patterson to Lorenzo
Thomas, Apr. 21, 1861, 2:586, Simon Cameron to Colonel Stone, Apr. 25, 1861, 2:600, Simon
Cameron to "all it may concern," May 23, 1861, ser. 3, 1:228; Donald, *Lincoln,* 265–67; Kamm,
"Thomas A. Scott," 2, 7, 9, 21, 22, 42; *York Gazette,* May 14, 1861.

4. Adj. Gen. Alexander L. Russell to Thomas A. Scott, July 31, 1861, Veterans' Affairs, Office
of the Adjutant General, Pennsylvania State Archives, Harrisburg, Pa., Letter Book; Papers of the
Governors 1858–1871, 4th ser., 8:408.

aster at Bull Run, Scott wired a general to *suggest* he prevent fleeing troops from entering Washington to prevent a public panic. During restoration of the Baltimore-Annapolis spur line, he could only *recommend* stationing a regiment as permanent guard. Cameron rectified that problem by asking Congress to create a new position of assistant secretary of war. Congress promptly agreed, and Cameron just as promptly named Thomas A. Scott to fill the $3,000-a-year job. Now, he could issue orders to reluctant generals and answer only to Cameron and Lincoln.[5]

Scott turned to south-central Pennsylvania to save the more than seventy bridges the Northern Central spanned on its Maryland corridor. York and Adams counties had economic impetus to preserve the rail line, and growing muster lists proved that men were ready to serve. All they needed was an organizer to shuffle them into a coherent military deck. York now provided its own superman, a businessman with forty years of political connections under his prodigious belt. That Alexander Small was a Democrat was an unpleasant fact Thomas A. Scott just had to tolerate.[6]

In 1805, Alex Small was born into a family whose name remained a York business byword into the late twentieth century. Business, however, was not initially on his mind. In 1824, he earned a medical degree and returned home to hang out his shingle. Along the way, he volunteered his medical skills at York's almshouse and served as staff surgeon for an army regiment. After eight years, Small walked away from the healing profession, reeled in by the twin lures of politics and business. Two runs at Congress failed, but the change of lifestyle placed him at the head of a manufacturing company and on the boards of many business and community ventures. (At his death in 1862, his net worth had reached nearly $70,000, a tidy sum when the counting of a man's worth unusually ended while still in three figures.)

In those chaotic April days, York turned to Alex Small, and he responded by organizing the collection of 15,400 rations in two days. When Camp Scott needed a man to spearhead the flow of matériel, Small had been the logical choice for camp commissary. Motivation to serve, if he needed any,

---

5. *O.R.,* Simon Cameron to Winfield Scott, May 6, 1861, 2:623; Thomas A. Scott to Joseph Mansfield, July 22, 1861, 2:754–55; ser. 3, 1:325–26; *Register of Officers and Agents, Civil, Military, and Naval, in the Service of the United States on the Thirtieth September 1861,* 101. The secretary of war's salary was $8,000. Scott established a schedule of charges the government had to pay the railroads, in effect setting the rates he paid himself. See *New York Times,* Aug. 9, 1862, for criticism of Scott's alleged price-fixing, and *Democratic Press,* Sept. 12, 1862, reprint of Scott's rebuttal to the *New York Times.* See also John E. Clark Jr., "Management in War: The Legacy of Civil War Railroads."

6. Gunnarsson, *Northern Central,* appendix 3, list of bridges.

may have come the month before when he witnessed the Pratt Street Riots. During his tenure, no one reported a hint of financial impropriety. The *York Gazette* complimented its fellow Democrat for operating the most cost-efficient campsite around, although they were light on comparative source material to make that statement.[7]

Small probably arranged financing for James Stahle's Ellsworth Zouaves. They hit the streets in June 1861 freshly uniformed and armed, so someone clearly had raised funds virtually overnight to pay for their gear. No record has been uncovered proving that Small was the Zouaves' benefactor, but the officers said as much by honoring him with a lifetime membership. When the Ellsworth Zouaves became the heart of Company A, 87th Pennsylvania, they called their Maryland base "Camp Small," and Alex Small was a frequent visitor. Upon his premature death on June 8, 1862, Company A paid him a heartfelt public tribute.[8]

Small connected with Thomas A. Scott and Simon Cameron through membership on the board of the Northern Central Railway. On August 13, 1861, Assistant Secretary of War Thomas A. Scott formally granted citizen Alexander Small permission to raise a regiment specifically pegged to guard the Northern Central Railway. Typically, the man who recruited a military unit also led it into the field, but York might have laughed envisioning their cigar-chomping favorite son commanding a regiment. Fifty-seven is an advanced age to initiate a military career, especially when a man's waistline closely matches his age inch for year. Small wisely declined offers to go into the field and looked elsewhere for leadership.[9]

Small turned to John William Schall to lead the regiment, a choice both logical and controversial. On the plus side, Schall was young but not too young, successful in business, and had the distinct advantage of being a graduate of Vermont's Norwich Military Academy. Schall's primary negative was that his roots were in Berks and Montgomery counties. He had moved to York a few years before the war but still considered Berks his home. While

7. *O.R.,* Alexander Small to Fitz-John Porter, Apr. 21, 1861, LI/1:359; Alexander Small to Jacob Stair, Apr. 17, 1861, Alexander Small ms. file, YCHT; *York Gazette,* May 28, 1861.

8. *Democratic Press,* June 13 and 20, 1862; *York Gazette,* Dec. 31, 1861, and June 17, 1862; Gunnarsson, *Northern Central,* 57. The men also called their grounds "Camp Small Jr." Gunnarsson claims the camp located at modern-day Cold Spring Lane was named for landowner Charles W. Small. The name had a conveniently dual purpose.

9. *Democratic Press,* June 13, 1862; *York Gazette,* July 23, 1861; Records of the Office of the Secretary of War: Letters Sent by the Secretary of War Relating to Military Affairs, NARA, Thomas A. Scott to Dr. Alexander Small, Aug. 13, 1861; Lewis Miller, *Sketches and Chronicles, The Reflections of a Nineteenth Century Pennsylvania German Folk Artist,* 121, 153.

he had integrated himself into the York community and risen to a command position with the local militia, there were lifelong residents who had a greater claim to the command. Schall rejected Alex Small's appointment, possibly because he knew it could lead to strained relations with other officers. Since he was in the midst of recruiting a company, captain's bars were sufficient—for the time being.[10]

The recipient of John Schall's largesse was York militiaman George Hay, viewed by a local newspaper as "one of the most efficient officers in the state." Hay had no formal military education, but somewhere in his household lay a stack of state militia commissions ranging from second lieutenant of infantry to captain of artillery to a recent promotion to major general of York County's force. To the York community, his face shined as brightly on the parade ground as Alex Small's did in a boardroom. Just as important, his roots wound as deeply into York's soil.[11]

Many a Yorker sat on furniture or stored books on shelves built by cabinet-maker George Hay, and more went to their eternal rest in one of his caskets. Hundreds had served under him in the antebellum militia. He had tried to lead a unit into the Mexican War, but his was the eleventh company in a state allotment of ten. When riots threatened Philadelphia, he took an outfit there to restore order, but nothing significant happened. Three months as captain with the 2nd Pennsylvania Infantry did not test his mettle in combat. Otherwise, the nearest he had come to battle was the day he was lounging by his shop window and a would-be assassin sent a bullet screaming past his head. Lack of battle experience was hardly unusual in that early stage of the war and little impediment to assuming leadership of a volunteer regiment. Indeed, he was more experienced in the art of leading men than many.[12]

George Hay proved popular with his men even though he expressed insecurity about their opinion of him and surprise when they offered praise. No extant communication speaks of him in anything but complimentary terms. "Gentleman" was a commonly used expression. A civilian visiting the regiment in the spring of 1863 reported, "Col. Hay is a great favorite here among

10. PA AGO, Civil War Muster Rolls and Related Records, 2nd Pa. mic. 3648; *Bucks County (Pa.) Gazette,* July 6, 1899; Prowell, *87th Pennsylvania,* 12, 270; *Biographical and Portrait Cyclopedia of Montgomery County, Pennsylvania,* edited by Henry Wilson Ruoff (Philadelphia: Biographical Publishing Company, 1895), 52–55; Norwich in the Civil War, www.norwich.edu/about/resources/nom/nis/alumni.htm. Norwich Academy is the country's oldest private military college. Unfortunately, a fire destroyed school records in 1867.

11. *Democratic Press,* June 8, 1858; George Hay File 12665, YCHT; *York Republican and Anti-Masonic Expositor,* Apr. 19, 1831; Prowell, *87th Pennsylvania,* 270.

12. "W" to the *York Republican,* April 23, 1863; George Hay Kain III, "George Hay: Citizen-Soldier from York, Pennsylvania." Hay lived Aug. 1, 1809–May 24, 1879.

the soldiers. It is seldom an officer is fortunate enough to have the universal respect and confidence of his command." He became a favorite of Gen. Robert Huston Milroy, too, who assigned Hay to a brigade command and with whom he exchanged postwar letters. The 12th West Virginia Infantry regimental history offers plaudits to his skill at drill instruction. When the men of the 1st Virginia Light Artillery (Union) heard the army was going to transfer them out of Hay's brigade in 1863, sixty soldiers signed a petition expressing eagerness to remain under his command.[13]

After a rupture forced his resignation in May 1863, Hay's subalterns gushed about his "courtesy and kindness" and "generous disposition." Eighth Corps headquarters in Baltimore thought enough of him to issue a permanent pass permitting his travel "on any good road from this city at all times." Until war's end, he regularly corresponded with the regiment, visited them in the field, and assisted wounded and sick comrades in obtaining transfers to York's U.S. Army Hospital. After the war, he continued to involve himself in militia affairs and reunions to the extent that his body permitted.[14]

George Hay never had an opportunity to prove himself in battle, but he knew how to instruct soldiers in the art of drill. A New Jersey soldier deemed the 87th Pennsylvania "the finest drilled regiment in the service."[15]

The regiment had a commander, and recruiting was lively; now, it needed a unit name. Not surprisingly, the "Thomas A. Scott Regiment of Pennsylvania Volunteers" became its official title, supposedly by directive of the War Department. Since the editor of the newspaper making the claim was Alexander Small's cousin, the progenitor of the regiment's title was more likely Small himself.[16]

The exuberance that had characterized recruiting in spring should have waned by August. The three-month men's experience had proved that army life was anything but the glorious existence described by April orators. Besides, anyone contemplating performing valiant feats in battle with the Thomas A. Scott Regiment was bound for disappointment. Nobody in Wash-

13. George Hay to his brother, Sept. 19, 1862; 1st Virginia Light Artillery (Union) to George Hay, Apr. 20, 1863; Robert H. Milroy to George Hay, Feb. 28, 1870, all from George Hay Kain III Collection; William Hewitt, *History of the Twelfth West Virginia Volunteer Infantry: The Part It Took in the War of the Rebellion 1861–1865,* chap. 2.

14. Photocopy of the original pass, Headquarters, Middle Department, 8th Army Corps, Office of the Provost Marshal, July 15, 1863, George Hay Kain III Collection; George Hay to Medical Director, David's Island Hospital, New York, July 25, 1864; Hay to Director, Philadelphia Hospitals, Aug. 23, 1864; *York Gazette,* Mar. 28, 1871, and Jan. 21, 1873.

15. Reunion Log of the 87th Pennsylvania, ms. 901, YCHT; John Newton Terrill, *Campaign of the Fourteenth New Jersey Volunteers,* 5, 48.

16. *York Gazette,* Aug. 20, 1861; *Hanover Spectator,* Dec. 20, 1861; *Gettysburg Compiler,* Feb. 17, 1862.

ington wanted them to fight, least of all Thomas A. Scott. Officially, the regiment had formed "to guard the property of the government or such lines of communication or property as may be in charge or under the control of the government."[17]

Recruits knew they were to be a "home guard" before they enlisted. Gettysburg's newspapers threw aside pleas to patriotism and lured men with promises of easy duty. No sleeping on the cold, hard ground for Adams County boys, the *Gettysburg Compiler* promised. They would be snoring away in "comfortable houses" before winter. The *Gettysburg Star and Banner* described the job as alternating two weeks on the railroad and two weeks off and rated the duty as "easy and pleasant." The *York Gazette* took a different path that may have repelled patriotic prospects, writing, "There is considerable objection among the volunteers enlisted for active service to the monotonous and tiresome duty of guarding railroads and government property. . . . The pay is the same as in the regular services."[18]

That was quite a recruiting slogan: Join the army and be bored. Expect no glory or anything to impress the young ladies, just carry out distasteful duties that "real" soldiers detested. Earn the same pay as "regulars," but harbor no fantasy about being a "real" soldier. Given the approach to the regiment's formation, it is inescapable that some men enlisted *because* of the promised easy duty. A year after entering into active service, someone verified that in a letter published by two area newspapers. The anonymous author, allegedly a member of the regiment, complained how officers had deceived them when they put them into active service "without the consent of the men . . . and contrary to their wish, as it was raised as a public guard regiment."[19]

A group of six men offers more evidence of the Scott Regiment's lure. In May 1861, nearly one hundred men, mostly from Adams County, enlisted in what became Company K, 1st Pennsylvania Reserves, a unit famed as the only hometown organization to fight in the battle of Gettysburg. Seven of those recruits refused to take the oath required to enter Federal service, and six of them reenlisted with the Scott Regiment. The army labeled them deserters but never punished any of them, so it tacitly approved their behavior even

17. Secretary of War Thomas A. Scott to Alexander Small, Aug. 13, 1861; Peter Nichol to George Ruggles, Mar. 19, 1865, CMSR of Albert D. Stouffer, Co. F, 87th Pa.; recollections of George Blotcher, YCHT. Blotcher used the expression "home guard."

18. Pension Records of Isaac G. Simmons, Co. E, 87th Pa.; *Gettysburg Compiler,* Sept. 9, 1861; *Star and Banner,* Sept. 13, 1861; *York Gazette,* Aug. 20, 1861.

19. *Gettysburg Compiler,* March 16, 1863, reprint from *Harrisburg Patriot and Union,* March 7, 1863.

though it never lifted the desertion charges. It must be noted that five of the six left the 87th Pennsylvania under honorable circumstances.[20]

George C. Blotcher, the regiment's best chronicler, was always bitter about some of his comrades' lack of enthusiasm but showered his greatest acrimony on the uncommitted officers recruited by this approach.[21]

"Our regiment was raised not like many others. . . . Those officers had not intended to go [to the front] because we were not called for actual duty and thought [it] best to resign. The old saying is, better be called a comrade than a dead hero."[22]

Blotcher no doubt had 1st Lt. William Frederick Frank among those in mind. Frank had served with the 16th Pennsylvania and then signed on with Solomon Myers's company. If Myers was unaware of Frank's poor attitude beforehand, he learned of it when Frank balked at leaving the railroad for active duty and allegedly began faking illness. Shortly thereafter, Frank left the army on a surgeon's certificate—ostensibly due to recurring malarial attacks. Civilian Frank soon publicly attacked soldier Myers, who returned fire with accusations of "Copperheadism," a peace-at-all-costs movement generally despised by soldiers in the field. A letter attacking Frank also appeared in a Harrisburg newspaper, one Myers might have penned.

> I am not at all surprised that the Copperhead Wm. F. Frank is trying to heap odium & even slander upon me. And no doubt, also, upon yourself, but I care not for all he can do against me . . . Drowning men grasp at straws & he knows he has a weak cause. Lt. Frank feigned sickness about 2 or 3 weeks after we left Baltimore for New Creek & was detailed but once as officer of camp guard after our regiment came into Virginia. He has been of no use since we left Baltimore. He was reported absent without leave from Oct 20th 1862 until he was discharged Jan 17th 1863.[23]

It is impossible to know how many in the regiment shared William Frank's uncommitted attitude, and many no doubt offered good service regardless.

20. CMSRs of John Gibson, Adam Holtzworth (reenlisted with the 107th Pa.), George Holtzworth, George T. Little, Zephaniah Rogers, Samuel Sheets, and William Zell, 30th Pa. (1st Pa. Reserves).

21. Pension Records of George Blotcher, Co. E, 87th Pa., statement of George Blotcher.

22. Recollections of George Blotcher.

23. Unknown to the *Harrisburg Telegraph*, March 24, 1863, letter dated March 16, 1863; Solomon Myers to George Hay, May 24, 1863, George Hay Kain III Collection. The *Telegraph* letter attacks William Frank and Copperheads in general. While it does not mention Frank by name, the inference mirrors Myers's letter.

But the presence of indifference to duty is hard to deny. Recruiters had made the possibility of battle seem remote and promised barracks superior to the living quarters some had in civilian life. Men had to travel only a few dozen miles from home to a post along a railroad that provided easy transportation home, with or without permission. One recruit was convinced that they would be living like "fiten cocks."[24]

Alexander Small added to staffing problems by omitting a critical step in the enrollment process: a medical examination. Availability of physicians was not an issue. Two of the Scott Regiment's field officers were qualified surgeons, and community physicians surely would have volunteered services. York and Adams counties provided the army with at least eleven surgeons and assistant surgeons, all of whom began service subsequent to the formation of the Scott Regiment. Small himself could have assisted with the rudimentary task, rusty though his medical skills might have become. While his was hardly the only regiment mustered without physical exams, Small was an experienced army surgeon who should have known better. Even though the short-term assignment was guarding a railroad, it was shortsighted to assume the men would never see combat.[25]

As a result, more than 11 percent of 87th Pennsylvania men who enlisted in 1861 left the army for illness or injury. By comparison, Cumberland and northwest York counties supplied most of Company H, 7th Pennsylvania Reserves, which stood recruits naked before examining physicians, who demanded demonstrations of stamina and agility. The 7th Reserves engaged in some of the war's worst fighting, yet Company H enjoyed a discharge rate for illness and injury less than half that of the 87th Pennsylvania. Medical exams paid off later in life, too. In virtually every age category, life expectancy among the war's survivors was up to seven years less for 87th Pennsylvania men than for other area soldiers enlisting in 1861. (See Appendix, "Soldier Life Expectancy.")[26]

24. Peter Free to his family, Dec. 11, 1861, Pension Records of Peter Free, Co. E, 87th Pa.; Johnston Hastings Skelly to his mother, Dec. 6, 1861, Pension Records of Johnston H. Skelly; personal receipts of Col. George Hay, George Hay Kain III Collection. Officers usually boarded in private homes or hotels. From December 7, 1861, through May 17, 1862, George Hay spent $89.43 for board and $113.25 to board his horse but fixed his host's broken sofa and cut $18.60 off his bill.

25. Known area surgeons were William D. Bailey (78th Pa.), Washington Burg (122nd Pa.), Thomas M. Curran (68th Pa.), Jared Free (83rd Pa.), Charles E. Goldsborough (5th Md.), Aug. Robert Nebinger (11th Pa. Cav.), William Prowell Nebinger (56th Pa.), Benedict M. Patterson (1st Pa. Light Art.), Luther L. Rewalt (21st Pa. Cav.), George Kerr Thompson (132nd Pa.), and Joseph A. Wolf (29th Pa.). All but Bailey and Burg were assistant surgeons.

26. The Scott Regiment's two officers with medical training were Capt. Jacob Hay, Co. A, and 1st Lt. John Edwin McIlvain, Co. K. CMSRs and Pension Records, where applicable, of all men of

Even a basic examination would have been sufficient to eliminate some physically inadequate recruits. Harrisburg resident John F. Walzer capped a fifteen-day army career by becoming the first of 214 87th Pennsylvania men discharged by surgeon's certificate. Joseph Hopson arrived blind in one eye and losing sight in the other, while Samuel E. Madlam showed up with a tumor on his arm. Since William B. Yeatts had no upper teeth, he could not bite open a charge to load his rifle. Jacob Lowe years before had cut the toes off his left foot, and Frederick Rinehart suffered from a leg ulcer, conditions that should have foretold both men's inability to march long distances. Charles Odenwalt enlisted with a bullet lodged in one lung, a condition that had to be common knowledge since a Scott Regiment comrade recently had put it there. Among these men, only Odenwalt was still a soldier six months after muster, and he never performed strenuous duties.[27]

Lewis V. Holter was a young man with no apparent physical shortcomings to preclude enrollment, but he had well-known psychological issues that should have kept him off the rolls. James Henry Blasser was not only Holter's commanding officer in the Scott Regiment, but also had been his schoolteacher before the war. Blasser described Holter as "nervous, of unequal temper, sometimes very violent seeming to lose control of himself" while others considered him "slow, [a] simpleton, weak physically." Army life changed nothing. Holter neither got the hang of drill nor accepted military authority. One too many broken rules forced the captain to order him bucked and gagged, a cruel punishment that had a man seated with hands tied in front, a stick over his arms and under his legs to lock all four appendages, and gagged. Released after an unknown time, Holter went berserk, screaming and fighting off men who tried to calm him. Slipping loose, he dived into the river and remained underwater. William Henry Harrison Welsh wrestled Holter to shore, or his story would have ended there.[28]

the 87th Pa. and Co. H, 36th Pa. (7th Pa. Reserves). Pension Records of veterans of Co. H, 36th Pa. include William H. Cook (deposition of John Irrgang, June 24, 1885), John W. Cook (deposition of Wilson O. Smith, May 28, 1894), and Joseph A. Durnbaugh (deposition of William Durnbaugh, Aug. 26, 1890). Pension Records of Henry S. Rannels, Battery E, 1st Pa. Light Art. (43rd Pa.). The last unit, partly recruited in York, also received physical examinations. For more on physical examinations, see Bell Irvin Wiley, *The Life of Billy Yank: The Common Soldier of the Union*, 23.

27. CMSRs: Samuel E. Madlam, Co. B; Frederick Rinehart, Co. C; Jacob E. Lowe, Co. D; Jacob B. Young, Co. F; Joseph B. Hopson, Lafayette B. Schlosser, and Jacob H. Peters, Co. H; William B. Yeatts, Co. I; Charles Odenwalt, Co. K, 87th Pa., and Joseph Hopson, Co. B, 130th Pa.; recollections of George Blotcher. After leaving the 87th Pennsylvania, Joseph Hopson enlisted with the 130th Pennsylvania and a month later was charging Bloody Lane at the battle of Antietam. The next day, he deserted. U.S. Census, York County, 1860.

28. Pension Records of Lewis V. Holter, Co. D, 87th Pa., depositions of James Henry Blasser, William H. H. Welsh, James B. Beck, Lewis V. Holter Sr., and James Moody, Nov. 21, 1882.

The army may have been grateful when Holter suffered an injury in a train accident. It gave his superiors an excuse to discharge him for "imbecility and general disability." Once home, solace came from a bottle, and fights with his father led to a suicide attempt. A stint with the emergency infantry during the Gettysburg crisis rejuvenated Holter's desire for army life, though, and he reenlisted in 1864, requesting assignment to his old company in the 87th Pennsylvania.[29]

Jaws dropped when Lewis Holter walked back into camp. A disbelieving Captain Edgar Monroe Ruhl grumbled loud enough for all to hear, "Here comes Holter again; he is not fit for the service." He lasted six months this time before the army sent him home for "general debility caused by masturbation." Holter's tentmate, James Hendrix, confirmed that "some of the boys were plagued about such a habit," but Holter argued that he "did not follow masturbation to an injurious extent." Surgeons then considered the practice potentially deadly. When Company C's John Weaver died, the 87th Pennsylvania surgeons listed "excessive onanism" as the cause of his fatal "softening of the brain."[30]

Most men, however, were fit to serve and eager to get on line, and Thomas A. Scott was just as eager to get them there. He pressured Alexander Small to replace "a good regiment now stationed on the Northern Central Railroad." This so-called good regiment was the 20th Indiana Infantry, which had emerged from the civilian womb only that July. While the men from Indiana would eventually endure some of the war's bloodiest moments, their experience in August 1861 was zero and their attitude rating not much higher. They nearly caused a riot in Indiana when they did not get the uniforms and arms they wanted and then behaved badly while along the Northern Central. Authorities considered them superior only because they had recruited them to fight while the Scott Regiment had developed as a home guard. After war had hardened volunteers, the difference was valid, but it hardly existed in mid-1861, when almost everyone held rookie status. Indeed, the Scott Regiment enlisted 158 men who had served in a three-month regiment, which was exactly 158 more than the 20th Indiana had in ranks. Then, as today, perception was reality, however false the conclusion. For much of their first

---

29. CMSR of Lewis V. Holter, 26th Pa. Militia; Pension Records of Lewis V. Holter, 87th Pa., discharge certificate and deposition of Lewis V. Holter, Nov. 15, 1882.

30. CMSR and Pension Records of Lewis V. Holter, deposition of Lewis Holter (father) Nov. 15, 1882. Violent tendencies persisted in Holter after the war. His father, who once had accosted schoolteacher James Blasser for being too strict with his son, now called on Sheriff James Blasser to arrest him. CMSR of John Weaver, Co. C, 87th Pa. Weaver died in the regimental hospital of what was likely typhoid or malarial fever March 8, 1864.

year of existence, the boys from York suffered derisive calls of "railroad sleeper guards," an insult that rankled George Blotcher to the end of his days.[31]

Thomas A. Scott was in such a hurry to free up the 20th Indiana that he bypassed typical enrollment procedure. Ordinarily, a regiment's recruiter enrolled his troops and sent them with accompanying paperwork to a "camp of rendezvous and instruction," in this case, Harrisburg's Camp Curtin. Instead, at the same time he was pressuring the governors of nine states to rush forces to Washington, Scott had the Quartermaster Department provision Alex Small's men directly and ordered mustering officers to York. When the procedure dragged, the adjutant general granted mustering authority to a regular army shavetail (second lieutenant) who needed lessons in mustering procedure.[32]

By September 15, half the regiment was formed and ready for active duty— by home guard standards. Engine number 85 waited at the station to pull railcars brimming with men and the excess baggage inherent to military neophytes. The band struck up "Yankee Doodle," and half the Scott Regiment marched to the rail station. Along the way, ladies wept and waved handkerchiefs, planted kisses on willing soldiers' cheeks, and dropped food bundles into their hands. At 8:30 A.M., after the obligatory speeches from men never destined to stand in the line of fire, the train steamed southward.[33]

Alex Small had seen to everything. Even the *York Republican* said he had "contributed greatly to the safe and speedy disembarkation and arrangement of the men," and it was disinclined to say anything good about a Democrat. Travel accommodations were hardly luxurious. Cars were the open type, and the men endured a shower of sparks and cinders throughout the trip. When they passed through Howard Tunnel in southern York County, many

31. Thomas A. Scott to Seth Thomas, Aug. 19, 1861, Secretary of War, p. 325; Craig L. Dunn, *Harvestfields of Death: The Twentieth Indiana Volunteers at Gettysburg;* recollections of George Blotcher; CMSRs of all members of the 87th Pa.

32. *O.R.,* General Order No. 58, Aug. 15, 1861, ser. 3, 1:412, General Order No. 61, ser. 3, 1:424–25, Secretary of War, Thomas A. Scott to Alexander Small, Aug. 13, 1861, Scott to Montgomery Meigs and to Seth Thomas, both Aug. 19, 1861; *Supplement to the Official Records of the Union and Confederate Armies Part II,* Record of Events, vol. 60, no. 72; Assistant Adjutant General to Lieutenant Baldwin, York, Pa., Sept. 9, 1861, Letters Sent by the Office of the Adjutant General's Office, Main ser., 1800–1890, RG-94, M565, roll 20, vol. 33, Sept. 4, 1860–Jan. 22, 1862, NARA; *Historical Dictionary of the U.S. Army, 1789–1903;* Card Records of Headstones Provided for Deceased Civil War Veterans, ca. 1879–ca. 1903, NARA. Second Lieutenant Henry Moore Baldwin, 5th U.S. Artillery, mustered that May 14, arrived with Capt. Rufus Terrill, who mustered some of Company A and let his protégé finish. Baldwin died Nov. 8, 1864, from wounds suffered at Cedar Creek, still just a second lieutenant.

33. *York Republican,* Sept. 19, 1861; *York Gazette,* Sept. 17, 1861; Gunnarsson, *Northern Central.* Newspaper accounts identified the engine as number 85, but it is not among the 1858 inventory of Northern Central engines. According to the 1873 inventory, Engine number 85 was built in 1864.

no doubt suffered some smoke inhalation. The boys still cheered when they crossed the Maryland line.[34]

Before the other five companies shipped out, they had an unpleasant duty to perform. Maryland recruit John Gibson was one of those who had refused oath with the 1st Pennsylvania Reserves, and now fate had multiplied his error. Before he even mustered into the Scott Regiment, typhoid fever made a widow of his pregnant wife and orphaned his daughter. Whatever Gibson's past, comrades paused for an act of respect they would perform often until others performed it for them.[35]

The second group of five companies left town with less fanfare, but local folk artist Lewis Miller captured the event on canvas. Some men took temporary assignment at regimental headquarters at Camp Dix, Cockeysville, Maryland, named for Maj. Gen. John Adams Dix, commander of the military department at Baltimore. If Dix felt honored, he nonetheless ignored the boys from York. Extant communication from his office mentions the Scott Regiment but once in a casual note to Gen. George B. McClellan that advised him the York men "have taken position . . . and have the bridges in charge."[36]

Once mustered into the service of the United States, the regiment had to take on a new name. Volunteer regiments assumed numbers within the state of origin in sequence of muster, and eighty-seven was next in line. Thomas A. Scott's railroad regiment became the 87th Regiment of Pennsylvania Volunteer Infantry, but "Scott" lingered until spring, when its namesake left the War Department. Then the title slipped into a historical footnote.

The regiment had a name, officers, and most of the equipment it needed. Now, the men had to learn to be soldiers. Like any organization, its efficiency depended principally on the character of its members. To know the 87th Pennsylvania, you have to get to know the boys from York and what motivated them to serve.

34. *York Republican,* Sept. 19, 1861. Howard Tunnel is located in southern York County.
35. Ibid.; Pension Records of John Gibson, 87th Pa.; CMSR of John Gibson, 30th Pa. Gibson has no service records with the 87th Pennsylvania.
36. John A. Dix to George B. McClellan, Sept. 19, 1861, Letters Sent—8th Corps, vol. 27; *O.R.,* Edwin Stanton's orders to John A. Dix, ser. 2, 3:426.

Chapter 4

The Rank and File

York and Adams counties proved their fidelity to the Union by offering about 7,000 men to military service over the course of the war. The 1860 census reveals the names of about 13,000 York County white males who would be of eligible military age the following year, and Adams County added approximately 5,000 potential recruits. Given the number of underage boys and overage men who enlisted and the many names absent from the 1860 census, it is fair to round up the number of the counties' available men to about 20,000. The Thomas A. Scott Regiment closed out September 1861 with 966 of those names on a roster that grew to 1,034 by year's end. Nearly 800 additional area men enrolled with other three-year regiments during 1861.[1]

Each man had his reasons for serving. "I have enlisted to fite for my cuntry and for a good caus," twenty-five-year-old Jacob G. Eppley wrote. William Henry Brenaman, age twenty when he enlisted, still believed enough in the cause after nearly three years in service to urge his civilian brother to "have the pleasure of helping to crush this wicked rebellion." Republican newspapers lauded patriotism and those who exhibited it. The *Hanover Spectator* praised the Stine and Stahl families for each putting three members into the 87th Pennsylvania, noting sarcastically, "Such instances are rare and present

---

1. U.S. Census, 1860, Pennsylvania, York and Adams Counties, manual count of white males ages 17–44. Four Adams County 1860 censuses are lost, and Newberry Township, York County, also appears to be missing people. For more on York's enlistments and draftees, see Mark A. Snell, "If They Would Know What I Know It Would Be Pretty Hard to Raise One Company in York: Recruiting, the Draft, and Society's Response in York County." The military eligibility age range was 21–45, but the minimum was ignored.

a striking contrast in comparison to some families." Henry Stine returned all the way from his midwestern home to serve with his brothers.[2]

There is no evidence to suggest opposition to slavery motivated area men to enlist. Extant pre-1863 letters are free of words such as "slave," "slavery," and "abolition." If "rights" appears, it is in reference to their own. Most statements on the war's purpose fell along the lines of those espoused by Gen. James Cooper, who deemed the war necessary "for the suppression of a wicked and unnatural rebellion."[3]

Passion had fueled many enlistments that April—*rage militaire* social historians call it. Nicholas A. Hahn had been brimming with it. Self-described as "a good, big boy," he was still awaiting his eighteenth birthday when he and several "playmates double-quicked before the mustering officer" of the ninety-day 16th Pennsylvania Infantry "to have some fun." Hahn retained enough enthusiasm to join the 87th Pennsylvania with ninety-four 16th Pennsylvania comrades.[4]

Carlisle-born Albert Dinkle Stouffer demonstrated *rage militaire* in a unique manner for the 87th Pennsylvania. His family had moved to Winchester, Virginia, before the war, so the eighteen-year-old followed the local crowd into the 31st Virginia Infantry. By September, his Yankee roots had kicked in, and he fled to York to enlist with the 87th Pennsylvania because the regiment was only going to guard railroads. Clearly, he found the thought of shooting old Virginia friends distasteful. He found little solace with his Yankee mates and spent most of his military service on detached duty, which is probably one reason he deserted the Union army. Although he returned without penalty under President Lincoln's amnesty proclamation, Lt. Peter Nichol distrusted Stouffer and as late as 1865 was trying to get him transferred. Nichol died in battle before that happened, and Stouffer mustered out honorably at the rank of corporal in spite of his desertion history.[5]

Rage militaire lived in seventeen-year-old Henry Shultz yet that September when he succumbed to youthful daydreams. Sneaking away in the middle of

2. Jacob G. Eppley to Gov. Andrew G. Curtin, July 11, 1862; William Brenaman to brother David, Jan. 31, 1864, Pension Records of William Brenaman, Co. C, 87th Pa.; *Hanover Spectator*, Oct. 25, 1861; Pension Records of Henry, Daniel, and George Stine, Co. G, 87th Pa.

3. General Orders No. 1, Army Records, General Orders and Special Orders, James Cooper's Brigade.

4. James M. McPherson, *For Cause and Comrades: Why Men Fought in the Civil War*, 16–17; Pension Records of Nicholas A. Hahn, Co. K, 87th Pa., Affidavit of June 10, 1913.

5. CMSR of Albert D. Stouffer, 31st Virginia, C.S.A., and Co. F, 87th Pa.; Pension Records of Albert D. Stouffer; Peter Nichol to George Ruggles, Mar. 19, 1865; Army Records, RG-393, part 2, Registers of Letters Received and Endorsements Sent, 3rd Brig., 3rd Div, 3rd A.C., Aug–Dec 1863, vol. 43, pp. 40–41, NARA.

the night, he donned clothing he had earlier hidden in the barn and walked to York to enlist. Jacob Shultz stormed after his son, but Henry said he would just sneak away again. As billions of fathers have learned by experience, arguing with a stubborn teenager can be pointless, so the elder Shultz reluctantly granted permission. Whatever Henry Shultz's actual age, his service records say he enlisted at the age of eighteen. He continued the lie right through the day they carved the wrong birth date into his tombstone.[6]

The passion of Ramsey Obediah Hannagan, on the other hand, should have ebbed long before the war started. The thirty-nine-year-old farmer and father of eight—with two more to come—had been a loyal member of the Crossroads Militia, so enlisting for real was the next logical step. Reportedly illiterate, he nonetheless received a sergeant's rank in the 87th Pennsylvania and later temporarily assumed first sergeant's duties when two higher-ranking sergeants were unavailable. Since paperwork was a major function of the first sergeant's job, someone had to have done it for him. When a second lieutenant's position opened in Company C, a surrogate wrote Governor Curtin a run-on letter begging for the promotion. It worked. Second lieutenant's bars became his, and Hannagan's name appears on a number of extant documents that someone must have written for him. He was such a good officer that the regiment offered him first lieutenant's bars, but this time he refused. He returned home from his faithful service with a leg wound that never healed, suffering a painful rupture and unable to work, and with a shortened life expectancy.[7]

Not everyone enlisted for positive reasons. Some joined to escape a civilian life that was going nowhere. Seventeen-year-old James Oren stated frankly that he joined up because he "didn't have a home," only to learn that military life was a step down in living arrangements. Chronic illness made the hospital his assignment for much of his first two years. When he finally went into the field, the Rebels seized him and shipped him off to Andersonville. He

---

6. This story came from conversations with Henry Shultz's grandson, Dr. Kenneth Shultz, still residing in York as of 2005. Dr. Shultz lived with his grandfather for twenty years and would argue about Henry's age. Ostensibly, Henry was born June 9, 1843, but the 1850–1880 censuses list him as six, fifteen, twenty-five, and thirty-five years of age, respectively. The Pension Office also questioned his date of birth, but Henry never offered clarification.

7. CMSR and Pension Records of Ramsey Hannagan, Co. C, 87th Pa. Infantry, testimony of Dr. Thomas M. Curren, June 23, 1877; CMSRs of David F. Hannagan (Ramsey's son), Co. C, 102nd Pa., Jeremiah M. Hannagan, Co. K, 166th Pa., John Hannagan, Co. B, 209th Pa., and Oliver Hannagan, Co. I, 166th Pa. Hannagan died in 1873 at the age of fifty-one. His last name is spelled a variety of ways. U.S. Census, 1860, Pennsylvania, York County, Springfield Township; diary of George Hay, George Hay Kain III Collection; Theodore A. Helwig to Col. L. B. Thomas, Dec. 1864, PA AGO, Muster Rolls.

returned home minus most of his teeth, his body covered with scabs and seeping sores.[8]

Twenty-year-old George Ignatius Francis Felty had a name heavier than the ninety-five-pound body that nature had somehow stretched to five feet, eight inches. Indentured at age nine by a widowed mother, he endured an abusive life paying off the obligation his family's poverty forced upon him. Joining the army must have seemed a comparative lark and may have put some spunk in him. He fathered twelve children and lived to the rare age of eighty-eight, dying only when struck down by a car as he crossed the street.[9]

John Ferdinand was another soul in search of a home, but he lived with the additional burden of being ugly enough to merit abuse on that point alone. "Bandy-legged, odd looking fellow, hare-lipped, cross-eyed, disfigured and rough looking all over, toed in as he walked" were just some ways acquaintances described him. His character may have been as distorted as his appearance, and no doubt the two were related. In the summer of 1863, "Old Ferdie," as mates called him, was a captive of the Confederacy at Richmond's Belle Isle prison camp. After many days of starvation rations, he snatched food from a helpless Ohioan and raced to the apparent safety of his mess tent to eat it. The Ohioan's comrades dived in after him and began administering a beating. Ferdie's shocked mates intervened, learned what had happened, and returned the stolen food. The incident taught Ferdie nothing. Before long, he stole rations from 87th comrade Valentine "Folly" Rouch. This time, no one stopped the beating, and no one regretted doing it.[10]

Irish immigrant Frank McAvoy was struggling in meager economic circumstances when he left New York City to follow the railroads in search of work. He landed in Baltimore and soon drifted northward into Pennsylvania, arriving in New Oxford on a day of high excitement. Anthony M. Martin, future adjutant of the 87th Pennsylvania, had turned his father's saloon into a recruiting station and was drawing men from all around. With no better work

8. CMSR and Pension Records of James Oren, Co. B, 87th Pa.; recollections of Michael Heiman, *York Gazette,* Feb. 20, 22, and 24, 1892.

9. Pension Records of George Felty, Co. I, 87th Pa.; *Gettysburg (Pa.) Times,* Oct. 30, 1929; Felty family lore courtesy of descendant Cheryl Lutz.

10. Pension Records of John Ferdinand, Co. G, 87th Pa., depositions of John Ferdinand, Charles F. Ropp, Thomas Ilgenfritz, and John Allen Wilt. During his pension process, Ferdinand alleged war had broken bones in his left hand, blinded one eye, and disabled a foot, but he found no witnesses to corroborate his claims. All witnesses thought he got what he deserved at Belle Isle. Pension Records of William Francis Eckert, Co. G, 87th Pa.; *Hanover (Pa.) Herald,* Oct. 13, 1883. Ironically, while a pension examiner investigating Ferdinand's case interviewed William Francis Eckert, Ferdinand's former sergeant, Eckert fell from his stool and died.

prospects in the immediate future and probably with a few drinks sloshing in
his belly, McAvoy decided to supply one of the few Irish brogues to a company of Pennsylvania "Dutchmen." He always managed to find Irishmen for
tentmates, though, even if he had to go outside the company. McAvoy was
no prize recruit and soon earned a reputation as "a tough case" of "dissipated
character" who "would resort to almost anything to get liquor."[11]

Henry W. Bowers was one of the regiment's many German-born members, having arrived in the United States shortly before the war and joined
a fight whose causes were none of his doing. A jumpy, "very noisy" little
fellow, according to George Blotcher, Bowers perhaps needed an outlet for
his nervous energy. He certainly needed an income. In the spring of 1864,
the regiment prepared for a campaign. While no one could know then that
they were headed for the bloodiest period of the war, they must have been
aware that something big surely was going to happen now that Ulysses S.
Grant was in charge. The night they broke camp, Bowers made out a will
and named a friend as beneficiary because he had no relatives in the country.
The beneficiary had to probate the will that autumn, an estate consisting of
one pocketbook.[12]

Dreams of feeling important motivated some to serve, but sometimes
dreams went bust. Michael Heiman had finished three months with the 16th
Pennsylvania and was lolling away a hot August day by one of York's center-
square market sheds. He saw handsome, blond-haired Lewis Maish approaching and soon was enduring a recruiting spiel. Maish wanted Heiman in the
company he was helping to recruit and almost guaranteed that his three-
month experience would win him stripes. Heiman was hooked. He signed
the enlistment papers and left for a few days to get his affairs in order. When
he returned, he discovered that the election for noncommissioned officers

11. *Map of Adams County from Actual Survey of G. M. Hopkins, C.E.* Jacob Martin owned the
Franklin House on the town square. Pension Records of Frank McAvoy, Co. I, 87th Pa., depositions
of Theodore A. Helwig ("dissipated character"), Finley Isaac Thomas (love of liquor), and James
Tearney ("tough case"); CMSRs and Pension Records, where applicable, of Alexander McManus,
James Rooney, and William Young, Co. I, and Robert McDonnell, Co. D, 87th Pa. These men of
Irish descent were all McAvoy's tentmates at various times.
12. Recollections of George Blotcher; Vital Statistics Card File, YCHT; CMSR of Henry W.
Bowers, Co. D, 87th Pa. Bowers was shot in the upper right arm at the third battle of Winchester,
leading to amputation and death. Other letters from 87th men contain premonitions of violence
in the 1864 campaigns: Alfred J. Jameson to his mother, Apr. 14, 1864, Pension Records of Alfred J.
Jameson, Co. A, 87th Pa.; Charles J. Barnitz to James Hersh, Apr. 19, 1864, James Hersh Papers,
CWMC; Thomas Oliver Crowl to William Fetrow, Apr. 21, 1864, and to his sister, May 3, 1864,
CWMC; David Gilbert Myers to his parents, May 3, 1864, Pension Records of David G. Myers,
Co. F, 87th Pa.

had been held in his absence and that most of the other men in his company were from Harrisburg and northern York County, strangers almost to a man. He never got those stripes.[13]

Age appears to have been a minor factor in bringing some men into the Thomas A. Scott Regiment, although arguably not for positive reasons and certainly not for legal ones. Of the 1,034 recruits who joined the Scott Regiment during 1861, only 5 of them reported being less than the legal age limit of eighteen and no doubt presented written permission from a parent. The actual count of underage recruits was 133, 13 percent of manpower, a rate rather higher than the 9 percent of boys enlisting in other regiments during 1861.[14]

Samuel Brenneman Gray's birth date of February 18, 1847 (he claimed 18), makes him the 87th Pennsylvania's youngest member authenticated. His adventure seeking put him through experiences no teenager should undergo, including two stints in Rebel prisons. Drummer Howard Stahl could also lay claim to being the youngest member, but his exact birth date could not be determined. He had no reason to lie about his age because he enlisted with brother Calvin and father, John Jacob, who nonetheless overstated his son's age by two years. Howard thrived well enough to beat cadences for the 67th Pennsylvania after his time with the 87th expired.[15]

Abraham B. Coble is another who may have qualified as the youngest member. "May" is the operative word because his claimed ages are many and diverse. The chart below demonstrates the various ages reported by or about Abraham Coble, illustrating how difficult it can be to determine birth dates for those born in the nineteenth century even when documentation is available.

13. Recollections of Michael Heiman, *York Gazette,* Feb. 20, 1892; Pension Records of Michael Heiman, Co. B, 87th Pa.; CMSRs of all men of Co. B, 87th Pa. Lewis Maish was selected first sergeant of Company B and promoted to second lieutenant May 26, 1863. Company B recruited only twelve men with military experience. Since a company had seventeen commissioned and noncommissioned officer positions, Maish's promise was realistic.

14. Benjamin Apthorp Gould, "Investigations in the Military and Anthropological Statistics of American Soldiers," *United States Sanitary Commission Memoirs of the War of the Rebellion: Statistical,* chap. 3, pp. 30–72. Gould examined 1,049,457 service records and found 1.5 percent were outside the age range 18–45, discounting routinely underage musicians. Statistics for south-central Pennsylvania soldiers confirm the findings for stated enlistment ages. See Wiley, *Billy Yank,* 299, for another contrary view of Gould's assertion. August V. Kautz, *The 1865 Customs of Service for Non-Commissioned Officers and Soldiers: A Handbook for the Rank and File of the Army,* 12.

15. CMSR and Pension Records of Samuel B. Gray, Co. E, 87th Pa.; U.S. Census, 1850–1880, Pennsylvania, York County, Lower Windsor Township; CMSRs and Pension Records of John J. Stahl, Calvin Stahl, and Howard Stahl, Co. G, 87th Pa.; CMSR of Howard Stahl, Co. K, 67th Pa. The 1850–1880 censuses list Howard Stahl's ages as three, thirteen, twenty-three, and three-three, respectively. John Jacob Stahl had three other sons who served in the Union army.

Source of Stated Age	Possible age at enlistment:
1860 census (July 17, 1860)--age 12	13
Death certificate DOB--July 25, 1847	14
Death certificate age--65-5-7 (May 31, 1846); CMSR at discharge Oct 1864--18	15
March 1901 pension deposition--56	16
DOB in pension application--July 25, 1844	17
1870 census--age 27	18
CMSR at enlistment	19
1850 census--age 9	20

Immaturity is a reasonable explanation for why boys enlisted. Sixteen-year-olds believe they will live forever. Overage men, though, should have outgrown such illusions and took great risk joining the army. Nevertheless, forty-one recruits had already experienced forty-six or more birthdays, and twenty looked back at the half-century mark. Among the forty-five-plus set, only three men honestly represented their years on Earth, and one of them was Col. George Hay, who, as a staff officer, was exempt from the upper age limit.[16]

John Shultz and William Young tied for the silver-hair award at fifty-eight years, although Shultz may have been sixty. Young told the recruiter he was forty-four; Shultz said forty-two. It soon became apparent that Young's stamina did not reflect his name, and the army assigned him to nursing duty. Even that light task did not help, and he died in 1864. On the other hand, Shultz, called "Pap" by mates, refused to admit he was over-the-hill. During the regiment's arduous trek over (West) Virginia's mountains in November 1862, the temperature dropped low enough to freeze the water in the men's canteens. Nonetheless, Shultz marched part of the way without shoes because of swollen feet, yet persevered while younger, well-shod men faded. A young comrade said, "I do not see how he stood it as he did." Another recalled, "He marched when younger people would have went for the ambulance train or

16. CMSRs of George Hay, George Washington Blasser, Co. D, and Henry Glatfelter Stroman, Co. G, 87th Pa. Blasser was fifty-two years old, but his service records contain no stated age.

hospital." A bullet in the buttock at Cold Harbor while he was squatting for nature's call halted his military career. Even with that wound—and the unmerciful teasing that angered him more than getting shot—he mustered out only nine days before expected time and lived another twenty-eight years.[17]

Pvt. Henry Glatfelter "Buggy" Stroman was forty-nine years old when he enlisted and the only noncommissioned man to admit to his advanced years. Why the army accepted him contrary to policy speaks to the poor discipline of recruiters. He was no Pap Shultz when it came to stamina and probably never had any interest in being a fighting man because he deserted just before the regiment went into the field in June 1862. Authorities arrested him and asked the regiment when they wanted him back. The regiment issued a terse response: Stroman was "not wanted—too aged and feeble for service." Instead of discharging him, they left him in custody until June 1864 when Lt. Robert Daniel mercifully obtained his release, allowing him to muster out that October. Technically, Henry Stroman spent three years in service, but he performed little real duty.[18]

Some older men joined the army to escape problems in civilian life. When Henry Armprister went off to war, he left behind a wife, seven children, and at least fifty-two birthdays. Bad habits he took with him. His commanding officer considered him a good soldier when sober, but that was a moot opinion since Armprister was "seldom ever sober." He went absent without leave and was hauled back to camp so often the captain tired of the chase and changed his status to "deserter." The Provost Guard returned him under arrest in October 1863, and that December a court-martial ordered him marched before the assembled brigade. The music was the disgraceful "Rogue's March," his head was shorn, the letter "D" appeared in India ink on his forehead, and around his neck hung a sign that labeled him "utterly worthless." Humiliating experience though it was, Armprister actually was twice fortunate. At the time of his trial, courts-martial were routinely sentencing deserters to death. His original sentence had dictated the "D" be *branded* on his forehead, but Gen. Joseph Carr took pity and ordered the words written with India ink.[19]

17. CMSR of William Young, Co. I, 87th Pa.; U.S. Census, 1860, Pennsylvania, York County; Vital Statistics Card File, YCHT; Pension Records of John Shultz, Co. F, 87th Pa., depositions of William Holtzworth, Zephaniah Rogers, Jerome Heidler, Charles Barnitz, Solomon Myers, Henry Coon, and William Aughenbaugh. For weather reports for the dates of the 1862 march, see Alfred J. Jameson to his mother, Nov. 19, 1862, Pension Records of Alfred J. Jameson, Thomas O. Crowl to his sister, Nov. 19, 1862, CWMC; and diary of Solomon Myers.

18. CMSR of Henry G. Stroman, Co. G, 87th Pa.

19. Thomas P. Lowry, *Don't Shoot That Boy! Abraham Lincoln and Military Justice,* 91, case of Sylvester Buel; York County Court Docket, 1856–1860, p. 164; Records of the Office of the Judge Advocate General, Court-Martial, Pvt. Henry Armprister, LL-1507, testimonies of Robert A.

The army had grown wiser by 1864. John McElroy, then at least forty-eight years old but claiming four years less, wanted to reenlist with Company F. The army balked because it already had relegated him to the ambulance corps due to physical infirmity and "advanced age." While they wanted men capable of offering good service, that was not a working definition of John McElroy, who made that fact clear a few weeks later when he died of natural causes.[20]

Pap Shultz aside, the presence of older soldiers was damaging to a regiment's efficiency. Most of the 87th's ancients began 1864 either as civilians or in their graves, with only one death coming by enemy fire. By contrast, only one-fourth of the underage group was gone by 1864 for reasons other than being killed or wounded in battle, and only six did not live to see the end of the war. These anecdotes and numbers confirm the fact that too much youth serves an army better than too much life experience.[21]

Lying about age was not limited to those outside the legal range. At least fifteen recruits between forty and forty-five years of age chopped up to thirteen years from their enlistment ages. Neither did the prevaricator have to be close to the upper age limit. Harvey James Harman claimed to be twenty-eight years old at enlistment, yet every other source says he was thirty-seven. His superior, Wells Abraham Farrah, likewise lowered his age by six years for no discernable reason. At least 113 men enlisting in 1861 gave ages that were wrong—according to the best data available—by at least three years. Over the life of the regiment, the number of men grew to 153, too large a count to assign exclusively to clerical error.[22]

At whatever age men enlisted, bloodlines lured many of them into army ranks and made the Thomas A. Scott Regiment very much a family affair. Nine members of the Little clan served, including a father and four sons.

Daniel and William C. Waldman; CMSR of Henry Armprister, Co. G, 87th Pa., and Co. E, 1st Pa. Light Art. Armprister reenlisted with the 1st Pa. Light Art. and completed that term. According to The Index Project (Thomas and Beverly Lowry, who have read and documented every court-martial in the National Archives), 390 convicted Union men had branding in their sentences and 345 were ordered tattooed with a "D." As of June 1, 2006, the Lowrys can be reached by e-mail at Civilwarjustice@aol.com.

20. "R.H.K" to the Star and Banner, Feb. 11, 1864, letter dated Feb. 2, 1864. McElroy died February 1, 1864. R. H. K.—likely Robert Hervey King, a Hunterstown, Adams County, man then serving as brigade clerk—described McElroy's funeral: "He was buried with military honors, the left wing of the Regiment in attendance. The coffin was draped with the Stars and Stripes under which he enlisted. The solemn notes of the funeral dirge reminds us that Death has again visited our company."

21. CMSRs of all men of the 87th Pa.

22. Tombstone of Harvey James Harman; Vital Statistic File, YCHT; Pension Records of Wells A. Farrah, Co. H, 87th Pa.; U.S. Census, 1850 and 1860, Pennsylvania, York County, Warrington Township; York County Commissioner, Recorder of Deeds, Military Enrollment List—1865, York County, York County Archives. Harman's reported date of birth is September 15, 1824.

Three Flinn brothers went off to war with brother-in-law Benjamin Sny-der, and a fourth Flinn brother followed three years later. Brothers Jacob and Matthew Foose enlisted as a pair and died in battle at virtually the same time. William Hamilton "Ham" Fahs came all the way from Lehigh County to serve under cousin John Fahs, and Philip Grove arrived from his Mifflin County home to enlist with brother Valentine. At least 184 members of the regiment could call one or more comrades "brother," and 15 could seek solace from their comrade-fathers in times of stress. Determining the identity of all the uncles and nephews, brothers-in-law, and cousins would keep a genealo-gist occupied for years.[23]

Family ties sometimes prompted rash decisions to enlist. John Englebert was a sixteen-year-old from Hunterstown, Adams County. Since he gave his real age at enlistment, we can assume he had parental permission to follow his brother-in-law Robert Hervey King into Company F. Nonetheless, Englebert deserted two days after mustering. The boy could not have been too hard to find. Robert King surely knew his whereabouts, as did the six other Company F men from Hunterstown, which was no more than a small collection of houses. Records do not reflect illness or an irate father dragging his underage son back home, but the army never arrested him. The lad made up for it a year later by joining the 138th Pennsylvania while still young enough to make his enlistment a violation of the Articles of War. Nonetheless, he completed the three-year term, drew a pension, and earned an honored gravesite in the Gettysburg National Cemetery. The 87th commanders may have recognized Englebert's inability and let him go home. The question is why they recruited boys like him at all.[24]

Family ties prompted some men to risk their health to serve with kin. Yorker Edward Nathaniel Kipp put in three months with a Pittsburgh reg-iment before enlisting with the 1st Pennsylvania Light Artillery, a unit that

23. CMSRs and Pension Records; U.S. Census, 1860, Pennsylvania, Adams County, Gettys-burg. Pension Records of William Hamilton Fahs, Co. A, 87th Pa. Identified father-son combina-tions enlisting in 1861 are Noah and Edgar Ruhl, George and James Blasser, Jacob and Samuel Gray, Oliver and Jacob Glassmyer, Granville and Nathaniel Jackson, John and Forest McElroy, John and Henry Clay Spangler, Adam and Eli Ream, John George and John Weaver, Henry and Charles Stroman, and Esias Z. Little with sons Charles Basil, Duncan, William Guynn, and David Forrest Little. Ongoing research has revealed, as of August 1, 2006, an additional 145 brothers, 6 fathers, and 13 sons of 87th Pennsylvania men who served with other regiments at some time during the Civil War.

24. Hopkins, *Map of Adams County,* 1858; U.S. Census, 1850 and 1860, Pennsylvania, Adams County; CMSR of John Englebert, Co. F, 87th Pa., Co. B, 138th Pa., and 2nd Battalion, Veteran Reserve Corps; Pension Records of John Englebert, 138th Pa. and Robert H. King, Co. F, 87th Pa. King married Englebert's sister Ann. For more on the Union army's dealing with deserters, see Lonn, *Desertion,* chaps. 3, 5, and 12.

had camped on York's Penn Commons just before the Scott Regiment took over. A bullet in the hip at the battle of Yorktown slowed him, but at Fair Oaks he suffered what may be a man's worst nightmare: a bullet through the penis. In pain and virtually unable to urinate, he was sent home by the army, a surgeon's certificate discharge in hand, to work out his physical malady with a civilian doctor. A week later, without telling anyone of his injury, he reenlisted with the 87th Pennsylvania to join three brothers already serving. The regiment immediately recognized his physical difficulty but assigned him to cooking duties instead of sending him home. Eventually, one of his brothers performed a catheterization to relieve his urinary blockage but surely instituted radical new pain in the process.[25]

The presence of family also led to some to positions of authority via that timeless path of advancement, nepotism. Cousins initially held three of the four command positions in Company H, and by the spring of 1862, Company D had two father-son pairs in command. Brothers eventually constituted part of the command structures of companies F and G, and the Hersh cousins rose to command Company I. Recruiters came from the well-to-do class, and success tended to encompass whole families, if only by osmosis.[26]

In examining the effect of politics as motivation to enlist, the question arises as to whether Republicans were more responsive to military service than Democrats. While we cannot know many men's party affiliations, we can examine districts' voting patterns and compare them to enlistment rates. The chart below lists voting districts for York and Adams counties with percentage of votes cast for Abraham Lincoln in 1860 and percentage of eligible men who enlisted in 1861.[27]

Of the counties' fifty-five townships and boroughs, thirteen sent double-digit percentages of their eligible men into service during 1861. Eight of those gave Abraham Lincoln a majority vote in 1860, so area Democratic support was not lacking. Neither did Republican districts necessarily respond well to

25. CMSRs of Edward N. Kipp, Co. A, 7th Pa., Battery E, 1st Pa. Light Art., and Co. E, 87th Pa.; Pension Records of Edward N. Kipp; CMSRs and Pension Records of Alexander Kipp and John Wesley Kipp, Co. A, and Peter Albert Kipp, Co. E, 87th Pa. After the war, the Kipps did not share last names. Edward assumed "Moore," which was either his mother's maiden or first married name. Alexander is buried as "Gibb," and often as not, they were all called "Gipp," typical Pennsylvania Dutch spelling variations due to a dialect that softened hard consonant sounds.

26. Twenty-five brothers-in-law, seven uncles and nephews, and twenty-eight sets of cousins were identified. Research outside immediate families was not exhaustive, so these counts are low.

27. *Gettysburg Compiler*, Nov. 12, 1860; U.S. Census, 1860, York and Adams counties; CMSRs for all York and Adams County men enlisting in 1861. York reported votes by township and borough, but Adams combined some districts.

Township or Borough	York County			
	87th 1861	Non-87th 1861	%Elig men enrl 1861	% Lincoln vote 1860
Carroll/Dillsburg	0	17	7.1%	42.7%
Chanceford	22	22	9.2%	42.2%
Codorus/Jefferson	3	3	2.0%	5.8%
Conewago	5	0	2.9%	53.1%
Dover	11	8	4.4%	25.9%
Fairview	2	27	6.1%	57.0%
Franklin	3	4	1.7%	53.9%
Glen Rock	14	5	30.2%	33.3%
Hanover	29	37	17.6%	62.1%
Heidelberg	6	11	4.9%	26.3%
Hellam	7	19	8.4%	56.9%
Hopewell	47	25	11.0%	50.4%
Jackson	2	1	0.6%	20.7%
Lewisberry	0	5	8.6%	81.4%
Lower Chanceford	7	11	4.7%	55.0%
Lower Windsor	13	16	7.6%	77.7%
Manchester	17	23	8.0%	57.1%
Manheim	3	2	1.2%	1.1%
Monaghan	7	11	9.8%	52.3%
Newberry	24	25	11.3%	74.6%
North Codorus	12	1	3.4%	18.4%
Paradise	1	1	0.5%	42.6%
Peach Bottom	0	9	2.0%	29.6%
Shrewsbury	48	10	11.4%	29.5%
Spring Garden	45	17	10.3%	40.3%
Springfield	21	2	4.8%	55.2%
Warrington	38	11	14.1%	66.7%
Washington	13	2	3.3%	45.5%
West Manchester	14	2	3.5%	37.6%
West Manheim	3	0	1.7%	25.8%
Windsor	7	5	3.6%	47.8%
Wrightsville	4	54	12.4%	41.8%
York Borough	279	144	26.0%	46.2%
York Township	19	11	7.3%	31.7%
Unknown	14	18		
TOTAL	740	559		

Township or Borough	Adams County			
	87th 1861	Non-87th 1861	%Elig men enrl 1861	% Lincoln vote 1860
Berwick	11	3	(1)	52.0%
Butler	5	5	4.3%	59.0%
Conewago	9	3	(1)	24.6%
Cumberland	11	7	8.7%	57.3%
Franklin	13	12	6.7%	47.6%
Freedom	4	4	8.7%	56.1%
Gettysburg	110	45	36.7%	53.5%
Hamilton	4	2	2.7%	34.5%
Hamiltonban	16	15	7.6%	55.6%
Hampton	0	0	0.0%	(2)
Huntington	4	3	3.1%	72.6%
Latimore	0	0	0.0%	(3)
Liberty	3	3	1.5%	(4)
Menallen	17	15	10.5%	75.3%
Mount Pleasant	11	1	4.0%	21.4%
Mountjoy	14	8	11.5%	43.3%
Oxford	36	3	15.7%	41.0%
Reading	9	4	5.5%	41.5%
Straban	17	1	8.8%	42.6%
Tyrone	3	2	2.7%	58.2%
Union	1	0	(1)	28.2%
Unknown	13	12		
TOTAL	311	148		

(1) - 1860 census data unavailable
(2) - Vote included with Reading
(3) - Vote included with Huntington
(4) - Vote included with Hamiltonban

recruiting calls. York County's Lewisberry Borough gave Lincoln the area's largest victory by percentage of vote but was initially stingy with manpower. By comparison, heavily Democratic Glen Rock was second only to Gettysburg in relative military participation. Southern York County's adjoining Hopewell and Shrewsbury townships enlisted virtually the same percentage of eligible men, but one voted slightly Republican and the other massively

Democratic. In Adams County, Republican Menallen Township sent 50 percent less of its eligible men than Democratic Oxford Township.[28]

Geography explains the differences. Democratic Glen Rock is but five miles north of the Maryland line, twenty-five miles closer than Republican Lewisberry. Both Hopewell and Shrewsbury townships border Maryland, so they responded equally. But being close to Maryland was still not the most decisive geographical factor that motivated enlistment. About 70 percent of 1861 enlistees came from a township or borough through which passed the Northern Central or one of its spur lines. Add York County's Hopewell Township and Adams County's Mount Pleasant and Berwick Townships, all in close proximity to a rail line, and the percentage increases to nearly 80 percent. The regiment's purpose was to guard the rail lines, and men responded to the call.

For whatever reason they came, by September, recruiters had molded nearly one thousand private male citizens of south-central Pennsylvania into a regiment. Election for commissioned and noncommissioned officers was among the first orders of business, a misguided practice that led to inexperienced soldiers being led by officers who had never seen battle. First, these neophyte officers had to learn to be soldiers themselves. That was a skill not all of them could master.

28. *York Gazette,* Nov. 20, 1860, and Apr. 23, 1861.

Chapter 5

Commanders and
Their Companies

Historian Reid Mitchell has observed that the company was an extension of a soldier's hometown community, that it became "the army for that soldier" (i.e., the group of men with whom each soldier ate, slept, fell into ranks, received orders, and fought). A detailed look at each company and its leadership sheds light on the 87th Pennsylvania's character. The chart below illustrates some of the regiment's demographics as of December 31, 1861.[1]

Companies A and K

These two companies had much in common. Recruits overwhelmingly came from York Borough, and their first captains eventually commanded the regiment. Once they got around to fighting, it was at opposite ends of a battle line, positions of honor awarded to the boys who literally were from York. Since the companies sprang from the same seed, they should have been identical. They were not, especially as to how much money the men could spend while on furlough. Only Company E had a lower net worth than Company K.[2]

Capt. James Alanza Stahle, a prominent member of the antebellum Worth Infantry, had to rise up on his tiptoes to stand face-to-face with many of

1. Mitchell, "The Northern Soldier and His Community"; Kemp, "Community and War."
2. James A. Stahle never formally commanded the 87th Pennsylvania but several times assumed that role in John Schall's absence or while Schall was acting as brigade commander.

Co	Primary Recruiting Area	First Captain	Muster Date	Cnt	Avg Net Worth	No Mar	Avg Age
Stf*	York Borough	n/a	Various	21	$3,356	14	28.6
A	York Borough	James Alanza Stahle	Sep 11	103	$4,133	37	21.8
B	Dauphin/Northern York Co	Jacob Detwiler	Sep 14	102	$884	34	25.5
C	Southern York Co	Andrew Jackson Fulton	Sep 14	102	$1,410	39	25.5
D	Southern York Co	Noah G. Ruhl	Sep 19	104	$921	35	25.7
E	York Area/Cumberland Co	Solomon Myers	Sep 13	100	$601	44	24.7
F	Gettysburg & vicinity	Charles Henry Buehler**	Sep 25	106	$1,386	37	26.3
G	Hanover & vicinity	Vincent C. S. Eckert	Sep 25	100	$613	31	26.0
H	Wellsville & vicinity	Ross Lewis Harman	Sep 19	102	$1,477	29	24.3
I	Eastern Adams Co	Thaddeus Stevens Pfeiffer	Sep 12	96	$2,230	18	23.8
K	York Borough & vicinity	John William Schall***	Sep 11	100	$576	25	23.5
			Averages ==>		$1,464		24.8

* Includes the band discharged August 31, 1862

** Replaced by William John Martin after Buehler's promotion to major

*** Replaced by John Alfred Albright after Schall's promotion to lieutenant colonel[3]

3. U.S. Census, 1860. "Cnt": Total men mustered; "No Mar": Number of married men; "Avg Net Worth": Sum of real estate and personal property from the 1860 census divided by "Cnt"; "Avg Age": Average of actual ages. Company I's value may be overstated because its principal township's census is unavailable. *Criteria for Calculating Net Worth:* (1) If the recruit stated no value on the 1860 census, his family's was used if the recruit was single and less than twenty-one years of age or living at home regardless of age. (2) In the absence of a stated value, $1.00 was used. (3) Recruits not found on the census were excluded.

his men, but a Prussian countenance and disciplinarian's bearing belied his diminutive size and sedate tailor's career. His Ellsworth Zouave Militia became the heart of Company A, which in turn became the darling of the regiment. The colorfully clad lads created a stir wherever they executed complex drill movements that "required a good deal of jumping & twisting around." Stahle remained at the helm until his promotion to major in early 1863.[4]

During Company A's posting in Melvale, Maryland, Union-loving Baltimore residents deemed Jim Stahle "skillful" and "indefatigable" and particularly appreciated his company's good behavior. When the regiment departed Baltimore in the spring of 1862, a York newspaper insisted that "the Zouaves under the admirable and persevering teaching of Captain James A. Stahle have attained a proficiency . . . excelled by none in the service." The author of the letter identified himself as "Zouave," so the opinion was hardly unbiased, but there were enough confirming opinions to support his case. Several months later, their parade ground skill so impressed Gen. Gustave Paul Cluseret that on the strength of Company A alone he declared the entire regiment "the best . . . in the U.S. regular or volunteer army." Also take Cluseret's rave review cautiously because he was then cajoling Governor Andrew Curtin to commission a friend in the 87th Pennsylvania.[5]

Many in Company A were sons of York's elite, which explains why the company had the regiment's top percentage of skilled professions and the highest average family worth. Less than one-fourth of the men gave farming or laboring as their profession. The company's average age was the regiment's youngest because Stahle wisely recruited only ten men age thirty or older, although among them was fifty-one-year-old fifer Henry Fink, who survived captivity and the war. Deep community roots allowed Stahle to tap into lifelong connections to fill ranks, but the Zouave uniforms gave him an enticing recruiting gimmick. Company A did not remain a Zouave unit for the duration but exactly when the company switched to standard uniforms could not be determined precisely. By the end of 1862, comrades were calling the 87th Pennsylvania the "Ragged Militia from Pennsylvania," and the regiment drew much-needed new uniforms in early December. By 1863, no extant account mentions the word *Zouave* in conjunction with the 87th Pennsylvania.[6]

4. Pension Records of William Hamilton Fahs, Co. A, 87th Pa., deposition of Greenbury S. Robinson, Dec. 7, 1888; Pension Records of James A. Stahle; *York Republican,* Sept. 19, 1861; *York Gazette,* July 1, 1862, citing the *Baltimore Clipper,* June 24, 1862. Stahle was five feet, four inches tall.

5. *York Gazette,* Nov. 4, 1862, letter from "Zouave," Oct. 23, 1862, and Dec. 2, 1862, letter from "York," Nov. 26, 1862; Gustave Paul Cluseret to Andrew G. Curtin, Nov. 26, 1862, PA AGO, Muster Rolls.

6. "York" to the *York Gazette,* Nov. 26, 1862, issue of Dec. 2, 1862; U.S. Census, 1860, Pennsylvania, York County, York Borough; Charles Edwin Skelly to his mother, Dec. 4, 1862, Pension

John William Schall performed but briefly as captain of Company K before leaping to lieutenant colonel. He earned universal respect throughout his tenure, esteem that lifted him to brigade command on several occasions. With no Zouave uniform to dangle before recruits and still relatively new to the area, Schall recruited more farmers and laborers than Stahle, which reflects supplementary recruiting in surrounding rural areas. He knew his job. Even with additional competition from Solomon Myers, Schall was so persuasive that he had recruited 117 men by August 22 and had the luxury of cherry-picking the most competent.[7]

Not all of Company K's officers were as steadfast as John Schall. Thirty-one-year-old John Edwin McIlvain was the son of a prosperous surgeon and had earned his own medical certificate in 1852. Nonetheless, when war came, he opted for a field officer's position rather than serve as a vitally needed surgeon. He first served as a private with the 2nd Pennsylvania Infantry and then as first lieutenant of Company K, 87th Pennsylvania, but stayed "on sociable, professional terms with [the medical staff]."[8]

McIlvain may have sought an active military role to counteract his Southern connections. Older sister Julia was the estranged wife of Benjamin Stoddert Ewell, initially colonel of the 32nd Virginia Infantry and later staff member for Confederate commander Joseph Eggleston Johnston. Julia McIlvain Ewell's brother-in-law became even better known: Richard Stoddert Ewell, Robert E. Lee's handpicked successor to Stonewall Jackson and conqueror of York in June 1863. Claims of Rebel-sympathizing residents were common in the area but no mention specific to John McIlvain could be found. He probably was a Union patriot but an arrogant one as he proved during the summer of 1862.[9]

Records of Charles E. Skelly, Co. F, 87th Pa. He wrote, "I was worse of[f] for pants than I ever was in my life." CMSR and Pension Records of Henry Fink, Co. A, 87th Pa.

7. John Schall to Samuel B. Thomas, Jan. 12, 1865, and George Hay to "all whom it may concern," undated, PA AGO, Muster Rolls; U.S. Census, 1860, York County; *Chester Times,* May 15, 1883; *York Republican,* Aug. 22, 1861. John Schall served as captain of Company K so briefly that the army never issued his captain's commission, which he filed to obtain immediately after leaving service. He continued military service with the Pennsylvania National Guard and rose to the rank of brigadier general during the Spanish-American War.

8. Pension Records of John E. McIlvain, Co. E, 87th Pa., deposition of Benjamin Tyson; Pension Records of Benjamin Tyson, Co. K, 87th Pa., deposition of Harrison Spangler and William Lesh; Court Docket 1856–1860, York County, p. 515. In 1859, McIlvain was arrested for disturbing the peace with seven future members of the 87th Pennsylvania. Lisa Heuvel, "The Peal That Wakes No Echo: Benjamin Ewell and the College of William and Mary."

9. Robert K. Krick, *Lee's Colonels,* 133; Edward W. Spangler, *The Annals of the Families of Caspar, Henry, Baltzer, and George Spangler,* 215, 221; Lisa Heuvel, "The Peal That Wakes No Echo"; 1860 Census, Pennsylvania, York County, York Borough. Benjamin Ewell met Julia McIlvain while en-

When the regiment shipped out on June 23 to what the men thought was to be active duty, last-minute orders switched their destination to mountain-bound New Creek, Virginia (now Keyser, West Virginia), ostensibly to prevent Richard Ewell from plundering military stores. Men learned that they were still "railroad sleeper guards," just in a more remote, dangerous part of the country and for a different rail line. The boys from York complained but settled in for the summer in a camp pitched "right on the bank of the river" where it was "swampy all around." Predictably, a heavy thunderstorm rushed a torrent downhill that threatened to wash them into the Potomac River. Typhoid fever struck soon afterward. With duty little more diverting than it had been along the railroad, morale drooped and sagged further when rumors reached them that the army had offered them active service and they had refused.[10]

McIlvain blamed the commanding officers and took the precarious step of voicing his complaints in a letter to Governor Andrew G. Curtin.

> Is such a thing possible as to move this Railroad Brigade Guard into active service either with [Maj. Gen. John] Pope or [Maj. Gen. George B.] McClellan? We have 900 active men, the best material to be found in York, Adams, & Dauphin Counties, the staff and a majority of the line officers of this regiment are cold, calculating speculators on the government treasury. They are of no earthly service here in this place . . . Your very humble & obedient servant . . . daily sees a military pantomime of the most striking character perpetrated by officers.

He added a postscript: "The writer of this is fully conscious that if Gov. Curtin would use it against him, the consequence would be annihilation."[11]

McIlvain avoided annihilation but resigned seven months later to take promotion to assistant surgeon of the 68th Pennsylvania Infantry. Whether the

---

gineering the Baltimore and Susquehanna Railroad, later the Northern Central Railway. They had separated prior to the war, and she lived in York in 1860. Their daughter remained with her father.

10. "Van" to the *York Gazette,* July 22, 1862, letter dated July 13, 1862; *York Republican,* July 1, 1862; recollections of James A. Stahle, *York Gazette,* Mar. 17, 1892; *O.R.,* Report of George B. McClellan, 11/1:49, John E. Wool to Edward M. Stanton, June 22, 1862, 12/3:424–25, John Pope to John Wool, July 1, 1862, 12/3:64, John Pope to Quartermaster, New Creek, Va., July 3, 1862, 12/3:62; Office of the Adjutant General, vol. 84, Letters and Telegrams Sent, Endorsements, and Special Orders, 1862, Army of Virginia, NARA; William Hartman to George Miller, July 5, 1862, George Miller Collection, YCHT; Alfred Jameson to his mother, July 4, 1862, Pension Records of Alfred Jameson, Co. A, 87th Pa.; *Star and Banner,* July 24, 1862, letter dated July 16, 1862. The regiment eventually moved camp uphill to drier ground.

11. John McIlvain to Andrew G. Curtin, July 27, 1862, PA AGO, Records of Applications for Military Positions, Vacancies, Appointments, and Resignations, and Commissions Issued, 1861–1865.

87th officers ever learned of his surreptitious letter is unknown, but he later apologized for his "bad streak" to Col. George Hay, the very man he had tacitly blasted in his letter to Governor Curtin. Although he initially seemed pleased by the new post, issues must not have been to McIlvain's liking with the 68th Pennsylvania either, because he resigned after six months due to "rheumatism of eight years standing." The two-year veteran so eager to get into active duty "suddenly" realized he had a long-term health problem that rendered him incapable of performing duty as an assistant surgeon.[12]

It is more likely that McIlvain was not a good surgeon, as the rest of his life demonstrates. Five months after he left the 68th Pennsylvania, he went to Baltimore and enlisted with the 1st Maryland Potomac Home Brigade Cavalry as a private, giving "bartender" as his profession. If he sought to hide his medical knowledge, he failed. The regiment promoted him to hospital steward, a position for which he should have been overqualified.[13]

After the war, McIlvain left York for a hospital steward's position at Oakland Carroll Hospital in Louisville, Kentucky, remaining there until 1869. Then, he enlisted as a private with the 6th U.S. Cavalry and remained at that lowly rank for nearly three years until the army again found out about his medical skills and promoted him to hospital steward. They assigned him to a post at Rock Island, Illinois, where he found both a job and a divorcée to his liking, marrying the latter and signing on with the former for another five-year stint. Once finished with this latest military service, he went to the Soldiers' Home in Milwaukee, Wisconsin, and again took work as a hospital steward and did not reach assistant surgeon's status for eight years. He eventually rose to first assistant surgeon but never became full surgeon. The kind eulogy the Soldiers' Home wrote at his death may be proof that he had found his niche, but it was not as a competent physician.[14]

Company B

Company B was a mongrel outfit of men independently recruited from two areas and expanded by a scattering of Yorkers such as Michael Heiman.

12. *Official Army Register of the Volunteer Force of the United States Army for the Years 1861, '62, '63, '64, '65*, part 3, 911; John E. McIlvain to George Hay, Apr. 5, 1863, George Hay Kain III Collection; CMSR of John McIlvain, 68th Pa.

13. CMSR of John McIlvain, 1st Potomac Home Guard. After McIlvain was promoted, he changed his life's work from bartender to druggist.

14. Pension Records of John E. McIlvain, Obituary by the Northwestern Branch, National Home for Disabled Volunteer Soldiers, General Orders No. 24, Apr. 21, 1892. McIlvain married Elizabeth Hill, née McCauly, October 3, 1874, literally on Rock Island.

John Crull, an experienced militiaman, pulled together some forty-five men from the Newberry Township area and brought them to York ahead of Jacob Detwiler's fifty boys from Dauphin and Perry counties. The combination virtually equaled the theoretical one hundred for a company, so they became martial bedfellows. Detwiler, a Harrisburg coal merchant, had a slight edge in manpower, and that gave him the election for captain. Crull settled for first lieutenant. Before long, the men regretted their decision.

Crull led most of Company B's drills and taught some unique maneuvers that instilled pride in the company. One movement so impressed Col. George Hay that he decided to show a delegation of York's upper crust what Company B could accomplish on the parade ground. Detwiler, however, wanted the limelight and told Lieutenant Crull to stand aside and let the captain direct his company that day. That did not sit well with the boys, so they plotted to humiliate him if the chance arose. Detwiler was about to give them that chance.

Drill started well enough until Detwiler decided to demonstrate Crull's unique movement. He shouted the order and completely botched it. Michael Heiman recalled:

> On any other occasion we might have executed the movement the captain had meant we should, but we were for playing a prank, so those of the company who should have gone to the right went to the left and others went to the right, bringing the whole company into confusion . . . [Detwiler] felt so vexed and humiliated that you could have knocked him down with a feather . . . He ordered us to our quarters and had the sergeant drill us for over an hour for his satisfaction and our punishment.[15]

Harassing Detwiler had not begun with that parade ground prank. Michael Heiman said it was virtually a nightly event. The playing of tattoo meant prepare to retire for the night, but that meant little to Company B, whose Cockeysville barracks often featured after-hours card games. Detwiler ordered the practice halted, but the boys ignored him. He posted a guard in the barracks with orders to make sure candles were snuffed out at the proper time. The idea might have worked if he had not given the job to George Kohr Toomey, an eighteen-year-old who, in Michael Heiman's words, "was from the country and hadn't been broken in yet." Precisely at 10:00 P.M., Toomey arrived and ordered lights out. Heiman recalled what happened next.

15. Recollections of Michael Heiman, *York Gazette,* Feb. 22, 1892; see Prowell, *87th Pennsylvania,* 20, for a sanitized version of this event.

The boys wished to finish a game they were playing and so kept on playing unmindful of Toomey's orders, reiterated again and again. This started the fun. While the one set continued playing, the others encouraged Toomey by cries of, "That's right Toomey. Make them put out their lights and go to sleep." Pretty soon shoes and other missiles began flying through the quarters. The lights were extinguished, even Toomey's, the usefulness of which was ended by a well aimed shot from a shoe. An awful chorus of noises now started up. Some crowed, others mewed and Toomey expostulated. Several times he grabbed offenders by the leg or foot, but they pretended to wake up suddenly and accused Toomey of disturbing their slumbers . . . It was very dark in the room and of course difficult for Toomey to locate those making the noises. Finally the sergeant slipped up, but his approach had been heard and when he was forward, those in the rear crowed, which he went to the rear those in the forward part crowed. The sergeant then wisely departed.[16]

Detwiler slept in a room separated from the men's barracks only by a thin wooden wall and heard everything. He sneaked in trying to catch the ringleaders but "fared no better than Toomey and the sergeant," Michael Heiman remembered with glee. Detwiler stormed out, raging on about reprisals he would dish out in the morning. Whatever punishment he meted out, if any, had no effect.[17]

The following spring, a bad situation worsened due to a trivial disagreement over hats. The boys hated their "high regulation military hats for dress" and turned in the crowns, "making low slouch hats out of them." Whatever his men wanted, Jacob Detwiler wanted the opposite, and he ordered crowns up. At dress parade, the boys saw companies A and F wearing crowns down and put their hats in the same condition. Detwiler threatened to punish anyone not obeying his order and complained to George Hay, who threatened arrest if they did not comply.

Company B marched with crowns down. No sooner had the parade ended than the entire company found itself under arrest and escorted back to barracks by Company A. The arrest did not bother them as much as Company A wearing their crowns turned down throughout the process.

When the captain of the guard arrived the next morning to detail some of Company B for duty, the boys refused to move. They reminded the captain that regulations forbade any soldier in a condition of arrest from standing guard, and they were all under arrest. Detwiler asked Adj. Jacob Emmett to plead his case. The boys countered with Pvt. William F. Spayd, a man loaded

16. Recollections of Michael Heiman, *York Gazette,* Feb. 22, 1892.
17. Ibid.

with what another ethnic group called *chutzpah*. Spayd informed Emmett that if Company A could wear their hats with crowns down, so could they. He held his hat in front of Emmett's face and punched his fist through, bursting the crown outward.

"There," Spayd said, "go tell the colonel that one fellow put his hat up."[18]

The next day, the company's forty worst troublemakers stood before a regimental court-martial. The defendants again chose William Spayd as the wrench to toss into the wheels of military justice. Spayd had done his homework and advised every man of his right to object to a different member of the court-martial board. By procedure, the challenged member of the court had to withdraw while the rest of the members discussed the validity of the objection. It did not take the court long to realize that every member was going to be challenged multiple times. Clueless what to do, the court called on George Hay for counsel. The colonel made no personal record of his reaction that has survived, but it had to be disgust because he told them to ignore the harassment and get on with the trial.[19]

The court presented charges of disobedience of orders and mutilation of uniforms, among others. While Detwiler had legitimate complaints against his company, he erred by concentrating on the trivial hat issue. He claimed that he had issued a written order about keeping the crowns up, but contrary testimony by Lt. John Crull and 1st Sgt. Samuel Finkle Keller humiliated him. The court adjourned to deliberate.

The finding of the court-martial was literally nothing. The men of Company B never heard another word about their hats and thereafter wore them however they wished. Michael Heiman claimed they lost their dreaded headgear a year later in (West) Virginia when they all blew into the Potomac River, a claim no doubt made with tongue firmly planted in cheek. Unknown to Heiman until years later, the court blamed Detwiler for Company B's disciplinary problems, determining that any officer unable to control his men should step aside. Detwiler surely had conversations on the subject with George Hay but retained his commission.[20]

Detwiler lasted as captain until July 21, 1863, when he resigned due to "valvular disease of the heart." A wag might suggest that his only heart problem was not having enough of one to be a military commander. He soon provided evidence of good cardiovascular health when he assumed a captaincy

18. Ibid.

19. Stephen Vincent Benet, *A Treatise of Military Law and the Practice of Courts-Martial*, 68–69; Wiley, *Billy Yank*, 196. As late as Aug. 1863, Gen. Nathaniel P. Banks could not organize a court-martial whose members had any knowledge of judicial procedure.

20. Recollections of Michael Heiman, *York Gazette*, Feb. 22, 1892. Heiman claimed John Albright, a court member, told him years later about the court's anti-Detwiler decision.

with the 53rd U.S. Colored Troops until a second resignation on August 16, 1864, returned him to Pennsylvania to recruit yet another regiment. That opportunity vanished when the new 199th Pennsylvania Infantry absorbed his recruits and had no position for a failed officer. Detwiler left the army forever on December 27, 1864, forced out by special order from the Adjutant General's Office.[21]

Whatever his shortcomings, Detwiler closed out his association with the 87th Pennsylvania in honorable fashion. Nine days after he left, he wrote glowing recommendations for Lewis Maish to become his replacement and Theodore A. Gardner to become second lieutenant. A month later, he wrote a plea to the commandant of Fort McHenry to release three Company B men caught deserting. So successful was that endeavor that none of their military records mentions the arrest. Ironically, one of them was none other than his old nemesis William Spayd.

In a strange twist, Company B had the regiment's second lowest desertion rate. That proverbial wag might speculate that the men were having too much fun to run away—at least while Jacob Detwiler was still in command.[22]

Companies C and D

These were the regiment's twins, two companies of men almost exclusively from southern York County, including that eager little railroad town of Glen Rock. Nearly 60 percent were farm boys or day laborers, men for whom dirt under the nails was a badge of honor. Many of their homes were so close to Maryland that they retrieved their mail across the state line. Mixed in were a few Marylanders who had temporarily shifted their homes to York County for employment reasons. They remained the most stalwart in the regiment. Company C had the lowest rate of desertion and Company D, the third lowest, in spite of suffering casualty rates among the regiment's highest.[23]

21. CMSR and Pension Records of Jacob Detwiler, Co. B, 87th Pa., and 53rd U.S. Colored Inf.
22. Jacob Detwiler to Andrew G. Curtin, July 30, 1863, and Aug. 12, 1863, PA AGO, Muster Rolls; Jacob Detwiler to Commander, Fort McHenry, Aug. 27, 1863, Records of the Adjutant General's Office, Muster Rolls, 87th Pennsylvania, Correspondence, NARA; CMSRs of William Zorger, Co. A, and William Spayd and John Gallagher, Co. B, 87th Pa. (the three men freed by Detwiler's plea); Court-Martial, William Spayd, LL-1508. At Mine Run, Spayd went AWOL and was court-martialed but received a relatively light sentence. Pension Records of Jacob Detwiler. Detwiler truly may have been ill. A witness said he returned home "a complete wreck." Whether physically or mentally, he did not say. Detwiler moved to Illinois and died at age forty-nine. For his obituary, see *Chicago Tribune,* Mar. 5, 1876.
23. Company D had a higher percentage of men from Hopewell Township. Maryland Line, Maryland, was the post office for the southern part of Hopewell.

Company C's first captain, Andrew Jackson Fulton, was a big man who intimidated recruits as he looked down at them with his black-whiskered face. Company C suffered the regiment's greatest number of killed and wounded, but none of that happened under Fulton's watch. After sixteen months with the 87th Pennsylvania, he took a transfer to command the 166th Pennsylvania Drafted Militia. He survived the war unscathed, but postwar life was less forgiving. While he was hunting in the fall of 1872, a falling rifle discharged and shot him through the groin, possibly severing his femoral artery. He bled to death in the woods of southern York County.[24]

The regiment's first battle casualty came from the ranks of Company C nine months after muster and a year before a bullet struck a second 87th man. On June 24, 1862, the day after the regiment reached New Creek, (West) Virginia, Pvt. Robert W. Keech was on picket duty when a small force of Rebels started taking shots. One struck Keech in the lower left leg, but he remained on the firing line. The price was falling ill with what surgeons determined to be "chronic hepatitis," a serious condition that soon had him on his way home with a medical discharge. Surgeons had not done their job well. Two months later, Keech started a three-year stint riding with the 11th Pennsylvania Cavalry.[25]

Shrewsbury Borough resident Noah G. Ruhl recruited and commanded Company D and eventually rose to the rank of major. Ruhl had the face of a Prussian nobleman, but his bank account was anything but aristocratic. Acquaintances described his family as "very poor, having but little of this world's goods and . . . compelled to labor for their daily bread." A store clerk by trade, Ruhl's stated net worth in 1860 was a meager $300 and that after settlement of his father's small estate had given him the wherewithal to purchase a house and store. Not only was he the regiment's poorest captain, he was poorer than many of his men. That alone made him a unique officer.[26]

---

24. Thomas E. Cochran to Gov. Andrew G. Curtin, Nov. 22, 1862, General Correspondence, carton 17; Thomas M. Vincent to Andrew G. Curtin, Dec. 6, 1862, Muster Rolls, PA AGO; Pension Records of Andrew J. Fulton, Co. H, 16th Pa. Mrs. Fulton's widow's pension is for the 16th Pennsylvania only. Dr. J. L. Free reported the bullet passed upward through Fulton's groin and lodged in his bowels, "killing him instantly." *York Gazette,* Nov. 12, 1872, claims Fulton was with two men when the accident happened and that death was instantaneous. Since groin and abdominal injuries are unlikely to be immediately fatal, the bullet likely struck the femoral artery, and he bled to death in minutes.

25. CMSR and Pension Records of Robert W. Keech, Co. C, 87th Pa., and Co. C, 11th Pa. Cav. Keech was discharged Aug. 21, 1862, and enlisted with the 11th on Oct. 25, 1862.

26. Pension Records of Edgar M. Ruhl, Co. D, 87th Pa., testimony of George Blasser, Noah Heiss, and James B. Koller, Jan. 21, 1882; U.S. Census, 1860, Pennsylvania, York County, Shrewsbury Borough. In 1860, Noah Ruhl lived with his mother.

Ruhl not only looked the part of a Prussian officer, he behaved like a stereo-typical one. David Christian Eberhart, a neighbor and comrade, described him in typically understated nineteenth-century manner: "There was a want of congeniality." Henry Seitz, Ruhl's second lieutenant, wrote in equally pas-sive voice, "Captain Ruhl is a man of that kind of disposition that any sugges-tions from an inferior officer or private is not relished by him." Ruhl had been a member of the court during Company B's farcical court-martial. Michael Heiman made a special point of protesting Ruhl's presence, claiming that no common soldier could ever receive justice by his hands. That memory still grated Heiman thirty-five years after the event.[27]

Ruhl's personal life may have helped turn him into a curmudgeon. He united in matrimony with Anna Maria—last name unknown—in 1840. If their marriage began in heaven, it took a precipitous tumble earthward. By 1857, he was only taking meals at home and sleeping elsewhere, possibly with Elizabeth Dietz down the street. Anna Ruhl referred to her as "Widow Dietz," but the 1860 census shows her cohabiting with a presumably breathing hus-band. In early 1858, Ruhl came home one last time, picked up his clothes, and said goodbye to their two children. He never spoke to his wife again except at their son's funeral when they argued over his estate. After the war, Noah Ruhl offered his family no financial support, Anna Ruhl requested none, and he would not have given it had she asked. "A perfect devil," he called her, yet their marriage had not been a shouting contest. Mostly, she scolded and he endured. So shriveled was their relationship that when he went off to war, he deeded his newly acquired property to Elizabeth Dietz so his wife could not claim it if he were killed.[28]

Edgar Monroe Ruhl remained with his mother throughout his parents' separation, supporting her and his sister on the meager income of a cigar maker. When the war began, he accompanied his father into the Thomas A. Scott Regiment, eventually to command Company D and, briefly, the 87th Pennsylvania. Edgar sent home money for his mother to purchase land and build a house, but she struggled to put food on the table. When Edgar died in battle, Mrs. Ruhl lost an income as well as a son. Estrangement from her

---

27. Henry Seitz to Franklin Geise, May 6, 1862, PA AGO, Muster Rolls; Pension Records of Edgar M. Ruhl, testimony of David C. Eberhart, Apr. 5, 1882; recollections of Michael Heiman, *York Gazette*, Feb. 22, 1892.

28. Pension Records of Edgar M. Ruhl, testimony of David C. Eberhart and Noah G. Ruhl, Apr. 5, 1882, Elizabeth Sandless and Mina Koller, Apr. 3, 1882, and Anna M. Ruhl, Mar. 29, 1883; U.S. Census, 1870, Pennsylvania, York County, Shrewsbury Borough. After the war, Noah Ruhl returned to Shrewsbury, a very small town, yet he and his wife never spoke. A career as a dry goods merchant increased his worth to more than $7,000.

husband continued into death. Father's and son's graves are side by side, but hers is nowhere near.[29]

In spite of his grouchy nature and near-impoverishment, Noah Ruhl was no Jacob Detwiler when it came to military matters. Men followed his orders no matter how much they might have disliked him personally because he possessed a strength of military character gleaned from five years of service in the regular army. Four years in the Seminole Indian wars and one in the Mexican War (serving as Noah R. Chapman) earned him a sergeant major's rank. That experience made him the only officer in the initial organization of the 87th Pennsylvania who had ever issued an order in battle.[30]

But Ruhl's insight into military discipline seemed lost on volunteers—at least until the shooting started. Only after ill health forced him to leave the army in mid-1864 did some realize that they had lost a valuable commander. A good argument can be made that Noah Ruhl should have been the first colonel of the Thomas A. Scott Regiment. He might have had a chance if only he had not committed two cardinal sins: He was not from York, and he was not middle class. Being a son-of-a-bitch was no impediment.[31]

Company E

Every organization needs one group it can count on to be there, not necessarily to perform headline-grabbing feats, but to be rock stable. That was Company E. It paid for that reputation with the regiment's highest casualty rate among pre-1863 recruits.

Solomon Myers took the reins in September 1861 and three years later still held the rank of captain, the regiment's only officer to finish his enlistment with the same rank he held when he entered. His performance prompted Lt. Col. James A. Stahle to describe Myers as "a faithful and energetic officer ever foremost in the discharge of his dutys." That Stahle said it to the governor

29. Pension Records of Edgar M. Ruhl, letters to his mother Nov. 21 and 22, 1863, and testimony of Noah Ruhl, Anna Mary Ruhl, George Blasser, Elizabeth Sandless (who claimed she lived with the Ruhls during their final breakup), Mina Koller, A. J. Koller (brother of Elizabeth Dietz), David Christian Eberhart, James H. Hendrix, and Eli McDonnel.

30. Registers of Enlistments in the United States Army 1798–1914, vol. 43, M233, roll 21, NARA. Ruhl probably used an alias during the Mexican War because he enlisted at age seventeen and was trying to escape detection by his parents. Segments of the microfilm of Mexican War enlistments are unreadable, which is perhaps why no record of his enlistment could be found. See Prowell, *87th Pennsylvania,* 274.

31. Theodore A. Helwig to Col. Samuel B. Thomas, Feb. 28, 1865; nine officers of the 87th Pennsylvania and Col. William Truex to "Whom It May Concern," undated but undoubtedly from Feb./Mar. 1865, PA AGO, Muster Rolls.

makes it even more of a plaudit, however generalized the compliment may have been. After the war, Justice of the Peace Solomon Myers assisted dozens of less educated former comrades in obtaining pensions until his death from stomach cancer in 1886.[32]

Company E was also a mongrel company, but comparison to Company B stops there. Isaac Hull, a mechanic appropriately from Mechanicsburg, Cumberland County, convinced two dozen fellow citizens to join him in a military experience and took them to York. Locked in a recruiting battle with James Stahle and John Schall, Solomon Myers latched onto Hull's recruits and then dipped into surrounding townships. Nearly half of his men were farmers and, with the exception of a concentration of carpenters, mostly unskilled workers, which gave Company E the regiment's lowest average family net worth. At the same time, it had the highest number of married men of any company.

Companies A and K may have had the honor of operating at opposite ends of the battle formation, but Myers's unit was the color company. In battle, it would march in the middle of the line, flags waving, the nucleus of the regiment. Teacher Solomon Myers was the perfect man for the duty, the senior captain whose health and resolve remained strong, officer of the day more often than anyone else, a diary-keeper who would leave behind a twenty-two-year legacy of daily weather reports.[33]

Isaac Hull, on the other hand, paid dearly for his patriotism. Nine months in Libby Prison and associated hellish hospitals made good health an elusive goal for the remainder of his life. He tried many postwar professions, but his body never allowed him to work steadily.[34]

Company F

This was the company from Gettysburg, the regiment's most famous postwar because of its celebrated hometown and the romanticized tale of Cpl. Johnston Hastings Skelly and Mary Virginia Wade, incorrectly known today

32. CMSRs of all members of the 87th Pennsylvania Infantry; James A. Stahle to Gov. Andrew G. Curtin, Jan. 25, 1864, PA AGO, Muster Rolls, 87th Pa., Correspondence.

33. Diary of Solomon Myers; Pension Records of Solomon Myers, Co. E, 87th Pa. Myers died September 14, 1886, of stomach cancer. Judging by the number of times his name appears in comrades' pension applications, he obviously spent many hours assisting those whose literacy level was beneath his own.

34. Pension Records of Isaac Hull, Co. E, 87th Pa. Seventeen Company E men resided in Cumberland County, and three Dauphin and two York County men from near Mechanicsburg were probably recruited by Hull.

as "Jennie." The unit began with seventy-seven men formed around the nucleus of the Independent Blues Militia Company. They camped on the York fairgrounds under command of state militia leader Charles Henry Buehler, who was still doing militia business even as he prepared to lead a company into Federal service. The boys from Gettysburg needed help from York in filling the rolls and got ten latecomers from southern York County who might have been with their friends in Company C or D had they enlisted sooner.[35]

Typical for a military commander in the war's early days, Buehler was successful in business and active with the antebellum militia. Before the war, he left his brother's *Adams Sentinel and General Advertiser* to become a thriving coal and lumber merchant. So popular was he with his men that one of them opined how any regiment under his command "would soon be the best company on the ground." His immediate promotion to major did not please the men of Company F, but they still named their Lutherville, Maryland, campsite in his honor. The men liked it even less when he accepted a colonel's commission with the 165th Pennsylvania Drafted Militia. By then, the 87th Pennsylvania was a long way from home in the wilds of (West) Virginia, from where the Skelly brothers offered opinions of Buehler's move as well as the caliber of drafted soldiers.[36]

> Buehler left here this evening for home and is a going to take command of the concrips [conscripts] as cornell. He will make a good one but he treat our company very bad by leaveing us after getting us out her[e].[37]

> I don't know wether he thinks he has a higher position or not but I think that Major in a volenteir Reg is as high a[s] Col. of drafted men.[38]

35. Jack Skelly's and Jennie Wade's well-known love story was omitted here because the author has nothing new to add. See Cindy L. Small, *The Jennie Wade Story* (Gettysburg: Thomas Publications, 1996). Charles H. Buehler to Gov. Andrew G. Curtin, Aug. 29, 1861, PA AGO, General Correspondence, container 9; *Gettysburg Compiler*, Mar. 24, 1896; CMSRs and Pension Records, where applicable, of Amos Burke, Samuel Emenheiser, William Flinn, William B. Fullerton, Jacob Hepburn Grove, George S. Markle, William McGonigal, Joshua Peeling, Edward Seitz, and Samuel Sprenkle, Co. F, 87th Pa. Charles Buehler's military career began shortly after the death of a son, which may be why his wife and other son often were with him in the field.
36. Peter Warren to "Dear friends," Sept. 1861, Skelly Family Papers, HCWRT; "Zoo-Zoo" to the *Gettysburg Compiler*, issue July 28, 1862, proclaims Buehler's popularity. "Zoo-Zoo," a nickname for Zouave, sent a number of letters to the *Gettysburg Compiler* and the *York Gazette*. He was probably James A. Stahle. CMSR of Charles H. Buehler, Co. F, 87th Pa.; Johnston Hastings Skelly to his mother, May 1861, and Dec. 7, 1862, Pension Records of Johnston H. Skelly.
37. Charles Edwin Skelly to his mother, Dec. 4, 1862, Pension Records of Charles E. Skelly.
38. Johnston Hastings Skelly to his mother, Dec. 7, 1862, Pension Records of Johnston H. Skelly, Co. F, 87th Pa.

Gettysburg grocer William John Martin took over for Buehler but was a pale imitation of his predecessor, no doubt suffering by comparison. He resigned June 11, 1862, because of "neglect of business at home and sickness in my family." Why Captain Martin felt he was unique in that regard he did not say. Probably he left because he did not take to command easily, if at all. As the spring of 1862 arrived, one of his men wrote, "We are commencing to like him better than ever. He has changed a grate deal in the last 2 months . . . and the men behave better." While that was a compliment to Martin's growth, it also shows that he had struggled with leadership.[39]

As soon as Gettysburg's newspaper editors heard of Martin's resignation, they geared up for a print fight—not that Gettysburg's opposing newspapers needed a reason to exchange insults. From the ensuing banter, we can assume that William Martin was a member of the Democratic Party. The *Adams Sentinel* reported the resignation with a tinge of sarcasm, saying that Martin "must have had a good reason for it."[40]

The *Star and Banner,* political soul mate in all things Republican, went for the jugular.

> The only reason given for this resignation, that we have heard, was the inactivity of the service in which the regiment was engaged. But this does not seem to be sufficient . . . We presume Mr. Martin has other good reasons for resigning which we would be pleased to make known. After having made about $1100 off the Government doing nothing, justice to Uncle Sam would seem to demand a further explanation.[41]

Journalistic claws unsheathed, the *Compiler* pounced to Martin's defense.

> It was currently rumored, and generally credited, that the Regiment was to be cutup for guard duty at various Hospitals. Long dissatisfied with the life of inactivity, to which the Regiment had been subjected, Captain Martin . . . sent in his resignation . . . The Republican papers here, impelled by partisan feelings of course, seek . . . to impeach the courage of Captain Martin.[42]

39. Charles E. Skelly to his mother, May 9, 1862, Skelly Family Papers, HCWRT; Charles Edwin Skelly to his mother, Dec. 9, 1861, Pension Records of Charles E. Skelly; CMSR of William J. Martin, Co. F, 87th Pa., letter of resignation June 16, 1862; George Hay to Andrew G. Curtin, June 11, 1862, PA AGO, Muster Rolls.
40. *Adams Sentinel,* June 24, 1862.
41. *Star and Banner,* June 25, 1862.
42. *Gettysburg Compiler,* June 30, 1862; CMSR of William J. Martin, Co. F, 87th Pa., resignation letter, June 16, 1862.

Back came the *Star and Banner,* words blazing.

> Aside from the simple statement, having direct reference to Captain Martin's resignation, we are authorized to say that the remarks of the *Compiler* are entirely gratuitous—not being authorized by Captain Martin or any one else. The *Compiler* makes it an occasion to attack the Republican party thus showing that it was more desirous of making party capital than of defending the Captain . . . The fact that the *Compiler,* a paper in sympathy with the traitors, undertakes to defend a Union soldier, is the very height of absurdity.[43]

Irish-born marble worker and businessman James Adair assumed command and was still at the helm when the regiment's three-year enlistment expired. Given the absence of any subsequent negative accounts, it is safe to assume that Adair supplied no fodder for scandal to the Gettysburg newspapers.[44]

Company G

This was a company with problems, and most of them started with its captain, Vincent C. S. Eckert, a man fastidious about keeping those two middle initials in his name. His was a prominent name in Hanover. Eckert Hall, located on the southwest corner of the town square, was the home for music and lecture lovers and purchased by V. C. S. Eckert to use as an armory for the Marion Rifles Militia. The former state legislator first made his money selling shoes. Then, in 1858, Eckert and Company Liquors announced its grand opening, specializing in "Pure Northeast Rum and Spanish bitters." That gave him the wherewithal to buy the *Hanover Gazette* and publish both English and German editions.[45]

Eckert did not serve in a three-month regiment, but that did not stop him from recruiting a company for three years' service. Fellow Hanover resident Henry Morningstar did serve for three months and also began recruiting a company for service as soon as he arrived home in July 1861. Though the town

43. *Star and Banner,* July 3, 1862.
44. CMSR and Pension Records of James Adair, Co. F, 87th Pa. After the war, Adair moved to the New York City area but returned often to Gettysburg for reunions. He died in 1910 from injuries sustained falling from a trolley car.
45. *Hanover Spectator,* Jan. 1, 1858, Sept. 2, 1859, June 1, 1860, and Apr. 20, 1893; *Fire Association of Philadelphia Maps; Daily Record,* Apr. 29, 1897. Based on names of Eckert ancestors, his two middle names were possibly "Conrad Sebastian."

had fielded two militia companies for many years, the two men found themselves shy of good bodies. Up against the influential Diller family recruiting
what became Company D, 76th Pennsylvania Infantry, Eckert and Morningstar had to join forces but still could not fill a company. Schoolteacher
Robert Alonzo Daniel saved them by recruiting some of his students and
other young men in York and joining the boys from Hanover. Balloting for
officers gave the captaincy to V. C. S. Eckert. Henry Morningstar and Robert
Daniel became first and second lieutenants, respectively.[46]

Like most newspaper editors of his time, V. C. S. Eckert was a target for
rival publications, but attacks on him were especially vitriolic. In a style that
would make a modern-day libel attorney drool, the rival *Hanover Spectator*
said of Eckert:

> V.C.S.A.S.S. Eckert . . . the brainless creature who presides over the col-
> umns of that miserable looking sheet called the Hanover *Gazette* . . . a
> man who is ready and willing to sell his influence to any corrupt scheme
> so that it puts money in his purse. Without the brains to originate any-
> thing or even to advocate a measure, he has a certain amount of *low
> cunning* that makes him useful to men of more brains and sounder judg-
> ment . . . We believe him to be a prodigious ass—ignorant, destitute of
> personal beauty and political honor or honesty.[47]

The invective was probably over the top, but Eckert's behavior during the
war demonstrates the verbal attack may have held some truth. For certain,
the 87th Pennsylvania history committee did not have pleasant memories of
him because it omitted his biography from the regimental history, one of only
two original captains so slighted. The committee had reasons.[48]

When a company had to draw unpleasant duty, Company G was apt to receive the unlucky selection. In May 1862, eight companies camped at Wood-
berry, Maryland, in preparation for active service, but Company G still
guarded the railroad. When the regiment visited Towson for a big celebration
in its honor, Company G was again stuck on guard and missed the festivities.
When, in May 1863, the regiment was returning to Winchester, Company G
was one of two left on detached duty at Bunker Hill, (West) Virginia.[49]

46. *Hanover Spectator,* Aug. 30, 1861, and Mar. 28, 1862. Conewago Township, Adams County,
adjacent to Hanover, supplied men to the company, but the township's 1860 census is missing.
CMSRs and Pension Records of all men of Co. D, 76th Pa. Brothers Cyrus F. and William Sly-
der Diller both held the rank of major in the 76th Pennsylvania, and sibling Luther Yost Diller
commanded Company D.

47. *Hanover Spectator,* Mar. 6, 1857, emphasis in original.

48. Prowell, *87th Pennsylvania.* Ross L. Harman's is the other missing biography.

49. *Gettysburg Compiler,* May 26, 1862; Thomas O. Crowl to his sister, June 16, 1863, CWMC.

Eckert went home on furlough in July 1862 with orders to return with a group of recruits. A newspaper account described him as "well and hearty," but by autumn, things were anything but well and hearty with the company. Eckert had both of his lieutenants under arrest for reasons that do not appear in either man's service records. Robert Daniel was a popular officer, but Henry Morningstar had an acerbic personality that may have conflicted with Eckert's. Whatever the charges, apparently they were serious enough to threaten dismissal from the service. Seventeen fellow officers appealed to George Hay for Morningstar's and Daniel's release, calling the accusations "insufficient to justify their removal from duty in our regiment and the Federal Army." Hay obviously intervened in the situation, because the regiment's division commander, Robert Huston Milroy, soon ordered Morningstar and Daniel returned to duty and Eckert home for fifteen days "on account of disability to do military duty." Eckert's disability does not appear to have been physical because, upon reaching Hanover, he turned immediately to recruiting, hardly an indication that he was suffering from severely depressed health. In March 1863, he once more returned to Hanover on furlough, and a newspaper declared him "hale and hearty and in the enjoyment of excellent health."[50]

Three months later, he was back at the helm of Company G and about to be tested by fire at the second battle of Winchester. Afterward, the *Hanover Spectator* claimed that witnesses spoke "in the highest terms of Captain V. C. S. Eckert and his men from Hanover who fought till it was considered madness to contend any longer." That may have been true for Company G but not for Eckert. On the second day of battle, he received orders to charge but would not move. He was too sick, he said. Too lame from a sprained ankle. Too deafened by the roar of battle. Too sunstruck. Too scorbutic and in pain. Morningstar and Daniel were present, but Eckert issued his subalterns no orders to take command.[51]

The fight came to them whether Eckert wanted it or not. Henry Morningstar's military career ended when he suffered a hernia jumping a ditch and could not get away. Ahead lay almost a year in a series of Rebel prisons. At Morris Island near Charleston, South Carolina, Morningstar was among a group placed in the line of fire in a Confederate attempt to halt Union

50. *Hanover Spectator,* July 18, 1862; Pension Records of Jerome Hair, deposition of Vincent C. S. Eckert, and pension records of John Stahl, deposition of Jacob Reed, both men Co. G, 87th Pa.; CMSRs of Henry Morningstar and Robert A. Daniel, Co. G, 87th Pa.; seventeen 87th Pennsylvania officers to George Hay, Oct. 8, 1862, George Hay Kain III Collection; Records, Special Orders No. 80, Oct. 20, 1862, and Special Orders No. 88, Oct. 31, 1862, Special Order Book, 8th Army Corps, Apr. 1862; *Hanover Spectator,* Nov. 21, 1862, and Mar. 27 and June 26, 1863.
51. *Hanover Spectator,* June 26, 1863; CMSR of Vincent C. S. Eckert, Co. G, 87th Pa.; Pension Records of Vincent C. S. Eckert, deposition of David P. Kerr.

artillery. While he was imprisoned, the army promoted him to captain solely for the purpose of opening the first lieutenant's spot for Robert Daniel. Henry Morningstar never exercised the rank and did not formally receive his captaincy until 1888.[52]

Eckert's failure at Winchester made those moves not only necessary but possible. What John Schall, by then colonel of the regiment, said to his reluctant captain is unknown, but shortly after Winchester, Eckert submitted his resignation for reasons of ill health. The regiment, brigade, and division brass all approved. All that remained was the endorsement of the corps commander, Maj. Gen. George Gordon Meade. While waiting for that to arrive, Schall approved Eckert's furlough to Washington "to settle his accounts with the government."[53]

George "Old Snapping Turtle" Meade took a dim view of officers who refused to advance in battle. On September 1, 1863, the Office of the Adjutant General issued a long series of diverse commands entitled Special Order No. 392. One of those orders dishonorably expelled Capt. Vincent C. S. Eckert from the Army of the United States. Eckert appealed and a year later, with the support of fellow officers, convinced the War Department to grant him an honorable discharge. The damage, however, had been done.[54]

Area newspapers barely mentioned Eckert's disgrace, but such events are impossible to keep secret. No extant account other than Eckert's pension depositions has yet emerged to explain what caused him to freeze in battle. The belated honorable discharge technically absolved him of guilt, but he lived the rest of his life as if ashamed of what he had done. He never again lived in Hanover, and no postwar reunion roll contains his name. He moved to Baltimore almost immediately after his return and two decades and a new wife later transplanted roots to Harrisburg. Although he had lived forty years in Hanover and still had family there, Vincent C. S. Eckert's remains lie in a Baltimore cemetery.[55]

The Eckert family may have provided the ultimate evidence of what they thought of their kin. Eckert's brother and 87th Pennsylvania comrade, Wil-

52. CMSR of Henry Morningstar; Office of the Adjutant General, RG-94, Bookmark M951 V.S.1865, NARA. Morningstar's promotion was retroactively made effective September 14, 1863.

53. Endorsements No. 14 and No. 27, Special Order Book, 8th Army Corps, Apr. 1862.

54. Records of the Adjutant General's Office, 1780s–1917, RG-94, Special Orders Issued from the Adjutant General's Office, 1863, vol. 2, no. 392, Sept. 1, 1863; CMSR of Vincent C. S. Eckert; Register of Letters Received, Secretary of War. While both index and register entries exist for the letter that fellow officers wrote in Eckert's defense, the letter itself is missing. Eckert's discharge is dated September 1, 1863.

55. *Gettysburg Compiler*, Nov. 16, 1863; *Star and Banner*, Nov. 19, 1863; ms. 901, YCHT; Pension Records of Vincent C. S. Eckert.

liam Francis "Frank" Eckert, preceded Vincent in death. In Frank Eckert's obituary, the family listed Dr. Henry Eckert as the only surviving brother.[56]

Company H

Like the placement of their respective letters in the alphabet, the men from Wellsville were one rung lower in the 87th Pennsylvania hierarchy than their Company G counterparts. When the Hanover boys missed the festivities at Towson, Company H partnered in loneliness. In May 1863, when two companies were detached to guard duty at Bunker Hill, (West) Virginia, Company H pitched tents alongside Company G. Company H's captain is the other original company commander lacking a biography in George Prowell's regimental history, and Prowell mentions the company less than any other. In part, that was because the company had no representative on the history committee, but it just as likely exhibits the frustration that once led James Stahle to write Governor Andrew G. Curtin, "We have a difficulty in that company that we have never had in any other."[57]

As always, a company starts with its commander, and forty-one-year-old Ross Lewis Harman built his company in a way that typifies the creation of a volunteer Civil War unit. Life had set him to farming, school teaching, and raising a family with an unusually soft hand, ventures he put on hold to urge others to fight for his Lincolnesque ideals. Nonetheless, boys from the Wellsville area signed enlistment papers knowing that Ross Harman was the best man to command them. He virtually filled a company even though recruiters from the 7th Pennsylvania Reserves had previously swept through the region. Unfamiliarity with military matters did not make him less qualified than thousands of others seeking commissions, but his son's brief biography paints a portrait of a man who may not have been up to issuing distasteful but necessary orders to lifelong acquaintances. That he was a gentleman seems certain. It is his ability as a military commander that is questionable.[58]

56. *Hanover Herald,* Oct. 13, 1883; Pension Records of Vincent C. S. Eckert and William Francis Eckert, Co. G, 87th Pa.; *Hanover Herald,* Oct. 13, 1883. Vincent C. S. Eckert's obituary appeared in the *Hanover (Pa.) Evening Herald,* Sept. 17, 1894, and the *Hanover Herald,* Sept. 22, 1894. The obituary briefly mentions his Civil War service without comment.

57. Thomas O. Crowl to his aunt and uncle, May 31, 1862, CWMC; Prowell, *87th Pennsylvania;* James A. Stahle to Samuel B. Thomas, A.A.G., Dec. 14, 1863, PA AGO. George R. Prowell mentioned Company G more often than H probably because Company G veteran John Clutter Hoffman was on the history committee.

58. CMSRs and Pension Records (where available) for all men who served with Co. H, 36th Pa.; recollections of Lane Scott Harman, Sept. 10, 1930. For comparisons to recruiting in other

Harman's problems came in no small part from health issues that rendered him useless on several occasions, the final time for three months. Neither did 2nd Lt. John Lawrence Shillito and 1st Sgt. Harvey James Harman bring much military savvy to the company. Their primary leadership qualifications were being Ross Harman's cousins. Only 1st Lt. Wells Abraham Farrah, an officer with the antebellum Washington Guards Militia, grew into the job and received plaudits in George Prowell's regimental history.[59]

Perhaps Ross Harman's greatest shortcoming was that he was not a member of an elite community in York or Adams County. Most other captains could call on friends in high places, luminaries such as Thaddeus Stevens, Thomas Cochran, or Governor Andrew Curtin. As a teacher, Harman was obviously a literate man, but otherwise he was a farmer from distant northwest York County. He did not live in York or Gettysburg and could not hop the cars and travel to either location. Company H came from an area that lacked mass transportation, and that kept folks from Wellsville necessarily aloof from "big city" political and social life.[60]

By early 1863, Ross Harman, Harvey Harman, and John Shillito were all civilians again. Shillito left the army first by reason of "a family in feeble health . . . who require the attention and protection of husband and father," reasons that sounded less like a man with a sick family than a man sick of the army. Ross Harman gave up in January 1863 and returned home "broken in health and incapacitated" because of "anasarca [swelling] dependent on diseased kidney." Harvey Harman resigned in March 1863, a departure not by choice. He was promoted to second lieutenant after Shillito's departure, but the job soon overwhelmed him, and he resigned due to "shortness of memory and want of sufficient military education filling the position of lieutenant." John Schall and George Hay added the word *incompetency* to his resignation letter.[61]

regiments, see Moe, *The Last Full Measure,* Dunn, *Harvestfields of Death,* O[smund] R[hodes] Howard Thomson and William H. Rauch, *History of the "Bucktails," Kane Rifle Regiment of the Pennsylvania Reserve Corps* (Dayton: Morningside House, Inc., 1988), and Kemp, "Community and War."

59. CMSR of Ross L. Harman, Co. H, 87th Pa.; recollections of Lane Scott Harman; Prowell, *87th Pennsylvania,* 73, 286–87; List of Officers, 1st Brigade, 4th Division, Pennsylvania State Militia, George Hay Kain III Collection.

60. The author's fraternal grandparents grew up not far from Wellsville and recalled that sense of isolation even as the twentieth century began.

61. CMSR and Pension Records of John Shillito, Co. H, 87th Pa.; U.S. Census, 1860; recollections of Lane Scott Harman; CMSR and Pension Records of Ross Lewis Harman, Co. H, 87th Pa.; CMSR of Harvey J. Harman, Co. H, 87th Pa., letter of resignation, Mar. 2, 1863; Circular, Jan. 28, 1863, Army Records, part 2, 8th Army Corps, Special Orders Apr. 1862–June 1863, vol. 2, NARA.

Wells Farrah stepped up to captain and was left to pick up the company's pieces, but the regimental brass were not going to allow another officer to rise from within Company H's ranks. "There is not a man in that company that a single officer in this regiment would select for any of the positions vacant in it," James Stahle wrote late in 1863. He obviously had felt the same way the previous January because the regiment flew in the face of tradition by looking outside the company to fill the first lieutenant's slot.[62]

They found Robert Samuel Slaymaker, a selection more political than practical. Rob, as friends called him, was the son of the wealthy York businessman and had enlisted with Company A. The regiment immediately detailed him as regimental clerk, and he never served mundane soldier functions and rarely saw anyone from his company. He worked closely with the adjutant at headquarters in Cockeysville, Maryland, learning the workings of command and becoming the regiment's fair-haired boy. Maj. Charles Buehler deemed him as "well qualified for any position the governor may assign him." When the regiment needed a "common" soldier to present a ceremonial sword to James Stahle, the regiment selected Cpl. Robert S. Slaymaker as its showpiece of choice.[63]

The clerk's job may have been a wise decision for reasons beyond his literacy. After Slaymaker's only battle experience, he returned to York and related his adventures to a family friend. The friend afterward wrote, "[Slaymaker] says [Col. John] Schall fought very bravely; but as he says the same with regard to the regiment, and I gather from what he says that he was considerably scared and took very good care of himself, perhaps what he says about their bravery is not very reliable." The critic who made that evaluation did so from the safety of home and without ever having experienced battle. Unfair an opinion as it was, it does indicate how one acquaintance assessed Rob Slaymaker's caliber as a fighting man.[64]

After the regimental quartermaster deserted and left accounts in a mess, Slaymaker's father began campaigning for his son to take the position and did not hesitate to call on Governor Curtin and evoke the names Hay, Schall, and

62. James A. Stahle to Asst. Adj. Gen. Samuel B. Thomas, Dec. 14, 1863, PA AGO, Muster Rolls.

63. Prowell, *History of York County,* 1:1006; Maj. C[harles]. H. Buehler to Adj. Gen. A. J. Russell, Oct. 9, 1862, PA AGO, Muster Rolls; *York Gazette,* July 1, 1862; Pension Records of Robert S. Slaymaker, Co. A, 87th Pa., deposition of Robert Slaymaker, Aug. 1881. The sword ceremony took place in Baltimore and apparently was a surprise to James Stahle.

64. James W. Latimer to brother Bartow, June 18 and 24, 1863, Latimer Family File 3577, YCHT; CMSR and Pension Records of Robert S. Slaymaker, Company A and H, 87th Pa., deposition of Robert Slaymaker, Aug. 1881, and Slaymaker to P. G. Clark, July 23, 1885.

Buehler in touting his son. That campaign went on hiatus when the position of sergeant major opened and the regiment dropped Rob into the job. He had held the rank only a few weeks when John Schall again asked Governor Curtin to approve the young man's promotion—this time to quartermaster and the first lieutenant's bars that went with it. The job was a virtual certainty until fate took a hand.[65]

Ross Harman's resignation took effect the day after Schall sent his letter to Governor Curtin, and the regiment threw Slaymaker into Company H as first lieutenant. The move infuriated the men, who complained that their new officer was "almost an entire stranger to the company." Whatever their shortcomings, the men of Company H had spent a year and a half together, developed pride and camaraderie, and now a stranger—a clerk, no less— would be their first lieutenant. Nonetheless, Slaymaker was in, and there was little they could do about it. The brass compromised and promoted Company H's Sgt. Michael S. Slothower to second lieutenant. Capt. Wells Farrah vaulted Cpl. Andrew Bentz Smith into the vital role of first sergeant, the first of two promotions Smith would come to regret.[66]

Slaymaker was adept at mathematics and claimed he could concentrate on a problem to the exclusion of everything around him. That was before he took a commission in Company H. Before the pressure mounted. Before blinding headaches struck and his powers of concentration faded. Before hearing the shocking news of his brother's death in battle. He kept his malady a secret, fearful that comrades would mock him for "playing off." Twenty years later, he admitted that "many a report went in to headquarters from my Regt. . . . when I was suffering from my head as no one but myself knew and was totally unfit for the work."[67]

Company H's situation unraveled on June 13, 1863. Bunker Hill, (West) Virginia, was a hamlet ten miles north of Winchester with a good water supply and a strategic location on the Valley Pike. It remained an inviting campsite for both sides throughout the war. Only four companies of infantry—G

65. Samuel R. Slaymaker to Gov. A. G. Curtin, Dec. 11, 1862, and John W. Schall to Adj. Gen. A. L. Russell, Jan. 17, 1863, PA AGO, Correspondence; CMSR of Robert S. Slaymaker; U.S. Census, 1860, Pennsylvania, York County; CMSR and Pension Records of Peter Ford, Quartermaster, 87th Pa. Ford, a successful dry goods merchant and George Hay's next-door neighbor, seemed ideal for quartermaster until he went home and did not return. The army dishonorably dismissed him but reversed itself May 11, 1864, dating his discharge Oct. 13, 1862.

66. Company H to Gov. Andrew G. Curtin, Nov. 18, 1863, PA AGO, Muster Rolls; CMSRs of Michael S. Slothower and Andrew B. Smith, Co. H, 87th Pa.

67. Pension Records of Robert Slaymaker, deposition of Robert Slaymaker, Aug. 1881; CMSR of Capt. Jonathan Smith Slaymaker, Co. C, 2nd Iowa. Jonathan Slaymaker had gone to Davenport, Iowa, just before the war and died at Fort Donelson, Tennessee, Feb. 15, 1862.

and H of the 87th Pennsylvania and A and I from the 116th Ohio—were stationed there as part of a defensive ring around Winchester. By contrast, an entire brigade and a battery of artillery guarded the Berryville outpost east of Winchester.[68]

The size of the Bunker Hill outpost would not have mattered had a large Confederate force not started moving down the valley toward Winchester in June 1863. Flush with success from the battle of Chancellorsville, Robert E. Lee set his Army of Northern Virginia in motion on a campaign that, unknown to anyone then, would culminate at a town named Gettysburg. Richard Stoddert Ewell's army closed in on the outnumbered Union force in and around Winchester and threatened the outpost at Berryville. A Union supply train parked there provided ripe fruit for Rebel plucking. The drivers hitched up and fled across country, bouncing along on narrow, winding roads, turning left at the village of Smithfield (now Middleway) to cross the Opequon River, with but one company of cavalry for protection. Bunker Hill was their immediate goal. There, they could strike the Valley Pike and scoot northward to the garrison at Martinsburg and escape into Pennsylvania if necessary. The Berryville outpost held out as long as possible but eventually had to fall back to Winchester. When the door opened, Rebel cavalry galloped after the prized wagon train.[69]

The train rumbled into Bunker Hill, horses well lathered and desperate for rest and water. The break had to be short-lived. A thousand or more Confederate cavalrymen were coming into view. Teamsters hustled to get away while the Pennsylvania and Ohio soldiers formed a thin defensive line and put an even thinner line of skirmishers to the front. The cavalry escort offered support for a time, but the wagon train was their primary responsibility. They soon were splashing through Mill Creek Ford on their way north. Amazingly, the wagon train made it to Harrisburg unscathed.[70]

68. Johnston H. Skelly to his mother, July 16, 1861, Pension Records of Johnston H. Skelly; *O.R.,* Joseph E. Johnston to Gen. S. Cooper, 2:934, Thomas J. Jackson to Joseph E. Johnston, 5:1092, Nathaniel P. Banks to C. S. Hamilton, 5:739–40, Report of Daniel Tyler, 27/2:17; Thomas F. Wildes, *Record of the One Hundred and Sixteenth Regiment Ohio Volunteers;* Prowell, *87th Pennsylvania,* 67. The 87th Pennsylvania regimental claims three hundred men were at Bunker Hill; the 116th Ohio regimental says two hundred. Manpower was light because Bunker Hill is north of Winchester and had less immediate exposure than Berryville.

69. Prowell, *87th Pennsylvania,* 67–69; Wildes, *Record of the One Hundred and Sixteenth Regiment Ohio,* 55; *O.R.,* Report of Daniel Tyler, 27/2:17; William H. Beach, *The First New York (Lincoln) Cavalry,* 231, 235. In the twentieth century, the Valley Pike became Route 11 and remained the principal north-south highway through the Shenandoah Valley until the construction of I-81. In 1863, a macadamized road was one that was covered in crushed stone, making it passable in wet weather but brutal for soldiers marching on poorly shod or bare feet.

70. Beach, *Lincoln Cavalry,* 235. The 1st New York Cavalry regimental history mentions no other troops at Bunker Hill. Prowell, *87th Pennsylvania,* 68. For images of Bunker Hill as it was

The four companies held almost until near dark, then fell back to two small brick churches they had prepared for defense. During the retro-movement, the Confederates inflicted stiff casualties on the 116th Ohio, whose regimental history barely mentions the 87th Pennsylvania. The omission may have been motivated by the Ohioans' casualty count of four killed, eleven wounded, and forty-two captured compared to only ten 87th casualties, two of whom died. The 87th lost its first officer to enemy fire when Michael Slothower fell that day and died the next. Rebels trapped his first cousin, Orderly Sgt. Andrew Bentz Smith, and sent him and seven other 87th captives to a farmhouse for their first night as prisoners. Sgt. John Myers Griffith fell wounded but made his way to a farmhouse and somehow convinced the woman of the house to hide him. He was still hiding there a month later when the husband returned home on furlough from the Confederate army but did not report him.

The rest of Bunker Hill's little force slipped through enemy lines and reached Winchester. There, they learned they had traded one hot spot for a much hotter one.[71]

The 87th Pennsylvania suffered its first battle death on June 13, a harmless eighteen-year-old drummer named Daniel H. Karnes. The Confederate army wanted more and coiled around Winchester all day on June 14. The 87th skirmished in town, but Company H strangely remained in the rifle pits. By nightfall, Gen. Robert Milroy knew he either must get away or be devoured. Whatever men could not carry they had to destroy. Sadly, that included all the 87th Pennsylvania's paperwork and George Blotcher's first diary. Milroy would try sneaking through a ravine, relying on the cover of darkness, then hit the Martinsburg Road to the Charles Town Road and slip away to Harpers Ferry. Orders whispered through ranks.[72]

---

then, see James E. Taylor, *The James E. Taylor Sketchbook: Leaves from a Special Artist's Sketchbook and Diary,* 176–77.

71. *O.R.,* General Return of Casualties, 27/1:194, Report of James Washburn, 27/2:67; Thomas O. Crowl to his sister, June 16, 1863, CWMC; James W. Latimer to brother Bartow, June 18 and 24, 1863, Latimer Family File, YCHT; Wildes, *Record of the One Hundred and Sixteenth Regiment Ohio,* 52, 56; CMSRs of all men of companies G and H, 87th Pa; Wilbur Sturtevant Nye, *Here Come the Rebels!* chap. 8; Pension Records of Robert S. Slaymaker, Slaymaker to William W. Dudely, Sept. 25, 1883, and Josiah Landen, Co. H, 87th Pa., deposition of Benjamin S. Kauffman, July 18, 1887; recollections of James A. Stahle, *York Gazette,* June 16, 1893. Stahle's memory failed him when he reported in his memoir that Michael Slothower died June 15 at Carter's Woods. John W. Schall to A. L. Russell, July 31, 1863, PA AGO, Muster Rolls. By the time of the second battle of Winchester, Robert Slaymaker and Michael Slothower had yet to muster at their new ranks. Shortly afterward, Schall sought to rectify that oversight so that Slaymaker's and Slothower's heirs could receive back pay.

72. CMSR of Daniel H. Karnes, Co. I, 87th Pa.; *O.R.,* Report of Noah G. Ruhl, June 28, 1863, 27/1:78–79, Report of Henry Peale, Nov. 10, 1863, 27/2:77–78. Slaymaker claimed, somewhat

Most men had fallen asleep in the rifle pits. John Schall ordered his officers awakened first so they could rouse their men, but no one saw fit to awaken Wells Farrah and Rob Slaymaker. By the time the two men returned to consciousness, Winchester was nearly Union-soldier-free. They overtook the regiment four miles from town near a farm owned by the Carter family, just shy of the road to Charles Town and near a rail depot called Stephenson's. Fighting was already under way. Rebel infantry, aligned along "a railroad cut masked by a body of woods," blocked the escape route. Two Rebel artillery pieces blasted away from a bridge that spanned the railroad, a bridge the Union boys had to cross if they were to reach the relative safety of Charles Town by the most direct route.[73]

Fighting surged back and forth until the sun sneaked over the horizon. Men on both sides reached into their ammunition pouches, came up empty-handed, and prepared for close-in combat. The two Rebel guns at the bridge had but two uninjured cannoneers and no healthy officers remaining. Sixty yards more and the boys from York would have snatched the cannons and punched a hole in the Rebel line. They might have done it if Stonewall Jackson's old brigade had not flooded onto the field just then. It was more than the exhausted Federals could withstand. Officers ordered every man for himself. The field soon was "dotted by scattered troops in all directions and the enemy close behind," George Blotcher remembered. He saw the 18th Connecticut stack arms and offer itself in surrender. He said he took "a few minutes"—more likely seconds—to let them know that he would not be joining them. Then, he ran.[74]

Most of the Union casualties that morning were captured. Capt. Wells Farrah became a statistic at Carter's Woods but was not counted among those captured. His body was never recovered.[75]

---

cryptically, that Company H did not fight on the 14th. Lorenzo D. Barnhart, *Reminiscences*, 110th Ohio Volunteer Infantry Web site, www.iwaynet.net/lsci/2ndwintr.htm (accessed Dec. 2, 2004). Charles Town, West Virginia, was then spelled "Charlestown," but the modern spelling is used here throughout.

73. James W. Latimer to brother Bartow, June 24, 1863, Latimer Family File, YCHT; *O.R.*, testimony of John W. Schall, Aug. 24, 25, and 28, 1863, 27/2:118–21, 136, Report of Edward Johnson, C.S.A., Aug. 18, 1863, 27/2:500–502, Report of George H. Steuart, C.S.A., June 19, 1863, 27/2:507–8, Report of Jesse Milton Williams, June 16, 1863, 27/2:512–13.

74. Recollections of George Blotcher.

75. *O.R.*, Report of Edward Johnson, C.S.A., 27/2:500–502, Record of Court of Inquiry, testimony of John W. Schall, 27/2:118–19. The modern bridge is just left of the 1863 bridge site as viewed from the Confederate perspective. The road trace is visible. *O.R.*, Return of Casualties at Winchester, Va., June 13–15, 1863, 27/2:53; testimony of John W. Schall, 27/2:119. Official summaries of the second battle of Winchester report 112 87th Pennsylvania casualties, and Schall reported 240. Neither count is correct. (See Appendix, "Casualties.")

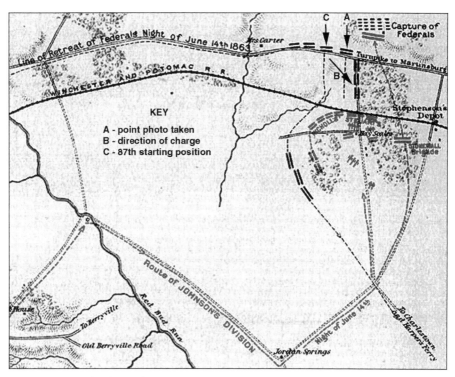

Carter's Woods (aka Stephenson's Depot) Battlefield. "Johnson's Division" shown on the map is the division Stonewall Jackson had commanded before being promoted to greater responsibilities. Jackson had died a month before the battle of Carter's Woods (*Atlas to Accompany the Official Records of the Union and Confederate Armies,* image 43, additions by the author).

Modern view of the field over which the 87th Pennsylvania attacked toward the Charles Town Road and Carter's Woods on the left. See Point "A" on the accompanying map (photo by the author).

"Our retreat nearly killed us," Pvt. Thomas Oliver Crowl wrote his sister after he reached Harpers Ferry, and he was not exaggerating. Tom and 130 comrades covered forty miles that day. Other men scattered to the mountains singly or in squad-sized units. Some got away only to delay their inevitable capture, while others faced days of hunger, fear, and confusion. Those wounded especially had trouble. George Washington Schriver had taken a bullet in the left arm but had the good fortune of escaping with a surgeon. In pain, he awakened the doctor about 1:00 A.M. June 16 and asked for treatment. The exhausted surgeon "growled a good bit but got his kit open and took out the bullet." Schriver's group eventually found Unionist farmers to prepare them meals, including one hearty repast on June 19 that made many sick from overeating.[76]

Another group maintained cohesion because it included James Stahle and Noah Ruhl and reached Bloody Run (modern-day Everett) on June 20 after five days without food. Rob Slaymaker was among them and wired home news of his safe status. The army gave Stahle's group the job of guarding prisoners at McConnellsburg. That chore completed and lacking further instructions, Stahle told his men to go home and await orders, something many had already done without permission. The *York Gazette* soon reported, "Members singly and in squads are roaming through the country seeking their way home."[77]

In Gettysburg, on June 19, diarists Sarah Broadhead and Salome Myers noted that ten 87th Pennsylvania stragglers were arriving on the Chambersburg Pike. Salome Myers was relieved that her uncle William Esaias Culp and cousin David Gilbert Myers were among them. Residents expressed either excitement and despair at their return, depending on the news the returning 87th men were able to offer individual families about their sons' welfare. Rumor had Company F's entire officer contingent killed or captured. It was not true, but no one could be certain of it then.[78]

By August, Rob Slaymaker had rejoined a fragment of the regiment—the one that included Tom Crowl—at Martinsburg, West Virginia, his mental state unchanged and he still too afraid of losing face to admit it. That changed in September when Assistant Surgeon Harris Steadman told Slaymaker that

76. Diary of George Washington Schriver.

77. Ibid.; Thomas O. Crowl to his sister, June 16, 1863, CWMC; CMSRs and Pension Records of Michael S. Slothower, Andrew B. Smith, and Robert S. Slaymaker, Co. H, and Henry Billmyer, Co. K, 87th Pa., deposition of William Henry Dixon; *York Gazette*, June 23, 1863.

78. Sarah Sites Rodgers, *The Ties to the Past: The Gettysburg Diaries of Salome Myers Stewart, 1854–1922*, 160; Sarah M. Broadhead, *The Diary of a Lady of Gettysburg, Pennsylvania from June 15 to July 15, 1863*, 6.

he had recognized his problem the first time they met and advised Slaymaker he should have resigned long ago. The blunt appraisal finally loosened his tongue, and he poured out his misery to Steadman. The assistant surgeon immediately filled out a discharge certificate while Slaymaker penned his resignation. The convenient excuse was "diarrhea," a condition the brass was not likely to investigate. It was also probably true.[79]

The last officer in Company H had gone down. That October, when 1st Sgt. Andrew Bentz Smith limped back from Belle Isle Prison, he commanded the company by default. The brass saw in Smith "a very gentlemanly soldier [who] done his duty as well as he knew how" and promoted him to first lieutenant. Smith may have earned his promotion, but his appointment may have been a concession to Company H because Colonels Schall and Stahle had already begun proceedings to promote Company I's 1st Lt. Anthony M. Martin to the captain's seat. The *Gettysburg Star and Banner* announced the promotion.[80]

No matter how hard Stahle and Schall pushed for Martin, he never assumed the position. Harrisburg refused to violate accepted procedure of promoting from within a company whenever possible. Martin instead accepted the rank of adjutant, a vaunted station within a regiment but at the rank of first lieutenant, not captain. Schall and Stahle continued to ignore Harrisburg's wishes and offered the captain's job to Company E's 1st Lt. Alexander Strickler. While he signed his name as captain of both Companies E and H for a time, Strickler also never assumed the job.[81]

Company H gained an ironic ally. Robert Slaymaker, writing from the comfort of home, expressed his feelings in a private letter to a former comrade, writing, "Poor Co. H has a hard time. Those in the field and those elsewhere seem doomed not to have justice done them. The ones in the field are knocked about not knowing who commands them. They have a new commander every few days."[82]

79. Pension Records of Robert S. Slaymaker, Co. A, 87th Pa., deposition of Robert Slaymaker, Aug. 1881.

80. CMSR and Pension Records of Andrew B. Smith, Co. H, 87th Pa., statements of Edward Wise, Jacob Hoffer, and John Hoffman; Court-Martial, Andrew B. Smith, LL-1369, case of testimony of James A. Stahle; John W. Schall to Alexander L. Russell, Nov. 7, 1863, PA AGO, Muster Rolls; *Star and Banner*, Nov. 19, 1863.

81. Samuel B. Thomas to Col. John W. Schall, Nov. 14, 1863, George Hay Kain III Collection; James A. Stahle to Alexander L. Russell, Dec. 6, 1863, and James A. Stahle to Samuel B. Thomas, A.A.G., Dec. 14, 1863, PA AGO, Correspondence; Lt. Col. James A. Stahle to Seth Thomas, Dec. 29, 1863, Bookmark Spu 18–1864; Muster Rolls of the 87th Pennsylvania Infantry, NARA, Correspondence, letter signed by all 87th Pennsylvania officers, Nov. 22, 1863.

82. Robert S. Slaymaker to John M. Griffith, Feb. 16, 1864, Bowman-Griffith Family Papers.

While Schall and Stahle worked to assign a captain, they were just as determined that the second lieutenant also would not come from within Company H's ranks. They turned to Sgt. Maj. Franklin Geise, who had enlisted with Company D and coveted a leadership role from day one. In early 1862, when ill health had forced out Company D's second lieutenant, Corporal Geise had applied for the position but had run into stone walls named Ruhl and Blasser, who both wanted their sons in command positions. Blood won. Geise lost.[83]

Frank Geise's writing shows that the auburn-haired farm boy was among the most erudite men in the regiment, and he gained those skills with a poor, German-speaking stonecutter for a father. Education came at the York Academy, an institution more commonly populated by sons of the elite, and that led to a postwar career embracing law and politics, including stints as prothonotary of York Borough. At his death, he held the post of mayor. During the war, his potential was not lost on George Hay and John Schall, who in late 1862 raised him from corporal to sergeant major. Now, in the aftermath of Winchester, they pegged him for second lieutenant of Company H.[84]

This time, Company H did not take it quietly. If the regimental brass would not listen, perhaps Harrisburg would. They wrote Governor Andrew G. Curtin a letter of complaint about Rob Slaymaker's previous tenure and the efforts to put Anthony Martin and Alexander Strickler in charge. On the subject of Frank Geise, they fired double loads of verbal canister.[85]

> We are again to have another stranger forced upon us, one who is distasteful to us in every respect and we believe utterly incompetent, the present Sergeant Major, Frank Geise, who is not a member of this company nor never has been. We make these statements under the impression that these appointments are not made in conformity with your orders as military regulations. We have on all occasions endeavored to do our duty as a company. Why it is that we are not used in this respect on equality we are not prepared to say. We are the only company in the regiment in which promotions have been made of entire strangers and not

83. CMSR of Franklin Geise (pronounced "Gise"), Co. D, 87th Pa.; John W. Schall to Alexander L. Russell, Nov. 17, 1863, PA AGO, Correspondence; Frank Geise to Andrew G. Curtin, May 7, 1862, PA AGO, Correspondence; CMSRs of James H. Blasser and Edgar M. Ruhl.

84. Franklin Geise to Andrew G. Curtin, May 7, 1862, PA AGO, Correspondence; *York Gazette,* May 2 and 6, 1900; Pension Records of Franklin Geise, Co. D, 87th Pa.; Frank Geise to George Hay, July 15, 1863, George Hay Kain III Collection. During the war, Geise claimed Democrats were "a rotten political party," yet later ran for public office as a Democrat, probably because he could not win in York as a Republican.

85. Company H to Gov. Andrew G. Curtin, Nov. 18, 1863, PA AGO, Muster Rolls. The letter does not mention Alexander Strickler by name but references Harrisburg's refusal to promote Anthony Martin.

members. We have men among us who we know to be competent and certainly deserving who have for more than two years applied themselves to the duties of a soldier.[86]

Nothing has emerged for us to know if Frank Geise was a hateful person or just Company H's scapegoat for the latest effort to install an outsider. He never married, which may reflect an inability to sustain personal relationships or a stubborn single-mindedness. His education may have made him appear haughty to Wellsville farm boys. In spite of the company's protests, John Schall and Jim Stahle tried until the following March to wedge Geise into Company H. In February 1864, Stahle made a special trip to Schall's home in Berks County while the colonel recuperated from diarrhea and goaded the commander into writing a letter requesting Geise's promotion. Geise made it academic when he wearied of the failed attempts and accepted a commission with the U.S. Colored Infantry.[87]

In the end, Company H won. Philip Gentzler, a carpenter from Warrington Township, sewed on the double-barred shoulder straps of captain, and Daniel Philip Lang Dietrich handled first lieutenant's chores until his death at the battle of Monocacy. The regimental history honors him with a biography.[88]

Robert Slaymaker found little happiness in a postwar life that exemplified a man searching for something that remained frustratingly out of reach. In the five years before the war, he had clerked in his father's foundry and no doubt would have inherited a substantial portion, if not all, of it. Instead, he found work in Boston, Massachusetts, but shortly returned to York, because he said, he did not like the New England climate. He married in 1866 and fathered a son, but the boy died at birth, and his wife passed on shortly afterward. He changed occupations four times in the years following his wife's death, including a year's stretch as a common laborer on his uncle's Kittanning, Pennsylvania, farm. He tried selling turbine water wheels for two years and

86. Company H to Gov. Andrew G. Curtin, Nov. 18, 1863, PA AGO, Correspondence. In Aug. 1864, five members of Company A wrote a similar letter to Governor Curtin protesting George Jonathan Chalfant's promotion. Daniel Bonge, Abraham Rhodes, Alexander Kipp, Emanuel C. Coleman, and Jacob Glassmyer to Andrew G. Curtin, Aug. 26, 1864, PA AGO, Correspondence.

87. *York Gazette,* May 2 and 6, 1900; Pension Records of Franklin Geise, Co. D, 87th Pa.; CMSR of Franklin Geise, Co. D, 87th Pa., Co. H, 32nd U.S. Colored Troops, and 54th New York; John W. Schall to A. L. Russell, Feb. 25, 1864, PA AGO, Muster Rolls; *Official Army Register;* Endorsements Sent, Army Records, Army of the Potomac, 1st Brigade, 3rd Division, 6th Army Corps, p. 64; John W. Schall to Alexander L. Russell, Feb. 25, 1864, PA AGO, Correspondence.

88. CMSRs of Philip Gentzler and Daniel Dietrich, Co. H, and William Esaias Culp, Co. F, 87th Pa. Culp mustered into Company F but briefly assumed command of Company H after Dietrich died at Monocacy. Prowell, *87th Pennsylvania,* 296.

then, ironically, moved to Winchester, Virginia, to sell agricultural products. A six-month stint in Chicago as a clerk for Cragin Brothers proved unrewarding, and the company fired him. Returning to Kittanning, he took work as a storekeeper, remarried, and finally started to pull his life together. He reached back for his mathematical ability and put it to good use at the profession of surveying. But a good night's sleep still eluded him. Concentration remained nearly impossible. At times, he said, he was "so much affected that it is impossible to calculate and study as my business requires. . . . My mind refuses to act."[89]

Robert Samuel Slaymaker was a casualty of war not counted in the statistics until science came to recognize the mental strain that men endure.

Company I

New Oxford is a small town in eastern Adams County. If it has gained any notoriety at all, it is due only to its proximity to Gettysburg. At the time of the Civil War, it was a handful of houses, small businesses, three churches, two hotel-taverns located on opposite corners of the town square, and an elite school called the New Oxford Collegiate and Medical Institute. As twenty-first–century drivers enter the town westbound on U.S. Route 30, they pass a street to their left called Pfeiffer Lane and just beyond, College Street. Both are short, narrow byways that only residents or deliverymen would have a reason to traverse. Few realize that they mark the site of a once highly respected school owned and operated by one of New Oxford's preeminent nineteenth-century families.[90]

The face of Dr. Michael Diedrich Gotlob Pfeiffer bore a prominent scar he had earned as a member of Prussia's Black Rifles, a daring unit that adopted the skull and crossbones for its insignia and tried to live up to it. Left for dead on the battlefield, Pfeiffer recovered to study medicine and decided his European Waterloo came shortly after Napoleon Bonaparte's. In 1818, he resigned the military to fulfill his dream of going to America. When he happened into the tiny village of Oxford—he would later be responsible for adding "New"—and heard everyone speaking German, he knew he had found a home. Two decades later, Dr. Pfeiffer opened a school to give boys "a thorough education

---

89. Pension Records of Robert S. Slaymaker, Co. A, 87th Pa., deposition of Robert Slaymaker, Aug. 1881; Slaymaker to P. G. Clark, July 23, 1885. Slaymaker's pension is with the Veterans' Administration, but a copy resides in the York County Heritage Trust library.

90. Hopkins, *Map of Adams County, Hopkins,* 1858. The Pfeiffer home was a block west of the Institute on the right of the York Pike.

without endangering their physical or moral health" which meant, in part, that he did not believe in corporal punishment. New Oxford folks ignored the school's long, formal name and just called it Dr. Pfeiffer's College. Along the way, Michael Pfeiffer became an ardent abolitionist "of the most pronounced and ultra type."[91]

On a cold January day in 1840, Sarah Pfeiffer bore her husband twin sons. One boy they christened with the quintessentially American name John Quincy Adams, but most folks called him "Quincy." The second son received the name of honored family friend Thaddeus Stevens, an abolitionist so unnerving to slaveholders that one Southerner concluded that Stevens "could shock the moral sense of mankind." That made Thaddeus Stevens comfortable in the Pfeiffer household, where his Underground Railroad activities were known and condoned, if not assisted. Stevens paid for his beliefs during the Confederate invasion of 1863 when Gen. Jubal Early delighted in destroying his ironworks.[92]

Thaddeus Stevens Pfeiffer—"Thad" to his friends—grew up in a privileged family immersed in the German ethics of hard work, education, dedication to duty, and abolition. If necessary, he would don a soldier's uniform to free the black man from bondage. Education came first, and Thad and Quincy joined their father's faculty as soon as they were prepared to pass on their accumulated knowledge. Quincy stayed home when war began, but Thad convinced others to follow him into the Oxford National Guards. When Alexander Small sent out the call, Thad responded in the way expected of prominent families' sons and took his company to York to join the Thomas A. Scott Regiment.[93]

Always attentive to detail, Thaddeus Pfeiffer never had anything resembling negative charges leveled against him and earned the position of acting

91. *Looking at the Past: New Oxford, Penna.,* 117, 120; J. Howard Wert, "Old Time Notes of Adams County," July 12, 1905, Pfeiffer Family Folder, Adams County Historical Society, Gettysburg, Pennsylvania; *New Oxford (Pa.) Item,* July 20, 1933, Charles F. Himes to his nephew John D. Keith, 1917, Pfeiffer Family Folder, Adams County Historical Society. Himes was an alumnus of Pfeiffer's school. *Hanover Spectator,* Mar. 24, 1847, and Apr. 7, 1880; John T. Reily, *History and Directory of the Boroughs of Adams County 1880.*

92. James Hersh to his mother, June 20, 1864, courtesy Walter Powell; Thaddeus Pfeiffer to Quincy Pfeiffer, Dec. 16, 1863, *Looking at the Past,* 126–27; R. C. Smedley, *History of the Underground Railroad in Chester and the Neighboring Counties of Pennsylvania,* 36; *Biographical Directory of the United States Congress; York Gazette,* Aug. 18, 1868; Colonel William H. Stewart, "The Trying Experience of the ex-President [Jefferson Davis] at Fort Monroe," *SHSP,* 27:344; "General J. A. Early's Report of the Gettysburg Campaign," 10:538. Vermont-born Thaddeus Stevens began his law career in Gettysburg in 1816 and later represented Lancaster in Congress as a Whig and Republican from 1849 until his death on Aug. 11, 1868.

93. *Star and Banner,* Aug. 30 and Sept. 13, 1861; *Hanover Citizen,* Sept. 5, 1861.

brigade inspector-general during the winter of 1863–1864. The influence of his father's medical knowledge gave him a special concern about men's health, something he looked to often. Two fatiguing years in the army, however, freed views he would never utter to anyone but his closest confidants. During the winter of 1863–1864, the draft again went into full swing and Quincy was talking about joining. Thad shot off a letter to his twin brother and underlined several words to make sure Quincy understood the importance of the issue.[94]

> I will not hear of such *foolishness*. I am best able to judge, and *you must not go*. Don't let a silly (and in your case, wicked) pride lead you into such a scrape . . . Nothing would make me *more miserable* than to see you in the Army. I assure you, if I could get out of the service with honor, I would do so tomorrow. I have it easy compared with others, but if you would see how the poor men and even the officers in the companies are brow beaten and trodden in the dust, you would lose your longing for the Army. *This is private* . . . Quincy, take my money and buy your release and believe me, *it is the greatest favor you can do me*.[95]

So weary of the army was the dutiful son that he urged his brother to pay the commutation fee to avoid the draft. But keep it quiet, Quince. Everyone must think that Thad wants to risk his life for the Union. Remember when you visited him in the fall of 1862? Recall struggling over the mountains of western Virginia and huddling together under three blankets yet still shivering? Do you recollect how once healthy men fell ill from exposure to the elements? That is the real army, Quince, not the one described by politicians or the one buried in your father's time-jaded memory. Don't become part of it. Above all, you must never tell anyone how your brother struggles each day with a crawling dread of death.[96]

Quincy and older brother Theodore enlisted anyway. Thad was in no position to stop them and, in a tragic way, probably motivated them. While

94. Thaddeus Pfeiffer to Lt. James Hersh, Sept. 1862, CWMC; *York Gazette,* Sept. 23, 1862, Chaplain to the *York Gazette,* Sept. 23, 1862, letter dated Sept. 3, 1862; Office of the Adjutant General, Volunteer Organizations—Civil War, Federal Muster Rolls, Correspondence, James A. Stahle to Capt. T. S. Pfeiffer.

95. Thaddeus Pfeiffer to brother Quincy, Dec. 16, 1863, *Looking at the Past,* 126–27. John Quincy Pfeiffer joined the 26th Pennsylvania Emergency Militia during the Gettysburg Campaign.

96. Ibid.; James Hersh to his mother, June 9, 1864, courtesy Walter Powell; *Star and Banner,* Dec. 4, 1862, Thaddeus Pfeiffer to his father, letter dated Nov. 19, 1862. Quincy had traveled with the regiment during the fall of 1862.

Thad was standing picket duty at the battle of Cold Harbor, a Confederate bullet destroyed the potential that was Thaddeus Pfeiffer. Quincy visited the regiment to search for his brother's remains but only had time to learn how Thad had died. The regiment had wanted to send his body back to New Oxford for burial, but circumstances made that impossible. Quincy had to wait a year and a half before he could claim Thad's body. In the meantime, he and Theodore could do their part in the war effort.[97]

"I fear his death will kill his father," friend James Hersh wrote his mother of Thad's passing. The tragedy did not kill Michael Pfeiffer nor did the death of Theodore that December, but the doctor closed the doors of his college forever. No doubt, he had pragmatic reasons for closing the school. Its useful life had ended, perhaps, but losing two sons in six months was surely more than "The Old War Horse" could bear.[98]

In the year 2000, Thaddeus Pfeiffer's photo hung on the wall of the Cold Harbor Battlefield visitor's center. To earn that honor, he had to suffer gut shot for a day before death freed him from his agony.[99]

97. James Hersh to his mother, June 20, 1864, courtesy Walter Powell; Zoo-Zoo to the *Gettysburg Compiler,* July 4, 1864, letter dated June 18, 1864.

98. James Hersh to his mother, June 9, 1864, courtesy Walter L. Powell; *Star and Banner,* Sept. 14, 1860; CMSRs of Thaddeus S. Pfeiffer, Co. I, 87th Pa., and John Theodore Pfeiffer and John Quincy Pfeiffer, Co. C, 202nd Pa. Quincy served as captain even though his military experience was eleven days as first lieutenant with the 26th Pennsylvania Emergency Militia. John Theodore Pfeiffer was a bugler wounded Oct. 8, 1864, at Salem Church, Virginia. He died that December.

99. CMSRs of Theodore Pfeiffer and John Q. Pfeiffer, Co. C, 202nd Pennsylvania; Pension Records of Thaddeus Pfeiffer. Quincy retrieved Thad's body in November 1865.

Chapter 6

Discipline Problems

D iscipline is an eternal issue in the military and was an especially per-
plexing problem with independent-minded Civil War volunteers.
Some members of the Scott Regiment got a head start on trouble shortly after setting up camp in York. Tom Crowl wrote about unnamed
comrades who caused an uproar in a local "hoar house," which was what folks
then called a building that stored ice. In this case, Tom's misspelling did not
convey his intended meaning. He did not detail what happened in the "hoar
house" but did relate how one man was shot, another knifed, and how irate
comrades afterward "bombarded the house, tore the windows out, and tore
things up inside a good bit." Area newspapers ignored the affair, as did the
York County judicial system.[1]

An incident like that at Tom's "hoar house" comes as no surprise to anyone who scans through five years of antebellum York County court dockets. Forty-one names appear there that later graced 87th Pennsylvania muster
rolls, several of them multiple times. Riot (disturbing the peace) and mali-
cious mischief were common charges. Two of the names were future 87th
officers Samuel Saylor and John Edwin McIlvain, arrested in company with
six future noncommissioned comrades for disrupting a school's choir practice. "Fornication and bastardy" and selling liquor put many before the court,
acts young men have always indulged in and doubtless forever will, however
the current state of jurisprudence might deal with them.[2]

1. Thomas O. Crowl to his uncle, Oct. 17, 1861, Pattee. The York County court docket does
not mention the incident.
2. Court Docket 1856–1860, York County, Nov. 1859 session, p. 515. The other future 87th
Pennsylvania choir-busters were Jonathan Barnitz, Joseph Henry, Charles Hyde, William Markley,
Henry Smallbrook, and John A. Wilson.

There were also many cases of assault and battery. Given the number of "not-guilty" verdicts and cases declared "no bill," losers of brawls no doubt brought some of the charges. There were serious cases, too. Isaac "Pud" Sweeney passed thirty days in the county jail for his assault. Moses Coble looked through bars for nine months, a light sentence considering that he attempted rape. George Lawrence Litz was the man who shot Charles Odenwalt in the chest during an 1858 altercation, but a jury somehow returned a not-guilty verdict.[3]

Adams County was not immune to run-amok youth, as New Oxford learned on December 27 and 28, 1858. Workmen from Hanover were erecting a house when, for reasons not explained, they got into an altercation with several local toughs. Tempers rose to such a pitch that fighting stretched into a second night "amidst yelling, throwing of stones, and brandishing of various weapons" that took out many of Mrs. Miley's hotel windows. Future 87th Pennsylvanians George Fleming, John Albert Dixon, and Charles Martin were among those arrested and sentenced to spend from six to nine months in Adams County Jail. After less than a month of incarceration, the three men escaped and emptied the jail of other inmates in the process. Fleming, known in the army as "Squaw," came back on his own "expressing a determination to serve out [his] sentence."[4]

The tendency for youth to challenge authority was just one reason why volunteer officers faced a monumental challenge. Throughout the army, officers too often themselves were ill equipped to lead. They generally had to rely on innate leadership skills, not formal training or experience. Noah Ruhl was the 87th Pennsylvania's only officer to have seen a battlefield, and the men's hatred of his gruff military demeanor in part reflected their military naïveté. Washington could have sprinkled experienced regulars throughout volunteer regiments to provide supervision but chose not to buck the traditional state-based militia concept. The regular army remained a separate organization. Since volunteers did most of the fighting, the absence of trained leadership no doubt cost lives.

3. *Democratic Press,* Aug. 10, 1858; Court Docket 1856–1860, York County, Nov. 1859 session, pp. 364–65; Pension Records of George Lawrence Litz, Co. H, and Charles Odenwalt, Co. K, 87th Pa.; *York Gazette,* Nov. 14 and 21, 1864; *Hanover Citizen,* Nov. 17, 1864. Litz had the tables turned on him after he returned from war. Convinced his wife had been cheating on him, he confronted his wife's alleged paramour, Leander H. Myers. This time, the doctor removed a bullet from Litz's chest.

4. *Gettysburg Compiler,* Jan. 3 and 24, and Feb. 28, 1859; Adams County Clerk of Courts, Quarter Session Docket 6, 1859. Fleming and Dixon were also fined $1.00, but another man received one year in jail and a fine of $.01. Prowell, *87th Pennsylvania,* 53.

Jacob Hay is just one example of poor officer material. He took a commission with the 87th Pennsylvania primarily because he was from a well educated, prominent medical family and had cared to serve in the antebellum militia. A surgeon by training, he is notable only because he was the first of the regiment's officers to opt out of service. He obviously thought himself well suited to command when he took the first lieutenant's role in Company A but soon realized that real army life was not like the merry overnight encampments of militia days. After just three months' service, Hay submitted his resignation due to "palpitations of the heart." He was a doctor. Who was going to argue? Hay returned home and lived another thirty-six years with his palpitating heart.[5]

Leadership issues began with the method of selecting officers in volunteer regiments. State governors, not the War Department, assigned volunteer staff officers the rank of colonel. The selection system for field-level leadership was even worse. During the first part of the war, the men elected the ranks of corporal through captain, essentially a popularity contest. The military has always insisted that a social gap between officers and enlisted men was necessary to maintain discipline, but the methods of selecting officers made that difficult to achieve. A typical result was an undisciplined and untrained environment that often led to disaster.[6]

Disciplined or not, by the end of September 1861, the entire 87th Pennsylvania was stationed along the Northern Central Railway and not much strained by the work. Thomas Crowl wrote, "We are all getting a long fine here, plenty to eat and nothing to do." George Washington Schriver penned in his diary, "Doing guard duty and fishing and catching a great many things that did not look like fish. Some had frocks on and some had feathers." Pvt. Peter Warren wrote his Gettysburg friends that he was getting "good living down here . . . It is better than any one got in the three months service." Pvt. Alfred Jameson told his parents, "Our greatest enemies here are mosquetoes and yellow jackets and they are too plenty. I never enjoyed myself better than I do at present." Small wonder that the *Hanover Spectator* announced the boys discovered that guarding a railroad "not as irksome as was at first supposed."[7]

5. CMSR of Jacob Hay, Co. A, 87th Pa., letter of resignation to Maj. Gen. John Dix, Nov. 20, 1861. CMSRs of David Ferguson McKinney, Assistant Surgeon, and William Francis McCurdy, Surgeon, 87th Pa. McKinney and McCurdy did not muster until mid-October and probably arrived after that. See McPherson, *For Cause and Comrades,* 135–38, for anecdotes about officers resigning and the pressures to do so.

6. Wiley, *Billy Yank,* 24–27.

7. Thomas O. Crowl to his uncle, Oct. 17, 1861, Pattee; diary of George Washington Schriver; Peter Warren to "Dear friends," Sept. 1861, Skelly Family Papers, HCWRT; Alfred Jameson to his

Men consumed their free time gathering chestnuts, fishing, trapping rabbits, entertaining visiting family members, and concerning themselves with sending laundry home to Mother. They bragged how they could leave virtually any time they wanted, an exaggeration but not wholly untrue. Six of them had the time to get married, one as far distant as Illinois. Come Christmas, Alexander Small provided Company A with ten turkeys for a carol-filled holiday feast held "at the elegant mansion of Mr. Gambrill of Woodbury." Throughout the regiment in newly erected barracks, men put up Christmas trees, which they decorated with an odd assortment of available items such as "boots, tin pans, whiskey bottles, one pack of cards with the ace of spades up for trump, haversacks and the Devil knows what else." Eggnog, apple toddy, and a host of other unnamed libations flowed freely, providing all with "a very high old time," pun certainly intended. While on duty, they drilled, stood guard, and policed camp but were a long way from the real soldiers that Washington did not believe they were anyway.[8]

Some spent free time getting into trouble and embarrassing the regiment. Respecting civilian property is a fundamental military discipline. That did not stop some of Company K from assuming Maryland's poultry population to be a flock of Southern sympathizers subject to arrest by any Union soldier. Andrew Miller accused comrade George J. Buzby of stealing chickens. Buzby denied it. Miller persisted. Tempers heated, and a shouting match ensued. Buzby picked up a rifle and shot Miller in the thigh. Within a month, Buzby was out of the army and on his way to a two-year sojourn in the penitentiary where chicken was seldom on the menu. The *Baltimore County Advocate* carried the story, but no York or Adams County newspaper did. In fact, the *Gettysburg Star and Banner* reported nothing but "favorable accounts of the regiment" during this period.[9]

The Miller-Buzby affair is an example of how personalities sometimes clash when men live in close confines. Irishman James Murray provides another. A stranger to Company F when he enlisted, Murray soon had mates wishing he had remained so. A bad attitude toward drill usually put him on the sidelines

---

mother, Sept. 23, 1861, and another undated letter, Pension Records of Alfred Jameson; *Hanover Spectator,* Oct. 25, 1861.

8. Joseph Helker to his cousin, Oct. 12 and Dec. 24, 1861, George Miller Collection; Peter Free to his family, Dec. 11, 1861, Pension Records of Peter Free, Co. E, 87th Pa.; Charles Edwin Skelly to his mother, Mar. 14, 1862, and May 9, 1862, Skelly Family Papers, HCWRT; Pension Records, where applicable, of all members of the 87th Pa. The six men known to have married before the end of 1861 are Peter S. Baum (Co. K), Jacob Deardorf (Co. F), Samuel Evans (Co. A), Philip Grove (Co. G), William Edie Patterson (Co. C), and William Schriver (Co. A).

9. *Baltimore County Advocate,* Oct. 19 and 26, 1861; *Star and Banner,* Oct. 31, 1861. The army discharged Buzby and, since he was from Baltimore County, allowed a Maryland court to try him.

during dress parades because he inevitably embarrassed the company. Time showed that he may have been the regiment's best fighting man, but comrades otherwise kept their distance, deeming him "treacherous." On at least one occasion, his threatening nature boiled into violence against one of the most timid men in Company F.

Thirty-seven-year-old Edward Little had a reputation as a likeable and "very inoffensive man," which made him a frequent target of jokes. Little could cook, though, and that alone made him valuable—and popular. In the spring of 1862, he stayed behind at their Lutherville camp to prepare dinner while the rest of the company traveled down the tracks to strut in full dress parade. James Murray went along but again sat on the sidelines during the presentation. Comrades recalled him acting especially surly that day. Throughout the return trip, he threw boards from the train with no concern as to whom they might hit. As soon as they got back, Murray hustled to the cookhouse and demanded coffee. Ed Little replied that it was not ready yet but he would let him know when it was.

That was not the answer Murray wanted to hear. He picked up a butcher knife and slashed Little's arm.

Stunned mates saw Little race from the mess tent holding his wounded arm, blood spurting between clenched fingers. No doctor was immediately available, so a mate staunched the bleeding and stitched the wound with common needle and thread. Murray realized he was in trouble and offered Little twenty dollars if he would keep quiet about the incident. Little did not admit to taking the bribe, but since the event does not appear in Murray's service records, he probably did. After the war, seven men testified to the incident, but a bullet at the battle of Cold Harbor in 1864 prevented Murray from giving evidence from his perspective.[10]

Most lapses to good order were nonviolent, which is not to say they could not be deadly. Twenty-year-old Edward Seitz enlisted late and did not arrive for duty at Company F headquarters until November 19. Two days later, he was dead. So, too, was David Forest Little, a seventeen-year-old from Gettysburg who passed into the next life in Seitz's company. The cause of their demise varied with the brand of whitewash used to write the report. "Camp fever" was the official reason. If true, it meant Seitz either had shown up with an advanced case or had contracted an amazingly virulent strain after his arrival. Stories spread that the boys had drunk poisoned milk given to them "by a Negro." The regiment would not admit that Seitz and Little actually

10. CMSR of James Murray, Co. F, 87th Pa.; Pension Records of Edward Little, Co. F, 87th Pa., depositions of Little and seven others taken during 1887.

had died from drinking too much of the liquor they bought from the black man.[11]

Michael Heiman recounted a tale amusing in the telling but one that demonstrates the dangerously lax discipline of the early days. Assigned to guard a railroad bridge, Heiman convinced his partner to stand watch alone while he went off to a corn-shucking party. As he was tearing off a husk, he heard someone call out his name and looked into the face of 1st Sgt. Levi Maish. Nothing happened then, but the next morning Maish ordered Heiman to spend his day off splitting rails, a punishment with the practical value of providing the camp with firewood. Pvt. Joseph Hummel joined him in punishment detail after a change of guard found him sleeping at his post. Regulations allowed both of them to be tied to a post and shot, but they only chopped wood.[12]

No matter how loose the discipline, some punishment techniques of that day were cruel enough to rip the soul from a man. We have already seen the effect bucking and gagging had on the psychologically troubled Lewis V. Holter, and Company B's Liborious "Levi" Gastrock provides another. Once again, Michael Heiman was in the middle of things. While Heiman and Hummel chopped wood on their punishment detail, the thirty-seven-year-old Gastrock lounged nearby and mocked them in his thick German accent.

"That's the way it goes," Gastrock said, grinning. "One, he sleeps on guard, he carries wood, and one he goes on to party, he *shplits* it."[13]

Irritating as the "Dutchman" was, Heiman and Hummel let him go until he wearied of his teasing. Picking up his rifle, Gastrock announced mockingly that he was free to go hunting while his two targets of abuse had to indulge in the sport of wood chopping. That was a mistake. Standing orders were that no one was to go farther than 100 yards from camp without permission. When Gastrock's foot hit yard 101, Heiman and Hummel sprinted for the sergeant and soon were part of a squad tracking down the wayward son of Company

11. CMSRs of Edward Seitz and David Forest Little, Co. F, 87th Pa.; *Baltimore County Advocate*, Dec. 7, 1861. The *Advocate* reported whiskey as the cause.

12. Recollections of Michael Heiman, *York Gazette*, Feb. 20, 1892; CMSR of Joseph Hummel, Co. B, 87th Pa. Hummel was captured near Petersburg, Virginia, June 23, 1864, and died of chronic diarrhea at Andersonville. Kautz, *Service Non-Commissioned*, 226–27. Article of War 46 (sleeping at post) permitted the death penalty, but Article 50 (abandonment of post) left punishment up to the court-martial. Prowell, *87th Pennsylvania*, 17, gives lip service to Heiman's abandonment of post without naming him. See Lowry, *Don't Shoot That Boy!* viii–x, for a then well-publicized account of Pvt. William Scott, sentenced to die for sleeping on guard.

13. The newspaper carrying Michael Heiman's story used phonetic spellings in paraphrasing Gastrock. That was a common practice then but avoided here except for "shplit."

B. Gastrock resisted arrest, "swore terribly in high German," and threatened his captors, but his five-foot-four-inch frame was probably no match for any one of them, much less all. The sergeant ordered Gastrock to assist Heiman and Hummel on the wood-chopping detail.

As soon as the sergeant left, Gastrock sat down and announced, "I'll be damned if I'll *shplit* wood."

Heiman again raced for the sergeant, who this time sent Cpl. Samuel Finkle Keller to handle Gastrock. Keller was the wrong man to resist. He was due for promotion to first sergeant, and a postwar life included a stint as high sheriff of Harrisburg. Leadership and law enforcement obviously appealed to him. Gastrock apparently did not know that because he refused orders to work. Keller ordered him bucked and gagged.

"The whole squad can't buck me!" Gastrock shouted.

Keller figured that he and Henry Eppley were enough of a squad, and he was right. They soon had Gastrock bound on the guardhouse floor, pleading for release. Heiman and Hummel peeked through the window.

"That's the way it goes," Heiman said, exaggerating his own German accent. "One, he sleeps on guard, he carries wood, and one he goes on to party, he *shplits* it, and one he goes hunting, he been bucked."

Tears rolled down Gastrock's face and brought a halt to the ridicule. Heiman lost any sense of satisfaction his revenge gained and recalled that Gastrock "never recovered from his humiliation and always had a forlorn and downcast look about him afterward." Whatever the experience might have done to Levi Gastrock's psyche, his military record was thereafter free of wrongdoing.[14]

Bureaucratic disorganization soon stuck pins in the regiment's morale balloon. Thanks to a paperwork foul-up, the paymaster did not know by December that the 87th Pennsylvania existed. Tom Crowl was certain that if payday did not arrive soon, men would revolt. "There is some of the men are taking french ferlows now allready," he predicted, and he was right. A gang hit Towson retailers with demands for free goods and liquor, at least once at the point of a gun, and made a general nuisance of themselves. After authorities arrested the perpetrators, the *Baltimore County Advocate* hoped "that hereafter the officers will allow none but decent men of the regiment to come to Towsontown." George Hay instituted damage control by holding drill for Towson residents and having the band perform concerts for the Union

14. Recollections of Michael Heiman, *York Gazette,* Feb. 20, 1892; CMSRs of Henry Eppley, Joseph Hummel, and Levi Gastrock, Co. B, 87th Pa., and Pension Records of Levi Gastrock. Eppley was five feet, eight inches tall and Hummel, five feet ten.

Relief Association. Again, York and Adams County newspapers avoided the incident.[15]

Even when payday became imminent, bad news came with it. Jack Skelly vented anger to his mother.

> We expect to get paid tommorrow but we have been fooled so much that we cant belief a word that is said . . . They only pay to the first of november and then they don't pay us any thing for the time we were in york before we were mustered into service. We don't [get] a cent for all the time that I was their . . . The boys are pretty cross about it. If I was out of this bulfrog regiment they would not fool me again if I live till I will get in another regiment.[16]

Morale sagged further thanks to a rumor mill that ground out misleading fodder. Men wrote home how they were about to march into active service to South Carolina, Florida, Fortress Monroe, Fort McHenry, or one of a myriad of other sites. Every movement was "imminent." The captain or lieutenant always said so. When nothing happened, Alfred Jameson became skeptical. "I cannot tell you if we are [leaving] or not," he wrote. "It has been talked about [in] the barracks for the last three weeks that we are to leave but I think it will stay at talking." One wag wrote, "One thing is certain, they cannot take us to all these places at the same time."[17]

Establishing unit esprit de corps was nearly impossible because the railroad guarding job necessarily spread them along thirty miles of track. Drill was the one military activity they had plenty of time to perform, but it was always in small units. At any given time, approximately half of the men were on guard duty, and two companies always served as headquarters guard. Not until eight months after muster did the entire regiment pitch tents on the same campground and drill together. Even then, they divided the next day and did not reunite for several more weeks.[18]

15. Robert S. Webb to Eli Slifer, Dec. 3, 1861, PA AGO, Muster Rolls; Thomas O. Crowl to his uncle, Dec. 1, 1861, Pattee; *Baltimore County Advocate,* Nov. 30, 1861, and May 10, 17, and 24, 1862. The Towson incident is not mentioned in any 87th Pennsylvania man's service records.

16. Pension Records of Johnston H. Skelly, letter to his mother, Dec. 6, 1861. Fourteen-year-old musician George Leighty had the most reason to be angry. The paymaster had no money for him.

17. Thomas O. Crowl to aunt and uncle, Oct. 17, 1861, Jan. 23 and Feb. 7, 1862, and to William Fetrow, Feb. 24, 1862, and to his sister, Mar. 22, 1862, CWMC; Joseph Helker to his cousin, Feb. 19, 1862, George Miller Collection; Pension Records of Alfred Jameson, letter to his mother, Mar. 12, 1862; *Hanover Citizen,* Feb. 13, 1862; Pension Records of Johnston H. Skelly, letter to his mother, Feb. 23, 1862; *Gettysburg Compiler,* Feb. 17, 1862; "Happy Family" to the *Star and Banner,* Mar. 13, 1862, letter dated Mar. 9, 1862.

18. Federal Muster Rolls, Report of the Organization and Proceedings of the 87th Regiment Pennsylvania Volunteers, Feb. 28, 1864, in compliance with the circular issued by the 3rd Brigade,

The good times of autumn faded into a winter of discontent. Years later, a graying John Clutter Hoffman remembered this period partly with chagrin but also with the wink that old men grant the foolishness of their youth. In honor of an 87th Pennsylvania reunion, he wrote a romanticized regimental history in verse he called "The Gallant 87th" and dedicated one stanza to that time.

> On "French leave" some pulled out for home,
> To other corps deserted some,
> The chance for glory seemed too glum
> In Gallant 87th.[19]

Col. George Hay soon made formal overtures to transfer the regiment to active service. Likely, he always had that in mind, but this was the proper time to strike. Maj. Charles Buehler contacted Adams County congressman Edward M. McPherson to impress on him how eager the regiment's two hundred Adams County men (i.e., voters) were to leave the railroad. Newspapers soon reported the regiment's desire for glory, but the boys had to wait several months for army gears to grind. Meanwhile, their new brigade commander, Gen. James Cooper, tried to convince them that they also serve who stand by railroad tracks and suffer abject boredom. He admitted their duty was "irksome" and "wearisome" but pleaded for them not to view it as "thankless or unimportant," adding, "Without obedience and discipline an army is but a mob." Many of the boys from York were proving him right.[20]

Once in the field, the absence of good discipline became deadly even without enemy gunfire. On June 23, 1862, the regiment, minus thirty-six men who deserted overnight, at last shipped out for what they thought was going to be active duty. Instead, last-minute orders landed them in New Creek, Virginia, (modern-day Keyser, West Virginia) for more of the same guard duty. They remained until orders on August 21 sent them after an actual enemy. In the field, misery replaced boredom. Three months out of the next four they

---

3rd Division, 3rd Army Corps, Feb. 23, 1864; Gunnarsson, *Northern Central,* 179–80; "Anonymous" to the *Star and Banner,* July 3, 1862, letter dated June 12, 1862; Josiah Daniel Diehl to Rebecca Diehl, June 13, 1862, mss. 12977 and 12978, YCHT.

19. John Clutter Hoffman, "The Gallant 87th"; Benjamin Frick File 30065, YCHT.

20. Charles H. Buehler to Edward M. McPherson, Jan. 20, 1862, George Hay Kain III Collection; *Hanover Citizen,* Feb. 13, 1862; *Gettysburg Compiler,* Feb. 17, 1862; *Adams Sentinel,* Apr. 25, 1862; *York Gazette,* Apr. 29, 1862. Edward McPherson briefly served as captain of Co. K, 1st Pennsylvania Reserves, but changed his mind and returned to Congress. At the time, the regiment had 176 Adams County men, 61 of whom were not old enough to vote. Warner, *Generals in Blue,* 90–91. Maryland-born James Cooper studied law in Gettysburg with Thaddeus Stevens and followed with a career in politics.

marched throughout the most rugged sections of what is now West Virginia chasing guerrillas, a journey that sent many men to the surgeon and some on the road home. According to Pvt. Joseph Helker, the roads they traveled were "the roughest and hardest . . . imaginable" and made a mile "twice as long as one of ours in Pa." They slept in snow, marched repeatedly through icy streams, and climbed over mountains that Pvt. Jacob Dovler considered "the bigist . . . you ever seen."[21]

They did all that on provisions that provided little sustenance, as Tom Crowl wrote his sister.

> We got scant a nough to eat and at night we were too tired to kook any thing . . . The water we had some times plenty and other times that scarce that we were nearly dead for it. In fact some times we took water that york county hogs wouldn't drink and we were ready to jump at it.[22]

After a much-needed respite in Clarksburg, the regiment returned to the town of Beverly on November 2 for the second of three visits. The year before, Gen. George B. McClellan had earned his reputation five miles up the road atop Rich Mountain, when his forces secured the vital Staunton-Parkersburg Turnpike for the Union. The strongly pro-Southern area did not react well to the Yankee victory, and most residents had fled by 1862. One Union soldier claimed there were only two families remaining in a five-mile radius, leaving the invading Yankees free to strip the once lively town of everything vital.[23]

An Ohioan who was there at the same time described the town as "a poor, miserable place" and wrote a letter to his wife explaining why he felt that way:

> As we pass a house and look in we see in place of a family in good style a house with windows broke in, broken down, dirty floors, boxes . . . , guns, knapsacks, soldiers . . . The old fireplace outside the fences tore down. In back in the yard horses and mules some dead, some living and fat and some might as well be dead. Such is Beverly, all caused by locofocoism north and south.[24]

21. Josiah Diehl to his mother, Sept. 5, 1862, mss. 12977 and 12978, YCHT; Joseph Helker to his cousin, Aug. 29, 1862, George Miller Collection; Pension Records of Jacob Dovler, Co. K, 87th Pa., letter to unknown, Sept. 12, 1862; *O.R.*, Correspondence, Battle of Rich Mountain, 2:201–11, Report of J. D. Imboden, Sept. 1, 1862, 12/3:949–53.

22. Thomas O. Crowl to his sister, Oct. 11, 1862, CWMC.

23. "Regulator" to the *Star and Banner*, Sept. 25, 1862, letter dated Sept. 9, 1862.

24. Josiah Staley to his wife, Nov. 4, 1862, Civil War Collection, MIC-17, roll 19, Ohio Historical Society; CMSR of Josiah Staley, Co. H, 123rd Ohio. Staley was captured at the battle of New Market, Virginia, May 15, 1864, and sent to Andersonville Prison. He received a parole December 13, 1864, but died that Christmas Day at Camp Parole, Annapolis, Maryland.

Alfred Jameson agreed, writing, "[I] never want to see the place any more if I can help it."[25]

All day November 4, 1862, tempers smoldered. Some men made no secret of wanting to reduce what was left of Beverly to ashes. The brass took the threats seriously enough to order the town off-limits and double the guard but failed to put the hotheads into line before trouble started.[26]

Albert Thompson Barnes was the leading 87th Pennsylvania bigmouth. Alcohol was not the cause. The off-limits dictum was sufficient on its own to rile him. Barnes had been complaining to tentmates all day and finally announced he was going into town in spite of what orders said. Friends George S. Anderson and Tempest Leichey Forrer tried to convince him otherwise, but Barnes's ire had flown beyond reason's reach. He stormed out of the tent and headed toward town, Anderson at his side trying to talk him back to earth. Their banter drew attention, and a crowd followed, tacking on rubberneckers as they went. Inevitably, it began assuming the characteristics of a mob.

Several 9th (West) Virginia guards stood in the way and tensed when they saw the gang of Pennsylvanians headed their direction. There had been "rivalry" between the two regiments, and they sensed trouble coming. Barnes stood face-to-face with a guard and demanded to be let into town. The guard reminded him of orders and refused. Barnes stepped back, fuming. George Anderson feared what Barnes might do next and offered a suggestion he later explained as an effort to save his tentmate's skin. Since it was dark, perhaps they could sneak into town by an unguarded alley. Barnes agreed, but the brass had foreseen this possibility and had guards blocking every entrance. Again he jawed with a guard, the mob egging him on this time. This guard also refused, and Barnes lost control. He grabbed the barrel of the guard's rifle and drove the butt deep into his stomach. Anderson yanked Barnes back. The sharp click of a musket pulled to full cock finally sobered Albert Barnes, and he stepped back again without Anderson's help.[27]

The situation might have ended there had the 87th Pennsylvania not recruited one man whose name has been lost to history, someone who decided then to pick up a rock and heave it at the guard. Sadly, the unknown soldier's aim was excellent. The missile smacked squarely on the guard's skull. Whether by anger or autonomic reaction, the guard's trigger finger jerked.

25. Alfred Jameson to his mother, Oct. 12, 1862, Pension Records of Alfred Jameson. The luxurious Goff house had become a hospital. The autograph of Joseph Fox, Co. G, 87th Pa., remains on one of the upstairs walls.

26. Pension Records of Albert T. Barnes, 87th Pa., deposition of George S. Anderson, stating, "There was great rivalry between my regiment and these West Virginia regiments" but offered no details on the nature of the rivalry or what had caused it.

27. Pension Records of Albert T. Barnes, deposition of George S. Anderson, 1892.

A bullet tore through Albert Barnes's belly, tossing him backward into a man just behind. They flopped hard to the ground, Barnes on top. Comrades lifted him off and discovered an exit wound in Barnes's back and an entry wound in the second man's stomach. Abraham Fox from Company E, one month past his seventeenth birthday, lay moaning, a bloodstain spreading across the front of his shirt.[28]

"Get your rifles!" someone shouted after they had recovered from the initial shock. The 12th (West) Virginia, also then at Beverly, remembered that the 87th camp flew into "a great commotion, like that of a disturbed hive of bees." Men snatched weapons and shouted to comrades washing clothes in the river to join in avenging two murders. No record found revealed what the Virginians were doing during all this, but it hardly could have been anything positive. A new mini-Civil War threatened to erupt in Beverly.[29]

"It was only with the greatest exertions that the officers managed to quiet them," Capt. Thaddeus Pfeiffer wrote with classic nineteenth-century understatement. By morning, the situation had calmed, but Barnes and Fox were dead. The army punished no one for the incident.[30]

Poor discipline was not unique to the 87th Pennsylvania, nor did misbehavior require a home-guard mentality. Given that the National Archives has about fifty thousand Union army general courts-martial transcripts on file, a complete recounting of weak discipline would fill several volumes, but here are a few examples:

- In August 1861, the Pennsylvania Bucktail Regiment told their colonel that were not going to leave camp until he issued them better firearms.[31]
- In 1861, Gen. Henry Wager Halleck wrote from Missouri: "Everything here is in such total disorganization and there is such a general lack of discipline." About that time, a captain complained to Ulysses S. Grant that the army in Cairo, Illinois, was "composed of boys, badly disciplined and drilled."[32]

28. Ibid. Barnes's mother was refused a pension because her son was not on duty when shot.

29. *History of the Twelfth West Virginia Volunteer Infantry.*

30. Thaddeus S. Pfeiffer to his father, *Star and Banner*, Dec. 4, 1862, letter dated Nov. 19, 1862; CMSRs and Pension Records of Albert T. Barnes, Co. H, and Abraham Fox, Co. E, 87th Pa.; recollections of George Blotcher. The ill-fated Abraham Fox was the brother of Joseph Fox, who had written his name on the Goff house wall. George Anderson claimed the West Virginia guard died, and George Blotcher likewise recalled another man dying, but a search of 9th and 12th West Virginia unit records revealed no one dying then or shortly thereafter other than by explicable causes.

31. Angelo Crapsey to Laroy Lyman, Aug. 3, 1861, Krista Lyman Collection, courtesy of Krista Lyman, Roulette, Pennsylvania; *Harrisburg Patriot and Union* and *Pennsylvania Daily Telegraph*, issues from mid-June through Aug. 1, 1861.

32. *O.R.,* Henry W. Halleck to George B. McClellan, Dec. 10, 1861, 8:818, J. C. Kelton to U. S. Grant, Dec. 18, 1861, 7:507.

- In August 1862, a general wrote from Winchester, Virginia, that his officers were so undisciplined that he recommended making an example of one of them.[33]
- An investigation into how Rebels captured an entire Union force at Gallatin, Tennessee, without firing a shot uncovered "the sleeping of sentinels on their posts appears to have been of no uncommon occurrence, and yet no punishment proportionate to this offense appears to have been inflicted."[34]
- Even as the war neared its conclusion, a frustrated general threw up his hands that officers of the 5th Tennessee Cavalry "seem to have no conception of their obligations and duties [and] have no control over their subordinates or men."[35]
- Edward L. Schroeder, a Yorker who bypassed the 87th Pennsylvania for a commission in a Maryland regiment, submitted his resignation due to "the utterly demoralizing and degenerate condition of the regiment."[36]

Mention these incidents to a World War II veteran, and he will shake his head in disbelief. The difference between the two wars is training and top-down organization. While most World War II participants were citizen-soldiers like their Civil War grandfathers and more likely to have been con-scripted, they were trained by professionals and expected to learn the same skills and disciplines as career military men. Civil War soldiers theoretically had to learn all that was contained in the *Manual of Arms* and the *School of the Soldier,* but the army left volunteer outfits to their own training devices. That often, if not usually, meant inexperienced officers leading inexperienced men. Ask that same World War II veteran about discipline, and he will likely say simply, "We did what we were told," something frequently not true for Civil War volunteers. The in-your-face drill instructor is a cliché of the modern Marine Corps' Parris Island, not York's Camp Scott. Some of that modern-day Marine Corps mentality would have come in handy during the Civil War. Advances in weaponry had made the old militia system obsolete, and weak discipline cost dearly in lives. The 87th Pennsylvania supplied its share.[37]

33. *O.R.,* Julius White to John Pope, Aug. 15, 1862, 12/3:574.

34. *O.R.,* Wadsworth Jenkins to H.C. McDowell, Aug. 23, 1862, 16/1:846; Lonn, *Desertion.* Lonn's work is primarily a survey of the *O.R.* and lacks interviews with, and accounts by, deserters, which would have put meat on an otherwise superb statistical skeleton. See also Wiley, *Billy Yank.*

35. *O.R.,* Robert H. Milroy to Asst. Adj. Gen. B. H. Polk, Jan. 16, 1865, 45/2:600, also referenced in Lonn, *Desertion,* 136.

36. CMSR and Pension Records of Edward L. Schroeder, Co. A, 5th Md.

37. See McPherson, *For Cause and Comrades,* chap. 1, for this respected historian's views on what made men enlist and fight within an undisciplined army.

Fitz-John Porter, shown here
as a major general
(Library of Congress)

Robert Patterson in younger days
(Library of Congress)

Thomas Alexander Scott (MOLLUS)

Alexander Small (*Genealogical Records of
George Small, Philip Albright, . . .*)

George Hay
(Gil Barret Collection)

John William Schall
(Roger Hunt Collection)

James Henry Blasser
(George R. Prowell, *History of the
87th Pennsylvania Volunteers*).

James Alanza Stahle
(Roger Hunt Collection)

Noah G. Ruhl
(Gil Barret Collection)

John Crull
(George R. Prowell, *History of the
87th Pennsylvania Volunteers*)

Isaac Hull (Gil Barret Collection)

Solomon Myers
(Gil Barret Collection)

Charles Henry Buehler
(George R. Prowell, *History of the
87th Pennsylvania Volunteers*)

Wells Abraham Farrah
(George R. Prowell,
*History of the 87th
Pennsylvania Volunteers*)

The church-forts, with modern-
day additions, that protected the
87th Pennsylvania and 116th
Ohio men at Bunker Hill.

Franklin Geise,
taken shortly before his death
(York County Heritage Trust)

Thaddeus Stevens Pfeiffer
(Gil Barret Collection)

Libby Prison in 1865, the James River flowing in the background.
The bottom half of the three-section building had not yet been painted white
when the boys from York arrived in June 1863 (Library of Congress).

Belle Isle, April 1865. This is what the boys from York would have seen had they been permitted to climb to the island's higher ground, except that tents would have been smothering the flat section of the island. Richmond and the remnants of the pilings of the recently burned Mayo Bridge are visible in the background (Library of Congress).

Andrew Bentz Smith,
a postwar image
(author's collection)

William Henry Lanius
as a baby-faced 1st sergeant
(courtesy of William Henry Lanius III)

Robert Huston Milroy
(Library of Congress)

Gustave Paul Cluseret
(Library of Congress)

David Christian Eberhart,
regimental chaplain and dentist
(George R. Prowell, *History of the
87th Pennsylvania Volunteers*)

Lew Wallace, savior of Washington,
author of *Ben Hur*, and nemesis of Billy the
Kid (Library of Congress)

James Brewerton Ricketts, the 87th
Pennsylvania's division commander
at Cold Harbor and Monocacy
(Library of Congress)

Beniah Keller Anstine, Co. C,
captured the day after Monocacy and
barely survived Danville Prison
(Gil Barret Collection).

Charles Frederick Haack, mortally wound-
ed at Monocacy while climbing a fence
(George R. Prowell, *History of the 87th
Pennsylvania Volunteers*).

Adjutant Anthony M. Martin,
mortally wounded at Monocacy
and died the day after the battle
(George R. Prowell, *History of the
87th Pennsylvania Volunteers*).

David Ferguson McKinney,
native Pennsylvania surgeon, who
returned to Frederick, Maryland,
to live out his life in splendor
(George R. Prowell, *History of the
87th Pennsylvania Volunteers*).

John Frederick Spangler, Co. A,
fatally wounded at Monocacy while
lying between his commanding officers
(Roger Hunt Collection).

Daniel Laumaster Welsh, Co. G, killed
at Monocacy and who allegedly gave a
dying farewell message to his family
(George R. Prowell, *History of the 87th
Pennsylvania Volunteers*).

Theodore Augustus Helwig
(author's collection)

Daniel Peter Reigle,
c. 1862, the regiment's only Medal of Honor
recipient, for his efforts at Cedar Creek
(Gettysburg National Military Park)

Edgar Monroe Ruhl
(Ronn Palm's Museum of Civil War Images)

James Tearney,
enlisted with the regiment as a
private and led it home as its colonel
(Gil Barret Collection)

Typical Union works in the Petersburg lines. Abatis protects the front of the fort (Library of Congress).

Typical Confederate works at Petersburg (Library of Congress)

The old men from York and their reunion at William Henry Lanius's home c. 1908.
Seated (l-r): Findley Isaac Thomas, James Alanza Stahle, John William Schall, unknown;
standing foreground: unknown, unknown, Charles Henry Stallman, unknown,
Samuel Saylor; far left background: David Ramsey Saylor.

Calvin Gilbert, veteran of Company F, was approaching his 100th birthday
when he explained to four Boy Scouts how his company had manufactured
many of the cannon displayed on the Gettysburg battlefield
(Gettysburg National Military Park).

The Pennsylvania Monument on the Monocacy battlefield, thirty-five feet of Vermont granite located behind what was the sunken road. It is the only battlefield monument that bears the name of the 87th Pennsylvania, and they must share it with the 138th and 67th Pennsylvania Regiments, the latter of which never got closer to the battlefield than John F. Staunton's train carried them (photo by the author).

Chapter 7

Desertion

Getting out of the army legally was much tougher than getting in. Officers could resign, but most enlisted men insistent on exiting the army took the easier but more perilous way out: they deserted. Sometimes the army changed the charge to a less-serious "absent without leave," but it was desertion just the same. Of the 1,034 men who enlisted with the 87th Pennsylvania Infantry during 1861, more than one-fourth left the regiment at least once without permission with the intent of remaining away for an extended time, if not forever. Their desertion rate was more than triple that of other area men enlisting in 1861, most of whom experienced more combat. Most of the 87th Pennsylvania desertions occurred during two time periods: the regiment's first year of existence and under special and more understandable circumstances following the second battle of Winchester.[1]

The First Year

To encourage men to enlist, the army paid a bounty (i.e., a signing bonus). Later in the war, bounties varied widely, leading the unscrupulous to enlist, accept what money was available up front, and then desert to another regiment to repeat the process. No one deserting the 87th Pennsylvania during the regiment's first year was a bounty jumper. Bounty amounts varied little if at all in the war's first year and were not substantial. A man joining the 87th received one hundred dollars to be paid only after discharge or to survivors in

---

1. CMSRs of all men of the 87th Pa.

the event of death. It was a grass-is-greener syndrome, not money, that gave some men wanderlust.

Some men managed to escape to another regiment by engaging in a little creative conspiracy. Privates Levi Spangler and Thomas Smith, for example, wheedled discharges from the regimental surgeon in January 1862 due to chronic health issues that gave them no chance of returning to active duty in the foreseeable future. Two weeks later, they joined the 107th Pennsylvania Infantry. That was a mistake. Smith ended up in the Invalid Corps, while Spangler returned home with a legitimate medical discharge and promptly died.[2]

The 76th and 114th Pennsylvania lured some men because both were Zouave regiments. The boys from York saw the popularity of James Stahle's Company A Zouaves, and here were entire regiments wearing the colorful uniform. Pvt. John H. Kindig, nicknamed "Reddy" for his hair color, deserted after just two weeks to join the 76th, one of three men to take the same escape route. The 87th Regiment dated his desertion a month after his enlistment with the 76th, so he had been gone for some time before they realized he was not coming back. The 76th was not a secure regiment for a York County man to join illegally. Wrightsville supplied much of Company I and Hanover generated Company D, making danger of discovery great. Kindig nevertheless completed his term, and the other two 87th deserters died well into their terms under honorable circumstances. Those who knew obviously kept quiet.[3]

Two of the men who deserted to the 114th Pennsylvania experienced difficulty with the 87th before they left, which no doubt motivated their decisions to depart. In the spring of 1862, the regiment court-martialed Pvt. Henry Smallbrook for an unknown offense and ordered him to forfeit a month's pay. Soon afterward, he fled to the 114th, completing a three-year enlistment and suffering a hand wound on day two at Gettysburg. Sgt. Thomas James Montgomery had received three promotions before his first Christmas in the army, but in mid-January the regiment ripped the sergeant's stripes from his sleeves. After an accident left him with a broken hip and foot, he went home on furlough to complete his recovery. Once restored to health, however, he

2. CMSRs of Levi M. Spangler and Thomas Smith, Co. B, 87th Pa. and Co. A, 107th Pa. Spangler enlisted at age forty-eight and Smith, at forty-seven. Both claimed forty-five. Spangler received a discharge from the 87th Pennsylvania January 12, 1862, and from the 107th April 10, 1863. He died of pneumonia in York May 3, 1863. Thomas Smith transferred to the Veteran Reserve (Invalid) Corps Mar. 1, 1864.

3. CMSR and Pension Records of John H. Kindig, Co. K, 87th Pa., and Co. E, 76th Pa. John J. Miller and Thomas H. Stevens, both of Co. D, were the other two men who deserted to the 76th. The 76th Pennsylvania was nicknamed "Keystone Zouaves" and the 114th, "Collis' Zouaves."

traveled to Lancaster and enlisted with the 114th Pennsylvania without mentioning his existing service obligation. When the illegal reenlistment turned up during his pension process, he offered the lame excuse that the 87th had left its Maryland camp and he did not know where it had gone.[4]

Sgt. Christian William Kehm was another who deserted to the 114th Pennsylvania. Once he was there, Capt. Edwin Forrest Kohler assigned Kehm as his first sergeant, which means either the two men had known each other before, Kehm had an engaging personality, or Kohler had no scruples about where he got an experienced man. Kohler's influence, however, could not keep Kehm out of trouble. By August, his stripes-and-diamond insignia was gone and shortly thereafter, so was he. He resurfaced in 1864 to take a plunge with the 2nd Pennsylvania Heavy Artillery as Christian *Kemp* because, he told a pension examiner, that was how everyone pronounced his name anyway. This enlistment he completed honorably, but a slip of the tongue nearly cost him his pension. During an interview, he naturally avoided any mention of the two regiments he had deserted. When the pension examiner asked where he had met his wife, Kehm said, "In Baltimore *while serving with another unit.*" The examiner never asked, "What other unit?" either missing Kehm's "oops" or choosing to ignore it, even though he put down Kehm's words, probably verbatim.[5]

Glamorous regiments did not motivate most men to jump ship, however. Why, then, did they desert? Unveiling their motives is challenging because relatively few detailed their reasons in writing. There are two rather obvious causes relevant to the entire army. First, more people will attempt anything that is easy to accomplish, and Civil War geography made desertion easier. A World War II GI wanting to desert in the Ardennes had nowhere to go, but Civil War soldiers often could walk home or reach a rail line and ride much of the way. Second, it is equally axiomatic that unlikelihood of punishment exacerbates rule breaking. For most of the war's first two years, the army arrested only a small percentage of deserters because it had no significant mechanism

---

4. CMSR and Pension Records of James Thomas Montgomery, Co. H, 114th Pa., deposition of James Montgomery, Jan. 23, 1900. Montgomery's service records give no reason for his reduction in rank. The Interior Department later granted him a pension but then denied his widow because of his desertion. His tombstone lists the 114th Pennsylvania. Court Docket 1856–1860, York County, pp. 226, 261. Before the war, Montgomery stood trial for assault and battery with the intent to kill. The court ruled not guilty but ordered him to pay court costs.

5. Kautz, *Service Non-Commissioned,* 131; CMSRs of Christian W. Kehm, Co. I, 87th Pa., Co. C, 114th Pa., and Battery L, 2nd Pa. Heavy Art.; Pension Records of Christian W. Kemp, Battery L, 2nd Pa. Heavy Art., emphasis added; Edward J. Hagerty, *Collis' Zouaves: The 114th Pennsylvania Volunteers in the Civil War,* 60; CMSR of Henry Lauer, Co. K, 87th Pa., and Co. I, 114th Pa. Lauer was the fourth 87th Pennsylvania man who jumped to the 114th Pennsylvania.

to capture them. That changed in large degree in early 1863 when the War Department established a provost marshal's office that soon reported upward of five thousand arrests each month. Even so, more men escaped capture than were caught. During the final two years of the war, Pennsylvania alone had twenty-four thousand men away from their posts.[6]

Men got away with desertion in part because home folks aided their escapes or, at least, did not report them. Ella Lonn, author of the first book-length treatise on Civil War desertion, wrote in 1928, "It is difficult . . . to understand the boldness with which the soldiers, men and officers showed their faces in their own homes." Available data for south-central Pennsylvania deserters validate her thesis. Twenty-nine-year-old John Denues fled the 87th Pennsylvania shortly after being broken to ranks but lived out his life in York County with two relatives who had completed terms with the regiment. We do not know how he was treated but clearly it was not harshly enough to force his departure. Likewise, all of those who survived the jump to the 76th and 114th regiments returned to their hometowns to live out their lives.[7]

A statistical search for sociological reasons as to why south-central Pennsylvania soldiers deserted proved almost fruitless with one exception: foreign birth. Immigrants not only deserted at a higher rate than native-born men, they also were less likely to return to active duty on their own. (See Appendix, "Personal Factors in Predicting Desertion.") This was not an isolated phenomenon. In August 1864, the 200th Pennsylvania Infantry came into existence staffed principally by York County men. Forty-two percent of the regiment's known foreign-born recruits deserted compared to less than 9 percent of native-born men. Reasons no doubt included immigrants' generally lower standard of living and the fact that the political and social causes that led to war affected them less.[8]

Age was the only other factor with even a minor influence in desertion. Thanks to the John Englebert-types who were too young for military life, underage boys deserted at a slightly higher percentage than their rate of participation, but the sample is small and the difference not great. The thirty to thirty-four age range also has a slight disproportion of deserters but represents only 9 percent of total participation. The eighteen to twenty-nine age range

6. Lonn, *Desertion*, 150–51, 233–34; CMSRs of all men of the 87th Pa. and all men from York and Adams counties who enlisted for three years during 1861.

7. U.S. Census, 1860–1880, Pennsylvania, York County, Spring Garden Township and York Borough; Vital Statistics Card File; Lonn, *Desertion*, 204.

8. CMSRs of all men of the 87th Pa. and 200th Pa. Ninety-five foreign-born men were identified enlisting with the 200th Pennsylvania. See Lonn, *Desertion*, 138, for generals' negative opinions of foreign-born soldiers.

had the most deserters because two-thirds of the men were in this age range, but the desertion rate was not disproportionate to participation.

The estimable James McPherson reasonably theorized that desertion rates were probably higher among married soldiers because they felt compelled to look after their families' welfare. Sensible as that hypothesis sounds, there is no statistical evidence that marital status provided any significant motivation for south-central Pennsylvanians to desert. Overall, about one-fourth of recruits were married, and about one-fourth of deserters were married. Combining marital status with personal assets produced one grouping with a slight trend toward desertion, that being non-87th men with valuations less than one thousand dollars. Otherwise, no grouping deserted in even small disproportion to its representation.[9]

Two other social factors, income and education, could have affected desertion rates. Logic dictates that men with money and education deserted less often because their reputations directly related to their ability to earn a living. Vincent C. S. Eckert's postwar life demonstrates how loss of community status apparently forced one successful man to leave the area. Poor, uneducated men, on the other hand, seldom performed as community leaders. Even if forced to relocate to escape arrest or censure, they could make a living much as before because their bodies were their tools. However logical the income argument may sound, no income group deserted disproportionately to its head count, although financially advantaged men perhaps represent too small a percentage of participation to offer a significant sample.

Ill health clearly was a major reason for desertion throughout the army, a fact that Ella Lonn surveyed statistically but did not study at the foot-soldier level. Sick men had little confidence in an army medical system staffed by surgeons unprepared by medical science and/or their ability to diagnose, much less treat, illness correctly. Surgeons might discharge one man with a condition that had a chance of improvement but force others who should have been bedridden to remain in service.

Forty-one-year-old Pvt. John Frederick Backoffer exemplified the latter. He was standing on a bridge one winter day in early 1862 and somehow failed to hear a train approaching. Fortunately, reality struck before the train, but the only escape left was jumping over the side of the bridge and holding on until the train passed. He leaped in time but grabbed nothing but air. The fall into the river might have been funny had he not ruptured a testicle, a painful and embarrassing injury that physicians then could not repair. When the 87th Pennsylvania left for active duty, the army ordered him along even

9. McPherson, *For Cause and Comrades*, 138.

though he found movement agonizing. Backoffer, who had become a United States citizen the day he enlisted, deserted.[10]

The army's handling of deserters returning to duty often verified that illness or injury had rendered them unfit to serve. Pvt. Israel Baublitz's tenure as deserter lasted six months until a York police officer tapped him on the shoulder, yet the army did not punish him. They detached him to teamster duty, a function routinely assigned to men physically unable to perform as frontline soldiers. Likewise, when Pvt. Alexander Crouch returned from desertion, the army immediately sent him to the Provost Guard, another dumping ground for the physically unfit.[11]

Ella Lonn defined a number of reasons why men deserted that are not applicable to the 87th Pennsylvania during their first year.

- Desertion to the enemy: In only one documented case did an 87th Pennsylvania man desert to the South and that in 1864 under unique circumstances examined later.
- The inability of men to endure war's hardships: By the soldiers' own admission, the 87th Pennsylvania's quarters were unusually comfortable. Guarding a bridge in the dead of winter is unpleasant and unhealthy but nowhere near as rigorous as active campaigning. Some men died of disease but not in great numbers and none of illness indigenous to an army camp. Those dying from foolish acts had only themselves to blame.[12]
- Inadequate supplies and firearms: Supplies were more than sufficient and personal items readily available. Some men actually reported gaining weight during the fall of 1861. While the 87th's first weapon was an old Harpers Ferry model musket converted from a flintlock, there was little need for a stellar rifle to guard railroad bridges. The only shots the men fired off the practice range took down a hapless cow and a lost horse that wandered near guard posts at night. Before the regiment went into the field, it received an issue of Enfield rifles.[13]
- War weariness: Hardly relevant in the 87th's case, although boredom was an issue. When it became an issue in 1863 and thereafter, few men deserted.

10. Lonn, *Desertion.* Lonn cited mostly generals. CMSR of John Frederick Backoffer, Co. H, 87th Pa.
11. CMSRs of Israel Baublitz, Co. D, and Alexander Crouch, Co. E, 87th Pa. It is clear from reading thousands of service records that unfit men were regularly assigned undemanding duty, especially during the war's last two years.
12. CMSRs of all men of the 87th Pa. Six men died of disease before July 1862, one from a lung ailment that likely was preexisting. Three died in accidents.
13. Johnston H. Skelly to his mother, Dec. 6, 1861, Pension Records of Johnston H. Skelly; Alfred Jameson to his mother, precise date unknown, Pension Records of Alfred Jameson; Prowell, *87th Pennsylvania,* 17–18.

- Cowardice: Again, irrelevant for the 87th during the early period. However, forty-four men deserted in 1862 after they heard the regiment was to enter active service. It is almost certain that they did so out of fear they *might* see action. Whether this was fear of injury or disgust over leaving a soft assignment is impossible to know.

Ella Lonn described three other reasons that clearly match the 87th Pennsylvania men's motivation to desert during their time along the railroad, the first two of which were discussed in a previous chapter: inadequate officers, caliber of recruits, and "An utter absence of a realization of the obligation incurred by enlistment."[14]

The 87th Pennsylvania offers several illustrations of Lonn's last reason. George S. Markle mustered in late February 1862 and fell ill almost immediately. He claimed that the surgeon pronounced him "unfit for service" and promised to issue a medical discharge. Three months later, Markle had heard nothing more on the subject but never made a second inquiry with the surgeon. When the regiment went west in June, he self-diagnosed total physical impairment and went home sans permission. A year later, he received a draft notice but the army rejected him for poor health, giving credence to his claim of disability. The army did not care. They found out where he was and sent him to prison.[15]

Jacob Deardorff deserted in May 1862, returned home, and astonishingly volunteered to substitute with the 165th Pennsylvania Drafted Militia that November. Clearly, the money the draftee paid him was too tempting to resist. The army uncovered his desertion and promptly arrested him, yet soon released him to begin a new life in Illinois, where his family had already moved and he had married the previous December. Records do not explain why he suffered no punishment for deserting and enlisting a second time contrary to the Articles of War. His actions demonstrate a man who viewed personal issues as outweighing military obligation. Years later he even applied for a pension based on his aborted service with the 87th. The Interior Department weighed his personal obligations with a different scale and said, "No!"[16]

14. Lonn, *Desertion,* 127–42.

15. CMSR of George S. Markle, Co. F, 87th Pa., statement of George S. Markle, undated but probably summer of 1864 since he made it at Prince Street Military Prison, Alexandria, Virginia, after his arrest June 23, 1864; Court-Martial, George S. Markle, LL-2415. The court sentenced Markle to return to duty and serve time missed while deserting as well as suffer financial penalties. A draft notice for a deserter was not strange because a local civilian representative compiled lists of eligible men with whom he'd had face-to-face contact.

16. CMSRs and Pension Records of Jacob Deardorff, Co. F, 87th Pa., and Co. D, 165th Pa.; *Gettysburg Compiler,* Nov. 10, 1862; *Adams Sentinel,* Nov. 11, 1862. Deardorff substituted for Cornelius Smith in the 165th Pa.

Marylander William Augustus Klingel said he deserted the 87th Pennsylvania because he knew no one in Company F and felt lonely, but others insisted his love of whiskey outweighed his sense of duty. In the two years following his desertion, he kept his family on the move to avoid arrest until the war's closing days, when he enlisted with the 8th Pennsylvania Cavalry as James P. Forsythe. Motivation to return to service may have come from guilt over two brothers who had served honorably, or he may have wearied of hearing his wife complain about their constant moving. A five-hundred-dollar bounty probably had something to do with it, too.[17]

Jacob Spotz escaped capture at Carter's Woods in June 1863 but injured a finger, so he wandered back to his Dallastown, York County, home to get his mother to nurse it. Mother Spotz was still tending her son's finger when the provost arrived that November and took him away. He swore he had never intended to desert, but neither had he reported his whereabouts to military authorities.[18]

Pvt. Enos Ignatius Alfersdorffer spent much of his seven months with the 87th Pennsylvania in hospitals. Finally pronounced fit and ordered back to duty, he left the hospital and vanished. Years later, he explained that he remained home because his leg had not healed from a gunshot wound. Who shot him and under what circumstances was a pertinent detail since the regiment did not engage in battle at any time during his tenure, and he would not have been with it even if it had. In fact, Alfersdorffer was shot in the leg and under honorable, albeit improper, circumstances. After he left the 87th, Alfersdorffer illegally enlisted with the 132nd Pennsylvania, and that took him to the battle of Fredericksburg, where he received his wound. One must wonder why he even mentioned his time with the 87th Pennsylvania during his pension process. However, successful completion of his second army term gave him the right to enter a postwar soldier's home and, ultimately, a Washington insane asylum.[19]

Peter A. McIntire experienced more than his share of bad luck but worsened his case by not communicating with authorities. Captured at Win-

---

17. CMSR of William A. Klingel, Co. F, 87th Pa., descriptive list of deserters; CMSR and Pension Records of James P. Forsythe, Co. G, 8th Pa. Cav., statement of William Klingel and deposition of Mary Jane Lambert Klingel. The Interior Department denied pensions to both Klingel and his widow and refused to honor his five-hundred-dollar bounty payment. His tombstone reflects his correct name and his cavalry service.

18. Pension Records of Jacob Spotz, Co. D, 87th Pa., deposition of Jacob Spotz, Sept. 5, 1887.

19. CMSR of Enos Ignatius Alfersdorffer, Co. D, 87th Pa., and Co. F, 132nd Pa.; Historical Registers of National Homes for Disabled Soldiers, Register of Members, 1867–1935, Central Branch, NM-29, entry 23, M1749, roll 29, entry 345. Alfersdorffer's last name was spelled a myriad of ways, but the version from the soldiers' home records is used here.

chester, he deserted from Camp Parole and remained illegally free until January 11, 1864. He was legitimately sick because the army sent him not to the guardhouse upon his return to duty, but to a hospital, where he stayed for three months. Back to active duty and captured again that July, he got lucky and received a parole after only nineteen days, but they were days in which he ate virtually nothing. He was sicker than before, and the army put him into the hospital at Camp Parole but shortly gave him a furlough home to recover and vote in the 1864 presidential election. On the way, bad luck multiplied when the train in which he was riding collided with another, and he was left with two smashed toes. McIntire spent seven weeks at home recuperating from the accident. Problem was, that was three weeks longer than his furlough allowed, and at no time did he attempt to brief the army on his situation. Somehow slipping the notice of local provost officials, he recovered sufficiently to return to Camp Parole, whereupon the army shipped him right back to York to muster out. Nineteen years later, he applied for commutation of rations for his time in captivity and was shocked to learn that his service records contained an unresolved desertion charge. The army should never have honorably discharged a soldier with an unresolved desertion charge on his record, so the pension office took its time investigating. McIntire eventually got his payment but only after several years' delay, all of which could have been avoided had he made the proper connection with the army at the time.[20]

All these men displayed naïveté about the individual responsibility they should have understood then and that is taken for granted by modern-day American soldiers and their families. Today, most of us know more than one person who served or is serving in the armed forces, and we accept military discipline as necessary. That was not true in April 1861 when the United States Army had only sixteen thousand men stationed primarily in the western states and territories. If folks knew Mexican War or War of 1812 veterans, they probably had been volunteers, not regulars. Washington had always kept the regular army small, partly for financial considerations, but also because the notion of a strong, centrally controlled army had struck fear into many Americans since the Revolutionary War. People trusted the local militia and its grab-your-gun-and-come-running concept for protection. Most south-central Pennsylvania men were self-employed farmers, laborers, craftsmen,

20. *York Gazette,* Oct. 4, 1864; George Hiner, claims agent, to the War Department, Feb. 16, 1883, Bookmark, Enlisted Branch, 3672 C1882; CMSR of Peter A. McIntire, Co. I, 87th Pa. Since the army did not feed men while they were prisoners of war, they could later receive a commutated value of the rations the army had never issued them.

small-business owners, or the sons of same, independent men innately suspicious of centralized authority. They carried that attitude into military service, often to their detriment.[21]

The army itself was sometimes derelict in reporting absences in a timely manner, and that led to false charges of desertion. Pvt. Conrad Gerecht's name hit the list of deserters on March 14, 1862. Some time later, they found him in a Baltimore hospital struggling against one of the many diseases that plagued Civil War armies. How he got there without someone knowing, or why the hospital did not contact the regiment sooner, his records do not reveal. The army was satisfied he got there legitimately and gave him a medical discharge.

The army was not only derelict about Luther Calvin Stouffer's status, it was confused. Service records list him as captured at the battle of Monocacy, deserted at Monocacy, and sick in the hospital during Monocacy, possibly because an 1863 court-martial for desertion made any of his subsequent actions suspicious. Whatever actually happened, the army could prove nothing wrong, and he mustered out honorably and on time with the rest of the regiment.[22]

Ella Lonn missed an important reason why men deserted. The word *worthless* appears often in soldiers' military records and not just because they deserted. In the motion picture *Glory,* the educated and sensitive Thomas Searles, played by Andre Braugher, was initially a worthless soldier humiliated by the gruff Irish sergeant major and Denzel Washington's Trip character. The fictional Searles used that shame as motivation to become a good soldier. In real life, many men—boys, often—improperly filtered by an inadequate enlistment process, became as "worthless" as superiors deemed them. Anyone with a bad self-image will be eager to escape his circumstances.

Pvt. Henry Tyson, for example, was subject to "falling fits." Either he suffered an epilepsy-like condition or he was simply "doppich," as the Pennsylvania "Dutch" call a clumsy person. Whatever his problem, he became one of those deemed "worthless" and ran away. Sixteen-year-old Henry S. Kidd spent his money "as fast as he gets it." That was part of the reason he wore a "worthless" label, however normal such behavior is for an unworldly teenager whose army pay was likely more money than he had ever possessed. He deserted in February 1862 but that August joined the 130th Pennsylvania

21. Kenneth W. Munden and Henry Putney Beers, *The Union: A Guide to Federal Archives Relating to the Civil War,* 242. See Baker, *Affairs of Party,* 153–56, for a description of Northern Democrats' fears of a standing army.
22. CMSRs of Conrad Gerecht, Co. F, and Luther C. Stouffer, Co. I, 87th Pa.

and, two years later, the 200th Pennsylvania. Clearly, Kidd wanted to serve but had lost interest in the 87th Pennsylvania.[23]

Character flaws have always prompted men to desert. Samuel Sheets was one of the "Company K Six" who refused muster with the 1st Pennsylvania Reserves and enlisted with the 87th. In December, he disappeared for two years until the army seized him attempting to enlist with the 3rd Maryland. Back he went to the Pennsylvania Reserves, which finally got Sam Sheets to complete an enlistment. German-born John Albert Dixon (aka Zimmerman), one of those convicted during the 1858 New Oxford riots, left on a pass from camp near Baltimore and never returned. He married during his escape but deserted his wife when he enlisted in the 4th Ohio Cavalry. Subsequent years included a string of illegal marriages and adulterous affairs that resulted in children born to several women. Obviously, no one could expect commitment to anything from Albert Zimmerman.[24]

Bestowing stripes on a man did not necessarily instill character. David Fox was the first of five sergeants to flee the 87th Pennsylvania's ranks. Two days after his December 1861 departure, he enlisted with the 99th Pennsylvania Infantry as a private, the only rank he ever held in that regiment. True to form, he deserted again but this time had to explain his reasons to a court-martial. Of the four other wayward sergeants in the 87th Pennsylvania, three enlisted with other regiments, and the fifth disappeared without a trace.[25]

One 87th Pennsylvania man's character flaws trumped all others. During the first week of December 1861, newspapers carried his heartbreaking story, an event that likely would have received small press had it occurred a year deeper into the war. It was tragic enough that it still touched some 87th veterans three decades later. In 1892, the *York Gazette* somberly recalled the event as the regiment's first violent death.[26]

Company K's assigned portion of the Northern Central was near the southern end of the line. Baltimore lay just down the tracks, an urban temptress that lured bored young men with siren songs of inexpensive women and *moments musicale* conducted by maestro alcohol. No one was more enticed than

23. *Glory,* Columbia/TriStar production, directed by Edward Zwick, screenplay by Kevin Jarre; Vital Statistics Card File; CMSR of Henry Tyson, Co. G, 87th Pa.; CMSRs and Pension Records of Henry S. Kidd, Co. E, 87th Pa., Co. B, 130th Pa., and Co. H, 200th Pa. Kidd was discharged from the 130th Pennsylvania by surgeon's certificate but completed his enlistment with the 200th.

24. CMSR of Samuel Sheets, Co. F, 87th Pa. Infantry, Co. K, 30th Pa., and 190th Pa; CMSR and Pension Records of John Albert Zimmerman, Co. I, 87th Pa. and 4th Ohio Cav.; CMSR and Pension Records of Jacob Shadle, Co. A, 87th Pa., 34th Ohio, and 36th Ohio.

25. CMSRs of all men of the 87th Pa.

26. *Hanover Citizen,* Dec. 5, 1861; *Democratic Press,* Dec. 6, 1861; *Baltimore County Advocate,* Dec. 19, 1861; *York Gazette,* Feb. 25, 1892.

Pvt. Benjamin Franklin Snyder, a man whose resistance level for liquor and women was well known to stand between nil and zero. November 29 was Snyder's second wedding anniversary, but it was unlikely he was celebrating. His marriage to Phebe Flinn had been the "shotgun" variety, and they do not appear in the 1860 census living together, although they had been together long enough during 1861 to make Phebe pregnant with their second child. Three of her brothers served with Company C, including Richmond Flinn, Snyder's boyhood pal and drinking buddy. Snyder instead opted to pass his army days with Company K. He had spent his anniversary building foundations for winter barracks but had enough energy left for a "French leave" and convinced two cronies to go along.[27]

That evening, Cpl. Daniel Heinrich Laumaster, commanding a guard post at the southernmost point within the regiment's responsibility, spotted Company K's three revelers crossing the bridge on their way into Baltimore. He did not attempt to stop them or check for valid passes. Hours later, two of them staggered back, grizzled veterans of one or more city watering holes. Laumaster noted that Benjamin Snyder's was the missing face.[28]

Morning came and with it a crew of excited railroad workers who informed Laumaster they had passed a dead soldier down the tracks. The corporal raced a squad to investigate and came upon a scene he wished he had never witnessed. A uniformed man lay across the rails, face crushed, brains oozing out the back of his skull, an arm and leg each smashed to a bloody pulp. A foot lay a short distance from the leg to which it had once been attached. The corpse's face was mangled beyond recognition, but Benjamin Snyder was the name that logically came to mind. They sent word to Company K at the Relay House.[29]

Capt. John Albright responded with first lieutenant and doctor John Edwin McIlvain. The doctor-lieutenant studied the mangled corpse and pro-

27. Pension Records of Benjamin Snyder, Co. K, 87th Pa., depositions of John Albright, May 19, 1882, Thomas Paley, May 16, 1882, Richmond Flinn, May 17, 1882, and statement of Phebe Flinn Snyder; Pension Records of Richmond Flinn, Co. C, 87th Pa., statement of William Bird; U.S. Census, 1850–1860, Pennsylvania, York County. Benjamin Snyder lived with and/or worked for William Shaw, as did brother-in-law and 87th comrade, Samuel Flinn. Benjamin and Phebe Snyder's first child, Ida, was born Feb. 8, 1860.

28. Pension Records of Benjamin Snyder, depositions of Daniel H. Laumaster and Henry Billmyer, May 19, 1882. Laumaster recalled that the two men with Snyder were Henry Billmyer and Billmyer's brother-in-law, Henry Stratemeier. Billmyer denied it, claiming he avoided Snyder and Stratemeier because they were "drinking men."

29. Pension Records of Benjamin Snyder, depositions of John Albright and Daniel H. Laumaster, May 19, 1882; Gunnarsson, *Northern Central*, 15, 48. Relay House in this instance was the connection point for the Union Bridge spur line, not the better-known Relay House on the Baltimore and Ohio line south of Baltimore.

nounced that it was certainly Benjamin Snyder. Not only was Snyder the only man missing from the company, McIlvain concluded, but the uniform and the corpse's height and body build perfectly matched Snyder's. With that pronouncement, those who accompanied the two officers knew "right away" that they were witnessing Benjamin Snyder's gory remains. They carted the body to Company K headquarters, covered it to frustrate the morbidly curious, and soon sent it home to an allegedly grieving widow.[30]

Phebe Snyder put her husband's remains to rest on a hilltop cemetery by a rural southern York County church and soon applied for a widow's pension. The story became even more tragic after Washington denied her application because her husband died while absent without leave.[31]

Sad the story was but with one serious flaw: The man crushed to death by a Northern Central Railway train on the morning of November 30, 1861, was not Benjamin Snyder.

The truth remained hidden from the world for a century until a family researcher began searching for an ancestor named Benjamin Taylor, an 1863 draftee into the 149th Pennsylvania Infantry who had served as both "Snyder" and "Schneider." "Snyder" is an Anglicized version of the German name "Schneider," but many translated "Schneider" directly into the English equivalent of "tailor" and shifted the spelling to "Taylor." This Benjamin Snyder permanently changed his name to Taylor and settled in Jefferson County after the war, married, and fathered eight children. Time and a successful life granted him pillar-of-community status, and he lived out his old age on a military pension.

The researcher uncovered early-twentieth-century Jefferson County newspapers that revealed Taylor's visit to his hometown in York County, the first, it claimed, since he had left there many years before. That drew the researcher into a conversation with a Snyder family member in York County. Comparing notes, they found that Benjamin Snyder and Benjamin Taylor had the same birth dates, parents' and guardian's names, and both came from sparsely populated Brogueville. They were obviously the same man.[32]

---

30. CMSR of John E. McIlvain, Co. K, 87th Pa.; Pension Records of Benjamin Snyder, depositions of John Albright, Franklin Ginter, and Henry Billmyer, May 19, 1882. Newspapers published contradictory details on the accident. *Hanover Citizen*, Dec. 5, 1861, said Snyder had a pass to Baltimore and "attempted to jump upon some of the outward-bound trains" and lost a foot. *York Democratic Press*, Dec. 6, 1861, reported that Snyder had fallen asleep on the tracks and lost both feet. *Baltimore County Advocate*, Dec. 7 and 19, 1861, claimed Snyder lost his left foot and right arm and put him into the *78th* Pennsylvania.

31. Card Records of Headstone Contracts and U.S. Soldiers; U.S. Census, 1900, Pennsylvania, York County, Hellam Township.

32. Pension Records of Benjamin Taylor, Co. F, 149th Pennsylvania Infantry.

We can never know why Snyder-Taylor abandoned his York County family. He apparently never related the incident because his descendants were shocked when they uncovered the event. His York County relatives also may not have known of his furtive escape. At least one of his sisters did not because she ordered a military headstone installed on his bogus grave a quarter century after the war. Following his desertion, he did not go far from York because he was drafted and enrolled with the 149th Pennsylvania in Carlisle under his real name. There is one revealing peek into his motives for deserting the army and his family: Not only was Benjamin Snyder's wife pregnant the night he faked his death, so was his lady friend Mary Bauman.[33]

The incident raises many questions, but one above all screams for an answer: If Benjamin Snyder does not lie beneath the York County grave marker bearing his name, who does? John McIlvain testified he had used the unique nature of the uniform to identify Snyder's body, plausible since uniforms at that early part of the war were not standardized. That means the victim was probably wearing Snyder's uniform. It is doubtful that Snyder happened on an unlucky soul just crushed by a train. Re-dressing a mangled corpse would have left telltale signs. It is also unlikely that he found a dead man, dressed him in his uniform, and placed him on the rails so the next train rendered identification impossible. The victim would had to have been of similar height and build, and Snyder was above average height. The ultimate question is, was he so desperate to escape his libido-driven conundrum that he committed murder to supply a double?

What is clear is that Benjamin Snyder successfully evaded a situation that was no one's responsibility but his. Only he could know how much his conscience bothered him.

Desertion after Second Winchester

The second battle of Winchester, June 13–15, 1863, nearly destroyed the 87th Pennsylvania, inflicting more than 40 percent of the total casualties it suffered during nearly four years of existence. On the good side, the overwhelming

---

33. Card Records of Headstone Contracts and U.S. Soldiers; U.S. Census, 1900, Pennsylvania, York County, Hellam Township. Susanna Snyder Shaw likely ordered the tombstone. Pension Records of Benjamin Snyder, deposition of Richmond Flinn, May 17, 1882; Snyder family lore courtesy Sam Snyder, descendant of Benjamin and Mary Bauman's bastard son, William Lemuel Snyder. The family contends that the Flinn brothers learned that Benjamin had been two-timing their sister and threatened to make his life miserable. Richmond Flinn did not attend Snyder's "funeral."

majority of casualties were those taken prisoner. Johnston Hastings "Jack" Skelly, "Jennie" Wade's alleged paramour, was among those few captured who did not escape with his life. The Winchester prisoner count included 293 87th Pennsylvania men out of roughly 4,000 captured, the overwhelming majority within a short period at Carter's Woods in the early morning of June 15.[34]

Confederate guards corralled many of the Union boys in the Winchester fort they had labored so long to build. In a few days, they were on a five-day, ration-scarce walk to the railhead at Staunton, Virginia, where they boarded a train for Richmond. On June 25, the train screeched to a halt in the Confederate capital and disgorged its Yankee cargo. Their destination was a tobacco warehouse once leased by merchants from that most Yankee of states, Maine. When the war began, Confederate authorities gave Luther and George Libby forty-eight hours to vacate and then installed bars in the windows to transform the brick structure into Libby Prison.[35]

Most captives were initially processed at Libby. Officers remained there and many from the 87th Pennsylvania were still looking at Libby's walls or those of another Southern prison when the calendar changed to 1865. After completing search and identification, guards herded enlisted men upstream to newly reopened Belle Isle to pass their days on the island's one flat section of land. The lucky ones got a ragged tent while others slept on the open ground without a blanket. Most of the 87th men who were captured at Winchester saw freedom no later than August, but some remained as late as October, fortunate to earn parole just before the near halt of prisoner exchanges damned them to the coldest Virginia winter in decades.[36]

Prison camp gave the boys from York a lot of time to think, and they had a lot on their minds. After he had driven the Federals from Winchester, Robert E. Lee continued north into Pennsylvania. The 87th Pennsylvanians

34. Federal Muster Rolls, Report of the Organization and Proceedings of the 87th Regiment Pennsylvania Volunteers. This report claimed 263 men and officers were captured at Carter's Woods. Service records generally do not list exact times of capture, so this number is nearly accurate. Prowell, *87th Pennsylvania*, 224, claimed only "about 200" men were captured at Winchester. CMSR of Johnston H. Skelly; Pension Records of Forest W. McElroy, Co. F, 87th Pa., deposition of William Thomas Ziegler. Ziegler was captured at Hancock, Maryland, one of many men taken prisoner away from the field of battle throughout June 15.

35. Sandra V. Parker, *Richmond's Civil War Prisons*, 9; "Libby Prison," Richmond Civil War Centennial Committee, 1961–1965, www.censusdiggins.com/prison_libby.html (accessed Apr. 11, 2004). Luther Libby still had a lease on the warehouse but left Richmond.

36. CMSRs of all men of the 87th Pa.; Pension Records of John W. Kipp, Co. A, 87th Pa., deposition of John W. Kipp, Dec. 15, 1868; *O.R.*, Henry W. Halleck, Summary of military operations, Nov. 15, 1863, ser. 2, 6:523–24, Benjamin F. Butler to E. M. Stanton, Nov. 18, 1863, ser. 2, 6:532–34. Decades later, some veterans only recalled their short stay in the more notorious Libby Prison even though they spent weeks on Belle Isle. Prisoner exchanges broke down in 1863 primarily due to Southern reluctance to treat black prisoners of war as equals.

soon heard that York had surrendered and the Wrightsville-Columbia Bridge lay in charred ruin. News of the battle of Gettysburg especially distressed the men in companies F and I. Were loved ones safe? Were their worldly possessions in Rebel hands? Would they return home to a land eviscerated by war?

Weeks passed before prisoner exchanges began. By the time they arrived at Camp Parole in Annapolis, Maryland, most men were physically ill and desperate to see home. They asked for furloughs, but authorities refused to grant leave to men they might have to call back to duty at any time. Many just skedaddled then, such as Pvt. Ephraim Coble, who deserted because he was in "enfeebled condition" after Belle Isle and "anxious to see his friends." As did many others, he returned to Camp Parole on his own. Other men approached camp officers to plead their cases and heard that if they were not soldier enough to get home on their own, they would have to remain. With this wink-and-nod approval, even obedient soldiers deserted. Long before the last 87th man arrived at Camp Parole, it was common knowledge that no one would suffer punishment as long as he did not stay beyond his exchange date. The trick was knowing when to return.[37]

Pvt. Henry Shultz, the underage lad who had defied his father to enlist, failed to learn the trick. He insisted that Capt. Vincent C. S. Eckert told him to go home and that he would inform Private Shultz when it was time to return. By then, the army had rid itself of Eckert, so Shultz bided his illegal vacation time waiting for word that never came. An arresting officer came instead, and Shultz's explanation did not fly with him. He remained in custody until January 25, 1864, when Lt. Robert A. Daniel obtained his release.[38]

Cpl. William F. Spayd and Pvt. Thomas Updegrove claimed the army listed them as killed in action, and they wanted to assure their mothers they were safe. Updegrove met his mother in Baltimore, so she knew early on that her son was breathing, but he continued on to Harrisburg and ultimate arrest. Spayd ended up in the guardhouse at Fort McHenry but escaped punishment thanks to his former captain, the tormented Jacob Detwiler.[39]

---

37. CMSR of Ephraim Coble, Co. H, 87th Pa.; Bookmark, R&P 661042, application for removal of desertion charge, c. 1900; Capt. R. M. Henderson to the Adjutant General's Office, Aug. 11, 1863, PA AGO, General Correspondence; Frank Geise to George Hay, July 15, 1863, George Hay Kain III Collection.

38. CMSR and Pension Records of Henry Shultz, Co. G, 87th Pa.

39. CMSR and Pension Records of Thomas Updegrove, Co. B, 87th Pa.; CMSRs of William F. Spayd and John Gallagher, Co. B, and William F. Zorger, Co. A, 87th Pa.; Jacob Detwiler to Commandant, Fort McHenry, Aug. 27, 1863, Federal Muster Rolls.

Pvt. Stephen McKinley Wilson arrived at Camp Parole and saw so many men suffering with malarial fevers that he begged for a furlough to escape the deadly environment. Denied, he went home anyway. Home cooking improved his health somewhat, so he started back for the regiment on foot, getting as far as Shrewsbury before his body forced him to rest at Noah Ruhl's house. Wilson related that tale twenty years after the war, but it was a lie. He never returned to the regiment because he was in jail. While home, he teamed up with a boyhood chum for a weeklong crime spree that soon had him convicted on two counts each of horse stealing and larceny. The misdemeanors earned him sixty days in York County Prison. The felonies landed him in Philadelphia's dreaded Eastern States Penitentiary for two three-year terms of solitary confinement and hard labor. The York County legal system was slow to communicate this fact to the army, and Wilson's status remained "missing in action" until April 1864.[40]

Pvt. Paul Mosebaugh told another incredulous story about his illegal trip home. That July, he arrived home sans furlough and bearing a self-diagnosis of "unfit for duty." He claimed that his father insisted he go to a friend's house in the country where he could better recuperate. On the assumption that authorities treated deserters arrested in civilian garb more harshly, he professed to have worn his uniform "constantly." That September, his sister paid a visit to his rural hideout to advise him that the army had ordered him back to duty, so he accompanied her home to retrieve the uniform his mother had washed. Mosebaugh never explained why or how the army sent orders to a deserter whose whereabouts they did not know or how he constantly wore the uniform his mother was washing miles away. When he went out to buy new shoestrings, a constable nabbed him. Pleas that he was already on his way back to camp failed to sway an officer eager to collect the thirty-dollar fee for collaring a deserter.[41]

Sgt. Benjamin Franklin Frick took off for home "on a French" immediately after the paymaster visited Camp Parole. Relieved to see all his friends safe and sound, he started back and dutifully reported to the Baltimore provost

40. CMSR of Stephen M. Wilson, Co. D, 87th Pa.; Stephen M. Wilson to J. C. Kelton, date unknown, Bookmark, Enlisted Branch, 4947-D-1884; York County Court Docket, 1860–1865; York County Sheriff's Office, Jail-Prisoner Boarding Record, 1863–1871. Daniel Overlander was Wilson's partner in crime. Overlander left York County Prison on bail and five days later enlisted with Co. B, 209th Pa. There is no further mention of him in York County court or prison records.

41. CMSR and Pension Records of Paul Mosebaugh, Co. E, 87th Pa., statement of Feb. 7, 1884. The War Department lifted the desertion charge, and Mosebaugh got his pension. Lonn, *Desertion,* 165–82. Initially, the government paid a finder's fee of $30.00 for the capture of a deserter but reduced that early in the war to $5.00 from which the agent had to pay expenses. Naturally, the capture of deserters went nearly to zero, so the fee reverted to $30.00.

marshal, who promptly slapped him in the guardhouse. After three hours behind bars, Frick explained the situation to the major in charge and got a break. He returned to Annapolis with pass in hand and wrote, "Bully for the major!" in his diary. Thanks to the charitable major, Frick's military records do not mention desertion.[42]

Pvt. William Harman Lutz was one of those rare individuals whose health was relatively good when he deserted Camp Parole but whose trip home destroyed his effectiveness as a soldier. When Lutz's southern York County friends heard about his return, they decided a celebration was in order and took possession of a carpenter shop near the William Ream farm for "a little apple butter frolic." They soon had the joint jumping, music courtesy of fiddler Bill Lutz, good times bolstered by the contents of liquor bottles whose subsequent empty condition came through no small effort on Lutz's part. When the party broke up, the staggering fiddler realized he could not make it home in his condition. That was no problem. The Reams had been friends since boyhood, and a son and three of Bill Ream's brothers were 87th Pennsylvania comrades. Lutz climbed into the hayloft to snatch a night's sleep.[43]

At dawn, as he did every day, Bill Ream headed to the barn to feed his livestock. This day, a strange sight greeted him: a blood-filled impression in the thick manure carpet and dark red rivulets on the stone wall next to it. Seeing nothing but the expected animal life, he went outside to search and saw a man trudging up the hill from the creek. It took him a moment to recognize Bill Lutz. A disgusting blood and manure stew dripped from his head onto his shirt. Ream asked what happened, but Lutz only knew that he had awakened on the barn floor with a head the size of a watermelon. By best guess, he rose during the night to relieve himself, fell through the hayloft, and smacked his head against the stone wall on the way down. He lay for hours in the fetid mattress and awoke so insensible that he had to crawl on all fours down to the creek to wash.[44]

The Reams cleaned up Lutz as best they could and that afternoon took him to a doctor, who picked a thumbnail-sized piece of bone from his skull. Thoughts of returning to duty vanished until September when the provost

42. Diary of Benjamin F. Frick, ms. 30065, YCHT; CMSR of Benjamin F. Frick, Co. A, 87th Pa.
43. Pension Records of William Lutz, Adam Ream, Eli Ream (1), Eli Ream (2), and Peter Ream, Co. C, 87th Pa. Lutz told the pension examiner that he had fallen while on his way back to the regiment but did not mention the party and heavy drinking that had preceded his accident.
44. Pension Records of William Lutz, depositions of William Lutz, June 5, 1894, and William Ream, June 6, 1894.

came calling and whisked him back to the regiment whatever his condition may have been. Surgeons, however, sent him straight to a hospital, and Bill Lutz never returned to active duty.[45]

The army was less forgiving of officers. At Winchester, Surgeon William Francis McCurdy was working at the Taylor Hotel hospital when the Rebel army marched into town. While bands played "The Bonnie Blue Flag" and Southern soldiers cheered the ladies of Winchester, McCurdy doctored until it was time to become just another prisoner of war. He had entered the army reportedly tilting the scales at 180 pounds but walked out of Libby Prison in late November a 115-pound wreck. A month later, he failed to return from a furlough, and the provost began searching Baltimore for him. They found him stumbling down a street, talking to himself, lost and unable to recall the name of his hotel. The army denied his resignation and sent him home with a dishonorable discharge.[46]

These are but a few stories about the 150 men of the 87th Pennsylvania captured at Winchester who walked away from the regiment without permission. A minimum of 33 returned either to serve little or no subsequent active role or to receive medical discharges. Unlike Bill Lutz, most had those conditions when they departed Camp Parole. Three of these men did not have to worry about the duty the army had waiting. Their Winchester experience killed them.[47]

Service records reveal only 22 post-Winchester deserters returning under arrest. A luckless Henry Clay Spangler made it all the way back to Virginia but not quite to the regiment when authorities arrested him. Eli Forrer and Valentine Myers were the only ones of this group to be court-martialed. In Forrer's case, that was understandable because he was still absent nine months after Winchester. Myers, however, acted no more egregiously than 149 others and less so than many. It is not without meaning that both men were members of Company H. Of those who returned on their own, none was court-martialed, including George Washington Ford, who should have been. Ford had deserted in May 1862 and returned under President Lincoln's amnesty proclamation a year later. A second illegal departure should have

45. Pension Records of William Lutz, deposition of William Lutz, June 5, 1894; Letters Received 1863–1864, Provost Marshal General's Bureau, 15th District of Pennsylvania, RG-110, box 46, NARA. Lutz was arrested Sept. 23, 1863.

46. CMSR and Pension Records of William F. McCurdy, Assistant Surgeon, 87th Pa., deposition of John Grover. McCurdy was also diagnosed with syphilis. Cornelia Peake McDonald, *A Woman's Civil War: A Diary with Reminiscences of the War from March 1862*.

47. CMSRs of all men of the 87th Pa.

been enough to put him before a court-martial, but he was a member of Company F, not H.[48]

Extant accounts make it clear that most of these men did not consider themselves deserters and were bent on returning, at least when they left Camp Parole. Decades later, many applied for pensions and were stunned when the Interior Department denied their claims because of unresolved desertion charges. While it is possible that some of these old men were feigning ignorance, it is unlikely they all were. In almost every case, for those who applied and who had honorably completed military service in some regiment, the War Department altered "desertion" to "absent without leave." The men got their pensions but only after a delay in the application process.[49]

The army did not forgive the seven 87th Pennsylvania men who had escaped capture at Winchester and then deserted. All of them stood before a court-martial, albeit sentences were not severe. Tom Crowl was one of them. A month after his escape from Winchester, his little piece of the 87th Pennsylvania was camped near Hagerstown, Maryland, little more than a day's hike over Cactoctin Mountain from Adams County. Another day or two of walking could get a fellow home. The enticement was too strong for him to resist.[50]

Tom spent what was probably an enjoyable two months at home until he turned himself over—he claimed—to two York police officers. After he had spent two days in the local jail, the provost took him on the standard south-central Pennsylvania deserter's prison tour: Carlisle's guardhouse, on to Camp Curtin for a day, and down the Northern Central to Baltimore, where Tom had an experience rare for a white man: He spent a night in a slave pen.[51]

The next night in Fort McHenry's guardhouse was a memorable and frightening one, an event he described to his sister.

> There we met with a very hard crowd. In the evening they took every damned thing we had a bout us and they took two blankets and done

48. CMSRs of George W. Ford, Co. F, Valentine Myers and Eli Forrer, Co. H, and Henry C. Spangler, Co. K, 87th Pa. There is no court-martial transcript in the National Archives for either Myers or Forrer, so any court-martial that may have transpired likely occurred at the regimental level.

49. Pension Records of all members of the 87th Pa.

50. CMSRs of all members of the 87th Pa.; Courts-Martial of George Long, Alburtus Ilgenfritz, and Thomas O. Crowl, all LL-1507. A perusal of court-martial group LL-1507 at the National Archives reveals many men from a variety of regiments who deserted for the same reasons as Tom.

51. Pension Records of Paul Mosebaugh, Co. E, 87th Pa. Mosebaugh described the same path of returning to the regiment. "Slave pen" was Tom Crowl's description.

what they cauled aniciate [initiate]. There would a bout ten take hold
of these blankets and put you in and toss you up a bout thirty feet in
the air in order to shake the things out of your pockets. They took every
damned thing I had.[52]

After a stay at Camp Distribution, Alexandria, Virginia, Tom arrived at
Culpeper, Virginia, with only the clothes on his body. The army informed
him that they had no clue where the 87th Pennsylvania was and sent him
back to Alexandria for eight more days of jail time while they searched. They
eventually found the regiment and returned Tom to Culpeper, where he wrote
a letter to his sister from the 3rd Division guardhouse.

"I do not know what the punishment will be but I supose it will be pretty
rough. Perhaps it may be death. If it is so I have only to die for a damed
negrow lover abe Lincoln. Dam his black soul. [If] I have to die I hope I will
and can haunt him till he closes his eyes and then I suppose hell will be our
doom."[53]

Tom had nothing to fear but damage to his pocketbook. The court-martial
settled on forfeiting his one hundred dollar bounty and all pay due and serving at half pay for the next six months.[54]

Sentences varied greatly for deserters even under similar circumstances.
The army inflicted public humiliation on Henry Armprister, as described
previously. Deserter David McCreary, whose postwar acts of violence demonstrated his lack of character, followed in the disgraced Armprister's footsteps
shortly afterward. For virtually identical offenses, however, courts-martial issued only fines and mere completion of missed service time to George S.
Markle and Benjamin Minnich. After Minnich took a bullet at the third
battle of Winchester, the army even returned his lost pay and bounty. These
quixotic sentences suggest that courts had decided the outcomes before trials
began.[55]

52. Thomas O. Crowl to his sister, Nov. 5, 1863, CWMC.

53. Ibid.

54. Ibid.; Court-Martial, Thomas O. Crowl, LL-1507. As a private, Crowl was paid $13.00
each month.

55. Courts-martial of Henry Armprister (LL-1507), David McCreary (LL-1508), and George S.
Markle; CMSR of Benjamin Minnich, Co. E, 87th Pa.; *York Gazette,* Oct. 16, 1866; *Democratic
Press,* Oct. 19 and 26, 1866; *True Democrat,* Oct. 23 and 30 and Nov. 2, 1866; and *Nashua and
Hillsborough Co. (N.H.) Advertiser,* May 22, 1873. On Oct. 10, 1866, McCreary knifed and nearly
killed former 87th comrade Joshua Daniel "Jesse" Diehl, who himself was later jailed in New
Hampshire for manslaughter.

Other Desertion Stories

One type of deserter universally felt the brunt of disdain: the man who fled during battle while comrades stood firm. Fortunately, the 87th had few such examples of overt cowardice and none at Winchester except for Vincent C. S. Eckert, although his fellow officers' fight to gain him an honorable discharge suggests the possibility of extenuating circumstances. Pvt. Franklin Dittenhaffer, on the other hand, ran from the field during the battle of Monocacy in July 1864, and no one in the 87th Pennsylvania ever saw him again. Nine months later and many miles from York, he collected a handsome bounty for enlisting with the 103rd Pennsylvania. He made no mention of the 87th Pennsylvania during his pension application process, and the government never found out. The deserter got his pension.[56]

Alexander Nauss was another documented deserter who received better treatment than he deserved. While in line charging up a hill at the battle of the Wilderness, he suddenly decided that the regiment needed water and that he was the only man who could fetch it. Nauss went all the way to Baltimore for water and was still there when arrested two months later. Col. John W. Schall presided at his court-martial, which may be why the court sentenced him only to make up missing time and lose pay and bounty. If Nauss did not kiss John Schall's boots beforehand, he should have afterward for saving him from a possible death sentence.[57]

Lt. James Hersh described Pvt. Daniel Heltzel as a man "so much afraid that he can't be kept in front [and] some way or other will make his way to the rear." He evoked pity, not scorn, from Hersh, but it is doubtful that his comrades viewed him as compassionately. Heltzel wiped away any animus when Rebels took him prisoner at Monocacy, and he died in captivity.[58]

Pvt. George Ambrose Warner offers the best-documented example of how 87th Pennsylvania men treated a comrade who deserted under fire. Sadly for him, he may have been innocent. Described as a "jerky and nervous" fellow from a family with a reputation for losing their tempers, the company may

56. CMSR of Franklin Dittenhaffer, Co. D, 87th Pa.; Pension Records of Franklin Dittenhaffer, Co. H, 103rd Pa.; Book Records of Union Volunteer Organizations, 103rd Pa., Descriptive Books, Independent Companies, RG-94, vol. 3 of 8. Dittenhaffer enlisted with the 103rd Pennsylvania March 28, 1865, in Greensburg, Washington County, the company's only York County man. He lied about his age, as he had with the 87th Pennsylvania. One hundred other York County men served with the 103rd, so his chances of discovery were high.

57. CMSR of Alexander Nauss, Co. B, 87th Pa.; Court-Martial, Alexander Nauss, LL-2439.

58. James Hersh to his mother, June 9, 1864, courtesy Walter Powell; CMSR and Pension Records of Daniel Heltzel, Co. I, 87th Pa. Heltzel died in Danville Prison.

have been waiting for him to do something out of line. At Mine Run, it happened.

On that freezing morning of November 30, 1863, the regiment waited to begin a charge that surely marked the last moments on Earth for many of them. The commanding general ordered the assault several times only to postpone it, building tension to the breaking point. With each delay, Capt. James Adair suspected Company F was shrinking and finally ordered 1st Sgt. John Henry Sheads to call roll. Sure enough, silence was the response to several names, George Warner's among them. To the relief of all, the generals called off the foolish charge. When the regiment fell back about 11:00 A.M., Company F found Warner a mile and a half in the rear cradling a bloodstained hand and insisting that the enemy shot him while he was serving picket duty.[59]

To a man, Company F knew that Warner had not been on the picket line. That had been Company K's job. He had vanished from Company F's position long before any retreat order arrived. Within earshot of all nearby, Captain Adair accused Warner of injuring himself to escape battle. Years later, former lieutenant William Baker called Warner "a shirk and a coward," a harsh opinion that may have been unfair. Another Gettysburg man, a veteran of the 138th Pennsylvania on the front line November 30, insisted that he had seen Warner there and saw him emerge bloody-handed from the woods. The skirmish line was not where Warner was supposed to have been, but it meant he had not bolted to the rear and that the enemy actually had shot him. Adding to strength of denial was the fact that not one Company F witness remembered seeing the powder burns on his hand that would have betrayed a self-inflicted wound.[60]

Trouble followed Warner home on his medical furlough after Mine Run. Neighbor George Willard kicked Warner's dog, causing Warner to fly into a rage. The situation became so tense that Willard rushed into his house and grabbed a pistol. Warner saw him coming, picked up a brick, and was ready to throw when a bullet tore through his arm. While a neighbor woman bandaged his wound, Warner quipped, "I have been shot twice, once for my country and once for my dog."[61]

59. Pension Records of George A. Warner, depositions of William Sheads, Oct. 1, 1890, and Feb. 4, 1891, and Mary J. Sheads, Feb. 4, 1891.

60. Pension Records of George A. Warner, depositions of John H. Sheads, Feb. 4, 1891, William Baker, Oct. 9, 1891, and Marcus J. Hamilton, Nov. 23, 1891. James Adair, lacking definitive evidence to the contrary, reported Warner as wounded. With one exception, no pension witness said anything good about Warner. Late in life, he flipped his story when he insisted that he had been with Company F when wounded and that his injury occurred after the order to retreat came.

61. Ibid.

Guilty or not, Warner returned to his life in Gettysburg and outlived every local Company F man except one. Whatever his reputation, he had no compunction about joining postwar reunions. What is clear from the story is what the men of the 87th Pennsylvania thought about a man they assumed had shirked his duty under fire.

Elias Bair tied with Benjamin Snyder for the regiment's most unique desertion, but totally different events motivated Bair's escapade. He was the only 87th Pennsylvania man taken prisoner at the battle of Harris Farm, a side event of the battle of Spotsylvania in May 1864. Already a veteran of Belle Isle Prison, Bair now had a rendezvous with Andersonville, a place where quick paroles were rare and death by starvation was an hourly event. By November, he was well on his way to adding his name to the death roll when Col. John G. O'Neil of the 10th Tennessee Infantry stopped by on a recruiting mission. O'Neil allegedly had convinced 250 Yankees from Millen Prison to join the Confederate army and was looking for more recruits. Switching sides meant fresh clothing, cleaner surroundings, and improved diet but at the price of becoming a traitor to the United States. Interested, healthy men at Andersonville were few and far between, but eight inmates agreed to go with O'Neil. Elias Bair was one of them.[62]

Their new comrades did not trust these turncoat Yankees and kept them unarmed and under guard on the belief that they had enlisted only to escape Andersonville. Their cynicism was wise. The first opportunity for these Yankee "Johnnys" to prove themselves came on December 28, 1864, near Egypt Station, Mississippi. Armed with muskets issued only the day before, some of them demonstrated the real reason they had joined the Confederate army when they slipped into Federal lines to report their circumstances and provide intelligence on Southern strength. They promised their group would offer no resistance if attacked, but there is disagreement about whether they did. One report said the turncoats threw down their weapons and surrendered. Another contended they killed twenty-three and wounded seventy-four Union men, surrendering only after being charged and overwhelmed.[63]

Whatever the truth of Egypt Station, the turncoats soon saw the inside of another prison—Yankee, this time—in Alton, Illinois. Confederate prison-

62. Diary of George Blotcher; CMSRs and Pension Records of Elias Bear, Co. E, 87th Pa., and 10th Tennessee, C.S.A.; William Marvel, *Andersonville: The Last Depot*, 223. Elias Bear's name may have been "Eli S. Bear"

63. *O.R.*, Report of John W. Noble, Jan. 13, 1865, ser. 2, 8:125–26, Maj. A. A. Hosmer to the Secretary of War, May 13, 1865, ser. 2, 8:554. Some sources deny there were Yankees in the 10th Tennessee, but Elias Bair's pension with the 87th Pennsylvania and his service record in the 10th Tennessee prove otherwise. See *Tennesseans in the Civil War*, excerpt available at www.tngenweb.org /civilwar/csainf/csa10.html (accessed Dec. 2, 2003).

ers would eventually be released, but Union traitors might have a date with a hangman's noose. The army saw an opportunity to turn these flip-flop Yankees to its advantage and made them an offer: join the 5th U.S. Infantry and fight Indians on the frontier or take your chances as prisoners of war. Elias Bair was among those who accepted the loaded offer, however reluctantly. Later, as a member of the 21st U.S. Infantry, Bare, as he then spelled his name, fought in the Arizona Indian wars. Somehow he managed to obtain an honorable discharge from the 87th Pennsylvania, a miracle of prestidigitation that someone claimed was due to his "fraudulent representations." The Interior Department agreed and revoked Bair's Civil War pension.[64]

Bair was one 87th Pennsylvania deserter who did not return to York County. In 1907, he lived in Maricopa County, Arizona, and later moved to the Soldiers' Home in Los Angeles, California, where he is bured in the national cemetery. Perhaps his experience in the Indian wars had made a westerner out of him. More likely, he needed to live out his life away from accusing eyes and wagging tongues.[65]

64. CMSR and Pension Records of Elias Bear. The "fraudulent representations" comment is in Bear's service records. See Marvel, *Andersonville,* 223–24, 300, for the similar escapades of Hiram Jepperson, Co. C, 5th N.H.

65. Pension Records of Elias Bear.

Chapter 8

Mine Run, Military Law, and Andrew B. Smith

November 20, 1863, was a happy day in the 87th Pennsylvania's camp. The paymaster had arrived, a visit that seldom occurred with the regularity army recruiters had promised. Men whipped off letters, stuffed envelopes with the cash so desperately needed at home, and put their mail into the care of regimental postmaster Edward Reinecker Herr, a two-year veteran then eight months shy of birthday number eighteen.[1]

Tom Crowl, still in the guardhouse for his desertion, wrote his family, explaining the need for haste.

> We have some very hard times at the preasant a count of fixing up for a battle. There will be a fight hear now in a few days and I expect it will be a very hard one. Lees army is laying on the south side of the Rapredan [Rapidan] River and entrenching them selves to a great extent . . . It is raining very hard and a good sign for three or four days. I supose we will have to move in a few days and it will be towards the enemy.[2]

---

1. David Gilbert Myers to his parents, Nov. 20, 1863, Pension Records of David G. Myers; Edward Rudy to his father, Nov. 20, 1863, Pension Records of Edward T. Rudy, Co. B, 87th Pa.; John Henry Martz to his mother, Nov. 21, 1863, Pension Records of John Martz, Co. I, 87th Pa.; Edgar Monroe Ruhl to his mother, Nov. 21, 1863, Pension Records of Edgar M. Ruhl, Co. D, 87th Pa.; CMSR and Pension Records of Edward R. Herr, Co. I, 87th Pa. Disclosure: Andrew Bentz Smith is the author's great granduncle. No one in the family, author included, had heard of him prior to uncovering the story told here.
2. Thomas O. Crowl to his family, Nov. 21, 1863, CWMC.

Gen. George G. Meade wanted to drive a wedge between the separated flanks of the Confederate army and defeat each singly before winter forced a hiatus from fighting. The potential was there for another great battle between Meade's Army of the Potomac and Lee's Army of Northern Virginia. To motivate his men, Meade had a telegram read announcing Ulysses S. Grant's victory at Chattanooga, Tennessee, in hopes his army would rise to the level of its western counterpart. Instead, continuing rain forced a forty-eight-hour delay in plans.[3]

The Army of the Potomac finally moved on November 26, but the wheels fell off Meade's wagon almost immediately. The Federals had to cross the Rapidan River to reach the enemy, which meant that the engineers first had to build bridges. The assembly technique is still in use: float pontoon boats and attach planks to them, one by one, until they span the river. Basic construction exercise that it was, 3rd Corps engineers made a classic blunder when they forgot to consider the recent heavy rains and arrived at the swollen Rapidan one pontoon short of reaching the opposite bank. The entire Union 3rd Corps had to wait while the engineers raced back to camp to retrieve another boat. That task finally completed, the artillery started crossing only to illuminate the next foul-up: heavy objects on wheels have difficulty climbing steep, rain-slicked riverbanks. Once more the 3rd Corps waited until the artillery pulled out to find a better crossing point.

After shivering for hours, the 525 remaining men of the 87th Pennsylvania Infantry crossed the Rapidan River on a weaving pontoon bridge and scrambled up the mud-greased embankment. The 3rd Corps plunged into the dense, scrubby woodland known as the Wilderness, an area made famous the year before by the battle of Chancellorsville and awaiting greater infamy under its own name five months hence. James Stahle commanded the regiment while John Schall was away battling a case of diarrhea. Andrew Bentz Smith, mustered as first lieutenant just ten days before, was at the helm of Company H but struggled to keep moving with a bad leg that had plagued him for a year and had grown worse at Belle Isle. Physical ailments would soon become the least of his problems. He was mere hours from falling under the

3. Osceola Lewis, *History of the One Hundred and Thirty-Eighth Regiment Pennsylvania Volunteer Infantry*, 48; Frederick Clark Floyd, *History of the Fortieth (Mozart) Regiment New York Volunteers*, 209; George G. Meade to his wife, Nov. 25, 1863, George Gordon Meade Collection, microform, U.S. Army Military History Institute, Carlisle, Pennsylvania; Circular, Nov. 25, 1863, Army of the Potomac, Special Orders Nov. 1862–Mar 1864, RG-393, Part 1, 606, NARA; Charles L. Peirson, "The Mine Run Affair," *Papers of the Military Historical Society of Massachusetts*, 14:62. James Longstreet's corps was not with the Army of Northern Virginia at Mine Run.

curse that had hovered above Company H for two years. The instrument of his demise would not be shells or .58-caliber bullets but the crushing weight of Civil War politics.[4]

Already-fading hopes of surprising the enemy disintegrated when a portion of the 3rd Corps realized it had gone three miles down the wrong road. The men had little choice but to return to the ford and settle in for an unscheduled overnight stay in brutally cold weather. No one had a tent, and the brass permitted no fires lest they betray presence and strength. By morning, Meade's army was "hardly in fit condition for a protracted struggle."[5]

The two armies stumbled into each other that morning. By 3:00 P.M., battle raged hot as the 87th Pennsylvania's brigade trudged through woodland so thick "you could not see a 100 yards in any direction." The men entered the field and crossed behind the Union line, emerging on the extreme left into the open pastureland of farmer Madison Payne. Their exposed position invited incoming fire, so brigade commander Col. Benjamin Franklin Smith ordered his men to file into position "under the cover of some irregularly shaped small hills." The 87th Pennsylvania anchored the brigade's right flank, which gave Jim Stahle the job of tying his regiment to the left flank of another already engaged on the bank of a ravine. That regiment was the 138th Pennsylvania, one with familiar faces from York and Adams counties, among them John Englebert, the boy who had deserted the 87th Pennsylvania more than two years before.[6]

The boys from York scrambled up the twenty-foot embankment and latched onto the left of the 138th. Once there, they knew they had problems. "The line of my regiment was formed in the shape of a horseshoe in a

4. Field Report, Nov. 26, 1863, Adj. Anthony M. Martin and Lt. Col. James A. Stahle, Federal Muster Rolls, Correspondence; *O.R.,* Report of William H. French, 29/1:735–36, Report of David B. Birney, 29/1:750–52, Report of Gouverneur K. Warren, 29/1:694–95; "Zoo-Zoo" to the *Gettysburg Compiler,* Dec. 14 and 21, 1863, two-part letter dated Dec. 5 and 6, 1863; CMSRs of John W. Schall and Andrew B. Smith, 87th Pa.; Special Order 297, Army of the Potomac, Special Orders, p. 591; diary of John E. Lowrey, 138th Pa., HCWRT. Lowrey, from Franklintown, York County, was mortally wounded Nov. 27 and buried in a garden near Robertson's Tavern at Locust Grove.

5. Lewis, *History of the One Hundred and Thirty-Eighth Pennsylvania,* 50–51; *O.R.,* Report of William H. French, 29/1:735–36, Report of Brig. Gen. Joseph B. Carr, 29/1:777, Report of Lt. Gen. Robert E. Lee, 29/1:825; "Zoo-Zoo" to the *Gettysburg Compiler,* Dec. 14 and 21, letter dated Dec. 5 and 6, 1863.

6. *O.R.,* Report of Benjamin F. Smith, 29/1:783–84, Court-Martial, Andrew B. Smith; CMSR and Pension Records of John Englebert, Co. B, 138th Pa. Northerners called the battle "Locust Grove" for the village a few miles distant that was George Meade's goal. "Orange Grove" was another name, but "Payne's Farm" is appropriate. For other examples of name variations, see *O.R.,* 29/1:730, 753, 779, 798–99, 853, which include the reports of Confederate officers Samuel S. Carroll, Peter Sides, Albert B. Jewett, William A. Ham, and John H. S. Funk.

very exposed situation," James Stahle reported afterward. The regiment had to form on a finger of land that jutted away, then curled back toward the action. Men on the left had to position themselves with their backs to the enemy and their faces in the line of fire from the regiment's right. They could not remain there, but to fall back meant realigning on muddy ground twenty feet below the battlefield. They had no choice and formed as best they could. Andrew Smith took his place "a few paces in the rear of the company."[7]

Rebel forces surged forward until "opposing lines became wrapt in one dense sheet of musketry," a 138th veteran recalled. The pressure built, but the 87th could not see the oncoming Confederates unless they streamed down the valley on their left. The 44th Virginia was in the process of doing the latter. Havoc threatened to reign, but even with the oncoming 44th Virginia, it was not coming from the left.[8]

"Fall back!" an officer in the 138th Pennsylvania shouted on the ridge above. The order meant only to reform a line in the rear and continue fighting, but battle transformed its meaning. The 138th began to break. The colonel screamed orders to stand firm, but no one heard or heeded them if he did. The colonel eventually got his regiment under control but not before chasing his men a good distance into the woods. Not before leaving bare the right flank of the 87th Pennsylvania.

Instinctively, men on the suddenly unprotected right of the 87th Pennsylvania started to inch back, and each one communicated panic to the man on his left that multiplied as a wave of fear swept down the line. The regiment's good order disintegrated like a line of tumbling dominoes. Then, to a man, the 87th Pennsylvania Infantry turned and ran into the woods.[9]

Andrew Smith encountered James Stahle in the woods "some one hundred or two hundred yards to the rear of the line of battle" attempting to rally troops who were showing little interest in fighting. Stahle ordered Smith to assist nearby officers in forming a defensive position. Smith's head swiveled

7. *O.R.,* Order of Battle, 29/1:220, Report of Benjamin F. Smith, 29/1:783–85, Report of John F. Staunton, 29/1:787–88, Report of David B. Birney, 29/1:750–52. General Birney ordered a brigade to cover the gap. Osceola Lewis, *History of the 138th Pennsylvania,* 52; Court-Martial, Orlando C. Farquhar, LL-1369, testimony of Moses M. Granger; Court-Martial, Andrew B. Smith, testimony of Franklin Geise and James A. Stahle and statement of Andrew B. Smith.

8. *O.R.,* Report of J. Warren Keifer, 29/1:781, Reports of Norvell Cobb, John C. Higginbotham, and William A. Witcher, C.S.A., 29/1:855–60; Lewis, *History of the 138th Pennsylvania;* J[ohn] H. Gilson, *Concise History of the One Hundred and Twenty-sixth Regiment, Ohio Volunteer Infantry,* 23.

9. Lewis, *History of the 138th Pennsylvania,* 53–54. The 138th history claims they retreated one hundred yards, but the terrain suggests that estimate may be conservative. Court-Martial, Andrew B. Smith, testimonies of James Stahle and Franklin Geise, and statement of Andrew B. Smith; *O.R.,* Report of John C. Higginbotham, 25th Va., 29/1:857.

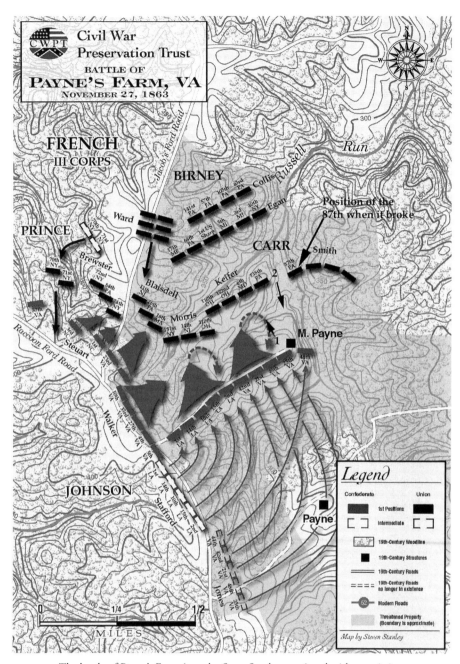

The battle of Payne's Farm (map by Steve Stanley, reprinted with permission
of the Civil War Preservation Trust, additions by the author: numbers
and arrows indicate positions and directions photos were taken).

1. The Union left as viewed from the Confederate right flank. The 138th Pennsylvania lay at the edge of the ravine (center) behind a fence that was there at the time, and more Union forces were in reserve on the distant high ground. Arrows point to the 87th's initial position.

2. This is what the 87th Pennsylvania's right flank saw when they reached higher ground (the arrow in photo 1). The regiment's left flank was virtually in their line of fire. Both distant buildings were built in the twentieth century but stand about where Madison Payne's farm buildings were in 1863 (photos by the author, March 19, 2003).

from side to side, looking for his company. He saw no more than a dozen men from any company and none from his own. Shells screamed in, shattering trees and transforming limbs into spears, sending men scurrying into the bowels of the Wilderness. Smith started into the woods to locate others. Stahle saw him leaving and shouted for him to rally his company.

Smith plunged his sword into its scabbard and shouted back, "My God, Colonel! I have no company any more!"[10]

Smith continued across the brow of a hill and spied Second Lieutenants Charles Henry Stallman and William Henry Lanius with the regimental color-bearer. Smith told them they should gather what men they could and move down to the fence line as Stahle had ordered. The three men managed to gather a group of unorganized soldiers and get back on line near another group of 87th Pennsylvania stragglers who were fighting near the 40th New York. They saw no sign of James Stahle and the rest of the regiment because they had since been ordered to the rear. As many as eighty 87th men remained on line until dark, among them Capt. Solomon Myers, shooting a rifle like a member of the rank and file.[11]

Night fell, and cries of the wounded replaced the crack of musketry. The residue of 87th Pennsylvania men left the battle line to rejoin their regiment. In the darkness of the Virginia Wilderness, on strange ground amidst thousands of soldiers, their haphazard search failed. As they stood in a group talking of what to do next, a soldier passed supporting a wounded comrade. He asked that someone please hold his injured friend while he slaked his thirst. When someone complied, the soldier disappeared into the darkness. Andrew Smith agreed to take the wounded man to the road and point him toward the hospital. The road was farther than Smith thought. By the time they reached it, the wounded man was in no condition to proceed alone, so Smith took him all the way to the hospital. When he returned to where he had left the group, the other men were gone, if he had even returned to the same spot. He located the provost marshal's tent and spoke to 87th comrade Theodore Cress Norris posted there, but Norris could not say where the regiment was. Smith continued to inquire without success until he ran into a squad of 87th men as lost as he, including a few from Company H and the regimental colors. He ordered his motley band to hunker down near the 138th Pennsylvania and 6th Maryland. When those regiments went to the rear at 4:00 A.M., Andrew Smith's lost squad fell in and found the regiment sometime after daylight.[12]

Two nights later, the boys from York might have been tempted to call their situation "hell" except it was much too cold for the devil. Frigid temperatures

10. Court-Martial, Andrew B. Smith, testimonies of Franklin Geise and James A. Stahle.

11. Court-Martial, Andrew B. Smith, testimony of Franklin Geise and statement of Andrew B. Smith; *O.R.,* Report of James A. Stahle, Dec. 3, 1864, 29/1:788; Prowell, *87th Pennsylvania,* 101; *Grand Army Scout and Soldier's Mail,* July 26, 1884, article by G. Norton Galloway.

12. Court-Martial, Andrew B. Smith, statement of Andrew Smith and testimonies of 1st Lt. Theodore Cress Norris, Pvt. George S. Anderson, 1st Lt. William Henry Lanius, and Pvt. John Lewis Ritter. The regiment had fallen back near Maj. Gen. William H. French's headquarters.

robbed men of the ability to speak coherently, and pickets had to change every half hour to avoid frostbite. Men went thirsty because the water froze in their canteens. George Meade had put his army through several maneuvers since the affair at Payne's Farm, but none had brought on a general conflict. "Grapevine telegraph," what a later generation of soldiers would call "scuttlebutt," said it was going to be for real this time. They were going to assault the Confederate line in the morning. Something besides weather concerned them: the sounds of an enemy chopping, building, entrenching, girding itself to withstand an assault. There would be a slaughter with the arrival of the sun. They would be the sheep.[13]

On the morning of November 30, 1863, Jim Stahle followed orders to place his regiment on the first assault line. He sent Company K three hundred yards forward as skirmishers, a trek from which three men never returned, including the Foose brothers. Federal artillery began shelling the Confederate works at 8:00 A.M. while the infantry waited for the order that would plunge them into battle. The order came, was countermanded, reissued, and cancelled once more. Nerves pushed toward the breaking point.[14]

Most military campaigns have at least one signature event, and this was it for the one known as Mine Run. A general, once bursting with confidence that he could carry the day, studied the Southern defensive line laid naked by daylight and knew how wrong he had been. Enemy soldiers had constructed strong works, thick abatis, and formed lines of fire ready to tear apart his flanks. They stood atop the breastworks motioning the Yankees to bring it on. The general told George Meade he would not make this suicidal assault, and Meade agreed. The Army of the Potomac returned to winter quarters at Brandy Station having accomplished nothing. Meade was certain—incorrectly—that he would become the latest in a long line of generals to lose command of the Army of the Potomac for directing another colossal waste of time and life.[15]

13. "Zoo-Zoo" to the *Gettysburg Compiler* Dec. 14 and 21, 1863, letter dated Dec. 5 and 6, 1863. See Martin F. Graham and George F. Skoch, *Mine Run: A Campaign of Lost Opportunities, October 21, 1863–May 1, 1864,* 74–76, for more descriptions of weather conditions on Nov. 29 and 30.

14. CMSRs and Pension Records of Jacob Foose, Matthew Foose, and David Hoffman, Co. K, 87th Pa.; Pension Records of George A. Warner, Co. F, 87th Pa., deposition of John H. Sheads; "Zoo-Zoo" to the *Gettysburg Compiler,* Dec. 14 and 21, 1863, letter dated Dec. 5 and 6, 1863; *O.R., * Report of Benjamin F. Smith, 29/1:785. The 126th Ohio was on the forward line with the 87th Pa.

15. Abatis was an obstacle soldiers built in front of an entrenchment to slow a charging enemy. It was generally constructed of tree branches tied or woven together and, if time permitted, each branch sharpened to make it more formidable. *O.R.,* Report of George G. Meade, 29/1:16, Report of Gouverneur K. Warren, 29/1:698; Graham and Skoch, *Mine Run,* 74–75; George Meade to his wife, Dec. 3, 1863, George Gordon Meade Collection. Gouverneur Kemble Warren was the general who changed his mind.

When the 87th Pennsylvania went into position on the morning of November 30, Andrew B. Smith was not in ranks and had been absent for two days. He reported to Colonel Stahle on December 2 with an explanation that could range anywhere from truth to fabrication. "When I left the ranks it was with the intention of rejoining it in a few minutes but . . . did not succeed in doing so, being too unwell. And after I was able to proceed I commenced my search for the Reg't and did not succeed in finding it until next day about 8 o'clock P.M. when I reported myself to the Lt. Col."[16]

Cowardice may have caused Smith to leave. Then again, he may have been telling the truth. Getting lost in the Wilderness among tens of thousands of soldiers was easy to do. "Too unwell" is all that we can know without uncovering new evidence. James Stahle did not accept the excuse and arrested Smith, who tendered his resignation the next day. Stahle passed it to brigade headquarters.[17]

It was not a good time to be asking favors of brigade commander Benjamin Franklin Smith. The Army of the Potomac was feeling heat for the aborted campaign, and Colonel Smith's performance on November 27 had been especially embarrassing. It had been his portion of the line that broke. Rumor said that only the timely arrival of the 6th Corps salvaged the situation. The rumor was untrue, but perception was reality even before mass media. Benjamin Smith had good excuses prepared: "I had no time to reconnoiter the ground over which I was passing . . . Most of the brigade was thrown in the tangled timber . . . The enemy was moving in heavy columns." His boss was working on a report that used the word *failed* describing Colonel Smith's execution, one that noted how the brigade's low casualty rate did not support any contention of being pressed by the enemy.[18]

If anyone was ever primed to find a scapegoat, Benjamin Smith was it. When the charges against Andrew Smith and his resignation came to hand the evening of December 3, he had one. Colonel Smith's recollection of Lieutenant Smith and the 87th Pennsylvania was fresh. He had endorsed four requests for Andrew Smith's promotion less than two weeks before and was

16. Court-Martial, Andrew B. Smith, statement of Andrew Smith.

17. Special Orders and Endorsements, Benjamin F. Smith, Dec. 3, 1863, Army Records, Army of the Potomac, 3rd Brig., 3rd Div., 3rd Corps, Aug–Dec 1863, vol. 40.

18. George G. Meade to his wife, Dec. 7 and 12, 1863, George Gordon Meade Collection. The *Washington Star* called Meade and his subordinates "hesitating generals." *O.R.,* Report of Joseph B. Carr, Dec. 4, 1863, 29/1:777–78, Report of Benjamin F. Smith, Dec. 3, 1863, 29/1:783–84, Report of Col. Norvell Cobb, C.S.A., 29/1:859–60; William F. Fox, *Regimental Losses in the American Civil War, 1861–1865,* 443–44. The 87th Pennsylvania's division did not suffer heavy losses on the Mine Run campaign. The Confederate attack at Payne's Farm petered out because their line became too extended and night was approaching, not due to the 6th Corps' arrival.

processing charges against two other 87th officers. The 87th Pennsylvania had formed the right of his brigade, and it had broken. No one claimed Andrew Smith was responsible, but he was convenient. Colonel Smith refused Lieutenant Smith's resignation on the technical grounds that it had not included proper documentation from the Ordnance Department. He added a terse order: Andrew Smith was to be "dishonorably discharged the service of the United States for cowardice."[19]

Andrew Bentz Smith's court-martial convened January 14, 1864, at the camp of the 3rd Division, 3rd Army Corps in Brandy Station, Virginia, Col. William Snyder Truex presiding. The court offered one charge—"misbehavior before the enemy"—and two specifications: Smith's so-called desertion on November 27 and his two-day disappearance from November 30 through the evening of December 2. Smith pleaded not guilty to the first specification and to the charge. History lost revealing information when he pled guilty to the second specification, guaranteeing there would be no testimony on where he was or what he did during those two lost days.[20]

Arresting officer James Stahle took the stand first. He agreed with Smith on what had happened November 27, but interpretations differed. Stahle's testimony was potentially damning to himself. When he said that he had "met the lieutenant coming to the rear," that could have meant either he was not with his men in battle or he ran faster than Smith to get to the rear. No one asked the question, although technically it did not matter. The specification against Smith was not that he had left the first line but his alleged refusal to rally men on a second defensive line. Stahle named Robert A. Daniel, Alexander Strickler, John Fahs, and Anthony M. Martin as the diligent few officers who had remained. He did not volunteer the whereabouts of the regiment's other officers or why he had not arrested them. The court asked if any other officer had been missing that day, and Stahle had to say yes. While Capt. Solomon Myers had reported his men the next morning the same as Smith, Stahle said that he did nothing punitive to Myers or anyone else because he "knew the quality of the men and that they had been doing their duty wherever they were." The only coward that day was Andrew Smith, the man Stahle himself had described as a "gentlemanly soldier" who had "done his duty as well as he knew how."[21]

19. Special Orders and Endorsements, Army Records, Army of the Potomac, 3rd Brigade, 3rd Division, 3rd Army Corps, p. 186. Endorsements of Stahle's requests for Smith's promotion occurred Nov. 19 and 20, 1863.

20. Court-Martial, Andrew B. Smith.

21. Ibid., testimony of James Stahle.

Sitting on the court-martial was none other than Solomon Myers. Since he had been just as lost as Smith on November 27 and on the field with him after the regiment broke, Myers should have testified for the defense. What today would be a conflict of interest was not then an issue, nor was the situation unique. In at least two other cases, Solomon Myers testified for the prosecution on the same court-martial on which he was empowered to render a verdict.[22]

Andrew Smith apparently had no legal counsel other than that offered by the judge advocate. Even had he procured an attorney, neither counsel nor the defendant could have asked questions during the trial. Procedure dictated that defendants write down questions and give them to the judge advocate to verbalize. Improvisatory response to testimony was difficult even for an experienced attorney. Nothing better evidences the absence of counsel than Smith's amateurish first question in cross-examination of James Stahle.[23]

"Are you certain that you saw me put my sword in the scabbard and retire?" Stahle said he was certain he had.[24]

The prosecution next called 1st Lt. Theodore Cress Norris, who had been serving with the provost marshal on November 27, and from whom Smith had sought assistance in locating the regiment. His testimony did no damage, proving only that Smith truly had been lost and eager to get back to where he belonged.[25]

But the next witness may have made Andrew Smith shudder when he entered the courtroom. Sgt. Maj. Franklin Geise, still lacking both lieutenant's bars and a reason to feel kindly toward anyone in Company H, was about to testify for the prosecution. If ever a man had an opportunity for revenge, it was Frank Geise. Instead, he delivered a surprise.

James Stahle had sworn under oath that Smith had been "more than usually excited" under fire. When asked to verify Smith's demeanor, Geise probably opened eyes when he testified, "[Smith] was not in the least excited." Stahle had stated that when he had first seen Smith he was in the company of "twenty or thirty men." To the same question, Geise replied, "At the time Lieutenant Colonel Stahle ordered Lieutenant Smith to rally the men I did not see a single man of the company." Stahle had testified that some of his officers had formed a defensive line in the rear and that Smith had refused to take part. When asked if there had been a defensive line formed, Geise said, "There

22. Courts-martial of Alburtus "Bertram" Ilgenfritz and George Long, both LL-1507 and both of Co. E, 87th Pa.
23. Benet, *Treatise,* 65, 112.
24. Court-Martial, Andrew B. Smith, cross-examination of James Stahle.
25. Ibid., testimony of Theodore C. Norris.

was not." On cross-examination, Smith asked Geise when the company and regiment reformed. He replied, "The regiment did not reform until the next morning when Lieutenant Smith and other men who had straggled joined us."[26]

Geise continued challenging Stahle's testimony. Stahle had said the regiment had broken because it had been reforming to the rear at the time the Confederates advanced. Geise's testimony and Smith's subsequent statement to the court agreed that the regiment had held position at Russell Run a short time before the 138th Pennsylvania collapsed. Geise made it clear that after the break on November 27, the regiment had been in chaos, scattered, and without leadership. Company H's most hated man had just contradicted almost all of Lt. Col. James Stahle's testimony.[27]

Smith opened his defense with Pvt. George S. Anderson, who testified that he had been with Smith in line of battle after the regiment bolted. Before that, Anderson had seen Smith talking with William Henry Lanius, Charles Stallman, and the color-bearer, bolstering Smith's claim that he had attempted to rally men back on line. Anderson was also among the group Smith had led back to the regiment in the morning and testified that the lieutenant had done all in his power to organize those lost and find the regiment.

Smith next called William Henry Lanius, who by then had been promoted to first lieutenant. Lanius verified that he had seen Smith in line of battle and that Solomon Myers also had been there. Smith's next questions were obviously intended to establish that not only had he returned to line of battle, but he had ordered Lanius and Stallman to come with him. Lanius's testimony likely came as much a surprise as Frank Geise's but in the opposite direction.

Smith asked, "How near was I to you, and did I say anything to you?"

Lanius said, "I remember of being within five or six feet of him but remember of no words passing between us."

"Do you recollect whether the colors were near us at that place?"

"I do not."

"Have you any recollection of Lieutenant Stallman being there?"

"I have no recollection of his being there at that time."[28]

Smith could only sit and listen to the judge advocate read the written questions and hear Henry Lanius claim loss of memory. Differing interpretations of events or time variances could explain the dichotomy, but so could perjury. If Smith was lying, he was a fool to call a popular officer to the stand knowing

26. Ibid., testimonies of James A. Stahle and Franklin Geise.
27. Ibid., testimony of Franklin Geise.
28. Ibid., testimony of William H. Lanius.

he would present contradictory evidence. George Anderson might have lied to save his commanding officer, but other witnesses verified his testimony. Henry Lanius was from one of York's "better" families and lauded for bravery at Carter's Woods. Only time stood between him and captain's bars. Smith's other witnesses were all privates.[29]

Lanius's testimony should have generated questions for the court to investigate. Either Smith told Lanius and Stallman to rally or he did not; either Stallman was with Lanius at the time and place Smith stated or he was not. Charles Stallman and the color-bearer could have testified one way or the other, but neither man was called to the stand. The army had sent Charles Stallman two hundred miles away to Carlisle on recruiting duty. Smith should have requested Stallman's return or called the color-bearer to the stand, but that would have required legal acumen a twenty-two-year-old saddle-maker from Kralltown clearly did not possess. The court, faced with a long list of cases to adjudicate, went to no lengths to find the truth.[30]

Henry Lanius eventually contradicted his testimony but waited thirty-five years to do it. During George Prowell's research for the regimental history, Lanius related what happened to him just after the regiment broke at Payne's Farm. He clearly remembered how he had been standing on the brow of the hill talking with Charles Stallman exactly as Andrew Smith had described it. The incident had remained fresh in Lanius's memory because while there, he had a brush with death, rendered even more vivid by a macabre joke. A shell fragment severed the strap to Lanius's haversack, and when the pack dropped to the ground, a nearby officer wisecracked how the Rebels had just cut off his base of supplies. If Lanius recalled this after thirty-five years, he certainly had it in his memory just weeks afterward.[31]

In yet another irony, Smith's case struck a sympathetic chord with that other Company H bone of contention, Robert S. Slaymaker, who a month after the trial discussed Smith's court-martial in a letter to a Company H comrade. "You I suppose heard Stahle had him court-martialed for cowardice. But when Stahle came to give in his evidence he had to give it in Smith's favor to save himself from incriminating himself on the same charge." Slaymaker had been present at neither the court-martial nor the battle of Payne's Farm, so he based his opinion on hearsay. Stahle's testimony hardly went "in Smith's favor," but Slaymaker's statement means that the idea of Smith's court-martial

---

29. Ibid., Smith's last witness, John Lewis Ritter, also verified George Anderson's testimony.
30. CMSR of Charles H. Stallman, Co. C, 87th Pa.
31. Prowell, *87th Pennsylvania,* 101.

being a rigged affair had a contemporaneous life that reached all the way to York.[32]

Andrew Smith was not the only 87th man who endured a court-martial for events that occurred during the Mine Run campaign. The others were rank and file tried for absence without leave, all claiming that they had been unable to keep up, and all returning on their own. Separate courts-martial found each man guilty, but none received a severe sentence. Ironically, while waiting for his own trial, Smith had to serve as prosecution witness in the cases of two men against whom he had pressed legitimate desertion charges prior to Mine Run. Even in the court transcripts' cold reflection of events, his testimony seems terse to the point of rudeness. Andrew Smith knew what was going to happen to him and had stopped caring.[33]

Despite Solomon Myers and shaky evidence, the court found Andrew Bentz Smith guilty on all charges and specifications. Military law required only a majority to convict, the ballot kept secret, and the written record of deliberation destroyed. We will likely never know how Myers voted or if he made an effort to salvage Smith's reputation. Myers made only brief mention of the verdict in his diary. Duty forbade him from revealing details, and he did not, even to himself. The court ordered Smith "to be cashiered" but in one way was merciful. They did not make his plight into a public spectacle nor, apparently, did they report it to south-central Pennsylvania's newspapers. Consult the Bates *History of Pennsylvania Volunteers* or Smith's card record in the *Pennsylvania Digital Archives,* and you will see only that his discharge occurred February 13, 1864.[34]

Because Smith pled guilty on the second charge, that verdict was a given, but was it sufficient to cause his dishonorable dismissal? Andrew B. Smith was one of six 87th Pennsylvania officers dishonorably dismissed from the service before June 1864 but the only one who endured a court-martial. In three other cases, fellow officers successfully assisted disgraced comrades in

32. Robert S. Slaymaker to John Myers Griffith, Feb. 16, 1864, Bowman-Griffith Family Papers.

33. Endorsements Sent, 3rd Division, 3rd Army Corps, p. 271; Courts-martial of 87th Pennsylvania men John Vogelsong, William Spayd, Martin Klinedinst, and David McCreary, all LL-1508. Andrew Smith testified in the Klinedinst and Wagner cases.

34. Benet, *Treatise,* 126–28; diary of Solomon Myers; Civil War Veterans' Card File, Pennsylvania State Archives, also available on the Pennsylvania Digital Archives Records Information Access System (ARIAS) at www.digitalarchives.state.pa.us/; Lowry, *Don't Shoot That Boy!* Courts-martial sometimes ordered soldiers' convictions and sentences published in their hometown newspapers. See Robert I. Alotta, *Stop the Evil: A Civil War History of Desertion and Murder* (San Rafael: Presidio Press, 1978), for the study of a Pennsylvania soldier court-martialed for desertion and murder and hanged for his crimes.

obtaining honorable discharges. No record emerged describing assistance for Smith.[35]

Andrew Smith may have been the only 87th Pennsylvania officer court-martialed for cowardice at the battle of Payne's Farm, but he was not the only one under arrest for that charge. Lt. Samuel Saylor also received a recommendation for dishonorable discharge from Col. Benjamin Smith for "misbehavior before the enemy." Like Smith, Saylor submitted his resignation, but his story got lost. While the 3rd Division endorsed his case for general court-martial the same day as Smith's, Saylor never stood before the military bar of justice. Special Order Number 26 forced him out of the army. His service records hint at drunkenness, but Benjamin Smith had said "cowardice," a charge timed so that any causative incident could only have taken place during Mine Run. No document found reveals why he did not face a court-martial, but one possibility stands out: Samuel Saylor was not a member of Company H.[36]

Capt. James Henry Blasser was another officer accused of improper conduct. Benjamin Smith approved Blasser for court-martial the same time as Smith and Saylor, yet after filing charges, the army granted him a ten-day furlough and never followed up with legal proceedings. Blasser was dishonorably dismissed the following May for being absent without leave, but the incident had nothing directly to do with Mine Run. The officer requesting the dismissal of both Saylor and Blasser was James Alanza Stahle, the same man who would later sign a clemency request on Blasser's behalf, something he would never do for Andrew Smith.[37]

35. CMSRs of all members of the 87th Pa. The other five officers dishonorably dismissed were: 1st Lt. Peter Ford (Feb. 22, 1863), Capt. Vincent C. S. Eckert (Aug. 6, 1863), 1st Lt. Samuel Saylor (Jan. 30, 1864), Surgeon William Francis McCurdy (Feb. 24, 1864), and Capt. James Henry Blasser (Mar. 30, 1864). The War Department later granted honorable discharges to Ford, Eckert, and Blasser.

36. Army Records, Charges and Specifications, Army of the Potomac, 3rd Division, 3rd Army Corps, 3rd Division, p. 267, and Letters Sent, p. 187. Consolidated Weekly Report of Aggregate Strength, Federal Muster Rolls; Special Orders and Endorsements, pp. 30, 33, and Endorsements Sent, vol. 89, p. 33. Samuel Saylor resigned Dec. 5, 1863, but Benjamin Smith refused it for the same technical reason he used for Andrew Smith. Saylor offered a second resignation January 27, 1864, and received a discharge January 30, 1864. James Stahle reported an honorable discharge for Saylor, but Saylor's service records say otherwise. He later served with the 149th Pennsylvania.

37. Register of Charges and Specifications, Army Records, pp. 260–61 and 264–65; CMSR of James H. Blasser; Army Records, Register of Letters Received and Endorsements Sent, vol. 42, pp. 328–29, furlough approved Feb. 27, 1864; James A. Stahle to Gen. Lorenzo Howard, Mar. 30, 1864, re: case of James Blasser, Bookmark, S774 v.s. 1864. The first attempt to press charges against James Blasser came back from division headquarters with unspecified corrections, but a second recommended court-martial. Records do not detail specific charges against Blasser.

Was James Stahle getting even with the troubling Company H, or was he succumbing to pressure from above? If the former, it went against all extant descriptions of him. George Blotcher, never hesitant to state the negative, considered Stahle a man who "had a good heart and a kind word for every soldier." Two known incidents support that. Shortly after the Smith case, Stahle met Privates Daniel Bonge and Alexander "Baldy" Bushdorf at a Baltimore train station as they headed home on veteran furloughs. They informed the colonel they were going to desert to join the navy and sought his advice. According to the two men, Stahle told them there would be no consequences so long as they served well, and events confirm it. They served as sailors under their real names but never faced justice. The second example occurred after the war, when Stahle assisted in the pension process of John Henry "Barber" Wolf, who had deserted the regiment not once, but twice.[38]

Andrew Bentz Smith returned to York County and the saddle business he had left behind in 1861, married, and fathered three children. The leg that troubled him in the army deteriorated steadily, undermining his health so severely that he had to cease working and move his family into his parents' home. On June 1875, a doctor amputated the diseased leg in hopes of saving his life, but it was too late. Smith died two weeks later at the age of thirty-four, a casualty of the Civil War as surely as if he had been shot dead in battle.[39]

38. Recollections of George Blotcher; CMSRs and Pension Records of Daniel Bonge and Alexander Bushdorf, Co. A, 87th Pa. and U.S. Navy; CMSR and Pension Records of John H. Wolf, Co. K, 87th Pa; Bookmark Eak6 1868.

39. Pension Records of Andrew B. Smith; Tax Rolls, York County, Franklin Township, 1866–1869, York County Archives, York, Pennsylvania. Taxes for the Andrew Smith family were $.52 in 1867, $.53 in 1869, and nothing the other two years. His widow had to send their children to a soldiers' orphanage. The Smiths' Adams County home, where they moved in the late 1860s, is now the East Berlin Fish and Game Association.

Chapter 9

South-Central
Pennsylvania and Race

Court cases made an indelible mark on the slavery debate, and none is better remembered than *Dred Scott v. John F. A. Sandford*. It was not, however, the first Supreme Court decision to address the issue of state versus federal rights with regard to slavery. Those same philosophies smashed head-on a decade before Dred Scott filed his first brief, and it all began in York County.[1]

In 1832, Maryland slave Margaret Morgan escaped with her children into York County. Five years later, her owner hired Edward Prigg to bring her back. Federal law said he could, but Pennsylvania law said that Morgan was free once she reached her twenty-eighth birthday. Once in Pennsylvania, she conceived and delivered another child, who, by state law, was free regardless of Morgan's status. Prigg approached York County justice Thomas Henderson for a warrant to seize the runaway, and Henderson dispatched a constable to make the arrest. By the time Morgan and her children stood before him, Henderson, for reasons not explained, had changed his mind and refused to continue the case. Without completed legal proceedings, Prigg did not have the authority to remove Morgan from the state. From Pennsylvania's perspective, he could never have license to remove the freeborn child, a fact

---

1. *Dred Scott v. Sandford,* in *Documents of American History,* 339–45; see Dred Scott Case, Touro College, Jacob D. Fuchsberg Law Center, www.tourolaw.edu/patch/Scott/; see also Africans in America, http://www.pbs.org/wgbh/aia/part4/4h2933t.html, and Supreme Court Historical Society, http://www.landmarkcases.org/dredscott/home.html (all sites accessed April–May 2004.

that may have motivated Judge Henderson's change of attitude. That did not stop Prigg from returning to Maryland with all captives in tow.[2]

York County issued a warrant for Prigg's arrest on a charge of kidnapping. He arrived for trial with an attorney supplied by the state of Maryland. A York County jury found him guilty based on three Pennsylvania laws that outlawed the kidnapping of any Negro or mulatto "to be kept . . . as a slave or servant for life." The verdict withstood the scrutiny of Pennsylvania's Supreme Court, but, by an eight to one majority, the United States Supreme Court reversed the decision, declaring Pennsylvania's laws unconstitutional and, by inference, all similar northern statutes. Sadly for Margaret Morgan, the Constitution made it painfully clear that she and all other runaways must be returned to slavery.[3]

On the surface, the Prigg decision seemed to resolve the legal dichotomy of federal versus state authority with regard to the return of escaped slaves. In reality, it muddied already murky political waters and offered something for everyone to hate. Abolitionists mourned the invalidation of states' personal-liberty laws, but slaveholders became even more infuriated by the Court's decree that the federal government must assume the sole responsibility of enforcing federal fugitive slave laws. This ruling effectively gave abolitionists a victory because runaways were less likely to be caught once reaching a free state when local law enforcement no longer had responsibility to detain them. Unintentionally, the Court had issued little more than another slavery compromise that only postponed the inevitable. The short-term result was implementation of the draconian Fugitive Slave Law of 1850 that helped increase sectional tensions to the breaking point.

The Prigg case was neither the only nor the first example of York County standing by its black residents. In 1825, slave catchers entered the state and seized a runaway named George. Not content with his capture, they soon had his blood streaming onto York County soil. The community could have ignored the situation, especially after the slavers smugly flashed a reward no-

2. Quarter Sessions Docket 1839–1844, York County, pp. 72–90, 221. Margaret Morgan's age is unknown, as is the number of her children, but she had at least one child before entering Pennsylvania. U.S. Census, 1840–1850, Harford County, Maryland. The 1850 census does not list the fifty-nine-year-old Edward Prigg as a slaveholder, but he did have one black servant. *York Republican,* Dec. 19, 1860.

3. Quarter Sessions Docket 1839–1844, York County, pp. 72–90. U.S. Constitution, art. 4, sec. 2, states, "No person held to service or Labour in one state . . . escaping into another, shall . . . be discharged from such Service or Labour, but shall be delivered up on Claim of the Party to whom such Service or Labour may be due." This section was removed by the Thirteenth Amendment.

tice for the runaway's return. Instead, the vigilantes found themselves in jail for assault and battery and rioting.[4]

York's most famous racially based case came to be known as the Conspiracy of 1803. It is significant because it reveals York's relatively balanced, nonviolent attitude toward black residents more than a half century before the Civil War.

When a stable burned down, the incident garnered no more than a small newspaper story in a time when wooden construction and open-flame lighting made fires common events. A week later, another blaze consumed three buildings and threatened the town with immolation, and citizens quelled another the following day before it did much damage. After five fires in nine days, the ugly word *arson* appeared in print. That became a certainty a week later when another barn went alight and took four buildings with it. The *York Recorder* used its largest type for the frightening headline "FIRE!" A reward for the arrest of the perpetrators started at two hundred, then jumped to three hundred dollars. Citizen groups patrolled streets, and the governor sent militia to assist. Terror continued until authorities arrested one of the perpetrators and the story rolled out. York County's jail soon held nineteen blacks and two whites on charges of arson. The near-immolation of the town stemmed from revenge-seeking after two blacks had been convicted—whether rightly or wrongly is uncertain—for attempting to poison their mistress.[5]

It was the perfect opportunity for the "white power structure," to use a modern-day term, to send these black troublemakers and their white supporters to prison or do worse. The event, however, took place in York, Pennsylvania, not the Tidewater region of Virginia, where twenty-eight years later angry whites would hang innocent blacks in the wake of Nat Turner's brutal slave revolt. No mobs surrounded York's jailhouse demanding vigilante justice, and no gangs dragged people from their homes in the dark of night. Of the twenty-one accused, the court released thirteen with stipulations and found two black men not guilty. Several blacks who were found guilty nonetheless walked free after posting bonds and pledging good behavior for a specified time, a sentence then commonly issued by the York court. Six defendants received harsh sentences in Eastern States Penitentiary, but their crimes had endangered lives and threatened the existence of an entire town. Rather than excoriate abolitionists over the issue, the *York Recorder* only admonished the local Abolition Society not to damage good principles with extremist behavior.[6]

4. James McClure, *Almost Forgotten: A Glimpse at Black History in York County, Pa.,* 18. The judge was Walter Franklin, uncle of York's own Maj. Gen. William Buel Franklin.
5. *York Recorder,* Mar. 2, 9, 16, and 23, 1803; Court Docket 1802–1806, York County, pp. 73–77. Only one defendant had slave status.
6. Quarter Sessions Docket, 1802–1806, York County, pp. 73–77; *York Recorder,* May 25, 1803.

Segregation came to York County in the twentieth century as it did to most northern communities, but the 1860 census shows that it was not common then. In rural Shrewsbury, for example, the homes of two white Low families surrounded the black James Simms house. The black Wilson family lived between the white Deaver and Brooks households in rural Fawn Township. In York Borough, the black Harris, Butler, and Robinson families lived in an otherwise white neighborhood. Wrightsville had the county's largest percentage of black residents thanks to employment opportunities generated by mining and river industries. Wrightsville's black families tended to live in clusters but not in one area of town.[7]

Adams County had a much smaller black population than York, and most lived in and around Gettysburg. Every student of the battle of Gettysburg knows about Abraham Bryan, the black farmer whose home still stands on Cemetery Ridge. They may not have noted that the black Craig family lived next door to the president of Pennsylvania (Gettysburg) College, that the black Fagen family resided between the white Bollinger and Thompson households, or that the shared home of the black Little and Redding families was sandwiched between the white Lightner and Paxton homesteads.[8]

Evidence points to nineteenth-century south-central Pennsylvania being a relatively good place for blacks to live by the standards of the time. While historian Jean Baker postulates how "generations of white Northerners saw blacks in a single public role—as victims of white mobs," that rabble was noticeably absent in York and Adams counties even during the Conspiracy of 1803. While the area hardly offered utopian islands of racial equality— the *York Democratic Press* alone proves otherwise—its history does not indicate harsh treatment of black residents. York Borough supported a separate black infrastructure, including a taxpayer-funded school for black children that opened in 1837. When someone torched the African Meeting House in 1841, York's chief burgess offered one hundred dollars for information leading to the perpetrator's arrest. Area newspapers continued to run ads for the return of indentured white servants long after reward notices for runaway slaves

7. U.S. Census, 1860, Pennsylvania, York County, Wrightsville. Wrightsville's black population was 13.6 percent of 1,156 residents.

8. University of Virginia Library Web site, Geostat Center, Collections, Historical Census Browser, *fisher.lib.virginia.edu/collections/stats/histcensus/* (accessed Feb. 2004). In 1850, Adams County had 25,426 white and 555 black residents; York County had 56,325 white and 1,125 blacks. In 1860, Adams had 27,532 whites and 474 blacks, and York had 66,834 whites and 1,366 blacks. U.S. Census, 1860, Pennsylvania, York and Adams counties; *Adams County History,* vol. 9, 2003, compiled by Larry Bolin; William A. Frassanito, *Early Photography at Gettysburg,* 229–30. Abram Bryan's home was headquarters for Union general Alexander Hays and in direct line of fire during Pickett's Charge.

vanished from print. York and Adams counties had always been places blacks risked their lives to reach, not escape. While the area had characteristics of the segregated society that later generations came to deem unacceptable, it did something the South avoided: it recognized blacks as worthy of at least some dignity.[9]

Reverend Hosea Easton, a black activist when the more notable Frederick Douglass was but a child, wrote, "The mechanical shops, stores, and school-rooms are all too small for the Negro's entrance as a man." He was right as often as not, but he should have come to York Borough and seen its black machinists, restaurant owners, blacksmiths, photographers, and schoolteach-ers. Personal service was not a job unique to blacks. Of 302 York Borough residents listing servant, washerwoman, coachman, or housekeeper as their occupation in the 1860 census, 263 were white. In Gettysburg, whites held 38 of 51 such jobs. Five of those men joined the 87th Pennsylvania.[10]

Barber was largely a black man's profession but one that provided steady income and growth potential. William C. Goodridge not only became York's most successful black man, he prospered more than most whites. The grand-son of a slave woman once owned by a signer of the Declaration of Inde-pendence, Goodridge maintained a running newspaper ad that bragged how he gave a shave "with a light hand and a keen razor." He must have lived up to the self-billing because he parlayed a tonsorial career into a flourishing entrepreneurship. By the 1850s, he owned a fleet of railcars and had erected a building on the town square that was York Borough's tallest. The Worth Infantry rented space there and always referred to their landlord as "*Mr. Goodridge.*"

It may have been no secret that the Goodridge house was a "baggage stop" on the Underground Railroad. Rumor said that he had used his building on the town square to hide an escapee from John Brown's Harpers Ferry raid. Harriet Tubman allegedly led fugitive groups through town, and it is likely that William Goodridge aided her. Runaways who entered York County often continued an odyssey that took them to Wrightsville and Columbia before heading to points north. Goodridge was the man with the railcars to facilitate freedom's flight.[11]

9. Baker, *Affairs of Party,* 245; *York Gazette,* July 20–Aug. 10, 1841, advertised a five-dollar reward for the return of a fifteen-year-old white indentured servant.
10. Baker, *Affairs of Party,* 245, citing Rev. Hosea Easton (1799–1837); U.S. Census, 1860, Penn-sylvania, York County, York Borough, and Adams County, Gettysburg; CMSRs and Pension Records, where applicable, of all men of the 87th Pennsylvania.
11. Prowell, *History of York County,* 1:595. Osborn Perry Anderson allegedly was the refugee from John Brown's raid. Worth Infantry; Smedley, *History of the Underground Railroad,* 46; Switala, *Un-derground Railroad,* 26–27, 100–110, 121–23. York constable William Yokum, code name "William

William and Evalina Goodridge raised a fine family in York, among them Glenalvin, a teacher in York's colored school and owner-operator of a photographic studio. The good life crashed around Glenalvin when a white woman accused him of rape, a charge that evoked gasps even from radical abolitionists. Evidence against him was classic he said/she said, and the alleged victim had waited three months to report the supposed incident. Her reported appetite for granting sexual favors, whether true or not, gave her a less-than-upright reputation and further eroded her credibility. When Glenalvin's attorney presented evidence that he had been elsewhere at the time of the alleged rape, a verdict of not guilty seemed assured.[12]

It is doubtful that any new evidence will arise to reveal the truth, but one lasting theory holds that Glenalvin was a victim of attempted extortion. If that was true, the Goodridge family refused to pay because the woman made good her threat to press charges. In spite of flimsy supporting evidence, the jury believed her, and the court denied a motion for retrial. The door of Eastern States Penitentiary slammed behind Glenalvin Goodridge. Ahead lay five years of hard labor and inadequate diet.[13]

York could have forgotten about Glenalvin. Instead, eighty-nine white York community leaders petitioned Governor Andrew Curtin to grant him a pardon, and some made pleas in individual letters. York County's district attorney told Curtin, "I have my doubts whether the same evidence would have convicted any white man in the county of the offense charged." He did not explain why he tried the case if he believed that.[14]

The pleas worked. Governor Curtin granted the pardon. Clearly, York's white leaders were not the type to lead mobs against their black neighbors.

The 87th Pennsylvania on Race

There is so little written evidence of 87th Pennsylvania men's views on racial matters that making a broad statement about their attitudes is prejudicial.

Penn," was an antebellum conductor on the Underground Railroad. Gettysburg and York Springs were Adams County's active Underground Railroad centers.

12. V. K. Keesey to Andrew G. Curtin, Dec. 1864, Records of the Department of State, RG-26, Clemency Files, Pennsylvania State Archives, Harrisburg, Pennsylvania. The alleged victim was Mary E. Smith.

13. Clemency Files; Court Docket, Aug. 1862 Session, p. 316; copies in file 21832, YCHT.

14. District Attorney W. C. Chapman to Andrew G. Curtin, Clemency Files. A copy of the court docket shows W. C. Chapman's name at the bottom of the findings. Clemency Files. The "Democrat" comment was written by G. H. Bressely with the concurrence of Judge Robert Fisher, Dr. Edward Pentz, and Chief Burgess David E. Small. Goodridge Family File 2360, YCHT; *York Gazette,* Dec. 27, 1864. Glenalvin J. Goodridge died of tuberculosis in 1867 in Minnesota.

Doubtless, few if any whites thought of black people as equals, including radical abolitionists. Life's experience in a race-and-class-oriented society had given them little reason to think any other way. Original material quoted in this book reflects some of those feelings. However unacceptable its content may be by today's standards, their words represent the opinions of just seven men: three newspaper editors already cited and four 87th Pennsylvania men referenced further on in this chapter.

Extant letters of 87th Pennsylvanians seldom mention race. Some men, however, imbedded racial references in their writing and no doubt their conversations, too. Swapping tales about alleged female conquests, Tom Crowl told a friend about the woeful dating possibilities during his first days in the army. "We have lots of girls down here," he wrote, "but they have black faces and what wight girls there is is that dambd dumb that they wipe ther arse with the same hand they cut there bread with." Teasing friends in Company H, Tom wrote in the same letter, "Jefferson Martin he is as cross as the Devil. I think that he will die some of these days with the mad fitts and we will have a negrow furnal [funeral] of him and J[ohn] Aker for the preacher." While stationed in New Creek during the summer of 1862, Tom wrote his family, "We thought it was very hot at Baltimore but it is twict as hot here. We are getting burned with the sun that we hardly know one an nother. We are all most as black as negros now."[15]

Two years later, the racial banter was not frivolous when Tom bragged to a friend about a sexual dalliance with a black woman. "I done a damned foolish trick," he wrote. "I married a wench down here as black as hell having chalk enough in her eyes to mark all creation and fat enough in her lips to grease my boots. Lord but wont I do greesing." Clearly, the "marriage" was a one-time financial arrangement that demonstrated how Tom's sexual needs overcame his low esteem of black women.[16]

Sgt. Maj. Frank Geise, Company H's object of scorn, was one of five 87th Pennsylvania men who accepted commissions with colored regiments. Geise trained black troops at Philadelphia's Camp William Penn but never led troops of any color into battle. Instead, the army took advantage of his education and assigned him as assistant provost marshal at Hilton Head, South Carolina. While there, he wrote a letter to George Hay describing the goings-on.[17]

15. Thomas O. Crowl to William Fetrow, Nov. 4, 1861, and to his aunt and uncle, June 26, 1862, Pattee; U.S. Census, 1860, Pennsylvania, York County. Jefferson Martin and John M. Aker, Co. H, were, respectively, residents of Monaghan and Warrington townships, York County.

16. Thomas O. Crowl to William Fetrow, Apr. 21, 1864, CWMC.

17. The other four 87th Pennsylvania men to serve in colored units were Jacob Detwiler, Co. B (53rd U.S.C.T.), Benjamin Franklin Frick, Co. A (39th U.S.C.T.), Samuel Fitz Nevin, Co. C (42nd U.S.C.T.), and Jesse Duncan Synder, Co. E (115th U.S.C.T.).

We are told that "the darkest hour is just before the dawn of day," and truly, Colonel, it seems to be so from what I see in this department, for it is nigger! Nigger!! Nigger!!! Everywhere—in the field; on the wharf; in the town; in the army; in the Quartermaster's Dept. All the work seems done by contrabands. Villages of contrabands numbering from 2 to 3000 have sprung up as if by magic on these islands since the commencement of this war.[18]

Geise's letter illustrates how even educated men freely used *nigger*. Indeed, Abraham Lincoln had used it sparingly during his famous antebellum debates with Stephen A. Douglas. So, too, did Frederick Douglass, on one occasion with near-jocularity in a letter to a white associate. However much the word inflames nerves today, it had yet to reach fire-starter status in 1864, and Frank Geise had not experienced a decades-long, televised civil rights movement to teach him otherwise. He was only punning within the context of his time and experience. While no white officer had to view black troops as equals to command them, it is doubtful that he would have applied for service in a colored regiment if he had held venomous racial views. His letter does not inherently express racial hatred however much it would if written a century later. Indeed, in the next sentence of his letter was: "On the whole I like this place much better than the Army of the Potomac."[19]

Abraham Lincoln's issuance of his Emancipation Proclamation raised some soldiers' ire. One 87th Pennsylvania man, an ardent Democrat, responding negatively but rationally, wrote "I do not believe the President's emancipation proclamation was called for and on the whole of its proceedings I do not think it will work out the good results which had been promised by it."[20]

Tom Crowl's response was far more emotional.

This Nigrow freedom is what is playing hell. This is a roug[h] thing that will destroy our army. We never enlisted to fight for Nigrows and that is all they are at now. We heared last evning that old Abe Lincoln was dead and I hope to god it is true and in hell as far as Virginia [i]s long. He is the very man that is a going to destroy our country. The nigrows in this place is that damned sassy that a white man can hardly walk the streets and our old General [Milroy] says that he thinks more of the Blacks then his soldiers. But if we get into battle he will stand a good chance of getting his infernal old gray head shot off. I will stay in the army till

18. Frank Geise to George Hay, Sept. 8, 1864, George Hay Kain III Collection.
19. Lincoln-Douglas Debates, www.nps.gov/liho/debate1.htm (accessed Feb. 18, 2004); William S. McFeely, *Frederick Douglass* (New York: W. W. Norton, 1991), 131; Frank Geise to George Hay, Sept. 8, 1864, George Hay Kain III Collection.
20. "F" to the *York Republican,* Apr. 1, 1863, letter dated Mar. 12, 1863.

I can get a chance then I mean to make tracks and the war ma[y] go to hell for me. I never intend to stay here and risk my life for these damned nigers.[21]

Tom Crowl's negative reaction was not only a response to the proclamation itself but to issues surrounding their new division commander, Brig. Gen. Robert Huston Milroy. The general was an abolitionist determined to enforce the Emancipation Proclamation when it went into effect January 1, 1863, although he was not above pressing "idle contrabands" into unpaid service repairing the Valley Pike. Milroy's confrontation with one of his brigade commanders sparked hot reaction.[22]

Frenchman Gustave Paul Cluseret, veteran of wars in Europe and Africa, had come to the United States to serve on the staff of Gen. George B. McClellan. A good performance at the battle of Cross Keys earned him a brevet promotion to brigadier general in spite of his poor command of spoken English. By November, he was serving in Robert Milroy's division in command of the 87th Pennsylvania's brigade. Milroy, the hard-bitten American abolitionist, soon clashed with Cluseret, the hard-bitten French mercenary. When two hardheaded men clash, the one in charge usually wins, and Cluseret found himself under arrest.[23]

Democratic newspapers related the causative event with melodramatic flare.

> [Cluseret] was not willing to allow his baggage and ambulance train to be filled with niggers, and the equipage left behind, and his soldiers obliged to walk, many of them with no covering for the feet. An eye witness related to me that on one occasion the train was filled with three "sable brothers," whilst the necessaries were left behind, and the soldiers on foot were obliged to guard the train and "free Americans," and that many of the soldiers were so worn out that they could scarcely drag their weary bodies along, and because the Brigadier remonstrated with the higher authorities [Milroy] and would and could not say *Amen*, he was suddenly relieved of his command.[24]

21. Thomas O. Crowl to his sister, Jan. 28, 1863, CWMC.

22. Warner, *Generals in Blue,* 326. Milroy received a major general's rank Mar. 10, 1863, to date Nov. 29, 1862.

23. *York Republican,* Apr. 13, 1863; *Appleton's Cyclopedia of American Biography,* edited by James Grant Wilson and John Fiske (New York: D. Appleton & Co., 1887–1889); Anthony M. Martin to George Hay, Nov. 23, 1862, George Hay Kain III Collection; Charles E. Skelly to his mother, Dec. 4, 1862, Pension Records of Charles E. Skelly.

24. *Gettysburg Compiler,* Mar. 16, 1863, citing the *Harrisburg Patriot and Union,* Mar. 7, 1863, emphasis in original; *Appleton's Cyclopedia.* Cluseret resigned and became strongly anti-Republican, his bitterness likely stemming from this incident.

The confrontation of generals threw accelerant onto a smoldering situation. One 87th man took Lincoln's proclamation and the Milroy-Cluseret incident as proof that Democrats had been right all along, that Republicans truly were plotting to swamp the North with cheap black labor to line their pockets. He vented to his brother.

> Milroy is here and he is bound not to leave without having all of us killed. He is a black harted Ablistionest. He has bill[s] pasted up here saying freedom to slaves. Well he has freed all of the Nigars as far as he went. He thinks more of one nigar then he dose of 10 soldiers for I have seen poor soldiers marching and hardly able to walk and the god dam nigars riding in wagons. I can tell you brother that I am tired soldering and nearly all the soldiers that's in our army on account of the freeing of nigars. I thought when I enlisted that I was in a good cause but now I see plain that I am fighting for nothing but the god dam nigars. So it is nothing but a money making nigar war. Don't be surprised if you here of the half of our army deserting after the[y] get paid. Thair is 5 months pay due to us. What would you say if I would leave? Do you think that I would break my oath? Have not the United States broken thair oaths?[25]

Racist as the men's words are, their bitterness sprouted from roots more complex than bigotry. None of the writers had volunteered to spend three years putting his life in danger to free slaves. Now, suddenly, a presidential edict thrust a new cause upon them that they, for right or wrong, did not want. That the Emancipation Proclamation was militarily pragmatic and morally beneficial was a viewpoint difficult for cold and ill, hungry and homesick soldiers to grasp, especially in the midst of a war that seemingly had stagnated into endlessness. If it were true that Milroy had ordered military equipment left behind and forced injured soldiers to walk to transport freed slaves, soldiers' anger would be understandable. Whether or not Milroy actually did that, the men believed he had.

Physical and emotional exhaustion was just as much to blame for their animus. A captain of the regiment, a supposed "ardent Lincoln supporter," admitted under condition of anonymity that "the men were not only tired out, but played out, and are looking anxiously for the end." Small wonder. When the regiment reached Winchester on Christmas Eve 1862, it had struggled three of the previous four months over the mountains of (West) Virginia

---

25. Unknown to his brother, Jan. 23, 1863, YCHT. Whoever donated the letter to the historical society tore off the signature, but the author was clearly an 87th Pennsylvania man, given the references in his letter. Efforts to match the handwriting to other 87th authors failed, and stated personal information is inadequate to determine the author's identity.

chasing an enemy that always eluded them. The baggage train lagged so far behind that for sixteen nights the men survived on half rations and slept on bare ground, each man with only a blanket for warmth, assuming he had one. After the bleakest Christmas of their lives, the boys from York faced an indeterminate time living in a Southern town whose citizens gave stray dogs more respect than they did Yankees. And General Milroy shut off furloughs. Rations were "the worst [they] ever got. Nothing but crackers, coffee and salt pork." Buying food was out of the question because it sold at exorbitant prices, not that high prices mattered. As one correspondent put it, "The pay-masters are all dead as far as we know." They would remain so for a total of eight months. Even if the men could tolerate being broke, it meant families at home were not receiving the financial assistance they needed to survive.[26]

Adding to their psychological burden was the growing Northern peace movement called "Copperheadism" that wanted to end the war now and re-turn to antebellum conditions. The *Harrisburg Patriot and Union* took up the peace banner and published a letter from an alleged member of the 87th Pennsylvania, probably 1st Lt. William Frederick Frank, a letter clearly de-signed to undercut morale. The *Gettysburg Compiler* excerpted it but notably omitted those parts italicized here.

> *Although the regiment has never participated in a battle . . . no men in the service will hail with more joy the day that will discharge them than the Eighty-seventh Pennsylvania, and* I feel firmly convinced that could as honest expression of opinion be had to day, three-fourths of the reg-iment would be found on the side of the "Union as it was" and the "Constitution as it is."[27]

26. *Gettysburg Compiler,* Mar. 16, 1863; John Jacobs to his father, Jan. 27, 1863, Pension Records of John Jacobs, Co. G, 87th Pa.; William B. Ramsey to unknown, probably April 1863, Pension Records of William Ramsey, Co. B, 87th Pa.; Charles Skelly to his mother, April 16, 1863, Pension Records of Charles E. Skelly, Co. F, 87th Pa.; Thomas O. Crowl to his sister, Feb. 16, 1863; "Zoo-Zoo" to the *Gettysburg Compiler,* Jan. 12, 1863, letter dated Jan. 5, 1863; "G. W." (possibly George Ambrose Warner) to the *Star and Banner,* Jan. 15, 1863, letter dated Jan. 2, 1863; "Old Regular" to the *Star and Banner,* Feb. 5, 1863, letter dated Jan. 26, 1863; "Anon" to the *Gettysburg Compiler,* Apr. 30, 1863, letter dated Mar. 24, 1863; Special Order 8, Jan. 15, 1863, Special Orders, 8th Army Corps, Apr. 1862–June 1863. For Winchester's hostility toward Yankees, see McDonald, *Woman's Civil War;* "Diary of Mrs. Hugh Lee"; Margaretta Barton Colt, *Defend the Valley: A Shenandoah Family in the Civil War* (New York: Orion Books, 1994); and Sarah Catherine "Kate" Sperry, "Sur-render? Never Surrender: July 13, 1861–December 3, 1865." Pretty Kate Sperry mesmerized men like the fictional Scarlett O'Hara and witnessed the 87th Pennsylvania's first battle on June 12, 1863, at Newtown, Virginia. Seeing the trap the Yankees had set, she frantically tried to wave off the oblivious Confederate cavalry, but they misinterpreted and waved back.
27. *Gettysburg Compiler,* Mar. 16, 1863, reprint from *Harrisburg Patriot and Union,* Mar. 7, 1863.

However much *Compiler* editor Henry John Stahle disliked the war, obviously he was disinclined to undermine the 87th Pennsylvania and the brother who served with it.

Democrats divided between war and peace factions: War Democrats versus Copperheads. Like the antiwar movements that later undermined efforts in Vietnam and Iraq, the Civil War's Copperhead movement called for an immediate peace, as if the two armies would simply go home and the political and social turmoil that caused the war would vanish with the last wisp of gunsmoke. Many soldiers knew that an unresolved end to the fighting would have rendered pointless all the sacrifices they had made. Enduring hellish circumstances for a cause is one thing. Enduring it for nothing, as proven by many Vietnam veterans, can have damning consequences.

The absence of support from supposed political comrades especially infuriated one War Democrat in the 87th Pennsylvania.

> My heart is often sick when I hear of dissension at home—my heart feels the want of harmony in this struggle. I love the Democratic Party, but oh! God, when I see men who call themselves Democrats, who abuse and misuse the word democracy for a cloak to hide their damnable purpose, my heart burns within me with indignation . . . I can be a Democrat and a Union man—but I hold that no man can be a true Democrat— a peace man and a rebel at the same time . . . Our country demands united action at this time and by the great God, the soldiers now in the service as volunteers will demand it from the people at home; if they do not give it to us, and if we ever have to return to our homes with defeat resting on our banners (because of their traitorous proceedings), you can rest assured there will be a day of reckoning.[28]

This emotional stew had a bitter taste to men struggling in the field, but their anger during the first half of 1863 was largely overreaction. Robert Milroy did not get his "infernal old gray head shot off" when the opportunity presented itself that June, and the threatened mass desertion was all talk. Only three men deserted the 87th Pennsylvania December 24, 1862–June 13, 1863, and one of them was so ill that he died shortly after leaving. Soldiers were more likely to direct threats of violence against Copperheads than Negroes. All this suggests that the black race was as much the latest scapegoat for soldiers' misery as a direct target of hatred. The entire Federal army proved that fact a year and a half later when they voted overwhelmingly to reelect Abraham Lincoln, who was running on a platform that recognized slavery as

---

28. "F" to the *York Republican,* Apr. 1, 1863, letter dated Mar. 12, 1863.

the cause of the war and called for its "complete extirpation from the soil of the republic."[29]

Outrage over the Emancipation Proclamation was not unique to the 87th Pennsylvania. Some took it to extremes, as the following examples show:

- An Ohio captain howled about fighting a "nigger war" and faced a court-martial for saying it too often.
- A slave-holding Union general from a border state said, "God damn the government. Let her go to hell. I will be found in the ranks fighting against her!" The army sent him packing for expressing his views so openly.
- Assuming that Lincoln's proclamation declared Negroes his equal, a New York lieutenant resigned his commission only to receive a dishonorable discharge instead.
- A California cavalryman deserted with his mount because he had promised to quit the war the day its cause became freedom for slaves. That adherence to principle put him before a firing squad.[30]

Lynching!

On July 3, 1863, York County experienced its only documented lynching during the nineteenth century, and an 87th Pennsylvania man played the key role. The circumstances, however, are far more complex than the inflammatory word *lynching* suggests. A fair study of the incident must examine facts within the context of events taking place at that time.

After its overwhelming victory at Winchester in June 1863, the Confederate army swarmed into Pennsylvania. As one arm of Robert E. Lee's force approached York, a committee of community leaders, including the recently resigned George Hay, rode the twelve miles west to Thomasville to meet them. The committee surrendered York and conceded to all demands for booty. Some still argue that the unprovoked surrender was unnecessary and cowardly, but that ignores the fact that the borough had virtually nothing but untrained militia for defense. Meanwhile, Rebels scattered throughout the region to conscript supplies they "bought" with Confederate scrip or promissory notes. One Rebel raiding party operated a few miles from Wellsville at

29. CMSRs of all men of the 87th Pa. The deserters were Andrew Luft (Co. A), Joseph Little (Co. D, and the man who died), and Albert King (Co. H). Platform of the National Union (Republican) Party 1864, in *Documents of American History*, 435.

30. Court-Martial, Capt. Benjamin Sells, 122nd Ohio, LL-1359; Lowry, *Don't Shoot That Boy!* cases of Brig. Gen. James G. Spears, 23, Lt. Edward H. Underhill (1st N.Y. Art.), 60–61, and Pvt. Thomas Clifton (2nd Ca. Cav.), 90.

the confluence of the Bermudian and Big Conewago creeks. The raiders used a slave to confiscate horses, a man residents claimed was as adept at locating concealed mounts as he was at insulting his victims, often doing the latter as he rode off on the victims' property.[31]

By June 30, the last of the Rebels had left the York area to reorganize near Gettysburg. Man-made thunder boomed on the horizon the next day, announcing that Robert E. Lee's move had turned into something more deadly than redeployment. When the thunder lasted two more days, it became clear that a battle like no other was taking place over there in Adams County. Citizens gathered to talk. Those living near Wellsville inevitably turned conversations to the recent robberies and only then realized the black Rebel was a common thread in the confiscations. Amazingly, someone had seen him that day walking alone, apparently having taken advantage of the chaos to escape his Rebel master.[32]

Onto the scene came Jeremiah Miley Spahr. The twenty-one-year-old had heeded Ross Harman's call in 1861 and had developed into one of the best soldiers in the 87th Pennsylvania. Not only had he earned sharpshooter's credentials, officers lauded him as a man "always ready for duty" who "would rather bear his suffering than go into hospital and be thought a 'hospital bummer.'" Spahr escaped capture at Carter's Woods and returned home—whether with leave or by desertion is not clear—and on the afternoon of July 3 was walking in the southwest corner of Warrington Township with at least five other men, including two of his brothers. Spahr carried his rifle, and the others probably carried firearms as well. Why they were there is subject to debate. One account claims they were looking for spoils of war, but that story is weak. The Rebels would have been unlikely to leave behind anything useful, and a veteran like Spahr should have known that. A second explanation is probably correct: The six men were looking for a horse thief at the request of local residents.[33]

31. Arguments still rage in York over what Confederate forces would have done had the town not surrendered—one side avers that, given Southern soldiers' behavior throughout the campaign, little or nothing different than the minimal damage and booty-taking that did occur. That view uses infallible hindsight and forgets that Wrightsville resisted and received a shelling. Four sources are used for the story of the lynching: *Hanover Citizen,* July 30, 1863; Clerk of Courts York County, Pennsylvania, Oyer and Terminer Papers No. 18, Aug. 1863 Session, York County Archives, York, Pennsylvania; *York Daily,* June 22, 1906, interview with an unnamed participant; recollections of Lane Scott Harman, June 30, 1930. Harman's account is at odds with the others and the least believable.

32. *Hanover Citizen,* July 30, 1863.

33. CMSR of Jeremiah M. Spahr, Co. H, 87th Pa.; Pension Records of Jeremiah Spahr, Co. H, 87th Pa., affidavit of Robert S. Slaymaker, June 6, 1889; *York Daily,* June 22, 1906; Clerk of Courts York County, Oyer and Terminer Papers No. 18, Aug. 1863 Session; *Hanover Citizen,* July

About the time Union forces were cutting down Gen. George Pickett's men, the six-man posse spied their quarry sitting on a bank along the state road (today's Harmony Grove Road), not far from Emig's Mill. Accounts diverge on what happened next. In a 1909 interview, an unnamed participant in the day's events claimed they agreed to hog-tie the black man and take him to York under arrest. All accounts agree that Jeremiah Spahr dissented because all accounts agree that he shot the black man. The reporter asked if anyone else fired, and the man replied sheepishly, "There must have been, for that darky was certainly pretty full of holes when we got up to him." A later account asserts the group tied up the black man, dragged him, and then hung him from a tree limb to use him for target practice. The account is dubious. The author wrote it sixty-seven years afterward and had not been present at the event. It also smacks of stereotyping based on postwar accounts of lynchings (i.e., that the method of death must have been a hanging). Whatever the killing technique, the black man was just as dead. The vigilantes hid the body in the bushes and agreed to say nothing about it.[34]

Such secrets are hard to keep. John Wells of *Wells*ville and Ross Harman's neighbor David Cadwallader got wind of the killing. They lived not far from the Quaker Meeting House that had spread its abolitionist influence throughout the area, and they took umbrage at the illegal killing of anyone. They reported the event, and a week later the coroner's office found the black man's body. He had been shot three times. Authorities charged Spahr with murder and his associates as accessories, implying that Spahr had fired all three rounds. John George Spahr posted a five-thousand-dollar bond against his property to ensure that his son would show up for the court date. The accused men had little to concern them. The court threw out the case. Jeremiah Spahr went back to the 87th Pennsylvania, and the other men went about their business.[35]

30, 1863; recollections of Lane Scott Harman. Prisoner-of-war records list Spahr's whereabouts as unknown between June 15 and Nov. 1, 1863. Lane Harman claimed Bill Spahr, "a rebel sympathizer who had been drafted into the army," was the central character. Jeremiah had a brother William who did not serve with any Pennsylvania regiment. Harman possibly confused William either with Jeremiah or William R. Smith, another man present. The *York Daily* wrongly claimed the main character, assumed here to be Jeremiah Spahr, had fought at Bull Run.

34. *York Daily,* June 22, 1906. The reporter used "naive," not "sheepish," but in a context that meant the same thing. Time of the event is a rough estimate based on statements made in this article. Recollections of Lane Scott Harman; *Hanover Citizen,* July 30, 1863. The *York Daily* and *Hanover Citizen* accounts mention only the shooting, and the court docket does not detail the method of killing. Technically, "lynching" does not refer to a specific form of execution, but hanging was the most common method.

35. U.S. Census, 1860, Pennsylvania, York, Warrington Township; Court Docket, Aug. 1863 session, Case 18. Charged were Jeremiah Spahr, Henry Spahr, Lewis Spahr, Levi Reiver, Lewis Reeser, and William R. Smith. Samuel Reiver, possibly kin to defendant Levi, also brought charges in the case. See U.S. Census, 1850, Pennsylvania, York County, Washington Township.

The killing would have been a despicable act under normal circumstances, and John Wells and David Cadwallader thought it so even given the atypical times. But was it justifiable under the state of affairs that existed then? Did the York judicial system handle the case properly? Was the absence of punishment for Spahr and the others a classic example of a racist community turning its back on the murder of a black man?

Whether or not the slave had carried a weapon, he was part of a massive invasion force; he had confiscated private property and reportedly mocked his victims while doing so. The entire event occurred under unique and terrifying circumstances—indeed to the sounds of a colossal battle that could have dissolved the Union and placed south-central Pennsylvania under the heel of an invading army. While Confederate soldiers had behaved well throughout the campaign, and twenty-twenty hindsight has shown that Robert E. Lee had no desire to subjugate the North, south-central Pennsylvanians could not have known that then. After viewing all the facts within context, York County handled the affair about as well as it could under the circumstances.[36]

As to a racist community turning its back on a black man, while it can never be argued that York practiced racial equality, it must be recalled that the county had a history of prosecuting crimes against blacks, not ignoring them. Only a year before, many of York's white leaders had worked hard to free Glenalvin Goodridge. But Spahr's victim had been an invader, and killing invaders during wartime is what a soldier is supposed to do. Had Jeremiah Spahr killed a white Confederate soldier instead of a slave, there would have been no prosecution at all. Why then should authorities have charged Spahr with murdering an aggressor because he happened to have been black?

Would Jeremiah Spahr have treated a white Rebel horse thief better? It is speculative, of course, and racism is a possibility, but Spahr did not need racism to motivate him. He was a dedicated soldier whose community was under assault by an enemy he had met in battle less than three weeks before, one that shattered his regiment, killed two company officers, and sent his first sergeant and nearly three hundred other comrades to Rebel prisons. It would be surprising had he not shot a white Rebel horse thief just as dead.

The Other Side

Not every man in the 87th Pennsylvania viewed blacks and the Emancipation Proclamation with disdain. Thaddeus Stevens Pfeiffer fits that mold if

---

36. Alfred Jessop to "Mrs. Jones," Feb. 9, 1930, ms. 11307, YCHT. Jessop lived in York at the time of the battle and recounted hearing gunfire almost thirty miles distant.

he had only half his namesake's abolitionist zeal, and his friend James Hersh likewise detested the practice of slavery.

Pvt. William Henry Brenaman demonstrated remarkable insight for a rural Winterstown farm boy and expressed himself well by any standard. Writing to his family from a freezing winter camp, he tried to convince a brother to take his turn at "soldogen."[37]

> I am writing this question at six or seven young and hearty chaps. I say, what will you call a man who refuses to shoulder his musket and fight for such a good government as we have? I call him a traitor to the United States government, that's so . . . I must say we are fighting a part for the niggros freedom and that is to abolish slavery. A great many look at this in a different way then I do but however I have said enough on this subject.[38]

William Brenaman had less than a year to say anything. Captured June 23, 1864, near Petersburg, Virginia, he died in Andersonville that September.[39]

Black men played a role in the 87th Pennsylvania as servants and cooks, but only two could be identified. A cook from York named Butler died at New Creek, (West) Virginia in late July 1862, but that is the only evidence uncovered. He may have been a neighbor to the one known black member of the regiment's support staff, Greenbury S. Robinson.[40]

Robinson maintained barbershops in both York Borough and New Oxford before the war and continued the tonsorial profession until age forced him to retire. He spent his life as an active member of the African Methodist Episcopal Church and served as a founding committee member for a new church in 1880. So respected were his contributions to the community that his death in 1908 merited a substantial front-page obituary in the *York Gazette*.[41]

When the Thomas A. Scott Regiment formed, Robinson signed on as servant for Company A and the regimental staff. Circumstances forced him to assume responsibilities that were more distasteful. Typhoid fever raged through the camp at New Creek in the summer of 1862. In the absence of sufficient medical personnel, any man might have to perform nursing duty,

37. CMSR and Pension Records of William H. Brenaman, Co. C, 87th Pa.; U.S. Census, 1850 and 1860, Pennsylvania, York County, Hopewell Township.

38. Pension Records of William H. Brenaman, letter to his brother David, Jan. 31, 1864.

39. CMSR of William H. Brenaman.

40. "Zouave" to the *Democratic Press,* Aug. 8, 1862, letter dated Aug. 5, 1862; U.S. Census, 1860, Pennsylvania, York County, York Borough.

41. U.S. Census, 1860, York County, York Borough, and Adams County, Oxford Township; *York Gazette,* Nov. 24, 1907, and Apr. 13, 1908; Black History File, YCHT.

and Robinson was no exception. Several of his charges became delirious with fever, and most went through periods in which they were unable to control bodily functions. Robinson recalled, "I was taking care of them all. I nursed & attended them altogether. Besides . . . [William Hamilton Fahs] I was nursing Benjamin Frick, Abram Frick . . . , John Welsh, Captain [James] Stahle, and [Samuel Finkle] Keller of Co. 'B.' They all had typhoid fever at that time . . . I used to have to clean [them] like . . . child[ren]."[42]

Robinson was still with the 87th Pennsylvania when the Confederate army approached Winchester in June 1863. During that phase of the war, a captured white soldier would go to a prison camp and see freedom within a relatively short time. A black captive might face more dire consequences. Robinson, though, had a natural advantage and the good sense to use it. Since he wore civilian clothing, he melted into Winchester's black population and walked away after the Confederate army left.

Green, as 87th Pennsylvania musician Charles Jacob Barnitz called him, returned to the regiment and remained until April 16, 1864, when he left with sutler Charlie Thomas. Unfortunately, he departed sixty-five dollars poorer thanks to the light-fingered efforts of an unidentified thief. The robbery and narrow escape at Winchester did not dull his enthusiasm for the army. He continued his service when he took work as a servant with the 39th U.S. Colored Troops.[43]

Black Angels of Mercy

Michael Heiman and James Oren were two members of the 87th Pennsylvania who learned the hard way to modify their views of the black population. They were among those taken prisoner on the dark day of June 23, 1864, near Petersburg, Virginia, and sent on their way to a temporary stay at Belle Isle Prison. Three weeks and an uncomfortable train ride to southwest Georgia later, they walked through the imposing log gates of Camp Sumter Stockade, better known as Andersonville. "Healthier boys never entered any prison," Heiman recalled. "There were only two in the lot that were over 22 years of age, but there were only six who lived to return home." Heiman's feet developed ugly yellow sores that washing in the putrid stockade stream only

---

42. Pension Records of William Hamilton Fahs, Co. A, 87th Pa., deposition of Greenbury S. Robinson, Dec. 7, 1888.
43. Charles Barnitz to James C. Hersh, Apr. 19, 1864, CWMC. Barnitz claimed that all the sutlers "left for parts unknown." CMSR of Benjamin F. Frick, Co. A, 87th Pa., and 39th U.S.C.T.

worsened. Sores soon covered Jim Oren's entire body and plagued him for three years.[44]

A few months after Heiman and Oren arrived in Andersonville, Confederate authorities became nervous. William Tecumseh Sherman's army was marching across Georgia. Southern leaders feared that a liberation of Andersonville would add thousands of Federal soldiers to the invading force, a shortsighted view that ignored most inmates' dismal physical condition. Authorities began emptying the prison, sending Heiman and Oren in a group that went to Millen, then Blackshear, and lastly, Thomasville, venues that were small improvement over Andersonville. False promises of exchange kept the men in line for a time, but few believed them after a while. When rumor said that they were going back to Andersonville, Heiman and Oren determined to escape or die doing it.[45]

December 22, 1864, was a cold night near Albany, Georgia. Southern guards huddled around a fire grabbing warmth and were not giving their charges necessary attention. Heiman and Oren noted this and simply walked into the woods unchallenged. Moments later, shouts trailed after the fugitives, followed by bullets that all missed. Heiman and Oren raced pell-mell through the darkness, bare feet pounding against rocks and stumps. Fading from fatigue and fear, they ran smack into an unseen corn shock and flopped to the ground. Gasping, confused, terrified, they had no idea where to go next, but go they must. By morning, they came to a road and picked a direction, stumbling on until they found a slave shack. Help us, they asked an old slave woman. She refused but promised she would not tell her master on them. They had to keep going but could not last long without help.

On Christmas Eve, they met "a lot of jolly slaves" who this time granted their request for a handout. Spareribs, cornbread, sweet potatoes, and cake filled their bellies. Amazingly, they held it down, quite a feat after six months on prison rations. The slaves gave them extra food and directions to "follow the seven stars" to Savannah, now controlled by General Sherman.

Christmas Day passed in a shack cooking some of the food the slaves had given them. The door suddenly swung open, and a white man stepped in. He wanted to know who they were and why they were there. Heiman and Oren tried to convince him they were Rebel soldiers going home on furlough. The man said he had just finished a three-month stint as an Andersonville guard and knew prisoners when he saw them. Instead of turning them in, he

---

44. Recollections of Michael Heiman, *York Gazette,* July 9, 10, 13, 15, 21–23, 1891; CMSRs and Pension Records of Michael Heiman and James Oren, Co. B, 87th Pa.

45. Charles Edwin Gotwalt, "Adventures of a Private in the American Civil War," YCHT.

surprised them with an invitation to supper and left, returning later with his children to gaze at the Yankee sideshow and reiterate his dinner invitation. After he left the second time, Heiman and Oren argued whether they should take the invitation. Oren wanted to attend, but Heiman felt uneasy. The debate grew heated until Oren fell into a brooding silence.

A rap at the door startled them. Two slaves entered, put their hats under their arms, and told Heiman that their master ordered them to bring the shoemaker to his house to work. Heiman was the shoemaker.

"What about me?" Oren asked, lifting his head.

"Massa will come for you," the slave said.

Heiman was suspicious and called one of the slaves aside to "ply him with questions." The slave admitted that his master wanted to arrest them but was afraid to do it by himself, what with all the other white men in Albany celebrating the holidays. Their master had sent them to separate Heiman from Oren, and then he would arrest them individually. Heiman knew they had to take a risk.

> I asked the darkies if it was possible for us to get away from there secretly. One of them agreed to take us out, and though we feared he might betray us, he took us safely through the woods, and at his home about four miles from the shanty, gave us supper. He then gave us information concerning the roads, and about 12 o'clock we left the place and set out . . . So ended our Christmas.

Slaves assisted Heiman and Oren three more times during the next few days but either gave faulty directions on how to reach Savannah or the escaped prisoners misunderstood. Instead of traveling due east to Savannah, they went southeast to Irwinville approximately eighty air miles from Andersonville. They reached Irwinville at night and by the next afternoon were again famished. More confident in approaching slaves now, they begged for food again, this time from several young girls.[46]

> They said they would get us some, though we must wait until they could bake some cornbread as they had none. So we remained quietly in the woods until evening and yet no one appeared with the food. Then we began to get tired of waiting and went to the slave cabin and entered. The wenches said they would get us something to eat immediately, so we warmed ourselves at the fire while they made preparations. Finally one

46. Irwinville, Irwin County, Georgia, was the place the fleeing Jefferson Davis was captured a few months later.

went out. The other one worked slowly on. The door was thrown open, two double-barreled guns thrust in, and a demand made to surrender. As it was useless to resist we complied. The party who arrested us consisted of four men, accompanied by three bloodhounds, one of the men being the master of the slaves who had betrayed us.

Instead of sending them back to prison, their captors put them to work. Their new lifestyle beat Andersonville, but they were still escaped prisoners in enemy territory. If anyone shot them dead, who would know? Who would care? With the help of a local woman sympathetic to the Union cause, Jim Oren made good his getaway but could not convince her to wait until Mike Heiman could join them. The woman introduced Oren to a band of other escaped prisoners and reluctant Southern conscripts hiding in a nearby swamp.

Heiman began feeling more uneasy about his situation. It came to a head one "pitchy dark" night as he lay awake in his cot.

> About 12 o'clock hoof beats sounded in the street below, and then a knock at the . . . door . . . It was not long before footsteps sounded in the hall and there was a rap at the door. I pretended to be asleep for some time, and when the rapping became more loud, arose and inquired what was wanted . . . There were men there then to take me back to prison. As I could do nothing but comply, I set off on foot, guarded by the two men who had come for me . . . As we journeyed along he suddenly turned to his companion and inquired:
>
> "What will we do if we meet them?"
>
> Said the other guard, "Well, if there's too many for us we'll have to surrender, I guess."
>
> I could not imagine what they were talking about. Afterward I found out. A large number of the "swamp men" had set out for Irwinville [Georgia] for the purpose of rescuing me; and that was what caused my sudden transfer. All the time the guards were apprehensive lest they should meet with this body of men.

Jim Oren had not forgotten his friend, but the rescue team had arrived too late. Michael Heiman again stared at the inside of Andersonville's log walls.

> Once more I was within the terrible stockade filled with miserable human beings, many dying of loathsome diseases, other awaiting death which would relieve them of their misery . . . No pen can adequately describe the horrors of the place. The only pleasant moments were those when sleep would visit the weary eyes, and the mind would wander in Dreamland. There were men in the stockade whose sufferings were thus intensified. In their waking moments starvation stared them in the face;

while in their dreams they sat down to well-filled tables of wholesome food, and choicest delicacies. Then they awoke to find all was but a vision which passed away and left them in a worse condition.

The inmate population was a fifth of what it had been when Heiman first arrived and made the stockade seem almost deserted. The food supply had not improved, though, and he again witnessed men "contending with maggots for a bone containing a little sustenance." Other 87th Pennsylvania men were there: Henry Shatzler, Charles Booth, Peter Bott, Christian List, and William Shuman. Life improved when they hooked up with some recently arrived Indiana men who had money to bribe guards for food the commissary never provided. But it was still Andersonville.[47]

Heiman urged the group to join him in another escape attempt. Their chance came when Confederate authorities again led them from the stockade and to the train station for what they assumed was another relocation. The date was April 14, 1865, the night that a famous actor, who had once attended school in York, would fire a bullet into President Lincoln's brain, and five days after Robert E. Lee had surrendered at Appomattox Court House. Had Heiman and company known then of Lee's surrender, they might have waited out the end of the war. Without that knowledge, Andersonville remained a reality too harsh not to escape.

As they neared the train, Heiman grabbed Shatzler's arm and pulled him under the cars. They waited, saw no action taken to stop them, and then crawled under the train station to wait. An Ohio man tagged along. As the train pulled out, the three men slipped into the Georgia woods. They awoke the next morning and looked into the trees at a half dozen snakes coiled in the branches above. They spent that day being terrified by snakes that seemed always to be lying in their path.

Slaves provided the first meal of this sojourn. They also gave escape directions that Heiman and company botched so badly they became lost in a swamp. Fortunately, the sounds of chanting field hands reached their ears, and they escaped by following the music. Once more, slaves saved them by leading them to the island in the swamp they had been unable to find on their own and then offered food and new directions on how to escape. Off the men went until they reached a bridge. A guard sprang into view and shouted for them to halt. He was black. Heiman's spirits skyrocketed. Only the Union army had black soldiers. This black man was not wearing a uniform, and Rebel soldiers stepped up behind him.

---

47. Recollections of Michael Heiman, *York Gazette,* July 13, 1891. Heiman's mess once gobbled down a large quantity of peanuts they purchased from a guard, no doubt making nourishment-starved intestines suffer.

"Hi, Mike!" The shout surprised Heiman as they walked into the Rebel camp: 87th Pennsylvania comrade Michael Fry Poet, and beside him, Henry Edgar Blaney. Both had jumped off the train from Andersonville but had soon been captured. They had a recent northern newspaper, and Heiman gobbled up the first real news he had seen in months. Only then did he understand something he had overheard a slave say. "The damn old fool oughter hole out a little longer," the slave had quoted his master saying. The sentence had meant nothing to Heiman then, but now he knew that the slave's master meant that Robert E. Lee had surrendered. The newspaper also told of Lincoln's assassination.

For the third time, Michael Heiman walked through the gates of Andersonville but this time only for an overnight stay. In the morning, they boarded a train bound for Macon and freedom. As they approached the city, they could see the fluttering Stars and Stripes, the view filling them with a joy that rendered them mute. They were not as happy about the Rebel uniforms the army gave them to wear, but, on a practical level, it beat their former rags. Best of all, there were old friends to revisit.

"Nice way to pass a comrade," the voice called to Heiman. It belonged to Jim Oren, alive and well—by Andersonville alumni standards.

It was good to be back in the Union army.

Michael Heiman returned home and opened a shoemaker's shop in York Borough. At the end of many a workday, he would close his shop and spin war tales to anyone who wanted to stay and listen. He was a regular reader of, and occasional contributor to, the *National Tribune,* a weekly national newspaper published by and for Union veterans. A *York Gazette* reporter eventually convinced him to put his stories into print. He no doubt embellished facts—events might have taken on added drama in his memory over time—but he related his tales with an assuredness that made them believable.[48]

Michael Heiman left Andersonville in April 1865, but it never left him. His body suffered the ravages of that stink hole until the day he died in 1910. Jim Oren passed on in 1922, an impoverished inmate of the National Soldiers' Home in Dayton, Ohio. Hopefully, they both remembered that not one of them would have returned had it not been for the support of dozens of slaves who risked their lives every time they assisted Yankee soldiers.[49]

---

48. *National Tribune,* Apr. 21, 1884, Michael Heiman's article on the battle of Cold Harbor.
49. Pension Records of James Oren and Michael Heiman.

Chapter 10

Winter Camp, the Overland Campaign, and Petersburg

A s 1864 arrived, the Union army stared at an ugly dilemma. Enlistments were going to expire throughout the year, and recruiting had long since slowed to a trickle. In the 87th Pennsylvania's case, it was a dry well. Lt. John Frederick Spangler went home to recruit after the second battle of Winchester and did not sign up one man in six months of trying.[1]

To entice men to reenlist, the army began offering what Tom Crowl called "great inducements," nothing more than that ageless incentive, money— "bounty," the army called it. A month-long furlough and the honor of wearing veteran volunteer stripes on their sleeves went with it. Actually, there were usually two bounties. Washington paid one, the value of which was nonnegotiable, although volunteers now received their bounty payments in three installments rather than in a lump sum after discharge. Local municipalities paid another, and those amounts and the payment method varied greatly. York County's Hopewell Township paid twenty-three men $300 each. The township borrowed to make payments and then tried to pay for it with a new tax it had difficulty collecting. Conewago Township in Adams County offered a mere $170. Bounties also increased with time and inadequate enrollment. George Blotcher stepped forward on the first call for veteran volunteers only to learn that he could have doubled his bounty payment had he waited a few weeks. The furlough was the carrot that lured Blotcher, though, not

---

1. James A. Stahle to Lorenzo Thomas, Jan. 25, 1864, Federal Muster Rolls. Stahle called Spangler "incompetent" and assigned Solomon Myers to replace him.

the money.[2] A year later, supply and demand gave John Dougherty $525 and William P. Edwards $680 in local payments to join the 87th Pennsylvania, amounts several times greater than a private's regular army pay and more than many civilians earned annually.

Every reenlistment counted against the district's draft quota. Reenlist enough veterans and/or recruit enough new volunteers and a district did not have to institute a draft. Gettysburg's recruiting drives were so successful that it drafted no one in 1864. If a region reached its manpower allocation, it could credit extra recruits to another district, perhaps even auctioning slots to the highest bidder. The army credited a number of 87th Pennsylvania reenlistments to a Lancaster township in which none of them resided, and the 200th Pennsylvania, formed in August 1864 with mostly York County men, applied enlistments to districts all over the state. If a district was not reaching its goal, it could up the bounty offer and lure men from other districts.[3]

Bounty even tantalized Tom Crowl. In addition, friends were reenlisting, and the tug of companionship teased him to remain in a situation that he detested. Two months of thought sobered him, though, as he wrote his sister.[4] "You want to know whether I have re-enlisted. When I become a idiot or damned fool, then I will go but no sooner. I know too well what soldiering is to be caught again . . . Dear Mary if you were a man . . . I would tell you in full what I think of this cursed war and enlisting. Therefor it will not do for me to write my opinon to you."[5]

In all, 193 men of the 87th Pennsylvania chose to become veteran volunteers, including 53 who had desertion charges on their records. Not all of them used their furloughs to good purpose, though. Joseph Ashley, who credited Lowell, Massachusetts, with his reenlistment, disappeared during his furlough, and several others opted to join the navy. Most, however, stayed until the army said, "Here's your discharge," or the Good Lord said, "Come home."[6]

2. Thomas O. Crowl to his sister, Jan. 10, 1864, CWMC; "Bill No. 9, An Act relating to the payment of bounties to volunteers in Hopewell Township, in the County of York," ms. 737.2, YCHT; *Adams Sentinel and General Advertiser*, Mar. 8, 1864; Pension Records of John Dougherty, new Co. G, and William P. Edwards, new Co. H, 87th Pa. See Kemp, "Community and War," 44–46, 55, for comparisons of bounties offered in two New England towns during 1862 and 1864.
3. CMSRs of all men in the 87th Pa. and 200th Pa.; J. Matthew Gallman with Susan Baker, "Gettysburg's Gettysburg: What the Battle Did to the Borough," in *The Gettysburg Nobody Knows,* edited by Gabor S. Boritt; recollections of George Blotcher; diary of George Blotcher; Snell, "If They Would Know What I Know." Examination of the service records of the 200th Pennsylvania reveals about half the men were credited to places in which they did not live.
4. Thomas O. Crowl to his sister, Jan. 10, 1864, CWMC.
5. Thomas O. Crowl to his sister, Mar. 27, 1864, Pattee.
6. CMSRs of all men of the 87th Pa.

There was finally time for some relaxation in a winter camp situated "about half way between Brandy Station and Culpeper." The men still had duties to perform, but they had enough free time to make this period seem a comparative vacation after active campaigning. Unlike during the regiment's days along the railroad, most of the troublemakers were long gone. Living conditions were primitive, but veterans had become geniuses at making the best of it. The men transformed Virginia forests into log huts that soon blanketed the plain.[7]

There was time to let off steam. One of the boys' favorite games was a benign version of the blanket toss used to rob Tom Crowl in Fort McHenry. The flyer would come "down spread out on all fours like a bull frog," and then back up he would go, repeating the flights until the next man took a turn. Capt. Solomon Myers elected to take a turn. He was a tall, heavy man, so it was with some strain that the men heaved him into the air. On the second throw, they tried to toss him higher. They succeeded. It was the catching part that gave them trouble. Myers hit the ground "more dead than alive" but suffered nothing more lethal than a bruised ego.[8]

There was time to renew the spirit, too, with a religious revival that swept the army. The 87th Pennsylvania's earlier extant correspondence makes no mention of formal religious exercises except to complain of the chaplains' "careless style" of approaching their duty in the field. That had much to do with the men who had served as chaplains.[9]

At the outbreak of war, the regiment's first chaplain, James Allen Brown, had been the acting president and professor of ancient languages at a seminary in Newberry, South Carolina. Faculty and students there wanted this Yankee preacher to state his loyalties. They had suspected all along that he was an ardent abolitionist, especially after he astonished the community by hiring white domestic servants. At a special assembly of faculty and students, Brown took to the pulpit to announce that he had been born and reared in the Union and wanted to die there. That was not a safe viewpoint to shout from the pulpit of a South Carolina church in 1861. The reverend wrote out his resignation and fled with his family, leaving behind most of their worldly goods, and returned to York where he had ministered a church in the 1840s.

7. "Typo" to the *Adams Sentinel,* Feb. 9, 1864, letter dated Jan. 30, 1864.

8. Recollections of George Blotcher. Solomon Myers mentioned nothing in his diary. He was five feet, ten inches tall.

9. Frank Geise to George Hay, July 15, 1863, George Hay Kain III Collection. See Wiley, *Billy Yank,* 262–74; and McPherson, *For Cause and Comrades,* 62–76, for further data on the role of chaplains in the military.

When the train taking them north crossed the Mason-Dixon line, Brown ordered his son to open the window and take a whiff of "free air."[10]

Unfortunately, Brown's tenure with the 87th was less provocative. He was a stiff, formal man, not the best personality for a field chaplain. He lasted less than a year before resigning to assume the chaplain's position of the U.S. Army Hospital at York. Two years later, he took the reins of Gettysburg's Lutheran Theological Seminary, where he remained until retirement.[11]

Brown's successor was bespectacled John Francis Baird, a man storyteller Washington Irving might have envisioned as a character in one of his tales. Baird, a Yorker, was serving a church in Cedarville, New Jersey, when the offer arrived from the regiment. He immediately accepted and joined the regiment at New Creek just before it moved into active service. But when the regiment reached Clarksburg, (West) Virginia, on August 28, he was more eager to sip tea with the town's upper crust than administer to his military flock. After a party and all-night stay at a new acquaintance's house, he awoke to find the regiment gone and his baggage with it. He tried to catch up on a borrowed horse, but pickets refused to let him out of town without a pass.[12]

Baird returned to his Clarksburg friend's home and wrote a letter to the *York Gazette* wondering what to do about his plight, as if some generous Yorker would rush to his side and lead him in the right direction. He said he had never enjoyed better health but was out of the army three months later on a surgeon's certificate. His problems may not have been physical. Baird returned to York a preacher without a church and surely embarrassed by a failed army experience his own hand had made public. He grew increasingly depressed and disappeared from his mother's home. Searches came up empty for three weeks until his body washed ashore in the Codorus Creek.[13]

Shrewsbury resident David Christian Eberhart followed Baird as chaplain. At Winchester in 1863, Gen. Robert Milroy granted him permission to take over the Episcopal Church as a military house of worship. When not min-istering to his flock, Eberhart doubled as regimental dentist. It was a useful

10. B. M. Zettler, *War Stories and School Day Incidents for the Children; Newberry College: 1856–1976, 120 Years of Service to the Lutheran Church and to South Carolina,* edited by Gordon C. Henry, 1976; CMSR of Rev. James A. Brown, Chaplain, 87th Pa., Resignation letter, July 3, 1862. Jacob Hay Brown, the boy who whiffed free air, rose to chief justice of the Pennsylvania Supreme Court. Brown family data courtesy of Jacob Hay Brown.

11. CMSR of James A. Brown, Chaplain, 87th Pa.; Abdel Ross Wentz, *Gettysburg Lutheran Theological Seminary,* vol. 1, *History, 1826–1965.*

12. Rev. John Francis Baird to Gov. Andrew G. Curtin, July 20, 1862; George Hay to Gov. Andrew G. Curtin, July 30, 1862, PA AGO, Muster Rolls of the 87th Pa., Correspondence; Rev. John F. Baird to the *York Gazette,* Sept. 23, 1862, letter dated Sept. 3, 1862.

13. *York Gazette,* Sept. 3, 1862, Apr. 14 and 21 and May 5, 1863.

combination. Given the rudimentary status of dentistry, prayer was no doubt important to Eberhart's patients. He frequently assisted the medical staff in the Taylor Hotel and once awakened next to seven corpses that had not been there when he fell asleep. He was hard at work when victorious Rebels rode into town on June 15. Chaplain status delayed but did not forestall Libby Prison, an experience that prevented his return to duty until April 1864.[14]

Cpl. Lawrence R. Kerber acted as unofficial chaplain during Eberhart's absence but exited the army on a surgeon's certificate in January 1864, leaving the 87th Pennsylvania without a spiritual leader during the army's religious revival. Pvt. Beniah Keller Anstine did not need one. He attended services at least once a night—more, duty permitting—and always recorded the sermon's topic in his diary. Faith later sustained him during a lengthy stay in Danville Prison.[15]

Alfred Jameson was another who felt his religious fervor warming with the weather and the increasing likelihood of battle. He wrote his mother:

> There has been a revival going on in our Brigade this whole winter. We have had preaching every night and three times on Sunday. Many have professed to have found the Savior. The building in which the meeting is held is a large log hut covered with canvas. It was built by the men of our Brigade. I enjoy these meeting in this humble hut more than I ever did in any carpeted church.[16]

A month later, Jameson told his family how his faith comforted him as the spring campaign neared.

> Perhaps this will be the last letter you will get from me in this camp. We are now preparing for a move. We sent our over-coats to Alexandria today. I think we will have some hard fighting before many weeks. Many men will fall. God only knows who they will be. I would like to see my home once again and enjoy its comforts. My prayer to Him is that he will guide me safely through all dangers, but if it should be His will that I should fall I hope to say, "Thy will be done." He knows what is best for me and I will submit to His will. If I shall fall it shall be in the cause of my Dear Saviour as well as my country.[17]

14. CMSR and Pension Records of David C. Eberhart, Chaplain, 87th Pa.; David C. Eberhart, "In the Enemy's Lines after Winchester," *Grand Army Scout and Soldier's Mail,* Oct. 13, 1883. Only four installments of Eberhart's five-part account were found.

15. Diary of Beniah Keller Anstine; CMSR of Beniah K. Anstine, Co. C, 87th Pa. Anstine was captured at the battle of Monocacy and imprisoned until Oct. 14, 1864.

16. Pension Records of Alfred Jameson, letter to his mother, Mar. 8, 1864.

17. Ibid.

Men coped with the specter of death by relying on faith and on the unrealistic confidence of youth. At Winchester the year before, Harrisburg native Edward T. Rudy had written, "There's a Reble force marching on this place but we ain't any ways afraid of that for we'll meet them when they come." The young man who addressed letters to "my dear father" and closed them with "your affectionate son" was wrong then and was again when he met the Rebels a year later. He died in Andersonville, a tragic event that his family claimed killed his father.[18]

Pvt. David Gilbert Myers was another jaunty lad from Gettysburg whose cockiness surely unnerved his parents when they read his letter announcing an impending movement.

> I may go into this fight and come out all wright and if not, if we never meet again on earth I hope that we may meet in heaven. Do not think that it troubles me any. When I go into any thing of the kind I expect to come by chance with the rest. I have no idea of dying yet. I expect to get out of the service safe with all the fighting we have to do this summer.[19]

They all would need whatever inner strength they could muster during what became the bloodiest period of the war.

The Wilderness

> Camp of the 87th Regiment Pa Vols
> May 3rd 1864
> Dear Sister
> I mean to let you know that we are to move tomorrow morning at four oclock. This is the commencment of our spring campaign. To where we to go to I can not tell but I suppose a cross the Rapidan River. Also we look for some very hard fighting. The reason of me writing this is because I don't supose where we are moving there will be a chance. Perhaps it may be the last letter that I can ever have the privilidge to send you and it may not but I hope it wont be so. I want you to write to me if I cant write to you. I may get your letters and I may not but risk some any how.
> Thomas Crowl[20]

18. Pension Records of Edward T. Rudy, Co. B, 87th Pa., letters to his father, May 23 and 27, and Nov. 20, 1863.

19. Pension Records of David G. Myers, letter to his parents, May 3, 1864.

20. Thomas O. Crowl to his sister, May 3, 1864, CWMC.

Tom Crowl was one of countless soldiers who whipped off letters that day. Ulysses S. Grant had ordered his huge Army of the Potomac to unwind from winter camp and head south to attack Robert E. Lee's Army of Northern Virginia. Grant's army was so immense that the 87th Pennsylvania did not cross the Rapidan River until twelve hours after the movement began. Thousands of men lightened their loads as they went. Not long into the march, Tom Crowl tossed away his blanket and knapsack. The quantity of new overcoats and blankets left by the side of the road surprised even General Grant. Cpl. John Keses saw "horseshoes by the hundred and enough old iron to employ half a dozen blacksmiths for a whole year."[21]

The Wilderness awaited as it had in the Mine Run campaign the previous November, a region of thick, scrubby growth in which no army could maneuver as Hardee's *Tactics* prescribed. Spring's budding foliage reduced vision so much that "we could not see the length of our regiment," John Keses recalled. Grant tried to get his army through this potential trap before Lee reacted, but he was too slow. The wily Southern commander met the Union army in the heart of the Wilderness and largely negated Grant's advantage in artillery and superior numbers. The dense vegetation guaranteed that U.S. Grant's first battle as supreme commander would be a bloody and confusing one.[22]

The 87th Pennsylvania remained in reserve on May 5 and never took part in the Wilderness's severest fighting. The boys from York left few recollections about their experiences. A recent history considered by many to be the battle's definitive tactical study does not index the 87th Pennsylvania at all and makes only two brief mentions of its brigade commander. Thirty 87th Pennsylvania men became casualties at the Wilderness, the highest rate in their brigade, and they did not shoot or capture themselves.[23]

The regiment was on the Fredericksburg Road standing in columns of fours when the shells starting flying on May 6. Men ducked each time a missile screamed overhead, prompting an unnamed regimental staff officer to scold them for cowardice. His lectures ended abruptly after a round zipped by his

---

21. *O.R.,* Report of Brig. Gen. William H. Morris, May 10, 1864, 36/1:722; David Gilbert Myers to his parents, May 3, 1864, Pension Records of David G. Myers; recollections of John Keses (these appear to be a series from an unknown newspaper, presumably in Connecticut, where he lived after the war); Ulysses S. Grant, *Personal Memoirs of U. S. Grant and Selected Letters 1839–1865,* 524; Thomas O. Crowl to his sister, May 3, 1864, CWMC.

22. William Joseph Hardee, *Rifle and Light Infantry Tactics.* Hardee wrote the book while a brevet first lieutenant in the U.S. Army but later became a Confederate general. Recollections of John Keses.

23. *O.R.,* Report of William H. Morris, May 10, 1864, 36/1:722–23; CMSRs of all men of the 87th Pa.; Gordon C. Rhea, *The Battle of the Wilderness, May 5–6, 1864* (Baton Rouge: Louisiana State University Press, 1994). William H. Morris was the 87th Pennsylvania's brigade commander.

head, and he ducked. Orders came to charge the Rebel battery that was be-deviling them. The charge failed, but one memory of it remained fresh in John Keses's mind years later.

> As we went forward over the ground strewn with dead and wounded I noticed a poor Yank lying in the middle of the Pike stone dead and his faithful dog waiting as it were for his master to wake up. What a contrast! The air alive with the noise of battle and the ground itself shaken with the conflict of thousands of men while in the thick of the fight a poor dog stands waiting for his owner to rouse from his last sleep. On we went until the enemy gave us grape and canister which not only set us back but made a horrible noise through the woods.[24]

Historians recognized the battle of the Wilderness as ending on May 6, but the 87th suffered eight casualties on May 7. David Gilbert Myers was one of them because he forgot the cardinal rule of pickets: Do not fall sleep. Exhaustion overruled common sense, and Myers and a few friends faded into dreams a short distance behind the picket line. Two rifle cracks awoke them at dawn. Amazingly, he was able to get a letter through to his parents explaining what had happened.

> I raise upon my knees to see what was the matter, then I seen three men. I could not tell whose men they were as they were dressed in a kind of a blueish grey. They had not seen us then yet until I began rubbing my eyes. Then one of them seen me and said come down here you damned Yankee you or I will blow your brains out of you. I got up and went to them and laughing said, You have me this time all the while expecting to have "my chunk" put out.[25]

Myers's "chunk" stayed whole, but he was a prisoner of the 61st Georgia. Weeks passed among his captors, time that seemed to give him a softer view of his enemy. He continued to get letters through, some routed to Gettysburg via Richmond and others hand-carried by an unnamed doctor.

> Us Yankees and the Confederates are getting very intimate. They will set and talk for hours and hours with us sometimes, the most of the talk about the war. The most of them have enlisted for during the war. There is a great many of them wishes this war was over. They say they would

24. Recollections of John Keses.
25. Ibid.

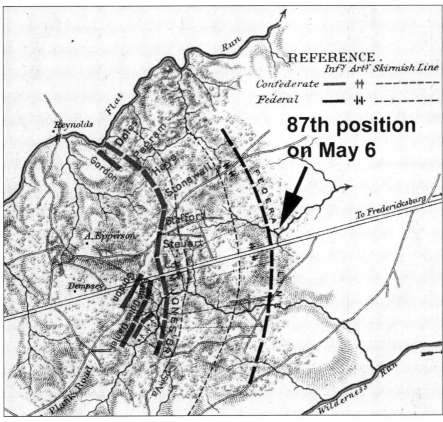

The Wilderness Battlefield, May 6, 1864 (*Atlas to Accompany the Official Records of the Union and Confederate Armies*, image 83, additions by the author).

not care which side would win, then again the largest portion of them say that they want to be parted from us entirely. They say that if only we would stay off their soil they would not bother us at all and then say they will fight if it must be for fourty years to come. They say they will never be brought under our government again. I do not know what to think of them sometimes. When I get talking to them about our country there is some of them wishes that they were there and some says they would sooner live in that Confederacy and have their wrights and be as poor as church mice sooner than to live under the old government and not have their wrights.[26]

26. Ibid.

Whatever his captors thought of David Myers, they had to follow orders and ship him to the prison stockade at Andersonville. You can visit him there today at grave number 9,893.[27]

Spotsylvania and Cold Harbor

A fifteen-hour march brought the 87th Pennsylvania to the next battlefield near Spotsylvania Court House. Once more, it was a relatively lucky regiment. While men died by the hundreds at the Mule Shoe salient and Bloody Angle, the 87th's brigade remained in a supporting role from May 8 until it left the area on the morning of May 22. Henry A. Ensinger's family did not agree the regiment was unengaged. An exploding shell drove hot shrapnel through his body, granting him the dubious honor of being the first 87th man killed on Ulysses S. Grant's Overland campaign.[28]

The regiment's principal memory of Spotsylvania inevitably revolved around the death of Maj. Gen. John Sedgwick. To assuage his men's fear, the general stood atop a breastwork in full view of the enemy and told all those within earshot that the Rebels could not hit an elephant from the distance where they lay. The words had little more than escaped his mouth when a bullet drilled into Sedgwick's skull, and he fell from the breastwork within sight of the 87th Pennsylvania. Pvt. Charles Edwin Gotwalt claimed he saw the entire incident, and Capt. Murray Samuel Cross alleged he helped carry Sedgwick's body to the rear.[29]

The section of the regiment most heavily engaged during the campaign was, ironically, the returning veteran volunteers. They had started back from veteran furlough on May 8 and missed the battle of the Wilderness. The army regrouped and rearmed the men at Alexandria and then sent them to Belle Plain, Virginia, to receive tents and rations and serve five days of picket duty. They headed back to the regiment on May 19 in the company of the 1st Maryland Infantry. By late afternoon, danger was coming their direction.[30]

27. CMSR of David G. Myers, Co. F, 87th Pa. At the author's last trip to Andersonville, David Myers's photo hung on the visitor center wall.

28. *O.R.,* Report of William H. Morris, May 10, 1864, 36/1:723; Pension Records of Abraham Benjamin Franklin Roat, Co. B, 87th Pa. Roat was lying beside Ensinger and injured by the same piece of shell. CMSR of William W. Walters, Co. B, 87th Pa. Walters could also lay claim as the first 87th man killed on the Overland campaign. Shot in the left foot at the Wilderness May 5 or 6, he died of tetanus in a Philadelphia hospital a month later.

29. Gotwalt, "Adventures"; CMSR and Pension Records of Murray S. Cross, Co. C, 87th Pa.

30. Diary of George Blotcher.

Suspicious that Grant was trying a flanking movement on the Confederate left, Robert E. Lee had ordered a "demonstration" to find out.

George Blotcher reported, "We formed a line of battle at once and firing commenced at once. We held them in check long enough till we received a strong reinforcement when the fight commenced with full force but being late in the evening by this time, the fire ceased and the enemy withdrew during the night without any booty but instead a loss."[31]

Blotcher's description makes the battle of Harris Farm seem insignificant. In the grand scheme of the Civil War, it was, but all things are relative. A large percentage of the 87th Pennsylvania's casualties credited to the battle of Spotsylvania occurred in this fight several miles from the more famous field of action.[32]

Grant's army continued its pursuit of the Rebels toward Richmond through intense heat. Thick clouds of dust raised by 200,000 feet tramping over drought-parched roads choked men, especially those cursed to march at the rear of the column. By the end of May, the Federals approached Cold Harbor, site of another furious conflict two years earlier that history recalls as Gaines' Mill. The luck that had kept the 87th Pennsylvania out of the worst fighting on this campaign was about to run out. Now it was their turn to take part in a full frontal assault. The men had charged into woods once before, at Carter's Woods, but that had been out of desperation against an unprepared enemy. On June 1, 1864, Rebels were well located behind sound breastworks, present in great numbers, and well supported by artillery. Gen. James Ricketts put the 87th Pennsylvania in the second of four lines of attack. Orders said, "Feel the touch of the elbow toward the centre, and when the works were reached the first line were to let the second pass, and finish up with the bayonet." The men stood in line for several hours before the final order came. When it did, they set off first "with dress parade precision," then double-quick, and finally, the last dash toward enemy lines.[33]

A reporter filed an eyewitness account.

> At about 6 o'clock [P.M.] an advance was ordered, and the whole line moved forward. A narrow belt of woods intervened between Ricketts' division and the enemy, and, on emerging from it into a ploughed field,

31. *O.R.,* Report of Richard S. Ewell, Mar. 20, 1865, 36/1:1073; diary of George Blotcher; Prowell, *87th Pennsylvania,* 139–40, account by Findley Isaac Thomas.

32. *O.R.,* Report of Stephen D. Ramseur, Aug. 3, 1864, 36/1:1082–83; CMSRs of all men of the 87th Pa.

33. James A. Stahle, "The Battle of Cold Harbor," *York Gazette,* June 1, 1892; *O.R.,* Report of George G. Meade, 36/1:194.

the position of the enemy was plainly visible on a wooded crest beyond. A heavy fire of musketry and artillery was immediately opened upon them by the rebels in their works, but through this deadly storm our men steadily advanced over the ploughed field, through an intervening swamp . . . and at the point of the bayonet drove the enemy from his earthworks, and held them during the night against repeated and furious assaults.[34]

Grant called off another scheduled charge the next day and waited until June 3 to launch an even greater attack. The 87th Pennsylvania was not involved in the worst of the fighting that developed, but conditions were hellish enough. The charge began at 4:30 A.M. but stumbled to a halt, forcing the boys from York to dig breastworks with tools George Blotcher had requisitioned that morning. At some places, Grant's men dug trenches only fifty yards from the enemy. "Zoo-Zoo" put his terror into words, a rare look at an account written as shells burst overhead.[35]

A terrible battle in progress. We have gained nothing yet to-day. The loss in our Brigade is heavy. Col. John W. Schall, commanding Brigade, wounded in arm—still on duty. Our loss in officers alone this morning is twenty in Brigade. Captain Pfeiffer is shot through the body; I fear will die. Co. F has just lost James Murray killed, Isaac Sheads and [Amos] Keefer wounded. The slaughter is terrible, and is not over. Our Regiment has the fourth line for once to-day. I have been in the front all the time nearly, but have always escaped. Our progress from this to Richmond will be slow, and cost many lives . . . I close as the firing is very hot. This is the 31st day of this campaign . . . God has watched over us, but our hour may come yet . . . Co. I has just had John Hale wounded in arm . . . Missing: Wm. Ogden, David G. Myers, Wm. Fullerton, supposed to be prisoners. In haste, ZOO-ZOO.[36]

The battle of Cold Harbor sank into trench warfare, foretelling the tactics associated with World War I. Men kept heads low, for to stand meant certain

34. P. Robertson, *National Tribune,* Mar. 20, 1884, citing a correspondent's story in the *New York Tribune,* June 2, 1864.

35. *O.R.,* Ulysses S. Grant to Henry Halleck, June 3, 1864, 2:00 P.M., 36/1:11, Report of William S. Truex, 36/1:727; diary of George Blotcher.

36. "Zoo-Zoo" to the *Gettysburg Compiler,* June 13, 1864, letter dated June 3, 1864; CMSRs and Pension Records, where applicable, of Isaac Sheads, David G. Myers, Amos Keefer, William Alexander Ogden, and William B. Fullerton, all Co. F, 87th Pa. Sheads died the day after Zoo-Zoo wrote this letter; Keefer survived but without his right arm; Fullerton was captured with David G. Myers but escaped. Ogden was captured while serving as dispatch-bearer, a position he earned due to his "perfect physical condition," according to a deposition of James Adair. Andersonville dramatically changed that condition.

death. By the time Grant pulled his army back on June 12, George Blotcher was so cramped he had difficulty rising.[37]

Tom Crowl wrote a letter from the trenches, one that stared wistfully ahead to September. "The expiration of my time is coming on slowly. There is something like seventy days yet . . . I still trust in god that I will get through safe but still there is big things to be done yet. But I think through July and August it will be to[o] warm to fight. Therefor I am still in hopes it will be to[o] hot for fighting. Hear is not any fun at all."[38]

Hellish as the 87th Pennsylvania's time was during the battles known as the Overland campaign, casualty figures show that the regiment suffered less than any other in the brigade, especially in terms of men killed. Cold Harbor casualties clearly delineate those who charged in the second line on June 1 from those who led the way.[39]

Battle	Regiments in the 1st Brig., 3rd Div., 6th Corps										Total	Total
	87th PA		14th NJ		106th NY		151st NY		10th VT			
	C	K	C	K	C	K	C	K	C	K	Cas	Killed
Wilderness	23	0	4	1	7	4	18	3	10	2	62	10
Spotsylvania	34	1	24	4	32	6	21	2	22	2	133	15
May 22 - June 1	2	0	6	1	4	0	6	2	1	0	19	3
Cold Harbor	28	5	125	29	111	23	36	14	134	28	434	99
Total * *	87	6	159	35	154	33	81	21	167	32	648	127
C = Casualties except killed K = Killed												
Tabulated from *O.R.*, 36: 127, 146, 160, 174.												

Petersburg

Cold Harbor mercifully ended, but what followed was still an ordeal, as Zoo-Zoo explained in words that reveal a man exhausted by war.

Bermuda Hundred, June 18, 1864
For several days we have been changing our base of operations, not with any hope of getting rid of the horrid din of battle, the shrieks of wounded men, and all the circumstances connected with war, but with the belief

37. Diary of George Blotcher.
38. Thomas O. Crowl to his sister, June 10, 1864, CWMC.
39. *O.R.,* sum of casualties from 36/1:127, 146, 160, and 174. Actual 87th Pennsylvania casualty counts totaled from individual CMSRs vary only slightly.

that this is the most practicable route to Richmond . . . Now our war-begrimed veterans, marching through dust and sand, short of rations, with scarcely any sleep, are brought here to bleed and die—to repair damages.

The little fighting Sixth [Corps], of course, had some of the heavy work to do—no less than that of guarding the rear of the army. Few persons can form any idea of the immense amount of work necessary to properly secure the safety of all the artillery, ambulance and wagon trains. After marching sixty hours in succession, we came in sight of the James River. At about five miles distant from Wilson's Landing, we commenced to fortify, getting our wagon trains inside the works as soon as possible. We would march a few hundred yards in the morning, fortify, and cook dinner—move again in the afternoon, fortify, and then cook supper, if making a little water hot and putting some mixture in called coffee, is what generally makes up that pleasant meal. So for a few days we proceeded in that slow, steady way, until the evening of the 16th inst., we suddenly marched on board the John Brooks and steamed away for City Point . . .

We reached here at daylight yesterday morning, marching all night. Oh, how weary the ear gets listening to the tramp, tramp, of those gallant men of ours—these friends, school mates, companions of our earlier and better years. Sun-browned, foot-sore, weary—how discipline has made them uncomplainingly dig, trench, cut, march, all for our common country. If the growlers and fault-finders at home could but see these five hundred smoke-begrimed, war-worn, veterans of ours file past them, after the battle, on the midnight march, they would hide their guilty heads in shame.

Forty-six days, covering almost a whole lifetime, have been passed through by these Pennsylvania boys, and still a hundred days remain for them of toil, work, fight and march, as by a recent order the term of the regiment will not expire until the 24th of September, making some of the men serve thirty days over their times. There is injustice in this.[40]

Fighting shifted from Richmond to Petersburg, Virginia, a rail center vital to the survival of the Confederate capital and where Lee's and Grant's armies would remain locked in struggle almost until the end. The siege of Petersburg was just beginning on June 22 when the 87th Pennsylvania took position west of Jerusalem Plank Road. Lt. Charles Henry Stallman commanded a battalion

40. Zoo-Zoo to the *Gettysburg Compiler,* July 4, 1864, letter dated June 18, 1864. For virtually identical sentiments expressed by a member of the 14th New Jersey, a regiment in the 87th's brigade, see Maj. Peter Vredenburgh to his father, June 4, 1864, in *Upon the Tented Field,* edited by Bernard Olsen.

of 125 men in support of a skirmish line that melted under unexpected Confederate pressure. Almost before anyone realized it, four pieces of artillery, Stallman, and 13 of his men fell into enemy hands, an affair that Ulysses S. Grant called "a stampede."

The experience of seeing comrades whisked away to Rebel prisons unnerved the boys from York, and the next day, those who had escaped that gruesome fate were tired and grumbling. They would have grumbled louder if they had known what was about to happen. Companies I and K were the lucky ones. They pulled duty elsewhere and missed one of the worst days the regiment would ever have to endure.[41]

Unfortunately for eighteen-year-old Charles Edwin Gotwalt, he served with Company A. The boy already had nearly three years of soldiering and a stay in Belle Isle Prison behind him but nothing could prepare him for what was coming. The regiment advanced through the pickets into the lead and all seemed well. Not more than five minutes later, the situation changed with shocking abruptness. The Rebel line broke through and nearly surrounded the 87th. Suddenly, it was every man for himself. Charlie Gotwalt searched for an escape route but soon realized that the Rebels had cut off any chance of escape. A hiding place seemed the next best option. There was a swamp nearby, one covered in tall grass that might hide a man. He tried digging into the ground, but bullets striking the mud in front of him ended that thought. He spied a shallow trench—probably a drainage ditch—and hunkered down, praying the tall grass would hide him until dark. Moments later, he heard a swishing sound, then another. The sound was coming closer. The grass disappeared in front of him. Young Charlie Gotwalt looked up at a Confederate officer standing before him, gripping the sword he had used as a scythe.

"Get out, you damn Yank!" the Rebel officer shouted.[42] Charlie had little choice but to comply with the sharply delivered order, and in a few days he found himself crammed onto a train headed to Andersonville. He had the company of sixty-eight 87th comrades.

Shortly after arriving, Charlie got advice from a long-term inmate: "Look up. If you look down, you'll be dead in three days." That advice did not

41. CMSRs of all men of the 87th Pa.; *O.R.,* Ulysses S. Grant to Henry Halleck, 40/1:13–14; Horatio Wright to George Meade, 40/2:314; Gotwalt, "Adventures"; diary of George Blotcher; James Hersh to his father, July 25, 1864, courtesy Walter Powell; Thomas O. Crowl to his sister, May 3, 1864, CWMC; "J.A.S." to the *Star and Banner,* Feb. 4, 1864, letter dated Jan. 28, 1864. "J.A.S." was possibly Joseph A. Simpson, the 87th's only Adams County man with those initials.

42. CMSR of Charles E. Gotwalt; obituary of Charles E. Gotwalt, *York Dispatch,* Sept. 19, 1938; Gotwalt, "Adventures"; *York Pennsylvanian,* July 9, 1864; *O.R.,* Samuel E. Pingree to Maj. C. A. Whittier, June 25, 1864, 40/2:415; Pension Records of Alfred J. Jameson, letter to his mother, July 1, 1864. Jameson escaped capture and witnessed events from a distance.

save his unidentified mentor, but Charlie used it to survive Andersonville and Millen prisons. Exchanged that December, he recovered sufficiently to attend Abraham Lincoln's second inaugural ceremony and shake the president's hand.

Andersonville did not take too much spunk from him. He fathered twelve children and lived until 1938. During his long life, he no doubt thought about the seventeen boys who went with him to Andersonville and who remain there yet today.[43]

43. Gotwalt, "Adventures"; CMSR and Pension Records of Charles E. Gotwalt. A Southern soldier took Gotwalt's rubber blanket. Adam Stifler to his wife, June 25, 1864, CWMC. Confederates robbed Stifler of his possessions while he lay wounded and helpless. The men recalled this affair as "Weldon Railroad," the same name as the better-known battle of the following month in which the 87th Pennsylvania did not take part.

Chapter 11

Monocacy

Ever the gambler, Robert E. Lee again dared split his army while his enemy stared him in the face. The strategy had worked well on several occasions and never more spectacularly than at Chancellorsville in May 1863. For this mission, Lee put irascible Lt. Gen. Jubal Anderson Early in charge and tasked him with protecting Lynchburg from a Yankee force and, if necessary, chasing the Yankees into Maryland. Early did his job well, driving one section of the Yankee army to Parkersburg, West Virginia, and trapping a second at Harpers Ferry. The Shenandoah Valley was open for the moment, which gave him the freedom to look eastward. Little more than open country lay between his army and Washington, lightly defended since Ulysses S. Grant had stripped the city's defenses to bolster the Army of the Potomac. If Early moved fast, he could be marching down Pennsylvania Avenue before Grant reacted.[1]

Early headed east and sent a cold wind of fear sweeping across southern Pennsylvania. For nearly three days, "a perfect stream of refugees" filled the streets of York and Gettysburg. Trains from several railroad lines chugged into town and steamed away packed with terrified citizens. Shopkeepers fled with wagonloads of goods and bankers emptied vaults. Farmers corralled livestock in preparation to flee or tucked animals into the hiding places they had used successfully a year before. Harrisburg's bridges became so jammed that military authorities denied passage to anyone without business in the state capital. Governor Curtin cancelled a trip to a Gettysburg Fourth of July celebration and put out a call for twelve thousand emergency volunteers, then twelve

---

1. *O.R.,* Report of Robert E. Lee, July 19, 1864, 37/1:346, Report of Jubal A. Early, July 14, 1864, 37/1:347.

thousand more. York's six-week-old *True Democrat,* a Republican newspaper despite its name, reduced issues to one page because the editor and four staff members had volunteered for guard duty. York molded together five emergency companies, a civilian defense force that had no chance of standing against battle-hardened Confederates. The *York Gazette* predicted doom and blasted Ulysses S. Grant for not having his lunch in Richmond by July 4 as it alleged he had promised.[2]

Northern hope for deliverance fell onto the thin shoulders of Maj. Gen. Lew Wallace, a man Chief of Staff Henry Wager Halleck and Commander in Chief Ulysses S. Grant had kept tucked away for two years since his late arrival nearly led to defeat at the battle of Shiloh. In early 1864, President Lincoln gave Wallace command of the military department headquartered in Baltimore, so far a peaceful assignment since the military clamped down on the city in 1861. Halleck had protested even that appointment and predicted that if Wallace's men saw combat, it would be "little better than murder." The ever-twisting path of war was about to test Halleck's prediction.[3]

Given the meager tools available to mount a defense, there seemed little hope that Wallace could be successful withstanding any significant Confederate assault. A few thousand militia and invalids made up most of his force, and Ulysses S. Grant had yet to offer assistance because he was unconvinced that Jubal Early posed any real threat to Washington. Not until July 5 did Henry Halleck convince Grant that the Confederate move was putting the nation's capital in jeopardy. Grant now moved quickly. Short term, the best he could offer was a small holding force, and he sent two brigades of Maj. Gen. James Brewerton Ricketts' division to Wallace. That included the 87th Pennsylvania.[4]

2. *Adams Sentinel,* July 5 and 12, 1864. Curtin was invited by Gettysburg lawyer David Wills, the same man who had invited Abraham Lincoln to speak the previous November at the dedication of the national cemetery. *York Gazette,* July 12, 1864; *Gettysburg Compiler,* July 11, 1864; *True Democrat,* July 19, 1864.

3. *O.R.,* Ulysses S. Grant to J. C. Kelton, Apr. 13, 1862, 10/1:177, Grant to Headquarters, Army of the Tennessee, Apr. 25, 1862, 10/1:174, Report of Lew Wallace, Apr. 12, 1862, 10/1:169–71, General Orders No. 97, 33:671, Henry W. Halleck to William T. Sherman, Apr. 29, 1864, 34/3:332–33; Grant, *Memoirs,* 236. Wallace insisted that confusing orders slowed his progress at Shiloh. Grant disagreed and regretted not relieving Wallace. In 1885, Grant changed his mind upon receipt of new information and added a footnote to his memoirs that exonerated Wallace. See Gloria Baker and Gail Stephens, "Honor Redeemed: Lew Wallace's Military Career and the Battle of Monocacy." Wallace is best known for authoring the novel *Ben Hur* and dealing with a New Mexico range war that involved Billy the Kid.

4. *O.R.,* Henry W. Halleck to Ulysses S. Grant, July 5, 1864, 40/3:82, 3:84; C. C. Augur to Colonel Gamble, C. H. Raymond to Colonel Gamble, and J. H. Taylor to Lieutenant Colonel Clendenin, July 4, 1864, 37/2:34–35.

The boys from York had a day off on July 5 and even merited a whiskey ration. The weather was blistering, so they took time to do laundry and no doubt got themselves as wet as their clothing. Near day's end, news arrived that the Rebels had captured Martinsburg, West Virginia, so it came as no surprise when a 3:00 A.M. blast of reveille sent dreams and them scampering. A dozen-mile march put them Baltimore-bound aboard the steamship *Columbia* and then by train to Monocacy Junction, just east of Frederick, Maryland, arriving by 8:00 P.M., July 8.[5]

At Monocacy Junction, the Baltimore and Ohio fed a spur line into Frederick, and nearby, three bridges carried the railroad and two roads across the Monocacy River on direct routes from the lower Shenandoah Valley to Washington and Baltimore. Two years before, the 87th Pennsylvania had come to this strategic river crossing when Washington feared that Stonewall Jackson was going to storm down the same path. Nothing had happened then and Pvt. Alfred Jameson did not think this trip would be any more eventful. He jotted off a quick letter to ask his mother why everyone was so frightened back home. "They need not be afraid that the rebels will pay them a visit," he assured her, "for we have force everywhere to match them." He was more concerned with getting Mom to send him five dollars.[6]

July 9 dawned with promises of a day better spent sipping a cool drink beneath a shade tree. The 87th Pennsylvania had marched to Frederick shortly after their arrival and spent most of a stormy night returning to Monocacy Junction via a strangely circuitous route. For the moment, they welcomed the heat to dry shoes and clothing. During breakfast, they watched farmers and slaves scamper through fields trying to take in as much wheat as possible before the shooting began.[7]

A short distance away, a New York lieutenant sat on the bank of the Monocacy enjoying the bucolic scenery like a vacationer. There was time to revisit a letter to his sister he had started four days before. "Bijou," as he signed himself, was as blasé about the situation as Alfred Jameson and spent much of his letter bragging about a recent promotion and gaudy pay increase. "I will not finish this letter until night," he wrote, "as we are likely to have a brush

5. Diary of George Blotcher; diary of Beniah Keller Anstine; Prowell, *87th Pennsylvania*, 175. Regiments arrived at different times. George Blotcher said he arrived at 4:00 P.M.

6. *O.R.*, J. W. Garrett to Edward M. Stanton, May 28, 1862, 12/3:274; unknown to the *Star and Banner*, July 3, 1862, letter dated June 12, 1862; *York Gazette*, June 3, 1862; *York Republican*, June 4, 1862; Thomas O. Crowl to aunt and uncle, May 31, 1862, CWMC; Pension Records of Alfred Jameson, letter to his mother, July 8, 1864; *York Pennsylvanian*, July 9, 1864.

7. Diary of Solomon Myers; *National Tribune*, Aug. 21, 1884, from "a paper prepared by request of Post Stannard, No. 2, Grand Army of the Republic, Burlington, Vt."; Glenn H. Worthington, *Fighting for Time: The Battle That Saved Washington*, 101.

with rebs just now and I shall want you to know the result." He returned to the letter two days and a different attitude later.

> By the blessing of God I am spared to finish this letter . . . [At] 9 A.M. the enemy attacked . . . & from that time until nearly sundown we were engaged in a battle as obstinately fought as any of the war . . . Amid such dreadful carnage, it seems almost impossible that any person could escape unharmed as I did . . . The fertile fields of the Monocacy must have been satiated with human gore.[8]

The 87th Pennsylvania's brigade held position near Gambrill Mill and a covered bridge, one of three bridges that drew armies to Monocacy Junction. About 8:00 A.M., Confederate forces approached from Frederick and spread across the field parallel to the river. Shells started raining down on Lew Wallace's men and claimed casualties in the 151st New York. George Prowell wrote in the 87th Pennsylvania regimental history that a round took out three 87th Pennsylvania boys from Company D, but contemporaneous accounts do not confirm that. Years later, James Stahle only recalled the New York injuries. Surely if he remembered the New Yorkers falling, he would have recalled his men's casualties.[9]

By midmorning, fighting extended from the junction to another bridge upriver where the National Road crossed the Monocacy. So far, Lew Wallace's militiamen and cavalrymen were doing most of the work and acquitting themselves better than expected. The Southerners realized that these Yankee militia boys were too well entrenched behind the river to be moved easily. They would have to use other methods to shake them loose.

Gen. John McCausland and his cavalry were selected to do the shaking. The steely-eyed Confederate general slipped downstream behind the cover of hills, pushed aside a small Federal cavalry unit he met while fording the Monocacy, and climbed to the summit of a hill crowned by the Worthington house. Six-year-old Glenn Worthington peeked through a cellar window all that day drinking in sights he would use nearly seventy years later to write the first major history of the day's fighting. McCausland studied the rolling, mostly treeless farm fields lying languid and dusty in the summer drought. Three-quarters of a mile away, the Thomas farm sat atop a low ridge that fate had transformed into a military objective. If McCausland could keep his presence secret a bit longer, he could fall on the Yankee flank and run those shaky

---

8. Abiel Teple LaForge, 106th N.Y., to his sister, multipart letter dated July 5–11, 1864, CWMC.

9. Prowell, *87th Pennsylvania,* 180; recollections of James A. Stahle, *York Gazette,* July 11, 1893; *York Dispatch,* Mar. 10, 1900. No contemporaneous diaries, letters, no newspaper account mentions morning casualties for the 87th, and service records do not identify men injured at that time.

militia boys off the field. Early's army would soon be moving on down the road to Washington.[10]

McCausland's judgment was flawed. Those were not amateurs he saw out there but the 87th Pennsylvania and other regiments of James Ricketts' division, and that brief clash with Union cavalry at the Monocacy had given away his presence. Lew Wallace had ordered James Ricketts to shift his men left to face this new challenge, a dangerous move that put Ricketts' line open to deadly enfilade artillery fire. Nonetheless, the disciplined veterans took only ten minutes—according to Wallace's forty-year-old memory—to position themselves from the Thomas farm to the covered bridge, now burning by Wallace's order to protect Ricketts' rear. The boys from York aligned near the gate of the farm lane, 10th Vermont on their left and the 14th New Jersey "behind a large hawthorne hedge" to the right. Ricketts then peeled off a skirmish line and sent it to a low ridge eight hundred yards forward. They ducked down behind a shrub-and-tree-covered fence along the Worthington/Thomas property line and waited.[11]

John McCausland, unaware of the picket line's existence, ordered his troops to dismount and proceed down the slope past the Worthington house. On they went, hard-as-nails cavalrymen expecting only militia as opposition, cluelessly approaching Ricketts' well-set trap. The last thing some of them remembered was wading through a field covered in waist-high corn and topping a small rise.[12]

Ricketts' men leaped to their feet and fired. McCausland's men "disappeared as if swallowed up in the earth," Glenn Worthington recalled. Dazed Southerners crawled toward the safety of a depression behind the cornfield, but Yankee pickets followed. The Worthingtons heard gunfire drawing closer, feet pounding past the house, and Southern officers cursing in vain trying to get their men to turn on the Yankees. The South's first try at flanking their enemy dissolved in failure.[13]

10. Worthington, *Fighting for Time*, 118. Given his youth at the time of battle and the passage of seventy years before publication, Worthington's accounts must be viewed cautiously. His father watched from upstairs and surely through his son's lifetime related stories that went through an evolutionary process.

11. *O.R.*, Report of William Emerson, July 12, 1864, 37/1:205, Special Orders No. 120, May 24, 1864, Report of Bradley T. Johnson, Aug. 10, 1864, 37/1:354–55; recollections of James A. Stahle, *York Gazette*, July 11, 1893; Lew Wallace, *An Autobiography*, 766–67; *National Tribune*, Apr. 15, 1886, article by Roderick A. Clark.

12. Worthington, *Fighting for Time*, 118.

13. Ibid., 118–120; Lew Wallace, *An Autobiography*, 766–67; Jubal Anderson Early, *Jubal Early's Memoirs: Autobiographical Sketch and Narrative of the War between the States*, 387–88. Both Worthington and Wallace agree that James Ricketts sat on his horse behind the skirmish line as McCausland's men approached. That is questionable. Division commanders usually did not command picket lines. More important, the pickets shot above bushes after standing. Anyone horsed would

McCausland took several hours before he tried again. This time, he brought a larger force and swung farther right to approach from behind a hill. The Federal skirmish line shifted left to meet the attack but was too late. McCausland had the tactical and numeric advantage this time. A half hour later, the Thomas house was in Confederate hands.[14]

That gave Ricketts' men an advantage because Confederate artillery fell silent to avoid hitting comrades. Lew Wallace decided to gamble. Winning this battle was unlikely, but at least he had to delay Jubal Early. Success meant salvaging his military reputation. Even a temporary triumph required holding the high ground around the Thomas farm. That meant someone was going to have to take it the hard way. Wallace rushed an aide to Ricketts with those instructions.[15]

William Henry Lanius, now boasting captain's bars and temporarily assigned to brigade staff, intercepted the aide and asked what was happening. When he heard the orders, he knew he should have passed the order up the chain of command. Instead, he wheeled his horse and galloped toward the regiments positioned at the head of the Thomas farm lane. Enemy fire zipped by him throughout the ride, but he reached his destination unscathed.

"Charge that hill!" Captain Lanius commanded two lieutenant colonels.[16]

Moments later, the now battle-hardened 87th Pennsylvania went shouting up the hill to its finest hour. The home guards had become heroes, and there were witnesses to prove it. "They did [it] in gallant style driving the enemy before them," an observing colonel afterward wrote. Lew Wallace remembered, "The effect was as if a sudden push had been given the enemy . . . Directly the whole opposing formation, catching the contagion of retreat, was going headlong in search of safety." Two New York regiments followed, a member of which later bragged how they also executed the charge "in splendid style." Decades later, Lew Wallace held fast to the memory of his regiments' battle

---

have been visible to McCausland's men, and all accounts agree that they were stunned by the attack.

14. There is a paucity of after-action reports on McCausland's attacks because many of his officers died. James Ricketts wrote only a timeline without details, and neither the 87th's brigade commander, William S. Truex, nor James Stahle wrote reports. See Edward Y. Goldsborough, *Early's Great Raid,* Frank E. Vandiver, *Jubal's Raid: General Early's Famous Attack on Washington in 1864,* and Douglas Southall Freeman, *Lee's Lieutenants: A Study in Command,* vol. 3, *Gettysburg to Appomattox.*

15. James B. Ricketts to Colonels William S. Truex and Matthew R. McClennan, July 9, 1864, 1:20 P.M., Monocacy National Battlefield Interpretive File; *O.R.,* Report of Lew Wallace, July 10, 1864, 37/1:193.

16. Recollections of James A. Stahle, *York Gazette,* July 11, 1893; Wallace, *Autobiography,* 780. Lew Wallace called Lanius's initiative "brilliantly done" but slyly added that, had the results not been as positive, "he might have heard from General Ricketts."

flags barely visible through the thickening haze of gunsmoke, and he recalled John McCausland's men racing in the direction whence they came.[17]

Maj. Gen. John C. Breckinridge, McCausland's immediate superior, watched from a safe distance and realized he needed a stronger force to finish the job. The Rebel general whose politics the *York Gazette* had lauded before the war now issued orders to kill some of its readership. The job fell to Maj. Gen. John Brown Gordon, a year beyond his journey into York County and the siege of Wrightsville. His thirty-six hundred infantrymen had been watching someone else fight for a change and groaned when ordered into action.[18]

Federals saw Confederate battle flags pop over the distant hill, two long, well-formed lines concentrating on the Union left. The 87th Pennsylvania shifted in that direction. James Stahle put 1st Lt. Charles Haack's Company K on the left with orders to hold at all costs. Solomon Myers led Company E to a nearby cornfield to shore up a weak spot, probably directly behind the Thomas house. The 14th New Jersey tacked onto the 87th's right, and the 10th Vermont and a company from the 8th Illinois Cavalry pushed left, ready to fire into the Rebel flank. Men from several regiments positioned themselves in and around the Thomas house.[19]

Lew Wallace watched the enemy approaching and shivered. Their lines were deep and long. His single line was so thin, and he had no reserves to buttress weak points. Continuing fighting at the junction and Washington Turnpike Bridge tied up forces there. Ricketts had one more brigade yet to arrive on the field. It was supposed to have made "all possible haste" getting here from Baltimore. Another thousand rifles would make a difference. Where were they? Wallace risked shifting three hundred or so men from the right to shore up the area around the Thomas farm, a move solidly in the category of damned-if-you-do/damned-if-you-don't.[20]

17. *O.R.,* Report of Col. William Emerson, July 12, 1864, 37/1:205; Wallace, *Autobiography,* 779–80; Lt. George Powell to the *Ogdensburgh (N.Y.) Daily Republican and Journal,* July 19, 1864, letter dated July 11, 1864. James Stahle commanded the 87th Pennsylvania at Monocacy while John Schall recuperated from his Cold Harbor arm wound.

18. Jubal A. Early, "Early's March to Washington in 1864," *Battles and Leaders of the Civil War,* vol. 4, *Retreat with Honor,* 496; John H. Worsham, *One of Jackson's Foot Cavalry,* edited by James I. Robertson, 151–55; John B. Gordon, *Reminiscences of the Civil War,* 310–13.

19. *National Tribune,* Apr. 15, 1886, letter from Roderick A. Clark; recollections of James A. Stahle, *York Gazette,* July 11, 1893; Pre-Battle Land Use Map, Monocacy National Battlefield.

20. Isaac Gordon Bradwell, *Under the Southern Cross: Soldier Life with Gordon Bradwell and the Army of Northern Virginia,* edited by Pharris Deloach Johnson, 179; Wallace, *Autobiography; O.R.,* Report of Maj. Gen. Lewis Wallace, Aug. 1864, 37/1:197; Court-Martial, John F. Staunton, NN-2456, testimony of James B. Ricketts. Wallace made repeated references to the missing brigade in his autobiography.

James Stahle recalled the moment of attack.

> We had hardly got into place before out of the woods and through an oat [hay] field came our foes charging in two lines. They moved in splendid order and excited our admiration by their splendid marching. Orders were at once given that not a shot should be fired until the enemy had reached a large oak tree a hundred yards distant from us, due west, and as that point was reached, with cheers, the firing began and it continued until the enemy was forced to seek the cover of the woods in order to form for another charge.[21]

Blistering Yankee fire felled a Rebel general and many subordinate officers. Southern confidence wavered, but these were veterans, ready to go forward again. This time, they would have company.[22]

A second Rebel wave, ironically led by a Yankee-born general named York, aimed at the Thomas house. Charles Spangler Welsh and sharpshooter Charles William Shultz fought from there, "Spang" Welsh inside, Shultz from the porch. An artillery round smashed into the house, then another, perhaps as many as six. An accurate count did not matter. There were enough to convince Welsh to get out of there. Rebels from that second wave met him at the front door. He was luckier than Charlie Shultz. Stretcher-bearers found him on the porch the next day with nine bullet holes in his body, one of which had shattered his spine. Shultz lingered until October 13, the day many comrades were home receiving discharges.[23]

George Blotcher felt a sledgehammer blow against his leg. The spent ball did not break flesh, but his leg became useless for the moment. A comrade with the royal Teutonic name of Ferdinand Frederick Stegenmyer assisted him from the field and rushed back to the fight. Blotcher never forgot Fred Stegenmyer. He never saw him again, either.[24]

21. Recollections of James A. Stahle, *York Gazette,* July 11, 1893.

22. Edwin Mortimer Haynes, *A History of the Tenth Regiment, Vermont Volunteers,* 202–3; George Washington Nichols, *A Soldier's Story of His Regiment (61st Georgia),* 171–72; Gordon, *Reminiscences,* 310–13; Wallace, *Autobiography;* Bradwell, *Under the Southern Cross,* 179; recollections of James A. Stahle, *York Gazette,* July 11, 1893. The unlucky Confederate general was Clement Anselm Evans, but he survived. Warner, *Generals in Gray,* 347–48. Brig. Gen. Zebulon York was born in Maine in 1819 but moved to Louisiana where he became a successful attorney and the owner of six plantations with 1,700 slaves.

23. Recollections of George Blotcher; CMSR and Pension Records of Charles W. Shultz, Co. E, and Charles Spangler Welsh, Co. F, 87th Pa. Welsh was known exclusively by his middle name. Peter Vredenburgh to his mother, July 12, 1864, *Upon the Tented Field.* Vredenburgh counted the artillery rounds from inside the house.

24. Diary of George Blotcher; CMSR of Frederick Stegenmyer, Co. E, 87th Pa. Blotcher's injury probably occurred before the battle's critical stage, or Stegenmyer would not have been able to leave the field, much less return.

The single line of Yankees could hold no longer. Back it went to a sunken road several hundred yards to the rear of the Thomas house, a natural breastwork reminiscent of Antietam's Bloody Lane. Lt. Charles Haack reached the fence along the road and discovered this mundane object became a monstrous obstacle when someone was shooting at you. A shell fragment split open his body as he reached the top rail. Before he could scream, a second round struck. Men pulled him over the fence and got him back to an ambulance. Life vanished two days later.[25]

A shell exploded in front of Martin James Klinedinst and sent shrapnel slicing through both legs. He did not feel much pain at first, but blood quickly filled his shoes. Another shell fragment tore through Henry Harrison Bortner's right thigh and lodged in his left. In between, it sliced through his right testicle. Another round shattered Charles William Sheads's jaw. He was better off than his cousin Elias. The shell that struck him tore off both of his feet.[26]

A shell shattered Henry Winters Kohler's gunstock and drove wood slivers into his foot. He grabbed at his foot and only then saw that one of his fingers terminated in a bloody stump. Eli Ream and Isaac Jesse Snyder offered to help him off the field, knowing that Kohler had been struggling with a rupture and could make no haste. He told his friends to tend to their Rebel business and limped off on his own. Kohler found Ream in good health after the battle, but Jess Snyder had made the ultimate sacrifice.[27]

The bullet that hit Adj. Anthony M. Martin struck a place soldiers dreaded: just above the hip and into his stomach. Chaplain David Eberhart was in the rear tending horses when he saw stretcher-bearers carrying Martin off the field. The adjutant gave the minister his sword and haversack to return to his family. Bearers carried him to a farmhouse and left him in the care of the family. The former student at Dr. Pfeiffer's New Oxford School survived twenty-four hours before death released him.[28]

25. Haynes, *Tenth Vermont*, 202–3; Nichols, *Soldier's Story*, 171–72; Gordon, *Reminiscences*, 310–13; Wallace, *Autobiography;* Bradwell, *Under the Southern Cross,* 179; CMSR and Pension Records of Charles F. Haack, Co. K, 87th Pa.; recollections of James A. Stahle, *York Gazette,* July 11, 1893; *York Gazette,* July 26, 1864. Haack was initially buried at Ellicott's Mills and later reinterred in York.

26. CMSRs and Pension Records of Henry H. Bortner, Co. C, 87th Pa., surgeon's certificate, Sept. 11, 1875; CMSR and Pension Records of Martin J. Klinedinst, Co. H, depositions of Feb. 13, 1882, and Apr. 21, 1888; CMSR and Pension Records of Elias J. Sheads, deposition of James Adair; CMSR and Pension Records of [Charles] William Sheads, Co. F, 87th Pa.; *Gettysburg Compiler,* July 18, 1864; *Adams Sentinel,* July 19, 1864. An epitaph by a comrade who saw Sheads die said simply, "He was a good man." It is impossible to trace the precise moment every injury occurred, but the timing of some can be inferred.

27. Pension Records of Henry W. Kohler, deposition of Eli Ream, Dec. 15, 1875; CMSR of Isaac Jesse Snyder, Co. C, 87th Pa.

28. Prowell, *87th Pennsylvania,* 186–87; Jacob Martin to James Hersh, July 20, 1864, CWMC. As of the close of 2005, Martin's sword was on display at the Monocacy Visitor's Center.

First Lieutenant John Frederick Spangler positioned himself between James Stahle and Noah Ruhl either to ask a question or make a comment. Stahle never learned which. Before Spangler could speak, a bullet ripped into his chest and lodged in his stomach (indicating they were lying on the ground or leaning forward against the fence). There was no time to get him away, so he lay suffering on the field for eighteen hours. Death came eight days later.[29]

A bullet struck Pvt. Anthony Wolf in the buttocks. Later generations of soldiers would call this "a million dollar wound," but Tony Wolf would have paid much more to have avoided it. The bullet did not stop in his buttock but shredded his bladder and ripped through the ileum, then passed through his large intestine and right kidney. It stopped against his spine. For five days, he lay in a field hospital with feces and urine oozing from the open wound, amazing surgeons that he survived so long before death relieved his suffering.[30]

Not all injuries came from Rebel bullets or shells. Pvt. Eli Israel Mowry was frantically loading and reloading his rifle when excitement caused him to shove his ramrod into the barrel at an angle. The rod bent, Mowry's hand slipped off, momentum propelling it downward. Abruptly his motion halted, and searing pain erupted. He looked down and saw his right hand skewered on the bayonet, the point protruding hideously through the back. The accident severed tendons that never healed.[31]

A third wave of Rebels hit the Yankee right near the river, and Lew Wallace's line collapsed. Their ammunition all but gone, Union boys ran back past Gambrill Mill toward the Baltimore Pike beyond. Confederates that had been banging away at the junction since morning began crossing the Monocacy and pressed the Union rear. Southern accounts said the Yankees fled like sheep. Many Northern reports called it an "orderly withdrawal." Southern versions were probably closer to the truth.[32]

James Stahle recalled that most of the 87th Pennsylvania's casualties occurred during this phase. Among them was Sgt. Daniel Laumaster Welsh, urging his men to stand a bit longer. He was firing his rifle when a minié ball

---

29. CMSR and Pension Records of John Frederick Spangler, Company A; *York Gazette*, Feb. 1892; Prowell, *87th Pennsylvania*, 187. Spangler's father traveled to Frederick and learned that John had been cared for by a Mrs. Doffler whom the elder Spangler eventually married.

30. CMSR of Anthony Wolf, Co. H, 87th Pa.; *Medical and Surgical History of the Civil War*, case 533; *The Monocacy Regiment: A Commemorative History of the Fourteenth New Jersey Infantry in the Civil War 1862–1865*, edited by David G. Martin, 83; Prowell, *87th Pennsylvania*, 186–88.

31. Pension Records of Eli Mowry, Co. I, 87th Pa.

32. *O.R.*, Report of Lew Wallace, July 10, 1864, 37/1:192; Peter Vredenburgh to his mother, July 12, 1864, *Upon the Tented Field*.

tore through his arm and lodged in his chest near his heart. Lt. Robert A. Daniel asked Welsh if he had a message for the folks at home.[33]

Welsh said, "Tell Mother I am dying."[34]

Confederates captured most of the prisoners from Ricketts' division near Gambrill Mill. Charles Augustus "Gus" Laumaster was destroying ammunition when the Rebels seized him. Beniah Keller Anstine and Francis Asbury Hersey managed to avoid capture but became separated from the regiment and spent a long, terrifying night hiding in the woods. Morning light revealed them to a Rebel patrol that sent them on their way to Danville Prison.[35]

Paul Mosebaugh did not fight that day. A respiratory ailment had sapped his strength, so his assignment was nursing the injured, probably at Gambrill Mill. He gave special attention to friend Henry Billmyer who arrived groaning from the effects of a leg wound from the same artillery round that hit Charles Haack. Moments later, a flood of blue uniforms racing past the mill told Mosebaugh he had to leave Billmyer to the mercies of the enemy.[36]

Visions of a Rebel prison brought George Blotcher's leg back to life. Instead of following the mass flight out the Baltimore Pike, he started walking east along the Baltimore and Ohio Railroad tracks, picking up stragglers as he went, possibly from the 10th Vermont. The refugees slept in a haymow that night and walked all the next day without eating. Blotcher went on alone the following day for reasons he never explained, once hiding when Rebel cavalry passed close by with a herd of cattle. An empty belly forced him to beg for food at a farmhouse, but he got lucky and picked a generous Union family. Good fortune stayed around one more day when he came across a railroad handcar and soon was pumping his way to the Relay House. He hopped a train to Baltimore and found the regiment, shocking comrades who had thought him dead or captured.[37]

33. Recollections of James A. Stahle, *York Gazette,* Feb. 1892.

34. Robert Alonzo Daniel to the *True Democrat,* Aug. 9, 1864, letter dated July 24, 1864. Daniel reported Welsh's full quote as, "Tell Mother I am dying but in the defense of our glorious nationality and the protection of that dear old flag." One must be dubious of these oft-reported but probably exaggerated, if not fictionalized, accounts of the dying as efforts by comrades to comfort a dead soldier's loved ones. If Daniel's estimate of the time of Welsh's fatal wounding is accurate, stopping to talk would have put him at great personal risk.

35. CMSR and Pension Records of Henry Billmyer, deposition of Charles A. Laumaster, Feb. 14, 1888; CMSR of Francis A. Hersey, Co. C, 87th Pa.; diary of Beniah Keller Anstine.

36. Pension Records of Henry Billmyer, Co. K, 87th Pa., statement of Henry Dobbins, June 16, 1884, and deposition of Paul Mosebaugh, Aug. 15, 1889.

37. Diary of George Blotcher. This was the Baltimore and Ohio's Relay House, not the Northern Central's. Blotcher wrote, "*We* [emphasis added] left on one of the B & O R. R. hand cars . . ." He did not clarify the membership of "we."

Noah Ruhl was leading a weary 87th Pennsylvania away from the battlefield when he saw a train approaching. Ricketts' missing brigade had finally arrived. The brigade's commander, Col. John F. Staunton, known to Ruhl from Winchester the previous year, got a briefing on what had happened and then ordered two companies off the train to cover the retreat. He hurried the train back to Monrovia, about eight miles from the battlefield.[38]

That may have been the only immediate action John Staunton took that day. His troop train had departed Baltimore at 7:45 A.M. on a fifty-nine-mile journey the Wheeling Express routinely covered in about two hours. While needing to take more care than a peacetime carrier, Staunton's train stopped too often for too long. He argued that he had been at the mercy of railroad officials on board, which speaks volumes about his leadership, a quality that several Union generals had long been certain he did not possess. A court-martial agreed and sent him home to Philadelphia in disgrace.[39]

The 87th Pennsylvania's surgeon, David Ferguson McKinney, stayed behind at his medical post at or near Gambrill Mill. When the Confederates left on July 10, they paroled him to serve his patients. McKinney's duties took him several miles distant to "Arcadia," a stately, hilltop home that necessity had transformed into a hospital. In spite of the gore he witnessed and doubtless created there, McKinney found the house and Frederick enchanting and returned after the war to buy Arcadia. He lived there until his death in 1915.[40]

Federal troops arrived later on the 10th and began the grisly tasks of burying the dead and retrieving the wounded. There was much to do. The Thomas farm was a virtual charnel house. Before the Confederates left, a Catholic priest serving as chaplain of the 14th Louisiana observed the carnage.

> On the crest of the hill where our men first attacked the enemy, we saw
> a regular line of Yankee bodies. A little in the rear they were to be seen

38. Court-Martial, John F. Staunton, Staunton to James B. Ricketts, Aug. 8, 1864. Gail Stephens of the Monocacy National Battlefield has studied the battle as much or more than anyone and believes, though admittedly without definitive proof, that Staunton's train never went beyond Monrovia.

39. Herbert H. Harwood Jr., *Impossible Challenge: The Baltimore and Ohio Railroad in Maryland,* 67; Court-Martial, John F. Staunton. Staunton was found guilty of "disobedience of orders" and "neglect of duty" but not guilty of "misbehavior before the enemy." *O.R.,* John Wool to Colonel Townsend, ser. 2, 4:489, B. F. Kelly to W. H. Cheesebrough, 25/2:131. Staunton's record included a charge of mistreating Confederate prisoners. Maj. Gen. Benjamin Franklin Kelly had once protested Staunton's promotion and insisted that they should instead look for "a good and efficient officer."

40. Pension Records of David Ferguson McKinney, Surgeon, 87th Pa; Benjamin Franklin Cooling, *Monocacy: The Battle That Saved Washington,* 161. Cooling misidentifies McKinney as "a local man." He was from Pinecreek Township, Clinton County, Pennsylvania, and living there at war's onset.

lying in every direction and position, some on their sides, some on their faces, some on their backs with their eyes and mouths open, the burning sun beating upon them, and their faces swarming with disgusting flies.[41]

Union veterans emphasized overwhelming Confederate numbers as the reason for their defeat at Monocacy. George Blotcher thought the odds so lop-sided that giving battle had been "folly." A New Jersey officer reported thirty thousand Rebels had attacked, and an Illinois cavalryman wondered why they had been sent there since "the Rebs outnumbered us 10 to 1." In truth, num-bers were not as grossly imbalanced as the defeated Yankees thought. Lew Wallace commanded an effective force of about six thousand. Jubal Early reported his infantry did not exceed ten thousand, a number confirmed by his staff member Henry Kyd Douglas. Eighty years later, famed southern historian Douglas Southall Freeman agreed and added four thousand cavalry and artillerymen to the Confederate head count. Authorities at the Monocacy National Battlefield concur with a total Confederate strength of about sixteen thousand, but Early detached two thousand cavalrymen to wreak havoc on some of the Northern Central Railway bridges the 87th Pennsylvania once had guarded. Given weaponry of the time, two-to-one odds were not neces-sarily overwhelming when attacking fixed defensive positions. Lew Wallace lost the battle because he had too much ground to cover with the force avail-able to him. The absence of John Staunton's brigade had been critical.[42]

Years later, Jubal Early expressed amusement at northern claims of his man-power and blamed headcount inflation on "the wild state of alarm and con-sternation into which my advance threw the authorities." He was correct. By the time news of his coming reached York, the *Gazette* reported Early's man-power at forty thousand, a "perfectly reliable" count, the *Gazette* claimed, be-cause it came one from employees of the Baltimore and Ohio Railroad "who have facilities for ascertaining the Rebel strength." The *Gettysburg Compiler* puffed up the count to forty-five thousand.[43]

There is, however, no disputing the South's overwhelming artillery advan-tage. Lew Wallace recalled, "The cannonading and the noise of bursting shells

41. James B. Sheeran, *Confederate Chaplain: A War Journal,* 94.

42. *O.R.,* J. McEntee to Col. G. H. Sharpe, June 28, 1864, 37/1:684, Adjutant General U.S. Army [Henry Halleck] to Maj. Gen. David Hunter, July 6, 1864, 37/1:177, Report of Jubal A. Early, July 14, 1864, 37/1:348–49; recollections of George Blotcher; Abiel Teple LaForge to his sister, July 5–11, 1864, CWMC; Edwin C. Bearss, *Documentation Troop Movement Maps: Battle of Monocacy,* 73, citing Silas D. Wesson, 8th Ill. Cav.; Henry Kyd Douglas, *I Rode with Stonewall,* 281–82; Freeman, *Lee's Lieutenants,* 3:558; Jubal A. Early, "The Advance on Washington," *SHSP,* 9:297–312; *Army of the Valley Returns,* comp. Gail Stephens, from reports in *O.R.* and accounts in Harvard's Library.

43. *York Gazette,* July 12, 1864; *Gettysburg Compiler,* July 18, 1864.

were furious—I had almost said infernal." Wallace had six three-inch rifled guns and one twenty-four-pound big gun disabled during the fight. The South had about thirty-five guns, many of larger caliber. A large percentage of 87th Pennsylvania casualties were shell wounds.[44]

Whatever the odds, Union veterans of Monocacy always claimed their sacrifice saved Washington. They have a point. Jubal Early's force reached Washington as planned but at least one day delayed and weakened by a loss of manpower and the physical exertion required to fight an entire day in summer's heat and humidity. Federal reinforcements arrived in Washington in time to stall Early's attack, forces that could not have arrived one day sooner. No less an authority than Ulysses S. Grant recognized Lew Wallace's effort as "a greater benefit to the cause than . . . a victory." As of May 2006, there are two major books on the battle of Monocacy, both subtitled "The Battle That Saved Washington," and a video subtitled "The Battle That Rescued Washington." No one wanted to believe that more than the veterans of the 87th Pennsylvania. William Henry Lanius spent years in an effort to have a monument erected on the battlefield.[45]

War offers many opportunities to twist history down a different path. Monocacy is hardly the Civil War's only example, but it is the subject here. What if Lew Wallace's men had been unable to reach Monacacy Junction by July 9, 1864, or had given up the defense of the junction as George Blotcher and others had argued?

A Confederate takeover of Washington would not have been tactically significant—Jubal Early admitted he could not have held the city with the force at his immediate disposal—but wars are not just about tactical victories. By mid-1864, the country was war-weary. Northern cries for peace had grown to cacophonous levels, fueled by casualty figures so gruesome that the Copperhead faction attached the pejorative "butcher" to Ulysses S. Grant. Now, President Lincoln was asking for more men for his military machine. The *Gettysburg Compiler* howled, "Seven hundred thousand men have been enlisted and drafted since the 17th of last October, and the cry still is—Give! Give!" The *York Gazette* claimed that the "desolating war, with its drain-

44. Wallace, *Autobiography,* 766–67; Early, "Advance on Washington," *SHSP,* 9:297–312; *O.R., Report of Lew Wallace,* July 10, 1864, 37/1:192; Henry Kyd Douglas, *I Rode with Stonewall,* 281–82; *Army of the Valley Returns,* comp. Gail Stephens.

45. Worthington, *Fighting for Time;* Cooling, *Monocacy; No Retreat from Destiny: The Battle That Rescued Washington* (Historical Entertainment and Lionheart Filmworks, 2006). See Brian Pohanka's introduction in the 1985 edition of Worthington's book for another view of the battle's historical importance. See also Grant, *Memoirs,* 606–7.

ing conscriptions and heavy taxation" would lead to "the total decimation of Pennsylvania."[46]

Abraham Lincoln's reelection that November came in no small part from an uplift in public morale generated by several small military successes during September and October. William T. Sherman made a major contribution to the Lincoln reelection campaign when he captured Atlanta, Georgia, in early September. Two weeks later, Lincoln gained more ground after the Union scored several victories in and around Winchester, Virginia. A mid-October victory at Middletown, Virginia, a battle known as Cedar Creek, put an exclamation point on both the fall political and military campaigns by snuffing out the Confederate army's existence in the Shenandoah Valley.

Had Jubal Early put the torch to Washington that July, Federal military strategy would likely have been altered, and those battles in Virginia might never have taken place. If nothing else, confidence in Ulysses S. Grant would have plummeted as the public added his name to a long list of military failures unable to subdue the Southern rebellion—and the only general to have lost Washington. After all, it had been his decision to weaken the capital's defenses to shore up the Army of the Potomac. Absent any other major military victory that different circumstances might have generated, the South would have maintained military pressure on northern Virginia and offset the great news from Georgia. Most important, the South would have bought time, its most precious ally.

Images of federal buildings lying in smoking ruin would have melted Abraham Lincoln's political ground into the consistency of quicksand. Shouts for instant peace assuredly would have risen to a volume too loud to ignore. Democrats likely would have gained control of the White House as well as one or both houses of Congress and made good their campaign promise of procuring a negotiated peace "at the earliest practicable moment." A rebuffed Abraham Lincoln would have remained president untl March but with authority drained by defeat. He might even have succumbed to reality and sought a negotiated peace himself.[47]

Peace without Northern victory would have been a devastating blow to the future development of the United States. A treaty either would have granted autonomy to the Confederacy or offered it major concessions to return to the Union. Black Americans in the South would have remained in bondage

46. *Gettysburg Compiler,* July 4, 1864; *York Gazette,* July 26 and Aug. 2, 1864.
47. Democratic Party Platform, 1864, *The Making of American Democracy: Reading and Documents,* edited by Ray Allen Billington, Bert James Loewenberg, and Samuel Hugh Brockunier (New York: Rinehart & Company, 1950), 368–69.

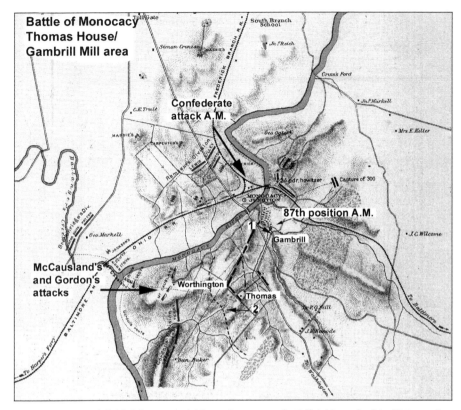

Monocacy Battlefield, July 9, 1864 (*Atlas to Accompany the Official Records of the Union and Confederate Armies,* image 83, additions by the author). The battle started in the morning as Confederate forces came from the direction of Frederick, then spread around the Union left.

for decades to come. Although Southern angst generated by Reconstruction would never have materialized—possibly ameliorating future race relations in the South—the issues of slavery's expansion into territories and the return of interstate runaways would have remained unresolved. Even when the states were reunited, secession or the threat of it would have become a viable option during all future state-versus-federal-rights confrontations—perhaps even within states that had geographical differences. It is realistic to envision a United States so splintered, so weakened, so susceptible to foreign intervention that it would be unlikely to exist today in anything like its present form, if at all.

Not for nothing did the boys from York and their comrades sacrifice themselves along the banks of the Monocacy River.

1. James Gambrill's mill and house. The 87th formed here in the morning and fled past it that afternoon (Monocacy National Battlefield).

2. View from the 87th Pennsylvania's position left of the Thomas house, facing John B. Gordon's approach over the distant hill. Sadly, Interstate 270 now cuts through the battlefield (photo by the author).

Chapter 12

Final Days of War

On August 7, 1864, Lt. James Hersh wrote from Harpers Ferry that the regiment was rested, regrouped, and ready to fight since its transfer to the Shenandoah Valley. Hersh had just returned from a Rebel prison and already made up his mind to go home the moment his enlistment ended. He was happy, though, that Phil Sheridan was going to take command in the valley. With a month left, the boys from York who had not reenlisted prayed that General Sheridan might end their military life as easily as it had started. The aggressive Phil Sheridan was not about to answer that prayer.[1]

Meanwhile, the War Department issued a directive that stunned almost every Union army officer who looked forward to going home. The army required a man receiving a commission or promotion to a higher commissioned rank to muster out at his old rank and remuster at the new one. A Washington bureaucrat decided that new muster meant the three-year enlistment period started anew and ordered the policy into action retroactively. With the swipe of a pen, he became one of the most hated men north of Virginia. Officers expressed "undisguised astonishment," a polite nineteenth-century expression roughly translated "[insert profanity here]." Under this regulation, Solomon Myers was the only 87th Pennsylvania officer eligible to muster out on time.[2]

This time, it was the 87th Pennsylvania officers who sent a protest letter to Governor Andrew Curtin. They had powerful support. Ulysses S. Grant advised Henry Halleck that "such a decision at this late day is of doubtful

---

1. James Hersh to his brother, Aug. 5, 1864, and his father, Aug. 7, 1864, courtesy Walter Powell.
2. Circular No. 61, War Department, PA AGO, Muster Rolls, box 54, folder 19.

expediency," and George G. Meade voiced similar objections. The generals had practical reasons for complaining. Men were refusing commissions if they had to remain in the army another three years. Several Company H sergeants, once so unhappy that they had missed out on promotions, now turned down offers of advancement. The War Department rescinded the onerous regulation in time for the officers of the 87th Pennsylvania to return to civilian life at the end of their original terms of service.[3]

Regimental demographics began changing that September and continued doing so throughout the following months. Recruits were arriving—sixty-four draftees and ninety-nine substitutes by year's end—but few were from York or Adams County. Draft rendezvous provided men who were more likely from Blair, Somerset, Bradford, Lycoming, or Bedford County. The following March, forty-eight more arrived, mostly volunteers, many from Lancaster County. By war's end, men from forty-six Pennsylvania counties had seen service with the 87th Pennsylvania. Overall, the new boys were younger, shorter, less apt to be married or of German heritage, and more likely to be unskilled workers. The 87th Pennsylvania was no longer "the boys from York."[4]

The regiment fought two battles that September. The first clash at Winchester on September 19 offered a cleansing experience when the men avenged their defeat of sixteen months earlier. For the first time, the men of the 87th Pennsylvania were able to say after a battle, "We won!" Victory came at a price. As many 87th men died in one day as in the previous three-day affair at Winchester, and the wounded count was two and a half times greater.[5]

The 87th's brigade charged across open ground at Winchester but advanced too far forward and had to fall back. A lull fell in the fighting, and some men stood around a house catching a little rest while awaiting the order that would send them back across the field. Rebel artillery did not rest, though. George Blotcher kept a sharp eye out for shells and stayed busy dodging them. One crashed through a nearby fence. Unfortunately for James Hanson Weakley,

---

3. Officers of the 87th Pennsylvania to Gov. Andrew G. Curtin, Aug. 21, 1864, PA AGO, Muster Rolls, box 54, folder 19; *O.R.,* Ulysses S. Grant to Henry Halleck, Sept. 9, 1864, 42/2:756, George G. Meade to Edwin Stanton, Sept. 10, 1864, 42/2:769; CMSRs of Solomon Myers and William E. Culp; anonymous 87th Pa. man to the *True Democrat,* Sept. 13, 1864, letter dated Sept. 3, 1864; PA AGO, Muster Rolls, John W. Schall to Samuel B. Thomas on the withdrawal of George Mowrer's and William F. Zorger's commissions, Aug. 14 and 25, 1864; Charles H. Buehler to an unknown general recommending William E. Culp for promotion, Aug. 31, 1864.

4. CMSRs and Pension Records, where applicable, of all men of the 87th Pa.; U.S. Census, 1850–1860, Pennsylvania, all counties. The statement of forty-six counties does not include the five companies that joined the regiment in March 1865.

5. CMSRs of all men of the 87th Pennsylvania.

he was standing just behind. The shell nearly tore him in half. No stretcher-bearers were available, so Blotcher and Cyrus Reher rolled Weakley onto a blanket and carried him to the hospital.[6]

Broken and sobbing, Weakley looked up at Blotcher and asked, "George, do you think I have to die?"

Blotcher hesitated but said, "I cannot see how you can get over this, Jim. There is no chance left for you."

The hospital was more than a mile to the rear, a journey that Weakley experienced in agonizing consciousness. Blotcher and Reher stopped several times to give him what relief was possible. They reached the hospital and said good-bye, then took time to drink a cup of coffee amidst piles of arms and legs deep enough to fill a wagon. They looked in on their wounded comrade before returning to the battle, but conversation for Jim Weakly had ended.[7]

Blotcher and Reher returned in time for the final charge that drove the Confederate army from Winchester. Years later, Blotcher recalled that day with the sense of glory that only the passage of time allows.

> This charge was made in open country. You could see for miles up and down the battle line like a half moon, and seeing all our colors waving in the air, it was a grand sight to behold, and in this condition our lines swept on unbroken for a good distance. But we came to a halt for a short time in order to give our cavalry a chance to make [a] dash on the retreating enemy, and they made a big haul of prisoners while doing so. After the cavalry had retired, our line swept on till we reached the Winchester Pike on the right side of Winchester, but during this charge we had to face all the enemy cannons and musketry, which was flying thick and fast, and several of our color bearers were wounded. At last the colors were picked up by Daniel Reigel, Company F, and he carried those colors through the balance of the engagement and all through the balance of the war.[8]

Three days later, one last fight closed out the military careers of many who should have gone home days before. Fisher's Hill was an eminence south of Winchester near Strasburg—more a ridge than a hill, actually. The Valley Pike ascended there, making it easy for even a small force to block that critical

---

6. Recollections of George Blotcher; *O.R.*, Report of William Emerson, Sept. 27, 1864, 43/1:231–32.

7. Recollections of George Blotcher. Blotcher doctored his diary years later, but the conversations are reasonable under the circumstances.

8. Ibid.

road. Confederate forces had withdrawn there after the Winchester battle. The Yankees went after them with well-executed vengeance, routing the thin Confederate line with a textbook example of a flanking maneuver. The 87th paid with four wounded, mostly minor injuries, but Valentine Myers's captors postponed his trip home by nine months. Nathaniel Vroman concluded a six-week army experience by being the only 87th man killed that day.[9]

For those who had not reenlisted, at last it was time to go home. The regiment received the order September 23 while at Woodstock, Virginia. George R. Prowell stated in the regimental history that 250 men left for home that day. The muster-out roll contained 326 names that October, but many men arrived from hospitals or detached service. On the return trip, some had their discharges rudely delayed. The second night out, near Harrisonburg, nine men were in advance of the regiment serving picket duty. "Mosby's men" swooped down and sidetracked their trip home through a prison camp at Salisbury, North Carolina, where they remained up to nine months. Henry Clay Pentz was the most jinxed of the group. He was nursing a wound from the Winchester fight.[10]

For the rest, folks at home were eagerly awaiting their return.

September 27, 1864, was a Tuesday, but the people of York only accomplished half their normal workload that day. The boys from York were coming home—some of them, at least. Community leaders met that morning and decided the town would shut its doors as soon as they heard the troop train arriving. About 1:00 P.M., the townspeople heard a distant locomotive whistle and rushed to the station to greet their returning sons with a restless sea of waving handkerchiefs and American flags. The army hospital band pumped out patriotic tunes in counterpoint to a chorus of bells pealing from

9. The bridge over Tumbling Run that carried the old roadway over Fisher's Hill is still visible, as is the road trace. It is beautifully drawn as it appeared then in *The James E. Taylor Sketchbook*, 455. CMSRs of all men of the 87th Pa. Nathaniel Vroman joined for duty Aug. 1, 1864. His name is also spelled "Veoman" and "Vooman."

10. PA AGO, Muster Rolls, Special Order No. 204, Sept. 23, 1864; diary of George Blotcher; CMSRs of all men of the 87th Pa.; Pension Records, where applicable, of the following men: William Denues, William Henry Clay Ginter, and Henry Clay Pentz, Co. A; Levi Mansberger and Peter Frysinger Zorger, Co. B; William Marques Wolf, Co. E; Solomon McMaster and Henry Swope, Co. I; Henry Clay Spangler and Thomas Gardner Taylor, Co. K, 87th Pa.; Prowell, *87th Pennsylvania*, 248. Prowell omitted McMaster and Taylor. The Confederate partisans may have been part of Lt. Col. John Singleton Mosby's force, but Federal soldiers in that part of Virginia tended to blame Mosby for all cavalry activity.

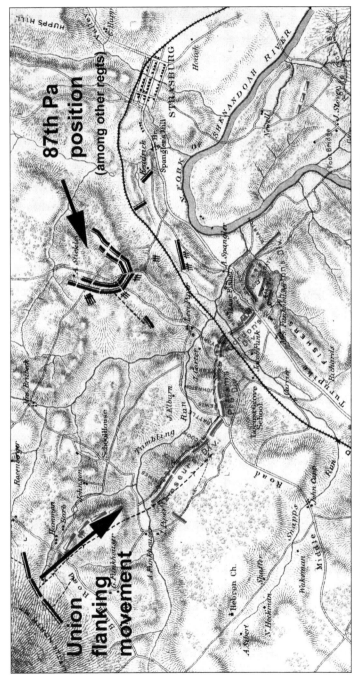

Battlefield at Fisher's Hill (*Atlas to Accompany the Official Records of the Union and Confederate Armies*, image 82, additions by the author).

every church steeple in town. "They look a little weather beaten," the *Adams Sentinel* reported, but they were home.[11]

These boys from York made one last march together, one that snaked through streets lined with cheering citizens. They halted in the town square and again endured speeches from men whose closest encounter with death was York's bloodless capitulation the year before. Old Camp Scott on the fairgrounds served as headquarters until muster-out, but the men were free to go home for a few days before returning for the final ceremony. John Schall got busy gathering up men scattered on detached duty or in hospitals.[12]

Meanwhile, York set out to prepare the finest celebration it could manage. The committee list quickly contained three hundred surnames that resembled an 87th Pennsylvania muster roll. The committee on table linen was up to the challenge of covering two 170-foot-long tables constructed by the committee on building tables. The knife-and-fork committee left no one lacking means to shovel enormous quantities of food into eager mouths, much of it put on plates by the committee on carving. The sumptuous feast took place in the hospital chapel on Penn Commons that rang with comradeship rather than fire-and-brimstone sermons. Of course, the boys had to listen to glass-lifting acclamations by big shots on the committee on toasts.[13]

At 5:00 P.M., October 13, 1864, their lives as soldiers ended. The paymaster was some days in arriving, but that was an old story. Money is an ephemeral article. Memories stay around until the last breath.[14]

The rest of the regiment was stuck in the field crunching hardtack, drinking dirty water, and yearning for an outhouse stocked with paper. Remaining on duty were:

138 of the original 193 Veteran Volunteers

119 of the 151 men who enrolled October 1861–May 1864; 7 mustered out by year's end

139 of the 178 men enrolled June–October 1864.[15]

11. *Cartridge Box* (U.S. Army Hospital, York, Pa.), Oct. 1, 1864; *York Gazette,* Oct. 4, 1864; *Adams Sentinel,* Oct. 4, 1864.

12. CMSR of George Feathers, Co. A, 87th Pa.; John Schall to Chief Surgeon, Haddington General Hospital, Oct. 5, 1864; CMSR of George Washington Meisenhelder, Co. B, 87th Pa.; John Schall to Surgeon in Charge, Chester Hospital, Oct. 5, 1864; *York Gazette,* Oct. 18, 1864.

13. *Cartridge Box,* Oct. 15, 1864; Prowell, *87th Pennsylvania,* 252–59.

14. *York Gazette,* Oct. 18, 1864.

15. CMSRs of all men of the 87th Pa.

Some of the 396 men were in hospitals, on detached service, or in Rebel prisons. However many were actually available to shoot at the enemy, regulations required them to consolidate to five companies and lose the name *regiment.* Companies F–K folded in reverse sequence into A–E. For the next six months, the army called them the 87th Pennsylvania *Battalion.*[16]

Maj. Theodore Augustus Helwig automatically became ranking officer, but he was a surgeon with no interest in field command. The army had assigned him to the 87th Pennsylvania that April after his experience with medical nightmares at Antietam and Chancellorsville. The German immigrant may have been the most erudite man ever to serve with the 87th Pennsylvania, demonstrating a command of written English few native Americans could match. The 87th's first surgeon, David Ferguson McKinney, often was unable to assist men in their postwar quests for pensions. McKinney clearly kept few records and frequently seemed disinterested, although 2nd Winchester destroyed many records. Helwig never failed to provide detailed accounts for men once under his care and often went the extra mile.[17]

Field command devolved to Capt. Edgar Monroe Ruhl, who had risen to command partly because Noah Ruhl had seen to his son's advancement. He also was the most senior field officer left, and it fell to him to write the regiment's after-action report for the most recent battle of Winchester. The terse account would be his first and last. Sometime after midnight on a frosty October night near Middletown, Virginia, Captain Ruhl busied himself with the day-to-day activities required of a commander. The battalion needed a quartermaster, so he wrote a recommendation for Sgt. William Esias Culp to take the job. Ruhl must have rushed it into the mail because he dated it October 19, and he would die before that day properly started. At dawn, the Confederate army pulled off the Civil War's version of "shock and awe" when it launched the war's greatest surprise attack. There, on a ridge overlooking the grand Belle Grove Plantation, 87th draftee Pvt. Simon Alfred Bendon, a

16. PA AGO, Muster Rolls, War Department Special Orders No. 86, Apr. 2, 1863, and No. 204, Sept. 23, 1864; Edgar M. Ruhl to the state adjutant general, Oct. 19, 1864; Federal Muster Rolls, R. I. Dodge to Colonel Cross, Sept. 30, 1864. Edgar Ruhl said there were 13 officers and 400 men. Prowell, *87th Pennsylvania,* 212, claims 200 but may have referred only to pre-1864 volunteers. Realignment merged companies thusly: K-A, I-B, H-C, and F-E. Years later, many veterans reported only their last company and not the one in which they spent three years.

17. CMSRs of Theodore A. Helwig, assistant surgeon and surgeon, 128th Pa. and 87th Pa., and David F. McKinney, surgeon, 87th Pa. Helwig's writing reveals his education. For examples, see Pension Records of Edgar M. Ruhl, Theodore A. Helwig to Mrs. Noah Ruhl, Oct. 22, 1864. See also Pension Records of Adam Henry Stifler, Co. C, 87th Pa., deposition of Theodore A. Helwig, Nov. 30, 1864; Theodore A. Helwig to Col. S. B. Thomas, Feb. 11, 1865, PA AGO. Obituary of Theodore A. Helwig, *Pottsville Republican,* Dec. 22, 1898.

wounded veteran of both Antietam and Chancellorsville, said that Company A "was nearly wiped off the face of the earth." One of those Rebel bullets drilled into Edgar Ruhl's chest and killed him almost instantly.[18]

The battle of Cedar Creek may have been a tragedy for the Ruhl family, but it proved a triumph for the Reigle clan. By afternoon, the Confederate onslaught had lost momentum, and Gen. Philip Sheridan made his famous ride to rally his army and break tired Southern forces. Cpl. Daniel Peter Reigle had carried the flag for the 87th Pennsylvania for the previous month while burdened by a wound suffered at Fisher's Hill. Flag-bearers had to be a stalwart lot; they got shot at appalling rates. Reigle stepped up his efforts at Cedar Creek when he saw an enemy counterpart waving his battle flag. He wanted that one and raced into the field, yelling for his comrades to follow, waving his flag to and fro. To his surprise, he found himself in a footrace with a New York lieutenant who had similar aims on the Rebel banner. Even carrying his own flag, Reigle was more fleet-footed and wrested the prize from the Confederate flag-bearer.[19]

Dan Reigle no doubt beamed when the division lined up for dress parade on October 22 and listened to a statement of commendation from division commander Col. Joseph Warren Keifer. Throughout the division, men heard "Corp. *David P. Reigler* [sic] . . . [cited] for bravery displayed upon the battlefield." It would have been more of an acclamation had Colonel Keifer's staff learned their hero's name before publicly patting him on the back.[20]

The 87th Pennsylvania had a hero. What it did not have was a commander. The army temporarily handed that job to 1st Lt. John Andrus Salsbury, 10th Vermont, a move that did not sit well with the Pennsylvanians. Principal Musician Lewis I. "Nut" Renaut let that fact be known by demonstrating why friends had given him his nickname. The Hanover resident had a long record of service, having responded at the first call in April 1861 to serve as musician with the 16th Pennsylvania and soon thereafter assumed the same

18. *O.R.*, Report of Edgar M. Ruhl, Sept. 26, 1864, 43/1:242, Report of John A. Salsbury, Nov. 1, 1864, 43/1:242; PA AGO, Muster Rolls, Edgar M. Ruhl to the state adjutant general, Oct. 19, 1864; Theodore A. Helwig to Mrs. N. G. Ruhl, Oct. 22, 1864, Pension Records of Edgar M. Ruhl; CMSR and pension records of Simon Alfred Bendon, Co. A, 87th Pa., and Co. K, 125th Pa.

19. Office of the Adjutant General, Regimental Descriptive and Order Book, 87th Pa., NARA, p. 43, Circular Oct. 22, 1864; George Powell to the *Ogdensburgh Daily Republican and Journal*, July 19, 1864, letter dated July 11, 1864, and "P.R." to the *Journal*, Nov. 8, 1864, letter dated Oct. 31, 1864. Thomas Shaw, 106th New York, was the man who lost the flag race to Reigle.

20. Regimental Descriptive and Order Book, 87th Pa., p. 43, Circular Oct. 22, 1864, emphasis added. Order books of the 14th New Jersey and 106th New York contain the same misspelling. See Medal of Honor Citations, www.army.mil/cmh-pg/mohciv.htm (accessed June 1, 2006); Biographical Directory of the United States Congress. J. Warren Keifer, as he was most often known, became Speaker of the House of Representatives in the 47th Congress.

role with the 87th Pennsylvania. Captured at Carter's Woods, he received his principal musician's rank shortly after returning to duty and soon reenlisted as a veteran volunteer. Trouble started on November 2 when Renaut decided to consume an alcoholic beverage and did not stop at one. When John Salsbury encountered him, Renaut was "crazy drunk" and "very noisy and boisterous." Salsbury grabbed Renaut, pushed him into his tent, and ordered him to stay put and calm down.

Renaut shouted, "I'll be damned if I will be commanded by any damned 10th Vermont son of a bitch!"

Salsbury ordered 2nd Lt. William Crosby Waldman, an original 87th man then acting as adjutant, to handle Renaut. Waldman made no effort to be subtle. He "clinched" Renault, who would have none of it. The fight was on. Renaut punched Waldman in the face at least twice and sank his teeth deep into Waldman's hand. When his mouth was not full of Waldman's body parts, Renaut screamed repeatedly, "I'll be the death of you!" Waldman kept a tight grip.

Renaut screamed, "I'll kill you, God damn you, as soon as I get loose!"

The noise carried to brigade headquarters, which sent word that things had better get quiet in the camp of the 87th Pennsylvania. Waldman somehow jammed a blanket into Renaut's mouth and kept it there until he quieted.

Renaut's drunken frenzy led him to a court-martial on charges of conduct prejudicial to good order, disobedience of orders, and striking a superior officer, on its own enough to put him before a firing squad. His only excuse was that he had been drunk and had not known what he was doing. The court, with no officers from the 87th Pennsylvania, apparently took his long service into consideration and sentenced him to the loss of four months' pay and four months at hard labor, the first two wearing a ball and chain. Backbreaking and impoverishing as the next four months were to be for Lewis Renaut, he would live, and he would leave the army with an honorable discharge.[21]

Clearly, someone acceptable to the battalion had to take command. Many men were interested, an attraction that lasted virtually until the regiment mustered out of service. James A. Stahle made overtures to command a col-

---

21. Court-Martial, Lewis I. Renaut, LL-3030; CMSR and Pension Records of Lewis I. Renaut, Co. G and D, 87th Pa. Maj. Gen. Truman Seymour authorized the sentence but scolded Salsbury and Waldman for dealing with Renaut themselves, asserting, "A commissioned officer always humiliates himself by a personal contest with a soldier . . ." Seymour expressed surprise at the leniency of the sentence but nonetheless approved it. Salsbury's middle name comes from several entries in http://worldconnect.rootsweb.com/cgi-bin/igm.cgi (accessed Feb. 2004). He wrote the 87th Pennsylvania's after-action report for the battle of Cedar Creek.

ored regiment and then tried to return as colonel of the 87th. The effort came too late, and Stahle remained a civilian. York's own Maj. Gen. William Buel Franklin noted that the 67th Pennsylvania was in similar stripped-down condition and suggested the two regiments consolidate with his younger brother Walter in command. Generals Truman Seymour and Horatio Wright got behind Walter L. Franklin's ambitions.[22]

With such heavy hitters pushing for consolidation and Walter Franklin's promotion, Pennsylvania could hardly avoid the issue. On December 4, Samuel Thomas, aide-de-camp to Governor Andrew Curtin, traveled to Washington to talk with the two regiments' officers. The 67th shipped out before he could catch them, but he met the 87th officers "at the foot of sixth street" just after their arrival. Speaking for both units, the 87th officers expressed interest in merging only if John Schall returned as colonel. They had no enthusiasm for Walter Franklin.[23]

Theodore Helwig shot off a letter to Andrew Curtin pleading with him not to assign a new colonel until John Schall made up his mind. Ten days later, Schall gave Helwig an answer. While admitting he harbored a yen to get back at the helm, Schall made it clear in his last paragraph that he did not plan to put bullets and diarrhea into his immediate future. "I have not yet done anything since my return home and present prospects are not very encouraging of doing much this winter. In fact I do not care much. We have excellent sleighing at this time, which affords good pastime . . . We also have fine skating, so you see I have turned out *considerable boy*."[24]

The regiment's officers bowed to the inevitable and formally requested that Walter Franklin become their commander. Theodore Helwig meanwhile pleaded the case of James Tearney for lieutenant colonel, but reversed himself when he learned that Noah Ruhl wanted the job. Ruhl campaigned for the position by obtaining a letter of recommendation from nine 87th officers and the regiment's brigade commander, William Snyder Truex. The state offered Ruhl the position, and he accepted. It made a formal offer of command to

22. James A. Stahle to Alexander L. Russell, Apr. 10, 1865, and to Andrew G. Curtin, Apr. 11, 1865, PA AGO, Muster Rolls; William B. Franklin to Andrew G. Curtin, Nov. 21, 1864, Truman Seymour to Andrew G. Curtin and Adj. General Russell, Nov. 28, 1864, and Horatio Wright to Andrew G. Curtin, Nov. 30, 1864, PA AGO. Truman Seymour became the 87th's division commander after James B. Ricketts fell seriously wounded at Cedar Creek.

23. Samuel B. Thomas to Andrew G. Curtin, Dec. 4, 1864, undated expense voucher, PA AGO, Muster Rolls. Thomas's expenses for the trip were $21.40. Prowell, *87th Pennsylvania*, 217–18.

24. John W. Schall to Theodore A. Helwig, Dec. 14, 1864, PA AGO, Muster Rolls. Emphasis in original.

Walter Franklin, who stunned everyone by turning down the offer in lieu of a staff position at lesser rank. He recommended Noah Ruhl in his stead.[25]

Walter Franklin's recommendation notwithstanding, Noah Ruhl stayed home, and James Tearney took command of the battalion, for most his tenure at the rank of captain, waiting several months before receiving a colonel's commission. Tearney had risen from a private in Company B and may have had the same issues with Ruhl as Michael Heiman. The regiment's erstwhile major remained a civilian, his no doubt pointed opinion lost to time. The merging of the 67th and 87th regiments also never happened because neither unit wanted to sacrifice its identity. They had fought and died as separate organizations and wanted history to remember them that way.[26]

In August 1864, south-central Pennsylvania sent nearly eight hundred fresh men to war in new regiments such as the 200th and 209th Infantry regiments. Many were relatives of 87th men, and some were 87th veterans who had gone home on surgeon's certificates. Several more were deserters subject to arrest if discovered. The army should have integrated these new men into existing regiments so they could profit from veterans' experience. Gen. George B. McClellan once declared that he would rather receive fifty thousand recruits into existing regiments than one hundred thousand in new ones. Secretary of War Edwin Stanton agreed but did little to change policy except to push recruits that direction by offering a three-dollar bounty to join an existing regiment. Since other recruits received two-dollar bounties anyway, a dollar offered little incentive.[27]

At the end of 1864, Washington at last began assigning recruits to existing regiments before allowing the creation of new ones. On March 15, 1865, Governor Andrew Curtin announced that Pennsylvania had sent 34 new companies into the field, 5 of them to the 87th Pennsylvania as new companies F–K. These were boys from counties such as Allegany, Lawrence, Bradford,

25. PA AGO, Muster Rolls, Theodore A. Helwig to Samuel B. Thomas, Feb. 28, 1865; 87th Pa. officers to "all whom it may concern," undated; Noah Ruhl to Samuel B. Thomas, Mar. 23, 1865; Officers of the 87th Pa. to Gov. Andrew G. Curtin, Jan. 31, 1865; Walter Franklin to Samuel B. Thomas, Mar. 28, 1865.

26. Prowell, *87th Pennsylvania*, 222; CMSRs of James Tearney, Co. B, 87th Pa., and Samuel S. Bulford, Co. K, 37th Pa. (8th Pa. Res.).

27. Pension indexes for the 87th Pennsylvania show at least thirteen men discharged for medical reasons who reenlisted with the 200th-209th Pennsylvania Infantry regiments. Most left the army in ill health a second time. The list is incomplete because it necessarily lacks anyone who did not apply for a pension. *O.R.,* General Orders No. 74, July 7, 1862, ser. 3, 2:206–7, Israel Washburn to Abraham Lincoln, July 28, 1862, ser. 3, 2:266, George B. McClellan to Gov. E. D. Morgan, July 15, 1862, ser. 3, 2:225–26, Edwin Stanton to Abraham Lincoln, Dec. 5, 1863, ser. 3, 2:1128–39, Edwin Stanton to John Brough, ser. 3, 4:1013, Thomas M. Vincent to R. J. Oglesby, ser. 3, 4:1049.

and Dauphin. Adams County supplied 20, but York County offered only 2. At least one-fourth of these 474 new men had seen previous service. That was a good thing because most arrived at the regiment mere hours before the final battle at Petersburg, Virginia.[28]

Although the 87th Pennsylvania had returned nearly to full strength, the army did not officially restore it to regimental status until April 30, 1865, and did not grant James Tearney his colonel's rank for another three weeks. One of the new officers, Samuel S. Bulford, fresh from three years with the 8th Pennsylvania Reserves, took over as lieutenant colonel. It was logical that the lieutenant colonel should come from the new half of the regiment, but that June, Zephaniah Hersh complained directly to the governor's office that he, not Bulford, should have received the commission. The governor disagreed, and Hersh stayed home nursing a serious leg wound that probably rendered him unfit for duty in any case. Two years later, the army did grant him a brevet major's commission for the gallantry he displayed at Petersburg on April 2, 1865.[29]

Last Battles

"Why you Yankee sons of bitches!" George Blotcher heard a Rebel picket shout. "Don't you come or we are set!"[30]

April 2, 1865, 4:00 A.M. It was raining. Had been all night. Bad weather did not stop the signal gun from firing and sending the Army of the Potomac pouring over their breastworks. The day before, Gen. Phil Sheridan had shut down the last viable rail line into Petersburg, Virginia, and now it was time to hold last rites over the Confederate stronghold. The 87th's brigade commander had placed the regiment on the left of the third line of battle because he assumed that half of the men were raw troops. It was not true, and the 87th proved it by racing through the front lines and into the lead of a Union tidal wave that swamped the thin Confederate skirmish line. Knowing the war was over, captured Southern pickets offered hands of friendship as soldiers sharing mutual respect. George Blotcher claimed he wept during the event.[31]

28. *O.R.*, A. G. Curtin to Edwin Stanton, ser. 3, 4:1238; Pension Records for all members, 87th Pa.; CMSRs of all men in new Companies F–K, 87th Pa., mustered March 1865.
29. CMSR of James Tearney; Prowell, *87th Pennsylvania,* 222; CMSR of Samuel S. Bulford; Zephaniah Hersh to Samuel B. Thomas, June 2, 1865, PA AGO, Muster Rolls.
30. Diary of George Blotcher.
31. *O.R.*, Report of William S. Truex, Apr. 11, 1865, 43/1:981–82, Report of James Tearney, Apr. 9, 1865, 43/1:990; diary of George Blotcher.

"Give those Yankee sons of bitches grape and canister!" a Rebel captain shouted. If Blotcher was still crying, he stopped when he heard that.[32]

German-born Augustus Hemple was one of the regiment's original men. Private Hemple had escaped every battle unscathed, but something unnerved him this time. He pulled George Blotcher aside before the charge and offered him all his worldly possessions—ten dollars and a watch—and begged him to give them to his mother when the war was over. Blotcher asked why.

Hemple said, "If we have to charge those works, I will never get alive over."

Blotcher refused, reminding Hemple that the Rebels would be sending bullets his way, too. When it was over, Blotcher regretted not having granted his friend's wish. He had to search Hemple's body to find the treasured articles.[33]

Union forces now had possession of the first line of Confederate breastworks. An hour's rest later, Ulysses S. Grant's army was on its way to snatching the Petersburg prize. The Confederates were not quitting yet. A shell cut Lt. Peter Nichol almost in half. A bullet cracked William Brison's skull, mangled one eye, and damaged the other. Pvt. Samuel William Shoemaker, a draftee, suffered a less glorious end to his day when he fell hard but nevertheless painfully into a ditch. After the war, Henry Shultz claimed that 2nd Lt. Samuel Wesley Keesey was the regiment's last battle fatality. Had they been able, Peter Nichol and Augustus Hemple might have joined an argument with draftees Porter Henry Fluck and William Henry Rice. Three of them died at unknown times on the field. Rice hung on until April 24 and earned the dubious distinction of being the regiment's last death from a battle wound.[34]

The inner Confederate works were empty the next day, and the Stars and Stripes rippled from a flagpole above Petersburg and the railroads that supplied Richmond. The Confederate capital began to evacuate, and Grant took off in pursuit of Robert E. Lee's withered army. Four days later, the 87th Pennsylvania fought its last battle when the men rushed downhill past a lonely house toward Sayler's Creek and slogged through the marsh surrounding the stream. Robert E. Lee lost one-fourth of his depleted Army of Northern Virginia that day, although the 87th Pennsylvania had little to do with it.[35]

32. Diary of George Blotcher.

33. CMSR of Augustus Hemple, Co. E, 87th Pa.; recollections of George Blotcher. Blotcher claimed he returned the items to Mrs. Hemple, who lost another son in the war.

34. Diary of George Blotcher; CMSRs of John Shadle and Porter Fluck, Co. C, William Brison, Augustus Hemple, Peter Nichol, and Samuel W. Shoemaker, Co. E, Zephaniah E. Hersh, Co. I, and Samuel W. Keesey (Geesey), Co. K, 87th Pa.; Prowell, *87th Pennsylvania,* 221. CMSR and Pension Records of William H. Rice, Co. A, 87th Pa. William Henry Rice was born in Edwards, New York, but lived in Bradford County, Pennsylvania, when drafted into service, mustering at the draft rendevous in Williamsport. He is buried in Arlington National Cemetery.

35. *O.R.,* Report of Ulysses S. Grant, July 22, 1865, 44/1:54, Report of Horatio Wright, Apr. 29, 1865, 46/1:905–9, Report of Richard S. Ewell, Dec. 20, 1865, 46/1:1292–95; Pension Records

The chase continued until April 9. George Blotcher always remembered the legions of slaves that followed them on that march, shouting praises of their Union liberators. The men ignored a rumor that Grant had sent Lee a peace proposal, preferring to believe that after they received official word. When the march halted and did not start again, they finally dared think this might be it. The day was beautiful and their spirits light as they waited.[36]

Then they heard that Lee had surrendered. George Blotcher never forgot the long night that followed:

> Cheer after cheer went up and everybody rejoiced which was kept up all night . . . Every body was wild and excitement ran high. Soldiers embraced each other in saying the war is over now and we can all go home . . . Army salutes were fired all this afternoon and all night . . . This was the greatest night I ever put in while in service. At this camp, nobody would or could sleep. If a soldier would lay down to take a nap, somebody would pull you out, and you had to put up with it with all such enjoyment and happiness never to be forgotten by any solder.[37]

Blotcher's mood reversed a week later. Abraham Lincoln was dead. Blotcher called it "a great calamity," adding, "Woe to the man that would use such language such that was often told against Abe Lincoln's mind."[38]

One of the new men learned Blotcher's warning through harsh experience. Sgt. Joshua R. Forrest said out loud, "I prayed for the death of Old Abe Lincoln for four years and do not regret it now that it occurred." The First Amendment protected him from reprisal, he said. A court-martial disagreed. They ripped the sergeant's stripes from his arm and sentenced him to carry a log five feet long around camp for six days, eight hours a day.[39]

Shooting had stopped in the Virginia theater, but soldiers march until their day of discharge. Union forces made a beeline for Danville, Virginia, the site of several prisons and the town to which Confederate leaders had fled after

of George W. Heckaman, Co. I, 87th Pa., affidavit of Henry Crist. While the 6th Corps played a principal role at Sayler's Creek, the 87th Pennsylvania was not heavily engaged. "Sayler" is spelled a variety of ways. As of December 2005, Amazon sold five books on the battle, all spelled "Sailor's." The spelling here is taken from the Sayler's Creek Web site www.saylerscreek.org (accessed June 1, 2006) and confirmed in *Confederate Veteran, Cumulative Index, 1893–1932*, vol. 3, *P-Z* (Wilmington: Broadfoot Publishing Co., 1986), 1789.

36. Recollections of George Blotcher.
37. Diary of George Blotcher.
38. Ibid.
39. Office of the Adjutant General, RG-94, Book Records of Union Volunteer Organizations, 87th Pa., Order Book, Companies G and H, vol. 3 of 4, May 23, 1865, NARA; CMSR of Joshua R. Forrest, Co. H, 87th Pa.

Richmond fell. On April 23, the 87th Pennsylvania put in twenty-two miles in unseasonably warm weather, much of it at a dogtrot. Two days later, they put up camp with eighteen miles behind them, yet George Blotcher thought it was "the easiest march we had for a long time." It seemed strange to him to be moving through Confederate territory without pickets in advance. Danville proved uneventful. Most prisoners were Federal stragglers caught grabbing spoils.[40]

During their final month of service, the men visited Richmond and marched in Washington's Grand Review, to the chagrin of many who suffered sunstroke. Officers began applying for discharges. Six men, four of them original members, were so eager to go home that they deserted. Veteran volunteer Andrew George Shull, in the army almost continuously since April 1861, had recently received a promotion to captain and requested a leave of absence to tend to family business. Denied, he left for home two days later and never returned, choosing a dishonorable discharge after more than four good years of service.

Pvt. William Augustus Knudson, an original man who had taken time off after his October 1864 discharge before reenlisting with the 87th, also threw it all away to leave early. So did Cpl. Richard Quinn, a veteran volunteer deserting for the second time and the only one of the six to be arrested. The army called Quinn a "straggler of the worst kind" and threatened capital punishment but limited retribution to a dishonorable discharge.[41]

Company C's Isaac Wagner lacked a discharge when he walked out of a Philadelphia hospital and signed up with the 7th U.S. Veteran Volunteers. Since serving under his real name was a problem, he gave the first one that came to mind: 87th Pennsylvania comrade William Waltamire, as Wagner misspelled it. He later served under that alias in the 4th U.S. Cavalry with two other 87th Pennsylvania veterans who never gave him away. Come pension time, though, he had a lot of explaining to do. So, too, did the real William Waltimyer, who had to prove that he was not the deserter.[42]

40. Recollections of George Blotcher; diary of George Blotcher; *O.R.,* Report of Horatio G. Wright, 43/1:1315.

41. Diary of George Blotcher; CMSRs and Pension Records of William A. Knudson, Hazzard P. McClure, and Jacob F. Ziegler, Co. A, Richard Quinn, Co. B, Jeremiah Frederick Bittner and Peter Shoemaker, Co. D, and Roland Curtain Dixon, Co. E, 87th Pa.; CMSR of Andrew G. Shull, Co. G, 16th Pa., and Co. G (then in Co. D), 87th Pa.; Andrew G. Shull to George D. Ruggles, Apr. 21, 1865.

42. CMSR and Pension Records of Isaac Wagner, Co. C, 87th Pa., 7th U.S. Vet. Vols., and 4th U.S. Cav. Enoch Christian Hartman and Andrew Kauffman Shive were Wagner's 87th Pennsylvania comrades in the 4th U.S. Cavalry. Wagner's pension file is among the largest in the National Archives, much of it spent explaining how he was not William Waltimire and why he had gone

The boys had been watching other regiments in their brigade going home and were bursting with anticipation. Their time came June 29, 1865. The next day, George Blotcher was home in Goldsboro, still in possession of his rifle, which he had purchased for six dollars. On July 2, he hopped a northbound freight for Camp Curtin and final muster. Old 87th comrades made the trip to Harrisburg to be "greeted with a great deal of joy and happiness . . . In such a state the day was spent and the last one to mingle together . . . perhaps on this side the grave." July 3 was even happier, for they were paid and civilians again. Most went home, but Blotcher and others stayed overnight in Harrisburg to "displace our soldier garb and make a citizen of ourself by stepping in a citizen garb which made quite a change in appearance to many."[43]

Blotcher made his last diary entry at his home in Goldsboro. "This morning I left Harrisburg for home and spent one of the happiest fourth of July for a good many years at home. And this ended my soldier life from August the 24th 1861."[44]

Memories and Change

Men returned to civilian life hoping to pick up where they had left off three or four years before. Instead, many found their military experience had done more than interrupt their lives. It had changed them forever. Not all the wounds were physical.

Even before the war, acquaintances described Jerome Hair as "a quiet man and a slow talker not given to conversation or even answering questions." Others considered him "a nervous man . . . [whose] arms and shoulders were afflicted with a nervous tremble or a twitching habit." Army comrades must have found his behavior odd, too, because he bunked alone throughout his time in the service. Sunstroke felled him in 1862, and he later claimed the experience rendered him unable to speak or think clearly. Others insisted that his mental problems came after a postwar drunken fall from a barn. Hair ended his military life in hospitals thanks to a bullet wound received at the battle of Cedar Creek.

After the war, Hair maintained no fixed address, although he made an Abbottstown tavern his hangout. The owner kept a jar of snakes preserved in

to prison for stealing from the Northern Central Railroad. He should not be confused with Isaac Wagner of Company G.

43. Diary of George Blotcher.
44. Ibid.

alcohol on the bar as a conversation piece. Broke and in an alcoholic fit, Hair pleaded for a drink. The bartender refused and told him to get out. Hair would not leave, so the bartender sent for the sheriff. Desperate for a drink, Hair seized the jar of snakes and began downing the disgusting contents. Sheriff Jacob Harman, Hair's onetime comrade in the 87th Pennsylvania, made the arrest.

In mid-1883, Jerome Hair entered the Virginia Soldiers' Home due to "rheumatism and nervous frustration" and was still there at his death in 1895. The hospital roster had a spot designated for the names of relatives or friends. Hair had left his blank.[45]

Daniel Blouse's postwar life may have been more hellish than his time in the army. By 1888, his family had no choice but to send him to the insane asylum in Harrisburg after "spells of hallucination . . . made him dangerous and attendants had to be with him to keep him from injuring his wife and daughter." George Henry Cleophas Brandt's alcoholic lifestyle led him to abuse his wife and her to seek a divorce. The former Mrs. Brandt did her best to forget she had ever known her ex-husband and could not—or would not—recall their wedding date. George Brandt died alone in a soldiers' home.[46]

Alburtus "Bertram" Ilgenfritz enlisted in 1861 as a drummer, but his army career was less than stellar. Two weeks after Carter's Woods, he fled from camp near Sharpsburg, Maryland, and returned under guard two months later. Years later, illiterate and with old age upon him, he received his first pension check. Funds did not go toward food or housing but for a wild spree that got him arrested for being drunk and disorderly. While in jail, Ilgenfritz gave up on life and made a futile attempt at suicide. He died alone, an inmate of the county almshouse.[47]

George Jonathan Chalfant was a popular fellow who, because of a death in the family, had not enlisted with the 87th Pennsylvania until August 1862. Nonetheless, he ended his military career with captain's bars on his shoulders, to the chagrin of others in Company A who complained yet again to the

45. CMSR and Pension Records of Jerome Hair, Co. I, 87th Pa., depositions of Thomas J. Shepherd and Jacob H. Schriver, Jan. 31, 1888, Jacob Harman, Aug. 13, 1889, John A. Wilt, July 25, 1889; Historical Registers of National Homes for Disabled Soldiers, Register of Members, 1867–1935, Southern Branch, Hampton, Va., NM-29, entry 69, M1749, roll 230, NARA. Hair's name was sometimes spelled "Herr."

46. Pension Records of Daniel Blouse, Co. B, 87th Pa., deposition of Dr. Ellridge Gerry; Pension Records of George H. C. Brandt, Co. K, 87th Pa., statement of Virginia V. Craig Brandt. The author states gratefully that he is not related to George Brandt. The author states gratefully that he is not related to George Henry Cleophas Brandt.

47. CMSR and Pension Records of Alburtus Ilgenfritz, Co. E, 87th Pa.; *York Dispatch,* Dec. 4, 1897.

governor that he did not deserve the captaincy as much as they. Chalfant's religious roots were Quaker, and he lies at rest in a Quaker cemetery, but neither his war career nor his end was peaceful. On April 12, 1878, he was traveling by train near Peru, Indiana, entered the water closet, and closed the door behind him. Shortly, a shot rang out. Conductors forced open the door and found Chalfant with a bullet hole in his heart. The family later said he died in a train accident but could not hide the suicide forever.[48]

An amputation is the most visible war disability and one that aging veterans often proclaimed as a proud sacrifice for their country. Thirteen 87th Pennsylvania men had an arm taken, six lost a leg, and seventeen learned to get by with at least one less finger. Not one of them held a rank higher than corporal. Poor James A. Fellers may have had the hardest luck when a bullet at 3rd Winchester cost him the lower portion of his left leg. By the following March, gangrene had begun creeping up the stump, and doctors had to amputate more of the leg to save his life.[49]

Pvt. George A. Welsh, shot in the left leg June 23, 1864, near Petersburg, Virginia, appeared to be fortunate when surgeons saved his limb. Most men suffering a wound as severe as Welsh's were not so lucky, especially if they received the injury during a major engagement when surgeons had to deal with thousands of wounded. Welsh's doctor gave a detailed report of treatment that appears to have been as agonizing an experience as being shot.

> George A. Welch Priv, Co E 87t Reg't Penn'a Vols, wounded in battle . . . by a Minnie ball causing a compound comminuted [pulverized] fracture of the femur in its upper third. The greater portion of the comminuted bone had been removed from the wound before he was admitted . . . At the time of admission, the wound was in a bad condition, being filled with maggots and considerably inflamed. The patient was placed upon a firm mattress with extension by means of a weight. The wound was carefully examined for comminuted bone but none found. It was then washed and after removing all maggots within reach, the wound was

48. John W. Schall to Samuel B. Thomas, Aug. 25, 1864, PA AGO, Muster Rolls; Daniel Bonge, Abraham Rhodes, Alexander Kipp, Emanuel C. Coleman, and Jacob Glassmyer to Andrew G. Curtin, Aug. 26, 1864, PA AGO, box 54, folder 15; "Zouave" to *York Gazette,* Nov. 4, 1862, letter dated Oct. 23, 1862; *York Gazette,* Apr. 19, 1878; Pension Records of George J. Chalfant and Simon Alfred Bendon, Co. A, 87th Pa.

49. CMSRs of all men of the 87th Pa. (especially James A. Fellers, Co. I). Pension Records for amputees often frustrate researchers. Until late in the nineteenth century, veterans filing for disability pensions had to prove that their army service led to their physical ailments. Because amputees' injuries were obvious, on that count, they were not required to offer much of the detail that historians crave.

washed with a solution of creosote [now recognized as a powerful car-
cinogen] for the purpose of destroying any maggots not within reach.
Ice dressing was then applied.[50]

Welsh would have been better off with the amputation. The bullet remained in him thirteen more years, and the leg never healed. In 1877, a doctor
at last removed the bullet, but Welsh's condition had deteriorated too much,
and he died shortly afterward.

Like George Welsh, many men kept damaged limbs that never functioned
efficiently, if at all. John Hoffman, postwar brother-in-law of the ill-fated
Andrew Bentz Smith, was a big man by the day's standards and had spent
his antebellum life building things. The battle of Carter's Woods changed his
skill set when one bullet tore into his thigh and a second one into his hand.
The leg wound broke no bones and was tolerable, but the hand never fully
functioned afterward.[51]

Bullets were not required for a man's life to be altered. George F. Prowell
came from a successful farming family near Lewisberry, York County, and returned home expecting to do his part, perhaps to inherit the farm. He quickly
learned that his body could no longer withstand the rigors of farm work.
Dysentery contracted at Belle Isle Prison had shriveled his strength, and two
years of rest and Mom's home cooking had failed to restore it. Clearly, a more
sedentary life was going to be necessary. On the advice of a doctor friend,
Prowell earned a medical degree and spent the next half century ministering
to the sick in Burnside, Clearfield County. He had one patient who suffered
with chronic dysentery until death: himself.[52]

Diarrhea and dysentery were companions to almost all soldiers at one time
or another. If Levi Gastrock thought bucking and gagging was cruel punishment, he learned that the ravages of dysentery were worse. He contracted it
the summer of 1862 and still had it at his death in 1886. Ever the brunt of jokes
since the episode with Michael Heiman, whenever the men saw him running
toward the sinks they laughed and said things like, "There goes Levi on the

50. Pension Records of George A. Welsh, or Welch, Co. E, 87th Pa., statement of Dr. J. B.
Garland, June 5, 1865. For the carcinogenic effects of creosote, see National Toxicology Program,
Department of Health and Human Services, http://ntp.niehs.nih.gov/ntpweb (accessed June 1,
2006).

51. Pension Records of John Hoffman, Co. H, 87th Pa., deposition of John Hoffman. In 1865,
Hoffman married the only sister of the ill-fated Andrew Bentz Smith. Hoffman stood five feet,
eleven inches tall and weighed about 170 pounds.

52. CMSR and Pension Records of George F. Prowell, Co. H, 87th Pa.; U.S. Census, Pennsylvania, York, Newberry Township. George F. Prowell is often confused with George Reeser Prowell,
author of the regimental history.

track again." There was nothing funny about the disease. Gastrock sometimes made the trip to the sinks ten to fifteen times a day and continued to do so much of his life. At least fifteen 87th Pennsylvania men died in service with diarrhea listed as at least a contributory cause. We cannot know how many men died prematurely because of dysentery's wasting effects.[53]

Hemorrhoids—piles, men called them—were among the most frequent complaints and no doubt associated with diarrhea. An affliction that is today resolved with an outpatient procedure was then incurable, its effects ranging from mildly uncomfortable to debilitating. Charles Gotwalt said that while a prisoner in Andersonville, his diarrheic evacuations caused his bowel to protrude from his anus, and he had to push it back inside each time. The "protruding bowel" was undoubtedly a hemorrhoid. Pvt. Thomas Price, among the regiment's forty-plus age crowd, bled so profusely from the anus that blood dripped from the bottom of his trousers and stained the seat of his pants. He insisted he could not march for at least a half hour after evacuation "in consequence of the protrusion of the bowel," again, hemorrhoids. The condition earned him a medical discharge in May 1863. Within a year, he was dead, adding his name to a long list of war casualties not included in the death toll.[54]

"Rupture" and "hernia" appear with surprising frequency in soldiers' pension applications and were another inoperable condition that kept men from gainful postwar employment. Only a truss promised any kind of relief, but often it did not help much. We perceive of nineteenth-century men as accustomed to physical effort. Why did so many suffer ruptures? Men were smaller then, averaging about five feet, seven inches in height. Weight is more difficult to know, but based on pension reporting, 130–140 pounds was common. In the field, a man often weighed less, particularly after a bout with diarrhea. The army had no plan of physical training for volunteers, and men existed largely on vitamin-deficient diets that weakened connective tissue. "Lift with your legs," commonsense technique that it is, was a method taught to future generations. Of course, war has indigenous reasons, such as a man sprinting over a rough meadow while someone shot at him.

Col. George Hay was the region's most prominent victim of rupture but far from the only one. Pvt. George H. Dittenhaffer, for some reason riding a horse on the retreat from 2nd Winchester, urged his mount over a fence. The horse responded well. Dittenhaffer did not. His groin smacked against

53. Pension Records of Liborious "Levi" Gastrock, Co. B, 87th Pa., deposition of John Rupp; Pension Records of John Lauck, Co. C, 87th Pa.
54. Pension Records of Charles E. Gotwalt, Co. A, and Thomas Price, Co. B, 87th Pa.

the pommel of the saddle when the horse touched ground. Pvt. Adam Morningstar, younger brother of Henry, suffered his rupture on the same retreat as his officer-brother. His mount was shank's mare and his leap just over a ditch, but the tearing of soft tissue put him on permanent teamster duty. Two days before the 87th's flight from Carter's Woods, Pvt. Thomas Ilgenfritz felt his groin snap when he fell from a log at Bunker Hill, the reason why he could not escape capture. Pvt. George Reuben Eichelberger, called "Old Dad" by comrades in spite of being only twenty-nine at enlistment, had a less romantic cause for his injury. Lifting a heavy load of wood caused an injury that sent him to the Annapolis Navy Yard for duty as a painter, but he was unable to perform even that less-strenuous work.[55]

Eye infections were medical issue exacerbated by unsanitary conditions. During the spring of 1864, many men reported vision problems that doctors called "chronic granular ophthalmia." The men called it "moon blindness," thinking the cause was sleeping with their faces toward the full moon. Tom Crowl was among the many sufferers. The condition became so severe for teamster William Miller that comrades would not "trust [him] to drive his team without close attention and directions from the wagon master." The condition was probably similar to that we today call "pink eye." With no way for doctors to stem infection, many suffered lifelong vision problems.[56]

Of those York County veterans reporting lingering service-related illnesses, relatively few were officers. Army life allowed them to sleep in tents or under roofs while on garrison duty, and they generally ate better. Furloughs were more readily available, and they could resign if army life became too uncomfortable. However, "reporting" is the key word. Officers did not apply for pensions as often as enlisted men because they tended to be more financially secure in old age. Thus, they were less likely to report chronic illnesses. Of those York or Adams County officers applying for pensions, the ravages of old age appear to have been a greater cause of disability than the long-term effects of war. Statistical analysis makes a different case. The average 87th Pennsylvania officer's life expectancy was fractionally less than that for the regiment as a whole and four years shorter than local commissioned men who served with other units.[57]

Compilation of life expectancy reveals other surprises. (See Appendix, "Life

55. CMSRs and Pension Records of George Hay, Staff, George H. Dittenhaffer, Co. C, Thomas Ilgenfritz, Adam Morningstar, Henry Morningstar, and George R. Eichelberger, Co. K, 87th Pa.

56. Pension Records of William Miller, Co. B, Richmond Flinn, Co. C, Thomas O. Crowl, Co. H, and Michael C. Morningstar, Co. K, 87th Pa.

57. Pension Records of all men of the 87th Pa. and the "non-87th" group. "Officers" here is defined as men who held a rank of at least second lieutenant at any point in the war.

Expectancy Tables.") Among war's survivors, the oldest recruits enjoyed a significantly longer life than those who enlisted before the age of eighteen. These underage boys had an average lifespan eleven years less than their oldest comrades. This occurred for both the 87th Pennsylvania's 1861 enlistees, the entire regiment, and for other area men enlisting in 1861. While young men had more strength to survive war's lasting effects, they also had to endure them longer. The older the man, the more apt he was to reach average life expectancy because he was already further along in life. Also, the army many times gave older men lighter duties, allowing them to serve as cooks, teamsters, or nurses.

If pain and disability went with being a veteran, for many, so did success, especially for commissioned officers. William Henry Lanius became a leading figure in York's economic scene in the lucrative fields of banking and transportation. Findley Isaac Thomas, a student at Dr. Pfeiffer's School when he enlisted, attended Dickinson Seminary after the war and was a bank vice president at retirement. William Henry Eicholtz made death his key to success when he moved to the cow town of Abilene, Kansas, and reportedly became the town's most prominent undertaker. Later, he expanded his business to Atchison, where he could "furnish either black or white hearse at reasonable charges." Paupers he buried for $13.50; indigent soldiers cost $20.50. Charles Zinn Denues took the same profession but remained in York to bury many of his former comrades.[58]

Gettysburg's John M. Warner wanted to serve in Company F with brother George of Mine Run infamy, but a boyhood accident had left him lame. Instead, he served as sutler for the 87th Pennsylvania, a civilian post he held until he was captured at Winchester in June 1863. A stay in Belle Isle Prison convinced him that the army was not his future. He returned to Gettysburg to begin a string of mercantile successes that resulted in terms on the boards of several Gettysburg concerns. As the twentieth century arrived, he wanted to leave a legacy and led a successful fund-raising effort to erect a hospital. Since he personally donated twenty-five thousand dollars, he got to name the building and honored his wife in the doing. The Annie M. Warner Hospital has since become the Gettysburg Hospital.[59]

James Stahle and Frank Geise entered the world of politics, but that opportunity was also available to the rank and file. William Thomas Radford Ziegler left the service wearing corporal's stripes but represented Gettysburg

58. *Gettysburg Compiler,* Jan. 29, 1895, and Jan. 16, 1900; *Atchison (KS) Daily Globe,* Dec. 20, 1887, and Jan. 21, 1888; Pension Records of Charles Z. Denues, Co. A, William H. Eicholtz, Co. B, and Findley I. Thomas, Co. I, 87th Pa.

59. Warner Family File, Adams County Historical Society; *Gettysburg Times,* Mar. 7, 1922.

in the state legislature and at Andersonville dedication ceremonies. Even when veterans lived mundane lives, newspapers sometimes stretched their reputations to enormous proportions. The obituary for railroad engineer William F. Baker expanded his war experience to include the battles of Gettysburg and Antietam. Newspapers regularly bestowed the rank of "captain" or "colonel" without regard to truth, especially when the man was of the same political persuasion as the editor.[60]

60. Pension Records of William H. Eicholtz, Co. B, Franklin Geise, Co. D, William T. Ziegler, Co. F, and Findley I. Thomas, Co. I, 87th Pa. *Martinsburg (WV) Herald,* Apr. 1899; CMSR and Pension Records of William F. Baker, Co. F, 87th Pa. At his death, Baker had been working in Martinsburg for some time as a railroad employee. York newspapers generally referred to Frank Geise as "Captain Geise" even though his highest rank had been first lieutenant.

Chapter 13

Postwar Politics and Reunions

The shooting war had ended but not the sniping between Democrats and Republicans. Politicians and their supporting newspapers kept firing as unrelentingly as before the war, just on different topics. Slavery was a dead issue by the end of 1865—the Thirteenth Amendment to the Constitution passed that year—and the state rights debate was shaken for the moment. Newspapers now churned political waters over the proposed Fourteenth and Fifteenth amendments, which promised equal protection for all races. The former amendment became law in 1868 and the latter in 1870 but only over the strenuous objections of the Democratic Party. The war had barely ended when the *York Gazette* wrote:

> This question of Negro suffrage is beginning to loom up before the American people . . . [and] will be the leading issue in our state elections. The question of African slavery, having been settled by the war, can no longer trouble us. It is now out of politics. With its departure the country has a good riddance, and the thirty years controversy about the institution of slavery is ended. But the Abolitionists are not satisfied with this. They are not content with the abolition of slavery . . . They must also, forsooth, have the Negro upon a social and political equality with the white man; they wish to give him the right of suffrage and, per consequence, make him eligible to office.[1]

John White Geary carried the Republican banner for governor of Pennsylvania during the election of 1866. Geary had political experience that spanned

---

1. *York Gazette,* June 13, 1865.

the country. The Mexican War veteran had organized California's post office and served as San Francisco's first American mayor. Later, he moved east to serve as governor of the Kansas Territory. He was a former Democrat, an abolitionist who did not believe in racial equality, and a former Civil War general. The Republican *True Democrat* made Geary the hero of every battle in which he had served. An enthusiastic rally on Gettysburg's Culp's Hill opened with former 87th Pennsylvanian Charles Henry Buehler's introduction of Geary as the man "who from yonder heights in July 1863 hurled back the armed hosts of treason." Exaggerated as the claims were, the political guns of Democratic candidate Hiester Clymer contained no such ammunition.[2]

Democrats infused race into politics no less than before the war. The *York Democratic Press* labeled the local Geary Soldiers' Club "York Boys in Blue-Black" and still called Republicans "abolitionists." When the *Gettysburg Compiler* printed stories of veteran meetings, they were often "*white* boys in blue" and were outraged by the thought of Negro equality. "Negroes in the ballot box," they wrote, "the negro in the jury box, the negro in the ladies' car, and the negro in the white school . . . Give the negroites your answer at the polls—No! No!! NO!!!" The *Democratic Press* headlined a Democratic meeting as a plea for "WHITE MAN'S GOVERNMENT," while the *York Gazette* adapted an old anti-Lincoln slogan to claim, "A vote for Geary is a vote for Negro despotism."[3]

The *Gazette* used astonishing illogic in a feature about federal funding to aid southern blacks.

> Coffee might be ten cents a pound cheaper if the national treasury was not robbed of eleven million dollars a year for the benefit of Geary's colored brethren in the South . . . If the slaves of the South were able to support themselves and their masters before their emancipation, why can't they support themselves alone now that they are free?[4]

By contrast, the Republican *Adams Sentinel* referred to soldiers' gatherings simply as "Gettysburg boys in blue" and did not automatically refer to their having a political agenda, although many did. Republican newspapers still lacked the conviction to declare strongly for racial equality, and the *Sentinel* tried to sidestep the issue altogether. "Negro suffrage . . . cannot be the issue

2. *True Democrat,* Aug. 21–Oct. 9, 1864; *Adams Sentinel,* Sept. 25, 1866; Warner, *Generals in Blue,* 169–70; John White Geary, *A Politician Goes to War: The Civil War Letters of John White Geary.*
3. *Democratic Press,* Aug. 17 and 24, 1866; *Gettysburg Compiler,* Sept. 24, Oct. 4, 1866, and Sept. 27, 1867; *York Gazette,* Aug. 28, 1866.
4. *York Gazette,* Oct. 2, 1866.

in the Pennsylvania canvass," it wrote, and asked their "Democratic friends to restrain themselves."[5]

The Republican *True Democrat* pressed for equality with politics to the fore and little reliance on the truth.

> Do you want to afford equal protection to all men? Vote for Geary . . .
> Do you wish to sustain the principles of liberty and freedom? Vote for
> Geary . . . If you wish to honor the men who made drinking cups from
> the skulls of our dead soldiers and trinkets for their women out of their
> bones, vote for Clymer.[6]

The *True Democrat* offered no proof that Democratic candidate Hiester Clymer had been a Southern sympathizer. Neither did it document when and where Confederate soldiers had indulged in ritualistic debauchery with Yankee remains. It continued its attack on the Democratic party as one obsessed by race.

> If all the negroes should die or emigrate, what would become of the
> Democracy [Democratic Party]? It would dwindle down like the little
> end of nothing whittled to a point and chopped off. This party breakfast
> on nigger, dine on nigger, sup on nigger and lunch on nigger. They have
> nigger served up in more ways than a French cook could cook a leg of
> mutton. They can twist the nigger into more shapes than a contortionist
> on his belly . . . He is the central figure of their platform . . . He inspires
> every speech of a Democratic orator . . . He *is* the Democratic Party.[7]

John Geary won the 1866 governor's race, so the *York Gazette* pulled out its 1860 Andrew Curtin headline to denigrate Geary's victory as one occurring due to "enormous frauds." South-central Pennsylvania went solidly Democratic, though, and remained a lost cause for Republicans for eighty years. Then, it flip-flopped into a virtual lost cause for Democrats.[8]

With new management, the passage of time, and the maturation of the journalistic profession, area newspapers' pointed opinions mellowed. The *York Gazette,* however, went to the opposite extreme. Under its mid-twentieth-century banner, the *Gazette and Daily,* it was reportedly the country's only

5. *Adams Sentinel,* Sept. 11, 1866.
6. *True Democrat,* Oct 9, 1866.
7. Ibid., Oct 2, 1866.
8. *York Gazette,* Oct. 23, 1866; United States Presidential Elections, http://www.uselectionatlas.org/RESULTS (accessed June 12, 2006).

newspaper to back the Socialist Party candidate in the 1948 presidential election.[9]

Active military organizations, veterans' groups, and the offspring units they engendered did not seem to care about the color of a comrade-in-arms when it came to offering military funerals. For example, the Gettysburg Guards provided a burial escort for 25th U.S. Colored Troop veteran William A. Thompson the same as it had for white veteran of the 3rd Pennsylvania Cavalry George W. King. The Sons of Veterans turned out on a crisp April morning to pay last respects to 127th U.S. Colored Troop veteran George W. Wagner just as it later would for the 87th Pennsylvania's Henry Swope. Society was still far from ready to accept equality, though. The burial ground for Gettysburg's colored veterans was all-black Sons of Goodwill (later Lincoln) Cemetery, not Evergreen or the National Cemetery. The Catholic Church's rule was the exception. Married into the faith, 43rd U.S. Colored Troop veteran Richard Myers lies at rest in Gettysburg's St. Francis Xavier Cemetery.[10]

Old Comrades

It did not take long after the war for the boys from York to get together. In mid-1866, George Hay called for a meeting of all veterans at the Union Engine House. Newspaper accounts gave no reason for the reunion and did not follow up, but the gathering was probably as much political as social. Veterans, including Harvey James Harman, the man who resigned from Company H due to incompetence, met another time in Gettysburg's Tate Hotel. James Hersh served on the executive committee of the Gettysburg Boys in Blue, an Adams County political organization. In 1887, former prisoners of war received an organizational charter with the prodigious and redundant name Pennsylvania State Association of Ex-Union Prisoners of War for the York County Association of Ex-Union Prisoners of War.[11]

As time passed and the veterans' hair became thinner and grayer, the men grew eager to reunite with old mates, some of whom they had not seen in

9. The *Gazette and Daily* is now the *York Daily Record* and takes a more moderate political stance.

10. Obituaries of George W. Wagner (aka Jones), William A. Thompson, and George W. King, *Gettysburg Compiler*, Apr. 30, 1895, and Nov. 5 and Dec. 31, 1902; obituary of Henry Swope, *Star and Sentinel*, Feb. 21, 1906, CMSRs of William A. Thompson, Co. D, 25th U.S.C.T., George W. King, Battery C, 3rd Pa. Heavy Art. (152nd Pa.), George W. Wagner, Co. I, 127th U.S.C.T., and Richard Myers, Co. K, 43rd U.S.C.T.; obituary of Richard Myers, *Adams County News*, Dec. 28, 1912; personal observation at St. Francis Xavier and Lincoln cemeteries. In 1938, Charles Parker, 3rd U.S.C.T., was reinterred in Gettysburg National Cemetery.

11. YCHT, ms. file 737; *Adams Sentinel*, Sept. 18, 1866; Meeting Itinerary, Sept. 25, 1866, George Hay Kain III Collection.

two decades. It was time to recall their war days as glorious now that many years separated them from eating army rations, sleeping on the cold ground, and breathing the pungent odor of gunsmoke and death. Old men who once had shot each other now began meeting amicably, sometimes shaking hands while reaching over the very stone walls they once had battled to possess. In the summer of 1888, Gettysburg held its first major gathering of veterans to celebrate the twenty-fifth anniversary of that great battle. Several of the old 87th men took the opportunity to meet in Corporal Skelly Post No. 9 of the Grand Army of the Republic "for the purpose of effecting a permanent regimental organization." John Schall became president of the new organization and gruff old Noah Ruhl, the vice president. "The reunion was a very enjoyable one after a separation of twenty-two years," a newspaper quoted an unnamed participant. Now, it was time for a real reunion.

On September 24, 1888, 87th Pennsylvania veterans, one traveling all the way from California, reunited in York, and Robert H. Milroy wired his greetings. Members of the old regimental band who still had credible embouchures and legs enough to march led the first of three parades through town. The mature boys from York sang "Auld Lang Syne" and "Rally 'round the Flag" with "hearty good will." "Marching through Georgia" was their favorite tune even though the only marching they did in that state was to a Rebel prison. An evening gab session they called "a camp fire" led to agreement to recognize their sacrifice at the battle of Monocacy and erect a monument there.[12]

The regiment reunited each of the next two years but then suspended gatherings until 1897. By then, not many were in condition to march any great distance. Chaplain David Christian Eberhart was blind and so feeble that he could no longer be there to recite the benediction. A decade later, members met again at William Henry Lanius's bungalow, 108 old men of an estimated 150 known still to be alive. From then on, reunions crossed regimental lines because no regiment had enough survivors for a good-sized reunion.[13]

Although they had discussed it often, not until 1904 did the veterans put forth a coordinated effort to erect a monument on the Monocacy battlefield. On the fortieth anniversary of the battle, fifty-nine veterans left York to attend memorial services on a field from which they once had fled in terror. Lew Wallace started from his home in Indiana, but failing health and summer heat forced him back home. The group appointed a monument association with Lew Wallace as president and York historian George Reeser Prowell as secretary. That committee in turn created a subcommittee to raise ten thousand dollars with William Henry Lanius as chairman. Monocacy veteran, histo-

12. YCHT, ms. file 901.
13. Ibid.

rian, and Massachusetts state senator Alfred Seelye Roe promised to gather matching funds.[14]

Lanius raised only five thousand dollars, but it was enough. On November 24, 1908, the monument was ready for unveiling ceremonies. Pennsylvania paid for everything that day, including a special six-car train to Frederick for those applying for a ticket and able to prove veteran status. The 87th Pennsylvania supplied 113 veterans. They placed the monument on a knoll just behind the sunken lane where they had made their last stand forty-four years earlier.[15] Henry Lanius delivered a heartfelt speech in the romantic style common to veterans long removed from bursting shells and screaming bullets.[16]

The day's events moved the *York Daily* to write:

> Vivid recollections yesterday crowded upon the surviving soldiers of that battle. Here a battery, there the rush of cavalry, to the right from a thicket the crackling fire of a skirmish line, to the left in a wheat field, the retreat of a broken Confederate rank, below a run flowing ominously red, they pictured it all under the inspiration of what was to many the first sight of those brown fields in all the time which has gone between that day and this.[17]

As time passed, age took its inevitable ravaging toll. The regiment's death rate peaked in 1913 with the passing of thirty-four veterans. The deadly influenza pandemic later that decade had minor effect because most of the boys from York were gone by then. Of the 1,349 men who served with the original organization of the 87th Pennsylvania, 134 are known to have lived to see flappers gyrate to scandalous jazz. George Blotcher died in 1924, but thirty of his former mates lasted long enough to experience the great stock market crash of 1929. Musician Calvin Gilbert lived five months into his hundredth year to earn the double distinction of being both Gettysburg's last living Civil War veteran and the 87th Pennsylvania's only known centenarian. Henry Shultz, the lad who had defied his father to enlist nearly eighty years before, joined Gilbert as the regiment's only other member still around to read newspaper accounts of Adolf Hitler's invasion of Poland. Gilbert survived that cataclysmic event by only ten days. When Shultz passed on January 27, 1940, ownership of the 87th Pennsylvania transferred into the hands of historians.[18]

14. *York Daily*, July 11, 1904, and Nov. 25, 1908; *York Gazette*, July 11, 1904.

15. A macadam road now runs between the knoll and the trace of the original lane.

16. YCHT, ms. file 901.

17. Ibid.; *York Daily, York Gazette,* and *York Dispatch,* all Nov. 25, 1908.

18. Pension Records of Calvin Gilbert, Co. F, and Henry Shultz, Co. G, 87th Pa.; *Gettysburg Times,* Sept. 14, 1939. Calvin Gilbert died September 11, 1939. Claims made here do not include men from the five companies that joined the regiment in March 1865.

Epilogue

Two Tales of Closure

Alfred Jameson, who had written so many letters to his family during the war, survived intact and returned home to work as a freight conductor on the Northern Central Railroad. In 1865, he proposed to his sweetheart, she said "yes," and the young couple looked forward to a June wedding. Days before the ceremony, Alfred was plying his trade on the railroad when, for reasons no one could explain, he stood atop a train while it was moving. Workers who found his body surmised that he never saw the bridge coming. On the day the Jameson family was to attend their son's wedding, they buried him instead.[1]

The 98th Pennsylvania Infantry was one of many regiments camped near Danville, Virginia, in May 1865. The army was sending men home one regiment at a time, and each man eagerly waited his turn. Pvt. George Crowl no doubt wanted to get home to celebrate his forty-fifth birthday with family and friends. He hoped that would include his son and fellow veteran, Tom. It would be good to hear his voice after so many months.

Free time was plentiful, so Crowl grabbed some to take a walk. He spotted a cemetery and ambled through the rows of graves, casually reading the names carved in the wooden headboards. Many were Union captives who had died in Danville's tobacco warehouse prison. Someone said there were fifteen hundred men buried in this graveyard. What he saw gave him no evidence to argue.

---

1. CMSR and Pension Records of Alfred J. Jameson; *York Gazette,* June 6, 1865.

Like any soldier, George Crowl had seen death often and witnessed the suffering that often preceded it. The names he saw in this graveyard meant nothing to him personally until one stopped him short. He read the head-board and then read it again. Suddenly, it was very personal. He stared at the crude grave marker, so shocked that he "scarcely knew what to do." Again and again, George Crowl read the words carved into the rough wood, hop-ing repetition would change them. But they remained "T. Crowl Co. H 87th Regt Pa."

George Crowl's thoughts may have returned to the last time he had seen his son. Before the battle of the Wilderness, he had surprised Tom with a visit to his shanty and was shocked to find a boy transformed into a full-bearded, veteran. Now, they met in a way George Crowl never had imagined. Writing his daughter, he asked her to relay the sad news to friends and family, saying simply, "Tell them that Thomas O. Crowl is dead." George Crowl discovered in a harsh way that his son had neither escaped the battlefield at Monocacy nor the stay in Danville Prison that followed. Like 620,000 of his brethren, Tom Crowl's spirit belongs to the ages, but his body is little more than one additional stroke on a statistician's notepad.[2]

2. Thomas O. Crowl to his sister, Apr. 21, 1864, CWMC; Pension Records of Thomas O. Crowl, consolidated with George Crowl, Co. G, 98th Pa.; George Crowl to his daughter, May 8, 1865; CMSR of Thomas O. Crowl. It is not known if Tom Crowl was wounded at Monocacy. Listing of the dead at Danville Cemetery on Interment.net, www.interment.net/data/us/va/danville/danvnat/index_ac.htm (accessed March 2003), has no Thomas O. Crowl but does have a "Thomas D. Crawl, Co. G, 67th Pennsylvania Infantry," who died September 18, 1864. This is undoubtedly Thomas O. Crowl, who also died September 18, 1864. His last name was often spelled "Crawl" or "Crall," and his court-martial records are indexed by that spelling because the indigenous south-central Pennsylvania accent avoids diphthongs, pronouncing "Crowl" as "Crawl." Confusing "D" with "O" or "C" with "G" was commonplace in documents of the era, and Tom served in Company C after regimental realignment. The 67th and 87th Pa. Regiments were also sometimes confused, e.g., *O.R.,* Report of David Zable, June 15, 1863, 27/2:514–15. Tom became a war victim again after death, this time from badly recorded personal data.

Appendix

P ersonal data displayed in the following charts and graphs were derived from any combination of sources listed in the bibliography. Data for the 87th Pennsylvania are solely for members of the original organization unless otherwise specified. Some statistics reflect the 87th Pennsylvania's enrollment during 1861 and are marked "1861," while others reflect enrollment 1862–1865 and are marked ">1861." Area men enlisting in 1861 with three-year regiments other than the 87th Pennsylvania are identified as "Non-87th."

Appendix

Professions, Age, and Physical Characteristics at Enlistment

Note: Professions were determined primarily from individual compiled military service records and secondarily from 1860 census records and 1862 and 1865 draft lists. "Wood worker" includes all forms of carpentry, cabinet making, etc.

Profession	87th 1861	Non-87th 1861	87th >1861	Profession	87th 1861	Non-87th 1861	87th >1861
Baker	0.5%	0.5%	0.3%	Military/seaman	0.2%	0.0%	1.2%
Bartender/waiter	0.2%	0.2%	0.0%	Miller	1.2%	1.2%	0.6%
Basket maker	0.5%	0.1%	0.0%	Miner/Quarryman	0.4%	1.2%	0.6%
Blacksmith	4.1%	4.7%	3.4%	Minister	0.1%	0.1%	0.3%
Boatman	0.5%	2.9%	1.5%	Misc skilled	0.7%	1.4%	0.3%
Brewer/Distiller	0.4%	0.4%	0.3%	Painter	2.1%	1.7%	1.2%
Brush maker	0.2%	0.0%	0.0%	Plasterer	1.5%	1.4%	0.9%
Businessman	0.2%	0.2%	0.3%	Printer	1.1%	1.2%	0.6%
Butcher	1.4%	1.1%	0.9%	Railroad worker	0.5%	0.9%	0.9%
Carriage Trade	3.1%	1.7%	1.5%	Saddle maker	0.9%	0.9%	0.3%
Clerical	2.1%	4.0%	0.6%	Servant	0.5%	0.6%	0.6%
Confectioner	0.3%	0.0%	0.0%	Shoemaker	4.6%	4.2%	2.8%
Cooper	1.3%	0.5%	2.1%	Student	0.4%	1.4%	0.3%
Factory worker	2.8%	1.6%	0.9%	Tailor	1.3%	2.0%	1.2%
Farmer/laborer	42.9%	40.4%	56.0%	Tanner	0.7%	0.0%	6.7%
Gentleman	0.2%	0.2%	0.0%	Teacher	0.7%	1.6%	1.5%
Hatter	0.5%	0.1%	0.0%	Teamster	0.0%	0.2%	1.5%
Lawyer	0.1%	0.5%	0.0%	Tin/whitesmith	1.2%	1.1%	0.0%
Locksmith	0.1%	0.0%	0.6%	Tobacco trade	1.7%	1.6%	0.9%
Lumberman	0.0%	0.1%	0.6%	Unknown	2.1%	2.0%	0.0%
Machinist	1.4%	1.9%	1.8%	Watchmaker	0.2%	0.2%	0.0%
Mason	4.1%	2.9%	0.3%	Weaver	0.6%	0.7%	0.0%
Medical/drug	0.4%	0.5%	1.5%	Whip maker	1.2%	0.9%	0.6%
Merchant	1.6%	1.1%	0.3%	Wood worker	8.9%	9.0%	4.3%

Age	87th 1861		Non-87th 1861		87th >1861	
	Stated	Actual	Stated	Actual	Stated	Actual
<18	0.5%	13.0%	0.8%	10.7%	3.6%	11.7%
18 - 24	62.9%	49.3%	59.9%	52.8%	49.8%	40.1%
25 - 29	16.1%	16.4%	16.0%	15.0%	21.0%	12.0%
30 - 34	9.1%	8.9%	8.1%	8.4%	11.3%	12.3%
35 - 39	5.0%	4.6%	6.3%	5.9%	11.0%	12.3%
40 - 45	6.0%	4.5%	5.8%	3.4%	11.7%	10.0%
46+	0.3%	3.3%	0.5%	2.9%	0.6%	2.3%
Unknown	0.3%	0.1%	2.8%	1.0%	0.6%	0.0%

Height	%87th 1861	%Non-87th 1861	%87th >1861	Overall Avg.
5' 0"-	0.1%	0.0%	0.6%	0.1%
5' 1"	0.2%	0.2%	0.3%	0.2%
5' 2"	0.9%	0.2%	0.3%	0.5%
5' 3"	2.0%	2.0%	4.2%	2.3%
5' 4"	3.9%	8.8%	9.3%	6.5%
5' 5"	7.5%	9.0%	13.8%	9.0%
5' 6"	11.9%	14.2%	16.7%	13.5%
5' 7"	12.3%	13.9%	18.3%	13.8%
5' 8"	17.3%	14.3%	12.5%	15.5%
5' 9"	9.4%	9.6%	9.0%	9.4%
5' 10"	8.3%	7.1%	6.7%	7.6%
5' 11"	5.2%	5.4%	2.9%	4.9%
6' 0"	1.7%	2.2%	2.2%	2.0%
6' 1"	0.5%	1.6%	0.3%	0.9%
6' 2"	0.4%	0.2%	1.0%	0.4%
6' 3"+	0.2%	0.0%	0.3%	0.1%
Unknown	18.1%	11.6%	1.6%	13.3%

Hair Color	%87th 1861	%Non-87th 1861	%87th >1861	Overall Avg.
Dark/Black/Brown	51.3%	59.0%	69.6%	56.8%
Light/Sandy	19.7%	24.9%	23.4%	22.2%
Auburn/Red	2.4%	2.6%	2.9%	2.6%
Gray	1.7%	1.3%	1.6%	1.6%
Unknown	24.9%	12.1%	2.6%	16.8%

Eye Color	% 87th 1861	% Non-87th 1861	%87th >1861	Overall Avg.
Dark/Black/Brown	18.2%	18.9%	12.8%	17.7%
Blue/Gray/Light/Hazel	57.6%	69.1%	84.3%	65.8%
Unknown	24.2%	12.0%	2.9%	16.5%

Casualties

All 87th Pennsylvania and Total Non-87th Battle Casualties

Head counts
87th Pa: 1,349
87th Mar 1865: 500
Non-87th 1861: 775

Battle	Killed	Wnd	Wnd/Capt	Capt	Capt/Died	TOTAL
Cedar Creek	7	24	0	9	2	42
Cold Harbor	4	35	0	1	1	41
Mine Run	4	11	0	0	0	15
Monocacy	17	32	2	25	8	84
Petersburg	5	10	0	1	0	16
Spotsylvania	1	30	0	2	0	33
Weldon Railroad	6	29	4	47	17	103
Wilderness	0	26	0	2	2	30
2nd Winchester	11	21	20	272	1	325
3rd Winchester	11	52	0	5	0	68
Other	2	21	0	26	0	49
TOTAL 87th	68	291	26	390	31	806
TOTAL Non-87th	83	183	30	108	45	449

Key
Killed: Died directly from battle wounds
Wnd: Wounded but survived
Wnd/Capt: Wounded and captured in the same battle
Capt: Captured but released
Capt/Died: Captured and died as a result of captivity

Note: Weldon Railroad Event took place June 22 and 23, 1864.

Non-Battle Casualties

Casualty	87th All	Non-87th
Deserted	104	49
Died	46	38
Dismissed	17	4
Illness/Injury	198	98
Resigned	15	17
Transfer	40	83
TOTAL	420	289

Men suffering casualties in different battles count once per casualty. Injuries in battle caused by accident (e.g., falls) are included with non-battle casualties, as are those sustained in shootings or explosions not enemy-inflicted. Transfers, technically not casualties but still losses to the sending regiment, are inflated for the non-87th group largely because Pennsylvania Reserve Corps men with unexpired terms of service routinely transferred to the 190th and 191st Pennsylvania on June 1, 1864.

Source: Individual Soldier Compiled Military Records

Life Expectancy Tables

Average Ages at Death Using Actual Enlistment Age

Enlistment Age	Including War Deaths			Survivors Only		
	87th Pa 1861	Non-87th Pa 1861	87th >1861	87th Pa 1861	Non-87th Pa 1861	87th >1861
<18	54.6	55.1	55.6	61.6	66.3	64.3
18 - 24	58.6	57.5	62.3	66.0	68.2	65.7
25 - 29	62.6	59.0	64.6	68.2	70.1	70.2
30 - 34	61.5	61.8	62.6	67.2	71.5	69.7
35 - 57	63.0	59.5	68.6	65.0	72.8	70.7
40 - 45	67.4	71.1	71.6	70.9	74.0	74.0
46+	65.0	72.8	71.8	72.7	75.8	77.9
TOTAL AVG	**59.4**	**58.6**	**63.6**	**66.2**	**69.5**	**68.1**

Average age at death for sixty-seven survivors who at any time held commissioned rank with the 87th Pennsylvania: 65.3

87th Pennsylvania Life Expectancy by Enlistment Year

Enlistment Year	All 87th	Headcnt	Survivors only
1861	59.4	939	66.2
1862	57.2	56	63.8
1863	77.4	4	77.4
1864	63.4	152	68.2
1865	71.4	38	71.4
TOTAL	**60.3**	**1,189**	**66.6**

Above statistics pertain only to those men for whom birth and death dates could be ascertained, i.e., "Head cnt." If only the year was known, June 30 was assumed. A "survivor" is defined as a man dying after 1865.

Personal Factors in Predicting Desertion

Actual Age at Enlistment

Actual Age	87th 1861		Non-87th 1861		87th >1861		Total	
	% of Men	% of Dstrs	% of Men	% of Dstrs	% of Men	% of Dstrs	% of Men	% of Dstrs
<18	13.0%	14.5%	10.7%	16.5%	11.7%	7.7%	11.9%	14.1%
18-24	49.3%	47.9%	52.8%	44.3%	40.1%	30.8%	49.3%	45.2%
25-29	16.4%	13.2%	15.0%	19.0%	12.0%	17.3%	15.3%	14.7%
30-34	8.9%	13.5%	8.4%	8.9%	12.3%	11.5%	9.2%	12.4%
35-39	4.6%	4.6%	5.9%	3.8%	12.3%	15.4%	6.2%	5.8%
40-45	4.5%	4.3%	3.4%	5.1%	10.0%	15.4%	4.9%	5.8%
46+	3.3%	1.7%	2.9%	1.3%	2.3%	1.9%	3.0%	1.6%
Unknown	0.1%	0.3%	1.0%	1.3%	0.0%	0.0%	0.4%	0.5%

Marital Status and Personal Worth at Enlistment

$1 - $999

	87th 1861		Non-87th 1861		87th All	
	% of Regt	% of dsrtrs	% of Regt	% of dsrtrs	% of Regt	% of dsrtrs
Married	18.2%	18.5%	13.5%	18.5%	17.2%	17.7%
Single	34.1%	34.0%	33.9%	28.4%	31.1%	32.7%
Unknown	0.5%	0.3%	1.0%	1.2%	0.5%	0.6%
TOTAL	52.8%	52.8%	48.4%	48.1%	48.8%	51.0%

$1,000 - $4,999

	87th 1861		Non-87th 1861		87th All	
	% of Regt	% of dsrtrs	% of Regt	% of dsrtrs	% of Regt	% of dsrtrs
Married	2.6%	2.0%	2.0%	1.2%	3.0%	2.0%
Single	13.8%	13.5%	10.7%	7.4%	13.5%	12.7%
Unknown	0.1%	0.0%	0.1%	2.5%	0.1%	0.0%
TOTAL	16.5%	15.5%	12.8%	11.1%	16.6%	14.6%

$5,000 - $9,999

	87th 1861		Non-87th 1861		87th All	
	% of Regt	% of dsrtrs	% of Regt	% of dsrtrs	% of Regt	% of dsrtrs
Married	0.4%	0.0%	0.6%	0.0%	0.4%	0.0%
Single	2.3%	1.7%	3.1%	3.7%	2.2%	1.4%
Unknown	0.0%	0.0%	0.1%	0.0%	0.0%	0.0%
TOTAL	2.7%	1.7%	3.8%	3.7%	2.7%	1.4%

$10,000+

	87th 1861		Non-87th 1861		87th All	
	% of Regt	% of dsrtrs	% of Regt	% of dsrtrs	% of Regt	% of dsrtrs
Married	0.6%	0.0%	0.4%	0.0%	0.5%	2.0%
Single	2.8%	1.7%	2.8%	2.5%	2.5%	12.7%
Unknown	0.0%	0.0%	0.0%	0.0%	0.0%	0.0%
TOTAL	3.4%	1.7%	3.1%	2.5%	3.0%	14.6%

Unknown

	87th 1861		Non-87th 1861		87th All	
	% of Regt	% of dsrtrs	% of Regt	% of dsrtrs	% of Regt	% of dsrtrs
Married	4.4%	4.0%	4.9%	4.9%	3.4%	3.4%
Single	18.9%	20.8%	21.6%	25.9%	14.6%	17.7%
Unknown	1.4%	3.6%	5.4%	3.7%	1.1%	3.1%
TOTAL	24.8%	28.4%	31.9%	34.6%	19.1%	24.2%

Marital Status and Personal Worth at Enlistment *continued*

	Total					
	87th 1861		Non-87th 1861		87th All	
	% of Regt	% of dsrtrs	% of Regt	% of dsrtrs	% of Regt	% of dsrtrs
Married	26.3%	24.4%	21.4%	24.7%	26.2%	24.5%
Single	71.9%	71.6%	72.0%	67.9%	70.6%	70.7%
Unknown	2.0%	4.0%	6.6%	7.4%	3.2%	4.8%
TOTAL	100.2%	100.0%	100.0%	100.0%	100.0%	100.0%

American-born Versus Foreign-born

	Head count	% Dsrtrs	% not return	% Court-martial
87th Native	1,116	24.8%	6.2%	1.3%
87th Foreign	230	33.9%	15.2%	0.4%
Non-87th Native	773	31.8%	4.0%	0.5%
Non-87th Foreign	59	2.2%	1.3%	0.0%
Total	2,178	16.3%	4.8%	0.7%

Selected Bibliography

Primary Sources

Adams County Commissioners. Minutes, 1841–1860. Adams County Historical Society, Gettysburg, Pennsylvania, MN #001.

Anstine, Beniah Keller. Diary. Typescript. Private collection.

Atlas of York Co. Pennsylvania Illustrated, from Surveys of Beach Nichols. Philadelphia: Pomeroy, Whitman & Co., 1876.

Atlas to Accompany the Official Records of the Union and Confederate Armies.
Washington, D.C.: Government Printing Office, 1891–1895; Carmel:
Guild Press of Indiana, 1999, CD-ROM.

Barnhart, Lorenzo D. "Reminiscences." 110th Ohio Volunteer Infantry, www
.iwaynet.net/~lsci/2ndwintr.htm.

Battles and Leaders of the Civil War. Secaucus: Castle Books, n.d.

Beach, William H. *The First New York (Lincoln) Cavalry.* New York: Lincoln
Cavalry Association, 1902.

Beidler, John Stoner. Diary. Edited by Charles Wilcox. Electronic copy. Private collection.

Blotcher, George. Diary, January 1, 1864–July 4, 1865. Library of the York
County Historical Trust, York, Pennsylvania.

———. Recollections. Library of the York County Historical Trust, York,
Pennsylvania.

Bowman-Griffith Family Papers. University of Washington Libraries Special
Collections, Seattle, Washington.

Bradwell, Isaac Gordon. *Under the Southern Cross: Soldier Life with Gordon
Bradwell and the Army of Northern Virginia.* Edited by Pharris Deloach
Johnson. Macon: Mercer University Press, 1979.

Broadhead, Sarah M. *The Diary of a Lady of Gettysburg Pennsylvania from June
15 to July 15, 1863.* Hershey: Gary T. Hawbaker, 1990.

Civil War Collection, 1804–1895. Ohio Historical Society, Columbus, Ohio.

Clerk of Courts, York County. Quarter Sessions Dockets, 1802–1866. York County Archives, York, Pennsylvania.

Crowl, Thomas O. Thomas O. Crowl Papers. Civil War Miscellaneous Collection, U.S. Army Military History Institute, Carlisle, Pennsylvania.

———. Thomas O. Crowl Civil War Letters. Historical Collections and Labor Archives, Special Collections, Pattee Library, Pennsylvania State University, University Park, Pennsylvania.

Douglas, Henry Kyd. *I Rode with Stonewall.* Chapel Hill: University of North Carolina Press, 1940; Marietta: Mockingbird Books, 1993.

Documents of American History. Vol. 1. 10th ed. Edited by Henry Steele Commager and Milton Cantor. Englewood Cliffs: Prentice Hall, 1988.

Early, Jubal Anderson. *Jubal Early's Memoirs: Autobiographical Sketch and Narrative of the War Between the States.* Baltimore: Nautical & Aviation Publishing Company of America, 1989.

———. "General J. A. Early's Report of the Gettysburg Campaign, with explanatory notes by Early added in 1872." In *Southern Historical Society Papers,* vol. 10, edited by R. A. Brock. Richmond: Southern Historical Society, 1904; Carmel: Guild Press of Indiana, CD-ROM, 1998.

———. "The Advance on Washington in 1864." In *Southern Historical Society Papers,* vol. 9, edited by R. A. Brock. Richmond: Southern Historical Society, 1904; Carmel: Guild Press of Indiana, CD-ROM, 1998.

Fire Association of Philadelphia Maps. New York: Sanborn-Perris Map Co., 1891.

Frassanito, William A. *Early Photography at Gettysburg.* Gettysburg: Thomas Publications, 1995.

Geary, John White. *A Politician Goes to War: The Civil War Letters of John White Geary.* Edited by William Alan Blair. University Park: Penn State University Press, 1995.

George Gordon Meade Collection. U.S. Army Military History Institute, Carlisle, Pennsylvania.

George Hay Kain III Collection. Manuscript file of the correspondence, diaries, and records of Colonel George Hay.

George Miller Collection. Library of the York County Historical Trust, York, Pennsylvania.

Gordon, John B. *Reminiscences of the Civil War.* Baton Rouge: Louisiana State University Press, 1993.

Gotwalt, Charles Edwin. "Adventures of a Private in the American Civil War." Edited by William Gotwalt. Typescript. Library of the York County Heritage Trust, York, Pennsylvania.

Grant, Ulysses S. *Personal Memoirs of U. S. Grant and Selected Letters 1839–1865.* New York: Library of America, 1990.

Hammond, James Henry. "Mudsill" speech to the United States Senate. Mar. 4, 1858. Electronic copy of text. Africans in America, www.pbs.org/wgbh/aia/part4/4h3439t.html.

Hardee, William Joseph. *Rifle and Light Infantry Tactics.* New York: J. O. Kane, 1862.

Harman, Lane Scott. "Recollections of the Harman Family." Typescript. Private collection.

Haynes, Edwin Mortimer. *A History of the Tenth Regiment, Vermont Volunteers.* 2nd ed. Rutland: Tuttle Co., Printers, 1894.

Heiman, Michael. Recollections. *York Gazette.* July 9–11, 13, 15, 21–23, 1891, Feb. 20, 22, 24, 1892.

Hersh, James. James Hersh Papers. Civil War Miscellaneous Collection, U.S. Army Military History Institute, Carlisle, Pennsylvania.

Hewitt, William. *History of the Twelfth West Virginia Volunteer Infantry: The Part It Took in the War of the Rebellion 1861–1865.* Twelfth West Virginia Association, 1892.

Historical Dictionary of the U.S. Army—1789–1903. Edited by Jerrold E. Brown. Westport: Greenwood Publishers, 2001.

Hoffman, John Clutter. "The Gallant 87th." Poem in souvenir program of the 1897 regimental reunion. York: Mundorf Publishing Co., 1897.

Kansas-Nebraska Act. Text. Avalon Project at Yale Law School, www.yale.edu/lawweb/avalon/avalon.htm.

Kautz, August V. *The 1865 Customs of Service for Non-Commissioned Officers and Soldiers: A Handbook for the Rank and File of the Army.* 2nd ed. J. B. Lippincott & Co., 1864; Mechanicsburg: Stackpole Books, 2002.

———. *Customs of Service for Officers of the Army: A Handbook of the Duties of Each Grade Lieutenant to Lieut.-General.* J. B. Lippincott, 1866; Mechanicsburg: Stackpole Books, 2002.

Keses, John. Recollections. Typescript. Private collection.

Keyes, Charles M. *The Military History of the 123d Regiment Ohio Volunteer Infantry.* Sandusky: Register Steam Press, 1874.

Krista Lyman Collection. Letters of Angelo Crapsey, 1st Pennsylvania Rifles.

Lee, Mrs. Hugh. Diary. Compiled by Sheila Phipps. Handley Library, Winchester, Virginia.

Lewis, Osceola. *History of the One Hundred and Thirty-Eighth Regiment Pennsylvania Volunteer Infantry.* Norristown: Wills, Iredell & Jenkins, 1866.

Lincoln-Douglas Debates. Electronic copy of text. U.S. Department of the Interior, National Park Service. Lincoln Home, www.nps.gov/liho/debates.htm.

Lowrey, John E. Diary. Harrisburg Civil War Round Table Collection, U.S.

Army Military History Institute, Carlisle Barracks, Carlisle, Pennsylvania.

Manuscript Files. Library of the York County Historical Trust, York, Pennsylvania.

Map of Adams County from Actual Survey of G. M. Hopkins, C.E. Philadelphia: M. S. & E. Converse, 1858.

McDonald, Cornelia Peake. *A Woman's Civil War: A Diary with Reminiscences of the War from March 1862.* Madison: University of Wisconsin Press, 1992.

Medical and Surgical History of the Civil War. Wilmington: Broadfoot Publishing, 1992.

Miller, Lewis. *Sketches and Chronicles, The Reflections of a Nineteenth Century Pennsylvania German Folk Artist.* York: Historical Society of York County, 1966.

The Monocacy Regiment: A Commemorative History of the Fourteenth New Jersey Infantry in the Civil War 1862–1865. Edited by David G. Martin. Hightstown: Longstreet House, 1987.

Munden, Kenneth W., and Henry Putney Beers. *The Union: A Guide to Federal Archives Relating to the Civil War.* Washington, D.C.: National Archives and Records Administration, 1998.

Myers, Solomon. Diary. Manuscript File 12740. Library of the York County Historical Trust, York, Pennsylvania.

Nichols, George Washington. *A Soldier's Story of His Regiment (61st Georgia).* Kennesaw: Continental Book Co., 1961.

Official Army Register of the Volunteer Force of the United States Army for the Years 1861, '62, '63, '64, '65. Part 3. Washington, D.C.: Adjutant General's Office, 1865.

Record Book and Memorabilia of the Worth Infantry. Rare Book Collection, Library of the York County Heritage Trust, York, Pennsylvania.

Register of Officers and Agents, Civil, Military, and Naval, in the Service of the United States on the Thirtieth September 1861. Washington, D.C.: Government Printing Office, 1862.

Rodgers, Sarah Sites. *The Ties to the Past: The Gettysburg Diaries of Salome Myers Stewart, 1854–1922.* Gettysburg: Thomas Publications, 1995.

Schriver, George Washington. Diary. In author's possession.

Sheeran, Rev. James B., C.SS.R. *Confederate Chaplain: A War Journal.* Edited by Joseph T. Durkin, S.J. Milwaukee: Bruce Publishing Co., 1960

Shetler, Charles. *West Virginia Civil War Literature: An Annotated Study.* Morgantown: West Virginia University Library, 1963.

Skelly Family Papers. Harrisburg Civil War Roundtable Collection, U.S. Army Military History Institute, Carlisle, Pennsylvania.

Sperry, Sarah Catherine "Kate." "Surrender? Never Surrender: July 13, 1861–Dec. 3, 1865." Typescript. Handley Library, Winchester, Virginia.

Stahle, James Alanza. Recollections. *York Gazette*. Mar. 17, 1891, June 1, 13–16, and July 11, 1893.

Supplement to the Official Records of the Union and Confederate Armies Part II. Record of Events. Wilmington: Broadfoot Publishing Co., 1992.

Taylor, James E. *The James E. Taylor Sketchbook: Leaves from a Special Artist's Sketchbook and Diary*. Edited by Dennis Frye, Martin F. Graham, and George F. Skoch. Dayton: Morningside House, 1989.

Terrill, John Newton. *Campaign of the Fourteenth New Jersey Volunteers*. New Brunswick: Daily Home News Press, 1884.

U.S. Bureau of the Census. United States Census, 1850–1900. Washington, D.C.

U.S. War Department. *The War of the Rebellion: A Compilation of the Official Records of the Union and Confederate Armies*. Compiled by Bvt. Lt. Col. Robert N. Scott. Washington, D.C.: Government Printing Office, 1880–1901; Carmel: Guild Press of Indiana, 2000, CD-ROM.

Vredenburgh, Peter. *Upon the Tented Field*. Edited by Bernard Olsen. Red Bank: Historic Projects, 1993.

Wallace, Lew. *An Autobiography*. New York: Harper & Brothers, 1906.

Wildes, Thomas F. *Record of the One Hundred and Sixteenth Regiment Ohio Volunteers*. Sandusky: I. F. Mack & Bros., 1884.

Worsham, John H. *One of Jackson's Foot Cavalry*. Edited by James I. Robertson. Wilmington: Broadfoot Publishing, 1987.

York County Assessment Office. Tax Rolls, 1866–1869. York County Archives, York, Pennsylvania.

York County Commissioner, Recorder of Deeds. Military Enrollment Lists, 1862 and 1865. York County Archives, York, Pennsylvania.

York County Sheriff's Office. Jail-Prisoner Boarding Record, 1863–1871. York County Archives, York, Pennsylvania.

Records in the National Archives

Card Records of Headstones Provided for Deceased Civil War Veterans, ca. 1879–ca. 1903, RG-92, M1845.

Department of the Interior. RG-15, Historical Registers of National Homes for Disabled Soldiers, Register of Members, 1867–1935.

———. RG-15, Pension Application Files, Civil War and Later.

Office of the Adjutant General. RG-94. Bookmarks.

———. RG-94, Book Records of Union Volunteer Organizations, Civil War, 87th Pennsylvania Infantry, Descriptive Books.

———. RG-94, Book Records of Union Volunteer Organizations, Civil War, 103rd Pennsylvania Infantry, Descriptive Books, Independent Companies.

———. RG-94, Compiled Military Service Records.

———. RG-94, Letters Received, 1805–1889.

———. RG-94, Letters Sent, 1800–1890.

———. RG-94, Muster Rolls of the 87th Pennsylvania Infantry.

———. RG-94, Regimental Letter Books of Volunteer Organizations, Civil War, 87th Pennsylvania Infantry.

———. RG-94, Registers of Enlistments in the United States Army, 1798–1914.

———. RG-94, Special Orders Issued from the Adjutant General's Office, 1863.

Preliminary Inventory of the Records of United States Army Continental Commands, 1821–1920. RG-393, Part 1, Army of the Potomac, Special Orders.

Preliminary Inventory of the Records of United States Army Continental Commands, 1821–1920. RG-393, Part 2, Army of the Potomac, 3rd Division, 3rd Army Corps, Register of Charges and Specifications.

Preliminary Inventory of the Records of United States Army Continental Commands, 1821–1920. RG-393, Part 2, Army of the Potomac, 6th Army Corps, Endorsements Sent.

Preliminary Inventory of the Records of United States Army Continental Commands, 1821–1920. RG-393, Part 2, E6766, Army of the Potomac, 3rd Brigade, 3rd Division, 3rd Army Corps, Aug–Dec 1863.

Preliminary Inventory of the Records of United States Army Continental Commands, 1821–1920. RG-393, Part 2, E7119, James Cooper's Brigade, General Orders and Special Orders.

Preliminary Inventory of the Records of United States Army Continental Commands, 1821–1920. RG-393, Part 2, E5804, Army of Virginia, Letters and Telegrams Sent, Endorsements, and Special Orders, 1862.

Preliminary Inventory of the Records of United States Army Continental Commands, 1821–1920. RG-393, Part 2, Middle Department, 8th Army Corps, Special Orders Apr. 1862–June 1863.

Provost Marshal General's Bureau, 15th District of Pennsylvania. RG-110, Letters Received 1863–1864.

Records of the Office of the Judge Advocate General. RG-153, Court-Martial Case Files.

Records of the Office of the Secretary of War. RG-107, Letters Sent by the Secretary of War Relating to Military Affairs.

Records in the Pennsylvania State Archives

Civil War Veterans Card File, 1861–1866. Pennsylvania Archives, Harrisburg, Pennsylvania. Electronic version available on Pennsylvania's Archives Records Information Access System (ARIAS), www.digitalarchives.state.pa.us/archive.asp.

Papers of the Governors, 1858–1871. Ser. 4. Vol. 8. Edited by W. W. Greist. Harrisburg: State of Pennsylvania, 1902.

Records of the Department of the Auditor General. Records Relating to Military Service, RG-2, 1–4762.

Records of the Department of Military and Veterans' Affairs. Office of the Adjutant General. RG-19, Records of Application for Military Positions, Vacancies, Appointments, and Resignations, and Commissions Issued, 1861–1865.

———. General Correspondence.

———. Letter Book.

———. Muster Rolls of the 87th Pennsylvania Infantry.

Records of the Department of State. RG-26, Clemency Files.

Secondary Sources

Baker, Gloria, and Gail Stephens. "Honor Redeemed: Lew Wallace's Military Career and the Battle of Monocacy." *North and South* 4, no. 2 (Jan. 2001).

Baker, Jean H. *Affairs of Party: The Political Culture of Northern Democrats in the Mid-Nineteenth Century.* Ithaca: Cornell University Press, 1983.

Bates, Samuel Penniman. *History of Pennsylvania Volunteers.* Harrisburg: State Printing Office, 1868.

Bearss, Edwin C. "Documentation Troop Movement Maps: Battle of Monocacy." Edited by Brett Spaulding. Frederick: Monocacy National Battlefield, 2003.

Benet, Stephen Vincent. *A Treatise of Military Law and the Practice of Courts-Martial.* New York: D. Van Nostrand, 1863.

Biographical Directory of the United States Congress, 1774–present. Electronic version at www.bioguide.congress.gov/biosearch/biosearch1.asp.

Boyd's Business Directory: The Counties of Pennsylvania, 1860.

Clark, John E., Jr. "Management in War: The Legacy of Civil War Railroads." *North and South* 5, no. 5 (July 2002).

Cooling, Benjamin Franklin. *Monocacy: The Battle That Saved Washington.* Shippensburg: White Mane Publishing, 2000.

Donald, David Herbert. *Lincoln.* New York: Touchstone, 1995.

Dred Scott v. Sandford (1857). Supreme Court Historical Society, www.land markcases.org/dredscott/home.html.

Dunn, Craig L. *Harvestfields of Death: The Twentieth Indiana Volunteers at Gettysburg.* Carmel: Guild Press, 1999.

Family Files. Adams County Historical Society, Gettysburg, Pennsylvania.

Family Files. Library of the York County Heritage Trust, York, Pennsylvania.

Floyd, Frederick Clark. *History of the Fortieth (Mozart) Regiment New York Volunteers.* Boston: F. H. Gilson Co., 1909.

Foner, Eric. *Free Soil, Free Labor, Free Men: The Ideology of the Republican Party before the Civil War.* New York: Oxford University Press, 1995.

Fox, William F. *Regimental Losses in the American Civil War, 1861–1865.* Albany: Albany Publishing Co., 1889; Guild Press, CD-ROM v. 1.6.

Freeman, Douglas Southall. *Lee's Lieutenants: A Study in Command.* Vol. 3, *Gettysburg to Appomattox.* New York: Charles Scribner's Sons, 1944.

Gallman, J. Matthew, with Susan Baker. "Gettysburg's Gettysburg: What the Battle Did to the Borough." In *The Gettysburg Nobody Knows,* edited by Gabor S. Boritt. New York: Oxford University Press, 1997.

Genealogical Records of George Small, Philip Albright . . . Philadelphia: J. B. Lippincott Co., 1905.

Gilson, J[ohn] H. *Concise History of the One Hundred and Twenty-sixth Regiment, Ohio Volunteer Infantry.* Salem: Walton, Steam Job and Label Printers, 1883.

Goldsborough, Edward Y. *Early's Great Raid.* Frederick: Historical Society of Frederick County, 1989.

Gould, Benjamin Apthorp. "Investigations in the Military and Anthropological Statistics of American Soldiers." In *United States Sanitary Commission Memoirs of the War of the Rebellion: Statistical.* Cambridge: Riverside Press, 1869.

Graham, Martin F., and George F. Skoch. *Mine Run: A Campaign of Lost Opportunities, October 21, 1863–May 1, 1864.* 2nd ed. Lynchburg: H. E. Howard, 1987.

Gunnarsson, Robert L. *The Story of the Northern Central Railway.* Sykesville: Greenberg Publishing Co., 1991.

Hagerty, Edward J. *Collis' Zouaves: The 114th Pennsylvania Volunteers in the Civil War.* Baton Rouge: Louisiana State University Press, 1997.

Harwood, Herbert H., Jr. *Impossible Challenge: The Baltimore and Ohio Railroad in Maryland.* Baltimore: Barnard, Roberts & Co., 1979.

Hatfield, Mark O. "John C. Breckinridge," *Vice Presidents of the United States.* Washington, D.C.: U.S. Government Printing Office, 1997.

Henry, Gordon C., ed. "Newberry College: 1856–1976, 120 Years of Service to the Lutheran Church and to South Carolina." Typescript.

Heuvel, Lisa. "The Peal That Wakes No Echo: Benjamin Ewell and the College of William and Mary." *Virginia Cavalcade* (Fall 1978).

Higginson, Thomas Wentworth. *Massachusetts in the Army and Navy during the War of 1861–65.* Boston: Wright & Potter Publishing Co., 1896.

Jenkins, Jeffery A., and Irwin Morris. "Spatial Voting Theory and Counterfactual Inference: John C. Breckinridge and the Presidential Election of 1860." Electronic copy. http://polmeth.wustl.edu/retrieve.php?id=67.

Kain, George Hay, III. "George Hay: Citizen-Soldier from York, Pennsylvania," 1996. Private collection.

Kamm, Samuel Richey. "The Civil War Career of Thomas A. Scott: A Dissertation in History." Ph.D. diss., University of Pennsylvania, 1940.

King, Elaine, William L. Ziegler, and H. Alvin Jones, eds. *Looking at the Past: New Oxford, Penna.* New Oxford: n.p., 1977.

Krick, Robert K. *Lee's Colonels.* 4th ed., rev. Dayton: Morningside House, 1992.

Livingood, James Weston. *The Philadelphia-Baltimore Trade Rivalry, 1780–1860.* Harrisburg: Commonwealth of Pennsylvania, The Pennsylvania Historical and Museum Commission, 1947.

Lonn, Ella. *Desertion during the Civil War.* Lincoln: University of Nebraska Press, 1928.

Lowry, Thomas P. *Don't Shoot That Boy! Abraham Lincoln and Military Justice.* Mason City: Savas Publishing Co., 1990.

Lowry, Thomas P., and Jack D. Welsh, M.D. *Tarnished Scalpels: The Court-Martials of Fifty Union Surgeons.* Mechanicsburg: Stackpole Books, 2000.

Marvel, William. *Andersonville: The Last Depot.* Chapel Hill: University of North Carolina Press, 1994.

McClure, James. *Almost Forgotten: A Glimpse at Black History in York County, Pa.* York: *York Daily Record*/York County Heritage Trust, 2002.

McPherson, James M. *For Cause and Comrades: Why Men Fought in the Civil War.* Oxford: Oxford University Press, 1997.

Meyer, Daniel. *Stephen A. Douglas and the American Union.* Chicago: University of Chicago Library, 1994. Electronic copy at Department of Special Collections, University of Chicago Library, www.lib.uchicago.edu/e/spcl/excat/douglasint.html.

Moe, Richard. *The Last Full Measure: The Life and Death of the First Minnesota Volunteers.* St. Paul: Minnesota Historical Society, 1993.

Nye, Wilbur Sturtevant. *Here Come the Rebels!* Dayton: Morningside Bookshop, 1988.

Papers of the Military Historical Society of Massachusetts. Wilmington: Broadfoot Publishing Co., 1990.

Parker, Sandra V. *Richmond's Civil War Prisons.* Lynchburg: H. E. Howard, 1990.

Prowell, George R. *History of the 87th Pennsylvania Volunteers.* York: Press of the York Daily, 1903; York County Historical Trust, 1994.

———. *History of York County.* Chicago: J. H. Beers & Co., 1907.

Randall, J. G., and David H. Donald. *The Civil War and Reconstruction.* 2nd ed. Lexington: D. C. Heath & Co., 1969.

Rebellion Record. Edited by Frank Moore. New York: D. Van Nostrand, 1861–1868; New York: Arno Press, 1977.

Reily, John T. *History and Directory of the Boroughs of Adams County 1880.* Gettysburg: J. E. Wible, 1880.

Richmond Civil War Centennial Committee, 1961–1965. "Libby Prison." Official Publication #12. Compiled by R. W. Wiatt, Jr. Electronic copy available on www. censusdiggins.com/prisonlibby.html.

Smedley, R. C. *History of the Underground Railroad in Chester and the Neighboring Counties of Pennsylvania.* Lancaster: Office of the *Lancaster Journal,* 1883.

Snell, Mark A. *From First to Last: The Life of Major General William B. Franklin.* New York: Fordham University Press, 2002.

———. "If They Would Know What I Know It Would Be Pretty Hard to Raise One Company in York: Recruiting, the Draft, and Society's Response in York County." In *Union Soldiers and the Northern Home Front,* edited by Paul A. Cimbala and Randall M. Miller. New York: Fordham University Press, 2002.

Spangler, Edward W. *The Annals of the Families of Caspar, Henry, Baltzer, and George Spangler.* York: York Daily Publishing Co., 1896; Salem: Higginson Book Co., n.d.

Stewart, William H. "The Trying Experience of the ex-President at Fort Monroe." In *Southern Historical Society Papers,* vol. 32, edited by R. A. Brock. Richmond: Southern Historical Society, 1904; Carmel: Guild Press of Indiana, CD-ROM, 1998.

Supreme Court Decisions, Touro College, Jacob D. Fuchsberg Law Center, www.tourolaw.edu/patch/Scott/.

Switala, William J. *Underground Railroad in Pennsylvania.* Mechanicsburg: Stackpole Books, 2001.

Vandiver, Frank E. *Jubal's Raid: General Early's Famous Attack on Washington in 1864*. New York: McGraw-Hill Book Co., 1960.

Vinovskis, Maris A., ed. *Toward a Social History of the American Civil War: Exploratory Essays*. Cambridge: Cambridge University Press.

Vital Statistics Card File, York County Heritage Trust Library, York, Pennsylvania.

Warner, Ezra. *Generals in Blue: Lives of the Union Commanders*. Baton Rouge: Louisiana State University Press, 1964.

————. *Generals in Gray: Lives of the Confederate Commanders*. Baton Rouge: Louisiana State University Press, 1959.

Wentz, Ross. *Gettysburg Lutheran Theological Seminary*. Vol. 1, *History, 1826–1965*. Harrisburg: Evangelical Press, 1965.

Wert, J. Howard. "Old Time Notes of Adams County," July 12, 1905. Pfeiffer Family Folder. Adams County Historical Society, Gettysburg, Pennsylvania.

Wiley, Bell Irvin. *The Life of Billy Yank: The Common Soldier of the Union*. Baton Rouge: Louisiana State University Press, 1952, revised 1971.

Worthington, Glenn H. *Fighting for Time: The Battle That Saved Washington*. Baltimore: Day Printing Co., 1932; Shippensburg: White Mane Publishing Co., 1985.

Zettler, B. M. *War Stories and School Day Incidents for the Children*. Smyrna: SoftPedal Publisher, 1993.

Newspapers

Adams (Pa.) Sentinel and General Advertiser, aka *Adams Sentinel, Star and Sentinel*

Atchison (Kan.) Daily Globe

Baltimore (Md.) American and Commercial Advertiser

Baltimore County (Md.) Advocate

Bucks County (Pa.) Gazette

Cartridge Box, The (U.S. Army Military Hospital, York, Pa.)

Chester (Pa.) Times

Chicago (Ill.) Tribune

Columbia (Pa.) Spy

Daily Baltimore (Md.) Republican

Gettysburg (Pa.) Compiler

Gettysburg (Pa.) Star and Banner

Gettysburg (Pa.) Times

Grand Army Scout and Soldier's Mail

Hanover (Pa.) Evening Herald
Hanover (Pa.) Herald
Hanover (Pa.) Spectator and Commercial Advertiser
Martinsburg (W. Va.) Herald
National Tribune
New Oxford (Pa.) Item
New York Times
News, The (Frederick, Md.)
Ogdensburgh (N.Y.) Daily Republican & Journal
Philadelphia (Pa.) Evening Bulletin
Pottsville (Pa.) Republican
True Democrat (York, Pa.)
Washington Star (Washington, D.C.)
York County (Pa.) Star and Wrightsville Advertiser
York (Pa.) Daily
York (Pa.) Daily Record
York (Pa.) Democratic Press
York (Pa.) Dispatch
York (Pa.) Gazette
York (Pa.) Pennsylvanian
York (Pa.) Recorder
York (Pa.) Republican, aka *Pennsylvania Republican, York Republican and Anti-Masonic Expositor, Weekly York Republican*

Photographic Collections

Gettysburg National Military Park, Gettysburg, Pennsylvania.
Gil Barret Collection, U.S. Army Military History Institute, Carlisle, Pennsylvania.
Military Order of the Loyal Legion of the United States (MOLLUS) Collection, U.S. Army Military History Institute, Carlisle, Pennsylvania.
Monocacy National Battlefield, Frederick, Maryland.
Roger Hunt Collection, U.S. Army Military History Institute, Carlisle, Pennsylvania.
Ronn Palm's Museum of Civil War Images, Gettysburg, Pennsylvania.

Index

87th Pennsylvania: amputations, 229, 230; battalion designation, 218, 233; Bunker Hill church-forts, 78, 105; Bunker Hill, detachment at, 70, 73; Bunker Hill skirmish, 76–78; casualties by battle, 246; casualty descriptions by individual soldier, 78, 79, 185, 186, 190–94, 198, 202–8, 213, 214, 231, 246, 247; casualty in battle, first, 63; companies F-K, March 1865, 222, 223; death from illness, first, 38; death in battle, first, 78; death in battle, last, 224; desertion, 115–39, 249–51; diarrhea and dysentery, 82, 84, 94 n12, 141, 230, 231; Emancipation Proclamation, reaction to, 163–65, 171; eye diseases, 35, 232; name of 87th assigned, 38; race, views of, 161–66, 171–73; religion, 181–84; reunions, postwar, 97, 238, 239; "Thomas A. Scott" name, 31, 32, 34–39, 44, 49, 64, 65, 86, 89, 172; Veteran Volunteers, 179, 180, 188, 217, 220, 226. *See also* Cedar Creek, battle of; Cold Harbor, battle of; Fisher's Hill, battle of; Harris Farm, battle of; Mine Run campaign; Monocacy, battle of; Petersburg, siege of; Sayler's Creek, battle of; Winchester, 2nd battle of, 3rd battle of; Desertion in 87th, causes of; Discipline issues in 87th; Emancipation Proclamation, other white reaction to; Enlistment ages in 87th; Enlistment motivations in 87th; Racial matters

Abatis, 112, 147
Adair, James, 69, 137
African Methodist Episcopal Church, 172
African Meeting House, 159
Aker, John, 162
Albany, GA, 174
Albright, John Alfred, 54, 126
Alfersdorffer, Enos Ignatius, 122
Anderson, George S., 99, 100, 151, 152
Annie M. Warner Hospital, 233
Anstine, Beniah Keller, 109, 183, 205
Armprister, Henry, xii, 46, 135
Articles of War, 48, 121
Ashley, Joseph, 180

Backoffer, John Henry, 119, 120
Bair, Elias, 138, 139
Baird, John Francis, 182
Baker, Jean, 159
Baker, William F., 137, 234
Baldwin, Henry Moore, 37, 37 n32
Baltimore and Ohio Railroad, 16, 197, 207
Barnes, Albert Thompson, 99, 100
Baublitz, Israel, 120
Bauman, Mary, 128
Bell, John, 12
Belle Grove Plantation, 218
Belle Plain, VA, 188
Bendon, Simon Alfred, 218
Bermuda Hundred, VA, 191–92
Beverly, WV, 98–100. *See also* Barnes, Albert Thompson; Goff, David, home and field hospital
"Bijou." *See* LaForge, Abiel Teple

Billmyer, Henry, 205
Blaney, Henry Edgar, 178
Blasser, George Washington, 48 n23, 83
Blasser, James Henry, 35, 48 n23, 103, 154
Blotcher, George C., xv, 33, 37, 43, 79, 155, 179, 189–91, 202, 205, 207, 208, 213, 214, 223–27, 240
Blouse, Daniel, 228
Bonge, Daniel, 155
Booth, Charles, 177
Bott, Peter, 177
Bounty payments, 115, 122, 135, 136, 179, 180, 222
Bowers, Henry W., 43
Branding, court-martial sentence of, 46, 47 n19
Brandt, George Henry Cleophus, 228
Brandy Station, VA, 147, 149, 181
Breckinridge, John Cabell, 8, 11–13, 201
Brenaman, William Henry, 39, 172
Brown, James Allen, 181, 182
Broadhead, Sarah, 81
Brown, John, 5, 6, 10, 11, 160
Buehler, Charles Henry, 67, 68, 75, 76, 97, 105, 236
Bulford, Samuel S., 223
Bunker Hill, WV, mentioned, 232; Gen. Robert Patterson stops at, 23
Bushdorf, Alexander, 155
Buzby, George J., 92

Cadwallader, David, 170, 171
Cairo, IL, 100
Cameron, Simon, 27–29
Camps, Union: Camp Curtin, 37, 134; Camp Distribution, 135; Camp Dix, 38; Camp Parole, 123, 130–34; Camp Scott, 21, 28, 101, 217; Camp William Penn, 162
Carr, Joseph, 46
Cedar Creek, battle of, 209, 218, 219, 227
Chalfant, George Jonathan, 228, 229
Clarksburg, WV, 98, 182
Cluseret, Gustave Paul, 55, 108, 164, 165
Clymer, Hiester, 236, 237
Coble, Abraham B., 44
Coble, Ephraim, 130
Coble, Moses, 90

Cockeysville, MD, 17, 18, 38, 59, 75
Cold Harbor, battle of, 189–91
Colored regiments: 39th U.S.C.T., 173; 43rd U.S.C.T., 238; 53rd U.S.C.T., 62; 127th U.S.C.T., 238
Columbia, PA, 25, 26, 160
Conspiracy of 1803, 158
Constitution: 14th Amendment, 235; 15th Amendment, 235; Democrats attack Republicans as anti-Constitution, 8, 166; permits slavery, 7; Prigg case, 157
Cooper, James, 40, 97
Copperhead peace movement, 33, 166, 167, 208
Crouch, Alexander, 120
Crowl, George, 241, 242
Crowl, Thomas Oliver, xv, 81, 89, 91, 95, 98, 134, 135, 140, 162–64, 179–81, 184, 185, 191, 232, 242
Crull, John, 59, 61, 104
Culp, William Esias, 13, 81, 218
Culp, John Wesley, 13
Culpeper, VA, 135, 181
Curtin, Andrew Gregg, 9, 18, 20, 41, 55, 57, 58, 73, 74, 76, 83, 161, 195, 212, 221, 222, 227

Daniel, Robert Alonzo, 46, 70–72, 130, 149, 205
Danville Prison, 109, 183, 205, 225, 241, 242
Danville, VA, 225, 226, 241
Deardorff, Jacob, 121
Democratic Party: area support for the war, 13, 15, 16, 49–52; area view of secession, 14; convention, 1860, 11, 12; fears influx of black labor, 7, 8, 10; Northern and Southern Democrats compared, 6, 7; Pennsylvania's Fusion ticket, election of 1860, 12; racial views, 6, 7, 159, 163–65, 235, 236; Republicans' opinion of, postwar 237; Republicans' opinion of, prewar, 6–9; War and Peace Democrats, 167
Dennison, William, 10
Denues, Charles Zinn, 233
Denues, John, 118
Department of Pennsylvania, 22

Desertion in 87th, causes of: age
factors, 48, 118–19, 249; boredom or
discouragement, 46, 97, 116, 117, 120,
122, 134, 155, 165; bounty jumping, 115,
116; character flaws, 125–28; eager to see
home, 131–33, 226; ease of deserting,
117, 118; feelings of worthlessness, 124,
125; ill health, 119, 120; inadequate
supplies, 120; income and social
position, 119; marital status, 119, 250;
mental instability, 133; supported by
homefolks, 118. *See also* Statistical charts
Detwiler, Jacob, 59–62, 65, 130
Diehl, Josiah Daniel "Jesse," 135 n55
Dieter, Jacob, 17
Dietrich, Daniel Philip Lang, 84
Discipline issues in 87th: ball and chain,
220; behavior problems, prewar, 89, 90;
bucking and gagging, 35, 95; experience
improves, 192, 199; frustration, 99, 100;
general discussion, 89–101; George R.
Prowell's approach to, xii; inactivity
causes problems, 91–93, 96; militia,
in antebellum, 16, 22; officers, 90, 91;
recruiting, 46, 91
Discipline, non-87th Pennsylvania men,
100–101
Dittenhaffer, Franklin, 136
Dittenhaffer, George, 231
Dix, John Adams, 38
Dixon, John Albert, 90, 125
Douglas, Henry Kyd, 207
Douglas, Stephen Arnold, 11, 12, 163
Douglass, Frederick, 160, 163
Dovler, Jacob, 98
Draft quotas, 180
Dred Scott case, 156
Duncan, Johnson Kelly, 13

Early, Jubal Anderson, 86, 195, 196, 200,
207–9
Eastern States Penitentiary, 131, 158, 161
Easton, Hosea, 160
Eberhart, David Christian, 64, 108, 182,
183, 203, 239
Eckert, David, 73
Eckert, Vincent C. S., 69–73, 119, 130, 136
Eckert, William Francis, 42 n10, 72, 73

Egerton, Charles Calvert, 18 n9
Egypt Station, battle of, 138
Eichelberger, George Reuben, 232
Eicholtz, William Henry, 233
Ellsworth Zouaves. *See* Militia
Emancipation Proclamation, other white
reaction to, 168, 236
Emmett, Jacob, 60, 61
Englebert, John, 48, 118, 142
Enlistment ages in 87th: actual versus
stated, 40, 41, 44, 245; ages of soldiers,
29, 34, 39–41, 44–47, 54, 55, 118, 119, 173,
233, 249; average by company, 54; effect
on life expectancy, 34; effect on older
men, 45–47; lying about age, 40, 45;
oldest enlistees, 45, 46; statistical charts,
245, 248, 249; youngest enlistees, 44
Enlistment motivations in 87th: age,
40, 41, 44, 45; bounty, 115, 179, 180;
desire for importance, 43; economic
conditions, 41–43; family ties, 44, 48,
49; geography, 52; patriotism, 22, 25,
39, 40; politics and social issues, 14,
40, 49–52, 73, 86, 163, 165; previous
military/militia experience, 41, 59, 63,
67, 69, 70; problems at home, 46;
promise of easy duty, 32, 33, 125; rage
militare, 40, 41; skill of recruiters, 53,
54, 56
Ensinger, Henry A., 188
Eppley, Henry, 95
Eppley, Jacob G., 39
Ewell, Benjamin Stoddert, 56
Ewell, Julia McIlvain, 56
Ewell, Richard Stoddert, 56, 57

Fahs, John, 48, 149
Fahs, William Hamilton, 48, 173
Farrah, Wells Abraham, 74–76, 79, 105
Fellers, James A., 229
Felty, George Ignatius Francis, 42
Ferdinand, John, 42
Fink, Henry, 55
Fisher's Hill, battle of, 214–16, 219
Flinn, Richmond, 126, 128 n33
Flinn (Snyder), Phebe, 126, 127
Fluck, Porter Henry, 224
Foose, Jacob, 48, 147

Foose, Matthew, 48, 147
Ford, George Washington, 133
Ford, Peter, 76 n65, 154 n35
Forrer, Eli, 133, 134 n48
Forrer, Tempest Leichey, 99
Forrest, Joshua R., 225
Forsythe, James P. *See* Klingel, William
    Augustus
Fort McHenry, Baltimore, MD, 9, 18, 62,
    96, 130, 134, 181
Fox, David, 125
Fox, Joseph I., 99 n25
Fox, Abraham, 100
Frank, William Frederick, 33, 166
Franklin, Walter L., 221, 222
Franklin, William Buel, 221
Frederick, MD, 110, 197, 198, 206, 210,
    240
Freeman, Douglas Southall, 207
Frick, Abraham, 173
Frick, Benjamin Franklin, xii, 131, 132, 173
Fugitive Slave Law, 10, 157
Fullerton, William, 190
Fulton, Andrew Jackson, 63

Gaines' Mill, battle of, 189
Gallatin, TN, 21 n15, 101
Gambrill Mill. *See* Monocacy, battle of
Gastrock, Liborious "Levi," 94, 95, 230,
    231
Geary, John White, 235–37
Geise, Franklin, 83, 84, 106, 150, 151, 162,
    163, 233
Gentzler, Philip, 84
Georgia regiments: 61st Infantry, 186
Gerecht, Conrad, 124
Gettysburg, battle of, 9, 13, 32, 77, 116,
    130, 169, 234
Gettysburg, PA, xi, 3, 4, 21, 51, 66, 81, 85,
    138, 159, 160, 195, 233, 238, 239
Gibson, John, 38
Gilbert, Calvin, 113, 240
Glassmyer, Jacob, 48 n23
Glassmyer, Oliver, 48 n23
Glen Rock, PA, 50, 51, 62
Goff, David, home and field hospital, 99
    n25, 100 n30. *See also* Beverly, WV
Goldsboro, PA, 227

Goodridge, Evalina, 161
Goodridge, Glenalvin, 161, 171
Goodridge, William C., 160, 161
Gordon, John Brown, 201
Gotwalt, Charles Edwin, 188, 193, 194, 231
Grant, Ulysses S., xii, 43, 100, 185, 189–92,
    193, 195, 196, 208, 209, 212, 224, 225
"Grapevine telegraph," 147
Gray, Jacob, 48 n23
Gray, Samuel Brenneman, 44, 48 n23
Griffith, John Myers, 78
Grove, Philip, 48, 92 n8

Haack, Charles Frederick, 109, 201, 203,
    205
Hagerstown, MD, 20 n14, 134
Hahn, Nicholas A., 40
Hair, Jerome, 227, 228
Hale, John, 190
Halleck, Henry Wager, 100, 196, 212
Hannagan, Ramsey Obediah, 41
Hanover, PA, xiv, 3, 21, 50, 69–73, 116, 219
Hanover Junction, PA, 19
Hantz Brothers Hardware, 17
Harman, Harvey James, 47, 74, 238
Harman, Jacob, 228
Harman, Ross Lewis, 73, 74, 76, 169, 170
Harris Farm, battle of, 138, 189
Hartman, Enoch Christian, 226 n42
Hay, George, 17, 18, 30, 31, 34 n24, 45,
    58–61, 71, 74, 83, 95, 97, 103, 168, 231,
    238
Hay, Jacob, 91
Heiman, Michael, xv, 43, 58–61, 64, 94,
    95, 173–78, 222
Helker, Joseph, 98
Heltzel, Daniel, 136
Helwig, Theodore Augustus, 110, 218, 221
Hemorrhoids (piles), 231
Hemple, Augustus, 224
Henderson, Thomas, 156
Hendrix, James H., 36
Hernia. *See* Rupture and hernia
Herr, Edward Reinecker, 140
Hersey, Francis Asbury, 205
Hersh, James, 39, 88, 136, 172, 212, 238
Hersh, Zephaniah E., 223
Hilton Head, SC, 162

Hoffman, Charles, 13
Hoffman, David N., 13
Hoffman, John, 230
Hoffman, John Clutter, 13, 97
Holter, Lewis V., 35, 36, 94
Hopson, Joseph B., 35
Howard Tunnel, 36
Hull, Isaac, 66, 104
Hummel, Joseph, 94, 95

Ilgenfritz, Alburtus "Bertram," 228
Ilgenfritz, Thomas, 232
Illinois regiments: 8th Cavalry, 201
Indiana regiments: 20th Infantry, 36, 37
Irwinville, GA, 175, 176

Jackson, Granville, 48 n23
Jackson, Nathaniel, 48 n23
Jameson, Alfred Jesse, xv, 91, 96, 99, 183,
    193 n42, 197, 241
James River, 106, 192
Johnston, Joseph Eggleston, 56

Kansas-Nebraska Act, 11
Karnes, Daniel H., 78
Keech, Robert W., 63
Keefer, Amos, 190
Keesey (Geesey), Samuel Wesley, 224
Kehm, Christian William, 117
Keifer, Joseph Warren, 219
Keller, Samuel Finkle, 61, 95, 173
Kerber, Lawrence R., 183
Keses, John, 185, 186
Kidd, Henry S., 124, 125
King, Albert, 168 n29
King, George W., 238
King, Robert Hervey, 47 n20, 48
Klinedinst, Martin James, 203
Klingel, William Augustus, 122
Knudson, William Augustus, 226
Kohler, Edwin Forrest, 117
Kohler, Henry Winters, 203
Kralltown, PA, 152

LaForge, Abiel Teple, 197, 198
Lanius, William Henry, 107, 113, 146, 151,
    152, 200, 208, 233, 239, 240
Lauer, Henry, 117 n5

Laumaster, Charles Augustus, 205
Laumaster, Daniel Heinrich, 110, 126, 204
Lee, Robert E., 77, 129, 168, 171, 177, 178,
    185, 189, 195, 224, 225
Leighty, Daniel, 96 n16
Libby, Luther and George, 129
Lincoln, Abraham, 7, 8, 10, 12, 13, 15, 21,
    27, 28, 49, 166, 167, 196; Democrats'
    opinion of, 7 n4, 8, 10, 208, 209;
    George Blotcher's opinion of, 225;
    Joshua R. Forrest's opinion of, 225;
    Tom Crowl's opinion of, 135, 163. See
    also Vote by county/district, 1860
List, Christian, 177
Little, Charles Basil, 48 n23
Little, David Forest, 48 n23
Little, Duncan, 48 n23
Little, Esias Z., 48 n23
Little, Joseph, 168 n29
Litz, George Lawrence, 90
Locofoco, 10, 98
Lonn, Ella, 118–21, 124
Lowe, Jacob, 35
Lutherville, MD, 67
Lutz, William Harman, 32, 133
Lynchburg, VA, 195

Macon, GA, 178
Madlam, Samuel E., 35
Maish, Levi, 43, 44 n13, 62, 94
Manassas Junction, VA, 22–24
Maps: Adams County in 1860, xxii; Battle
    of Monocacy, 210; Battle of Payne's
    Farm, 144; Battle of the Wilderness,
    187; Carter's Woods, 80; Fisher's Hill,
    216; South Central Pennsylvania and Its
    Railroads, xxiii; York County in 1860,
    xxii
Markle, George S., 121, 135
Martin, Anthony M., 42, 82, 83, 109, 149,
    203
Martin, Charles, 90
Martin, Jefferson, 162
Martin, William John, 54, 68, 69
Martinsburg, WV, 77, 81, 197
Maryland regiments: 1st Infantry, 188; 1st
    Potomac Home Brigade Cavalry, 58;
    3rd Infantry, 125; 6th Infantry, 146

McAvoy, Frank, 42, 43
McCausland, John, 198–201
McClellan, George Brinton, 38, 57, 98, 222
McCurdy, William Francis, 91 n5, 133
McElroy, Forest W., 129 n34
McElroy, John, 47, 48 n23
McIlhenny, John Taughinbaugh, 22, 23
McIlvain, John Edwin, 56–58, 89, 126–28
McIntire, Peter A., 122, 123
McKinney, David Ferguson, 110, 206, 218
McPherson, Edward M., 97
Meade, George Gordon, 72, 141, 142, 147, 213
Medal of Honor recipient. *See* Reigle, Daniel Peter
Militia, xi, 1, 3, 5, 16–19, 22, 25, 27, 30, 31, 41, 55, 59, 63, 67, 69, 70, 74, 86, 90, 91, 121, 158, 160, 168, 196, 198, 199; 26th Pennsylvania Militia, 87 n95, 88; Crossroads Militia, 41; Ellsworth Zouaves, 55; Independent Blues Militia, 67; Marion Rifles, 69; Washington Guards, 74; Worth Infantry, 16–18, 160; York Rifles, 16, 25
Miller, Andrew, 92
Miller, Lewis, 38
Miller, William, 232
Milroy, Robert Huston, 31, 71, 78, 108, 163–67, 182, 239
Mine Run campaign (incl. battle of Payne's Farm), 137, 140–55
Minnich, Benjamin, 135
Mitchell, Reid, 53
Monocacy, battle of: analysis of outcome, 207–10; Gambrill Mill, 198, 204–6, 210, 211; Gordon's attack, 201–5, 210; McCausland's attack, 198–200, 210; missing Union brigade, 201, 206; Monocacy Junction, 197, 198, 208; Pennsylvania monument, 114, 239; Pennsylvania's reaction to invasion, 195, 196; reflections by veterans, 239; sunken road, 203; Thomas house, 200–203, 210; Worthington house, 198, 199
Montgomery, Thomas James, 116
Morgan, Margaret. *See* Prigg case
Morningstar, Adam, 232
Morningstar, Henry, 69–72
Mosebaugh, Paul, 131, 205
Mowrey, Eli Israel, 294
Murray, James, 92, 93, 190
Myers, David Gilbert, 81, 104, 184, 186, 188, 190
Myers, Richard, 238
Myers, Salome, 81
Myers, Solomon, 1, 19, 20, 23, 33, 56, 65–66, 146, 149, 150, 153, 179 n1, 181, 201, 212
Myers, Valentine, 133, 215

National Road, 198
Nauss, Alexander, 136
New Creek, VA (Keyser, WV), 33, 57, 63, 97, 162, 172, 182
New Jersey regiments: 14th Infantry, 199, 201, 219
New Oxford, PA, 3, 42, 85, 90, 125, 172
New Oxford Collegiate and Medical Institute, 85, 86, 88, 203, 233
New York regiments: 40th Infantry, 146; 106th Infantry, 219 n19; 151st Infantry, 198
Newspapers, described, 5, 6
Newspapers cited: *Adams (PA) Sentinel and General Advertiser,* aka *Adams Sentinel* and *Star and Sentinel,* 10, 67, 68, 217, 236; *Baltimore County Advocate,* 92, 95, 127 n30; *Daily Baltimore Republican,* 1; *Gazette and Daily,* 237; *Gettysburg Compiler,* 8–11, 15, 32, 68, 69, 166, 167, 207, 208, 236; *Gettysburg Star and Banner,* 9, 10, 15, 22, 32, 68, 69, 82, 92; *Hanover Gazette,* 69, 70; *Hanover Spectator,* 39, 70, 71, 91; *National Tribune,* 178; *True Democrat,* 196, 236, 237; *York County Star and Wrightsville Advertiser,* 15; *York Daily,* 240; *York Democratic Press,* 7, 8, 10, 15, 159, 246; *York Gazette,* 8, 9, 14, 15, 29, 32, 81, 125, 172, 178, 182, 196, 201, 207, 208, 235–37; *York Recorder,* 158; *York Republican,* aka *Pennsylvania Republican, York Republican and Anti-Masonic Expositor,* and *Weekly York Republican,* 10, 11, 37
Nichol, Peter, 40, 224

Norris, Theodore Cress, 146, 150
Northern Central Railway, 2, 16, 19, 21,
    27–29, 36, 52, 91, 125, 127, 134, 207, 241

Odenwalt, Charles, 35, 90
Odgen, William, 190
Ohio regiments: 4th Cavalry, 125; 116th
    Infantry, 77, 105
O'Neil, John G., 138
Oren, James, 41, 173–78

P. A. and S. Small's Hardware, 17
Parkersburg, WV, 195
Patterson, Robert, 22–25, 102
Payne's Farm, battle of. *See* Mine Run
    campaign
Payne, Madison, 142
Pennsylvania Railroad, 16, 27
Pennsylvania regiments: 2nd Heavy
    Artillery, 117; 2nd Infantry, 21, 23, 26,
    56; 11th Cavalry, 63; 16th Infantry, 21,
    23, 26, 33, 40, 43, 219; 30th Infantry (1st
    Reserves), xiv, 32, 38, 49, 97 n20, 125;
    36th Infantry (7th Reserves), xiv, 73;
    41st Infantry (12th Reserves), xiv; 43rd
    (1st Light Artillery), xiv, 48–49; 67th
    Infantry, 44, 114, 221, 222, 242 n2; 76th
    Infantry, xiv, 70, 116 n3; 99th Infantry,
    125; 103rd Infantry, 136; 114th Infantry,
    116–18; 130th Infantry, 124; 132nd
    Infantry, 122; 138th Infantry, 48, 114,
    137, 142, 143, 145, 146, 151; 165th Drafted
    Militia, 67, 121; 166th Drafted Militia,
    63; 199th Infantry, 62; 200th Infantry,
    118, 125, 180, 222; 209th Infantry, 222
Pentz, Henry Clay, 215
Peru, IN, 229
Petersburg, siege of: xii, 112, 192–93, 194,
    223, 224; Jerusalem Plank Road, aka
    Weldon Railroad, 192–93
Pfeiffer, John Quincy Adams, 87, 88
Pfeiffer, John Theodore, 88
Pfeiffer, Michael Diedrich Gotlob, 85, 86,
    88
Pfeiffer, Sarah, 86
Pfeiffer, Thaddeus Stevens, 86–88, 100,
    106, 171, 190
Philadelphia, PA, 7, 30, 131, 162, 206, 226

Poet, Michael Fry, 178
Popular sovereignty, 11
Porter, Fitz-John, 18–21, 102
Pratt Street Riots, 2, 18, 21, 29
Price, Thomas, 231
Prigg case, 156, 157
Prison camps: Alton, IL, 138; Anderson-
    ville, GA, 41, 138, 172–74, 176–78,
    184, 188, 193–94, 231, 234; Belle Isle,
    Richmond, VA, 42, 82, 107, 129, 130,
    138, 141, 173, 193, 230, 233; Blackshear,
    GA, 174; Libby, Richmond, VA, 66,
    106, 129, 133, 183; Millen, GA, 138, 174,
    194; Salisbury, NC, 215; Thomasville,
    GA, 174
Prowell, George F., 230
Prowell, George Reeser, xii, xiii, 73, 198,
    215, 239

Quaker Meeting House (Wellsville, PA),
    170
Quinn, Richard, 226

Racial matters: area's attitude toward
    blacks, 7, 156–61, 168–71; area's attitude
    toward German immigrants, 8;
    lynching, 168–71; segregation, 159, 160.
    See also 87th Pennsylvania: race, views
    of
Rapidan River, 140, 141, 184, 185
Railroads, military use and dangers of, 26.
    See also individual railroad companies
Ream, Adam, 48 n23
Ream, Eli, 48 n23, 203
Ream, William, 43, 132
Reher, Cyrus, 214
Reigle, Daniel Peter, 111, 219
Relay House: Baltimore and Ohio
    Railroad, 205; Northern Central
    Railway, 126
Republicans: attack Democrats, 10, 11;
    Democrats' opinion of, postwar, 235;
    Democrats' opinion of, prewar, 6–9,
    165; description of ideals, 9–12
Rice, William Henry, 224
Rich Mountain, 98
Ricketts, James Brewerton, 109, 189, 196,
    199–201, 205, 206

Rinehart, Frederick, 35
Robinson, Greenbury S. (servant), 159, 172, 173
Rock Island, IL, 58
Roe, Alfred Seelye, 240
Rouch, Valentine, 42
Rudy, Edwin T., 184
Ruhl, Anna Maria, 64, 65
Ruhl, Edgar Monroe, 36, 64, 104, 218
Ruhl, Noah G., 63–65, 81, 83, 90, 104, 204, 206, 218, 221, 222, 239
Rupture and hernia, 31, 41, 119, 203, 231, 232
Russell Run. *See* Mine Run campaign

Saint Francis Xavier Cemetery, 238
Salsbury, John Andrus, 219, 220
Savannah, GA, 174, 175
Sayler's Creek, battle of, 224, 225 n35
Saylor, David Ramsey, 113
Saylor, Samuel, 89, 113, 154
Schall, John William, 29, 30, 56, 66, 72, 75, 76, 79, 82–84, 103, 113, 136, 141, 190, 217, 221, 239
Schroeder, Edward L., 101
Scott, Thomas Alexander, 26–29, 32, 36–38, 102
Scott, Winfield, 19, 20, 24
Sectional rivalry, 5–7
Sedgwick, John, 188
Seitz, Edward, 93
Seitz, Henry, 64
Seymour, Truman, 220 n21, 221
Shatzler, Henry, 177
Shaw, Thomas, 219 n19
Sheads, Charles William, 203
Sheads, Elias J., 203
Sheads, Isaac I., 190
Sheads, John Henry, 137
Sheets, Samuel, 125
Sheridan, Philip Henry, xii, 212, 219, 223
Sherman, William Tecumseh, 174
Shillito, John Lawrence, 74
Shive, Andrew Kauffman, 226 n42
Shoemaker, Samuel William, 224
Shull, Andrew George, 226
Shultz, Charles William, 202
Shultz, Henry, 40, 41, 130, 224, 240

Shultz, John, 45–47
Shuman, William, 177
Skelly, Charles Edwin, xv
Skelly, John Hastings, xv, 13, 66, 67, 96, 129
Slaves and slavery, 3–11, 13, 14, 40, 80, 134, 156–60, 165, 168, 169, 171, 172, 174–78, 197, 202 n22, 210, 225, 235, 236
Slaymaker, Jonathan, 76 n67
Slaymaker, Robert Samuel, 75, 76, 79, 81, 82, 84–85, 152
Slothower, Michael S., 76, 78
Small, Alexander, 28–31, 34, 36, 37, 86, 92, 102
Small, James. *See* Small's News Depot
Smallbrook, Henry, 89 n2, 116
Small's News Depot, 2, 16
Smith, Andrew Bentz, 76, 78, 82, 107, 140–55
Smith, Benjamin Franklin, 142, 148, 154
Smith, Thomas, 116
Snyder, Benjamin Franklin, 48, 126–28, 138
Snyder, Isaac Jesse, 203
Snyder, William Lemuel, 128 n33
Spahr, Jeremiah Miley, 169–71
Spangler, Henry Clay, 133
Spangler, John Frederick, 110, 179, 204
Spangler, Levi M., 116
Spayd, William F., 60–62, 130
Sperry, Sarah Catherine "Kate," 166 n26
Stahl, Calvin, 44
Stahl, Howard, 44
Stahl, John Jacob, 39, 44
Stahle, Henry John, 9, 11, 167. *See also Gettysburg Compiler*
Stahle, James Alanza, 9, 25, 53, 55, 56, 65, 66, 73, 75, 78 n71, 81, 82, 83, 84, 103, 113, 141–51, 154, 155, 173, 198, 201, 202, 204, 220, 221, 233
Stallman, Charles Henry, 113, 146, 151, 152, 192–93
Stanton, Edward McMasters, 222
State rights, 6, 8, 13, 235
Statistical charts: 87th Pennsylvania Characteristics as of Dec. 31, 1861, 54; Age, of recruits, 245; Casualties, Battle, 87th Pennsylvania, 246; Casualties,

Non-Battle, 87th Pennsylvania, 247; Casualties, Overland Campaign, 191; Abraham B. Coble, ages reported, 45; Desertion, Factors in Predicting, 249–51; Life Expectancy, 248; Occupations, 244; Physical Characteristics of Recruits, 245, 246; Voting patterns vs. enlistment rates by political entity 50, 51
Staunton-Parkersburg Turnpike, 98
Staunton, John F., 206
Steadman, Harris, 81, 82
Stegenmyer, Ferdinand Frederick, 202
Stevens, Thaddeus, 74, 86
Stine, Henry, 40
Stouffer, Albert Dinkle, 40
Strickler, Alexander, 82, 83, 149
Susquehanna and Tidewater Canal, 3
Sweeney, Isaac, 90
Swope, Henry, 238

Taylor Hotel. See Winchester, VA
Tearney, James, 111, 222, 223
Tennessee regiments C.S.A.: 5th Cavalry, 101; 10th Infantry, 138
Thomas, Charlie (sutler), 173
Thomas, Findley Isaac, 113, 233
Thomas, Samuel, 221
Thomas A. Scott Regiment. See 87th Pennsylvania, Thomas A. Scott name
Thomasville, PA, 168
Toomey, George Kohr, 59, 60
Towson, MD, 70, 73, 95, 96 n15
Training, comparison of Civil War to World War II, 101
Truex, William Snyder, 149, 221
Tubman, Harriet, 160
Turner, Nat, 158
Tyson, Henry, 124

Underground Railroad, 4, 8, 12, 86, 160
Updegrove, Thomas, 130
U.S. regiments: 4th Cavalry, 226; 5th Infantry, 139; 6th Cavalry, 58; 7th Veteran Infantry, 226; 21st Infantry, 139

Valley Pike, 76, 77, 164, 214
Vermont regiments: 10th Infantry, 199, 201, 205, 219

Veteran Volunteers. See 87th Pennsylvania: Veteran Volunteers
Virginia regiments C.S.A.: 2nd Infantry, 13, 56; 31st Infantry, 40; 44th Infantry, 143
Vote by county/district, 1860, 50, 51
Vroman, Nathaniel, 215

Wade, Mary Virginia "Jennie," 66–67, 129
Wagner, Isaac, 226
Wallace, Lew, 196, 199, 200, 201, 207, 208, 239
Waltimyer, William, 226
Walzer, John F., 35
Wantz, George, 17
Warner, George Ambrose, 136–38, 166 n26, 233
Warner, John M. (sutler), 233
Warren, Gouvernor Kimble, 147 n15
Weakley, James Hanson, 213, 214
Wells, John, 170, 171
Wellsville, PA, 73, 74, 84, 168
Welsh, George A., 229, 230
Welsh, Charles Spangler, 202
Welsh, Daniel Laumaster, 204, 205
Welsh, William Henry Harrison, 35
West Virginia regiments: 1st Light Artillery, 31; 9th Infantry, 99; 12th Infantry, 31, 100
Willard, George, 137
Wilson, Stephen McKinley, 131
Wilson's Landing, VA, 192
Winchester: 2nd battle of, 13, 72, 77–81, 168, 218, 231, 233; 3rd battle of, 135, 209, 213, 214, 229
Winchester, VA: attitude toward Union soldiers, 166; events of July 1861; mentioned, xv, 173, 182, 206; Taylor Hotel, 133, 183; Union troops imprisoned at, 129. See also Patterson, Robert
Wolf, Anthony, 104
Wolf, John Henry, 155
Woodbury, MD, 70
Woodstock, VA, 215
Worthington, Glenn, 198, 199
Wrightsville, PA, xiv, 3, 25, 50, 116, 159, 160, 201

Wrightsville-Columbia Bridge, 26, 130
Wynkoop, George Campbell, 18–21

Yeatts, William B., 35
York, Confederate invasion of, 6, 130
York, Zebulon, 202, 202 n22

Ziegler, William Thomas Radford, 129 n34
Zoo-Zoo, 67 n36, 190–92
Zimmerman, John Albert. *See* Dixon, John Albert

About the Author

Dennis W. Brandt is a freelance author-historian. His other works include *Shattering the Truth: The Slandering of Abraham Lincoln.*